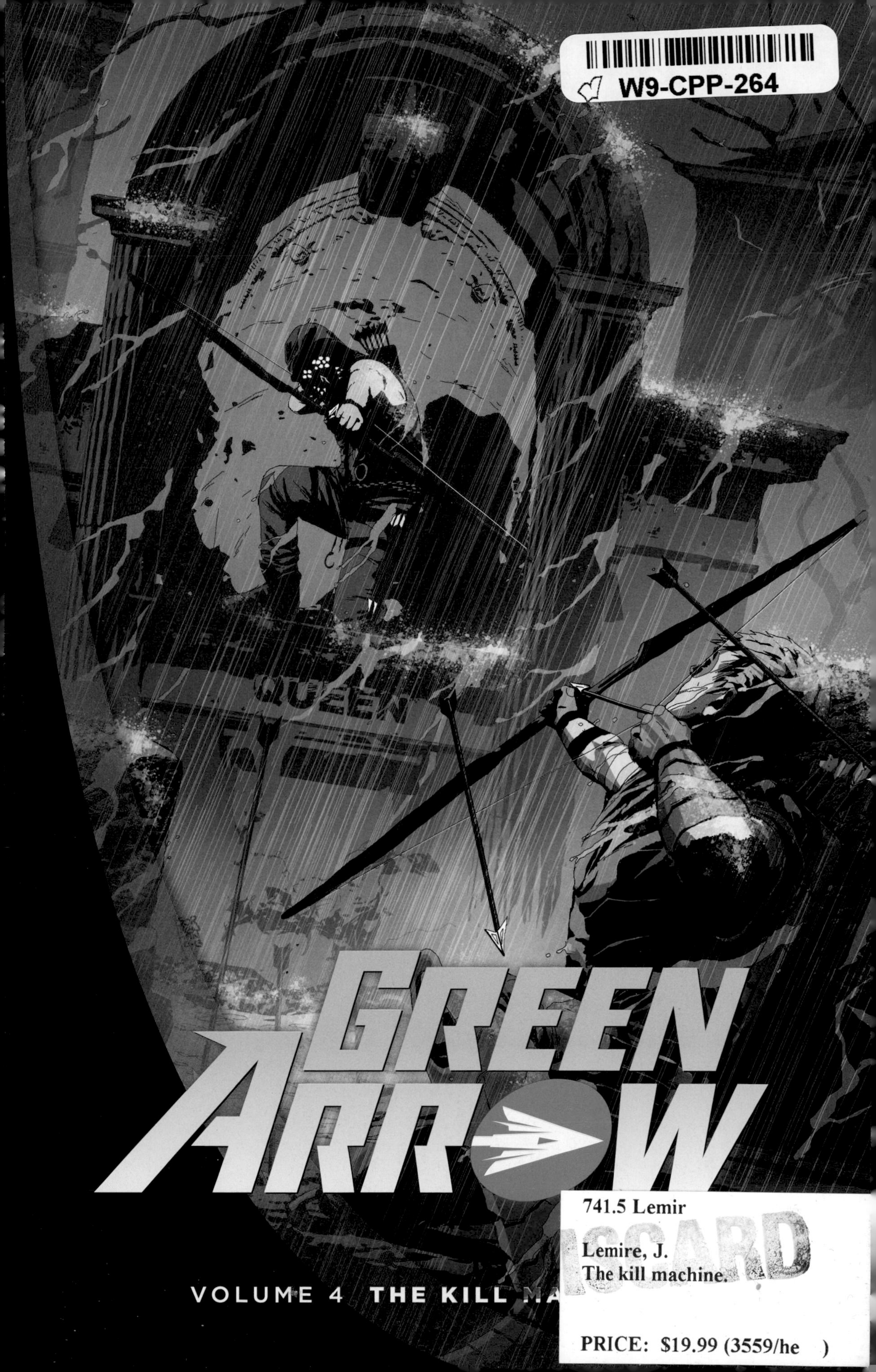
QUEEN
GREEN ARROW
VOLUME 4 THE KILL MA

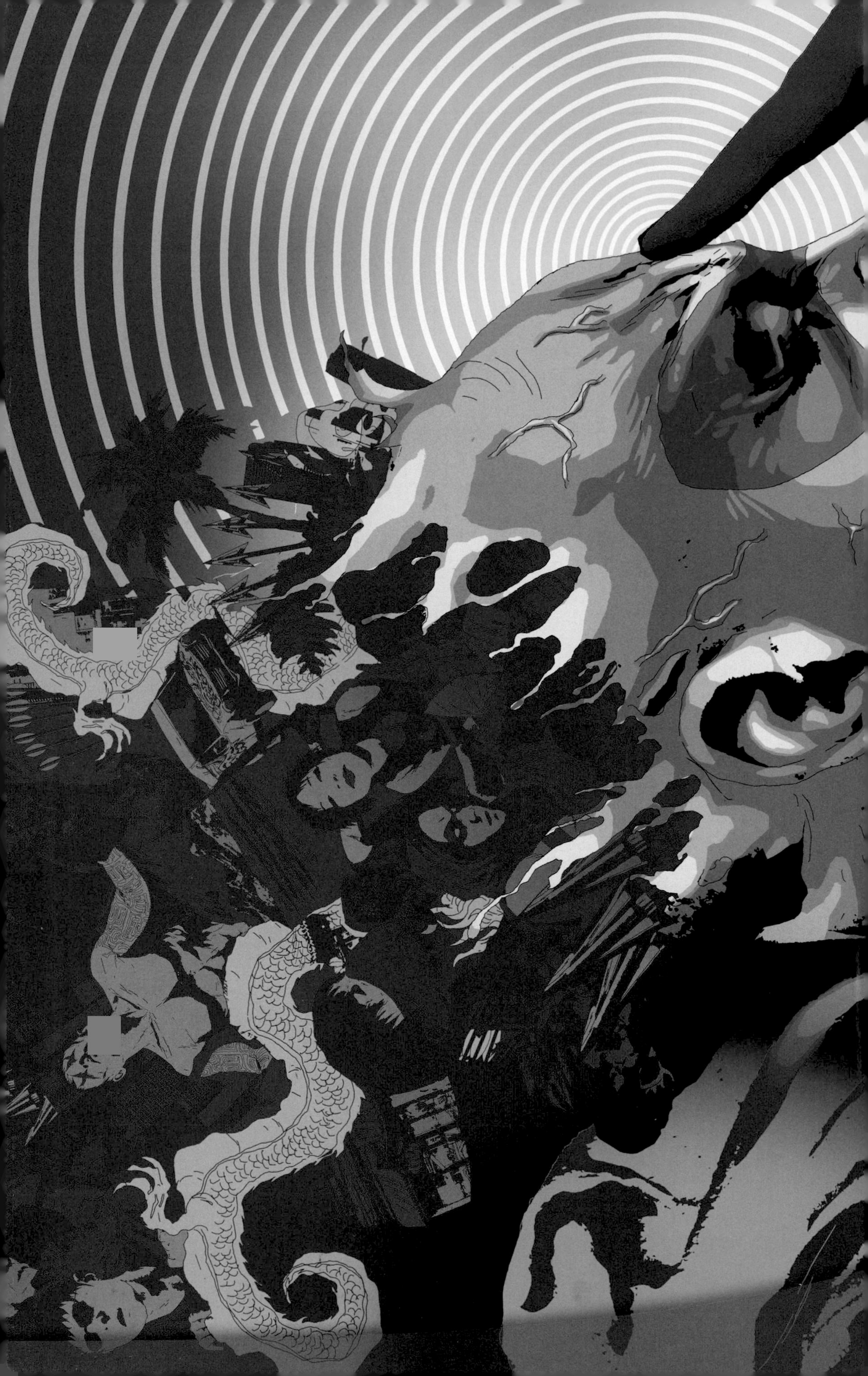

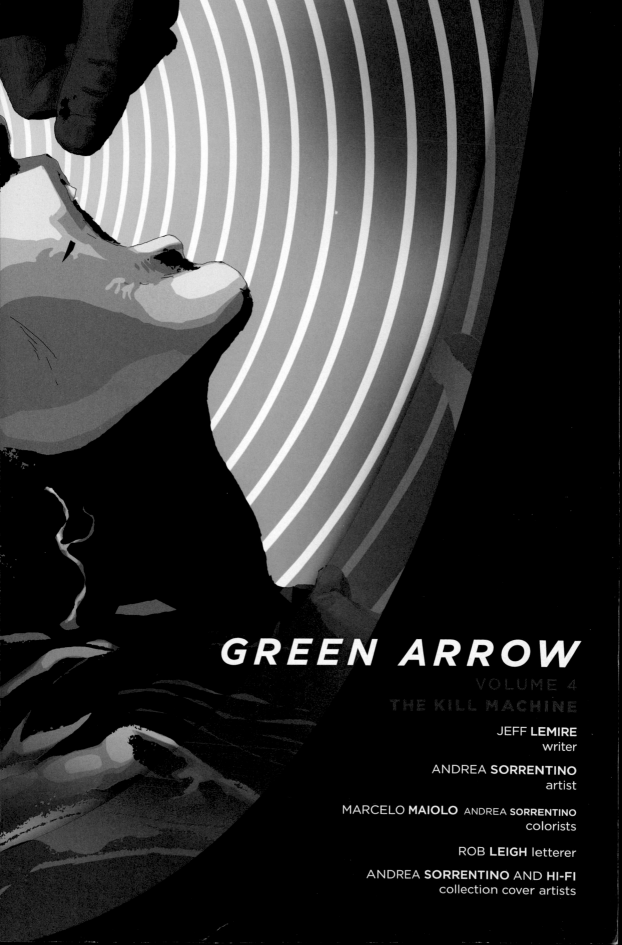

GREEN ARROW

VOLUME 4
THE KILL MACHINE

JEFF **LEMIRE**
writer

ANDREA **SORRENTINO**
artist

MARCELO **MAIOLO** ANDREA **SORRENTINO**
colorists

ROB **LEIGH** letterer

ANDREA **SORRENTINO** AND **HI-FI**
collection cover artists

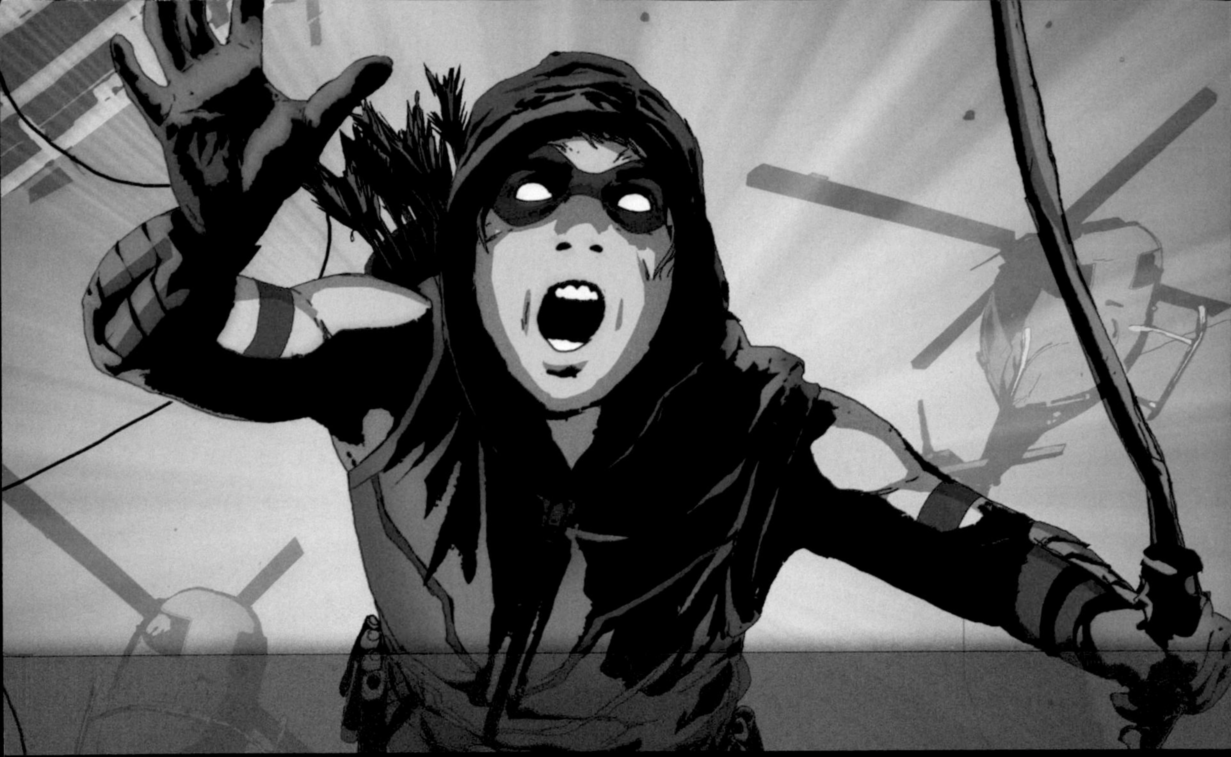

MATT IDELSON BRIAN CUNNINGHAM JOEY CAVALIERI WIL MOSS Editors - Original Series
HARVEY RICHARDS Associate Editor - Original Series KATE STEWART Assistant Editor - Original Series ROWENA YOW Editor
ROBBIN BROSTERMAN Design Director - Books ROBBIE BIEDERMAN Publication Design

BOB HARRAS Senior VP - Editor-in-Chief, DC Comics

DIANE NELSON President DAN DIDIO and JIM LEE Co-Publishers
GEOFF JOHNS Chief Creative Officer
JOHN ROOD Executive VP - Sales, Marketing and Business Development
AMY GENKINS Senior VP - Business and Legal Affairs NAIRI GARDINER Senior VP - Finance
JEFF BOISON VP - Publishing Planning MARK CHIARELLO VP - Art Direction and Design
JOHN CUNNINGHAM VP - Marketing TERRI CUNNINGHAM VP - Editorial Administration
ALISON GILL Senior VP - Manufacturing and Operations HANK KANALZ Senior VP - Vertigo and Integrated Publishing
JAY KOGAN VP - Business and Legal Affairs, Publishing JACK MAHAN VP - Business Affairs, Talent
NICK NAPOLITANO VP - Manufacturing Administration SUE POHJA VP - Book Sales
COURTNEY SIMMONS Senior VP - Publicity BOB WAYNE Senior VP - Sales

GREEN ARROW VOLUME 4: THE KILL MACHINE

DC Comics, 1700 Broadway, New York, NY 10019
A Warner Bros. Entertainment Company.
Printed by RR Donnelley, Salem, VA, USA. 2/14/14. First Printing.
ISBN: 978-1-4012-4690-7

SUSTAINABLE FORESTRY INITIATIVE
Certified Chain of Custody
At Least 20% Certified Forest Content
www.sfiprogram.org
SFI-01042
APPLIES TO TEXT STOCK ONLY

Library of Congress Cataloging-in-Publication Data

Lemire, Jeff, author.
Green Arrow. Volume 4, The Kill Machine / Jeff Lemire, Andrea Sorrentino.
pages cm
Summary: "Jeff Lemire and Andrea Sorrentino begin their ground-breaking saga in the fourth volume of Green Arrow! A mysterious villian called Komodo knows Oliver's secrets and uses them to rob Oliver of all his wealth and his company. Now on the run from this seemingly unstoppable force, Oliver finds himself in a mystery involving the island where he first became Green Arrow and his father! Everything will change for the Emerald Archer in this new beginning for the character. This volume collects Green Arrow #17-24 and 23.1"— Provided by publisher.
ISBN 978-1-4012-4690-7 (paperback)
1. Graphic novels. I. Sorrentino, Andrea, illustrator. II. Title. III. Title: Kill Machine.
PN6728.G725L46 2014
741.5'973—dc23
2013045547

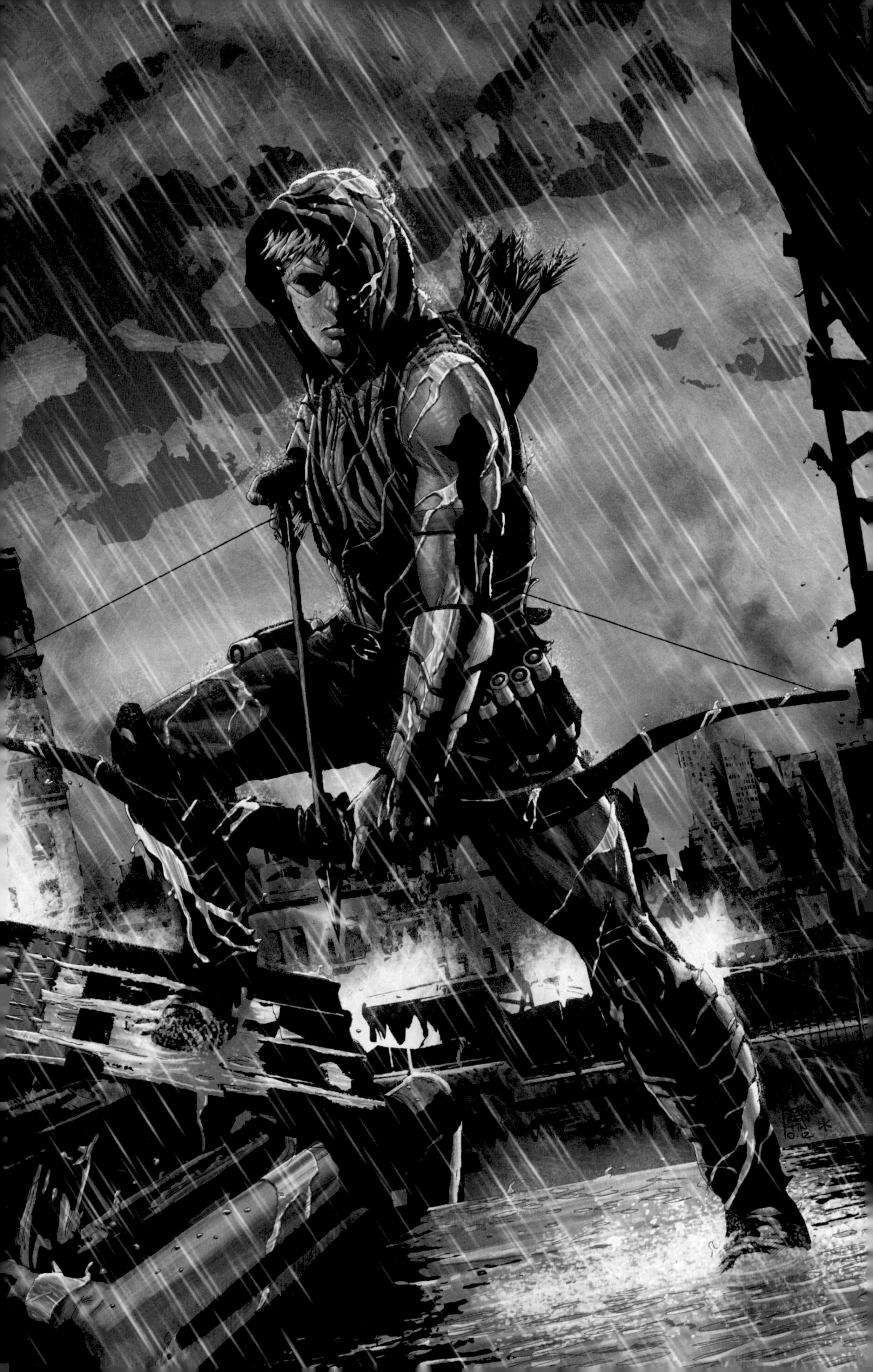

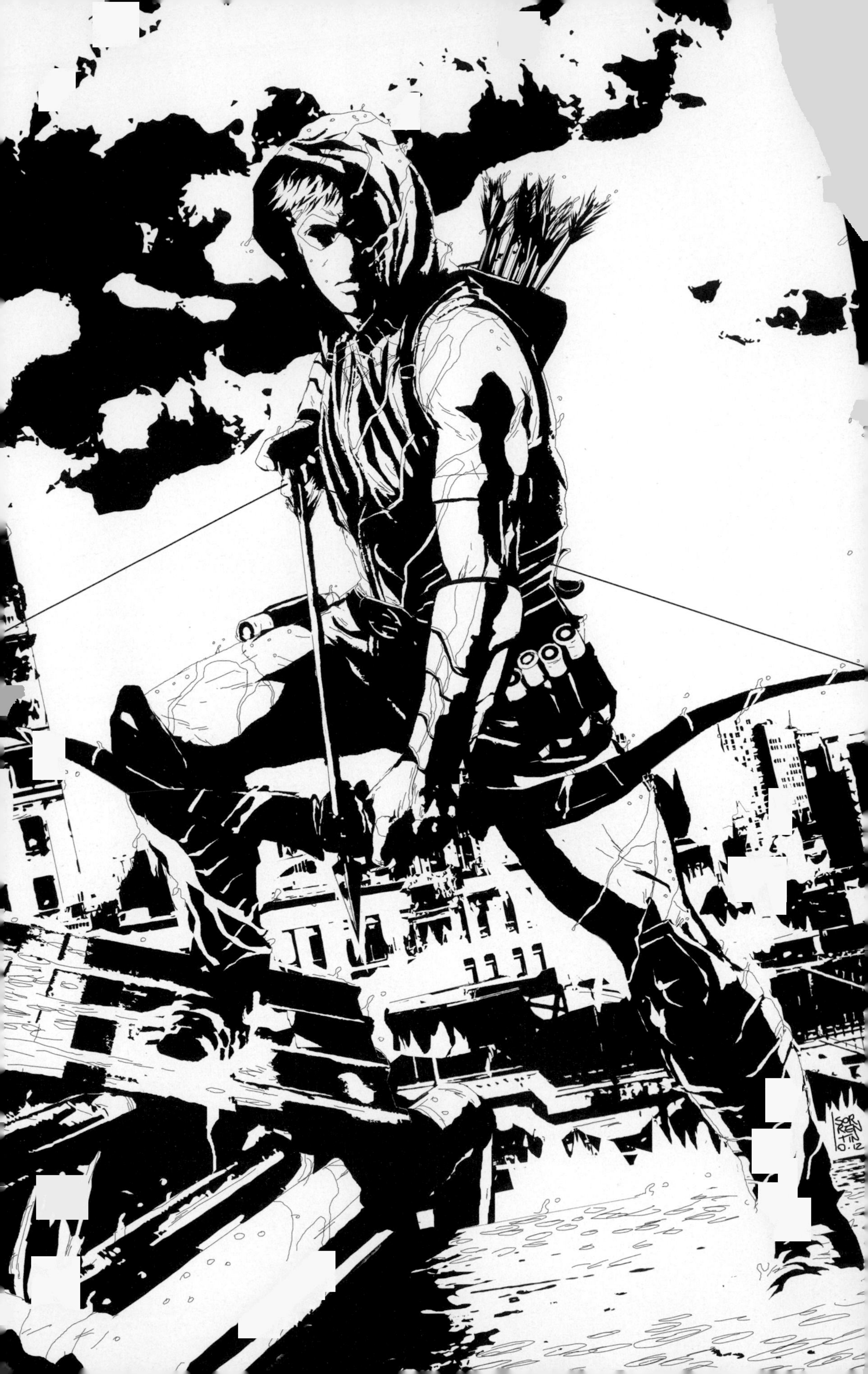
SOR
REN
TIN
O.12

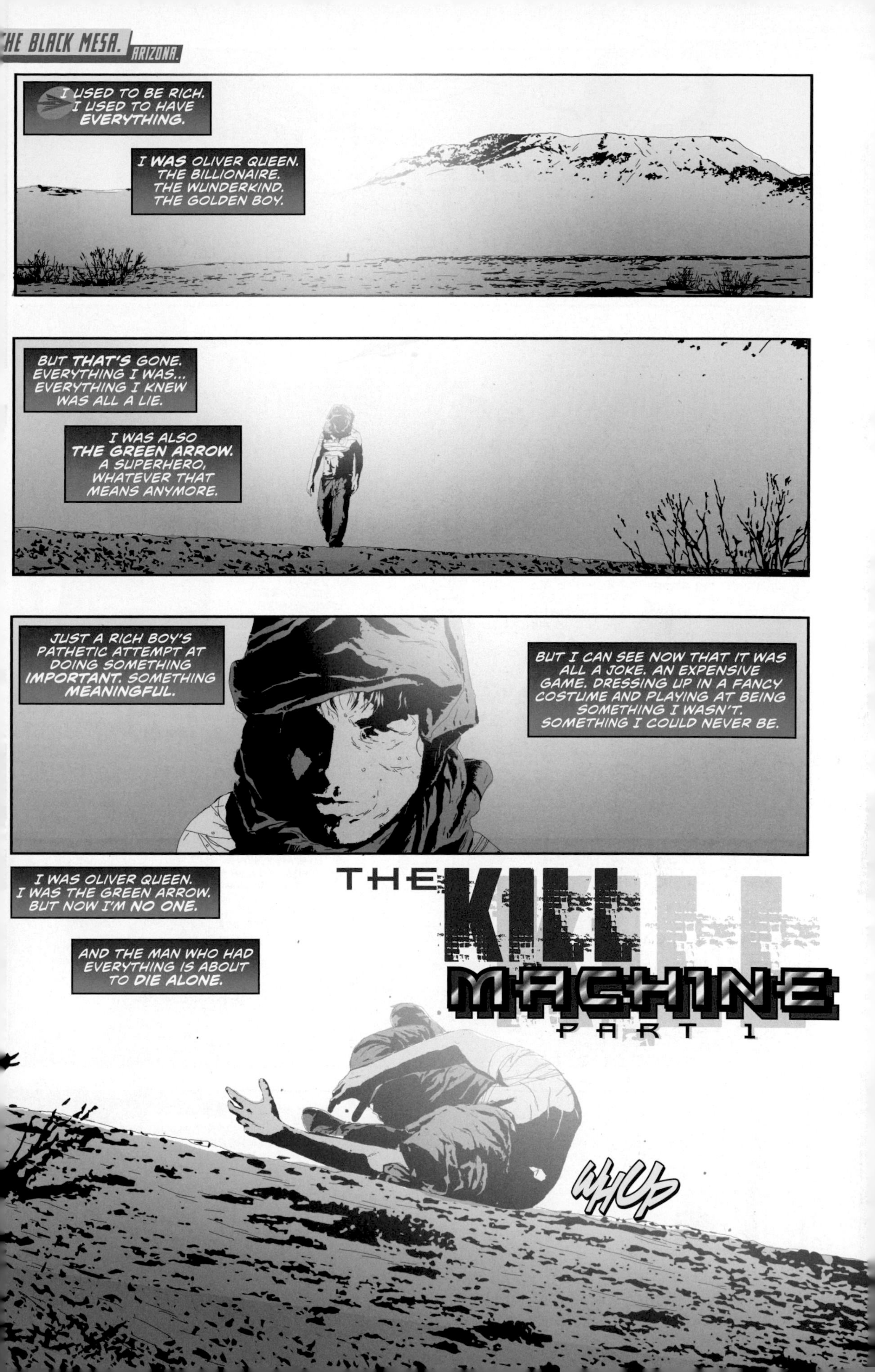
THE BLACK MESA. ARIZONA.
I USED TO BE RICH. I USED TO HAVE EVERYTHING.
I WAS OLIVER QUEEN. THE BILLIONAIRE. THE WUNDERKIND. THE GOLDEN BOY.
BUT THAT'S GONE. EVERYTHING I WAS... EVERYTHING I KNEW WAS ALL A LIE.
I WAS ALSO THE GREEN ARROW. A SUPERHERO, WHATEVER THAT MEANS ANYMORE.
JUST A RICH BOY'S PATHETIC ATTEMPT AT DOING SOMETHING IMPORTANT. SOMETHING MEANINGFUL.
BUT I CAN SEE NOW THAT IT WAS ALL A JOKE. AN EXPENSIVE GAME. DRESSING UP IN A FANCY COSTUME AND PLAYING AT BEING SOMETHING I WASN'T. SOMETHING I COULD NEVER BE.
I WAS OLIVER QUEEN. I WAS THE GREEN ARROW. BUT NOW I'M NO ONE.
AND THE MAN WHO HAD EVERYTHING IS ABOUT TO DIE ALONE.
THE KILL MACHINE PART 1
WHUD

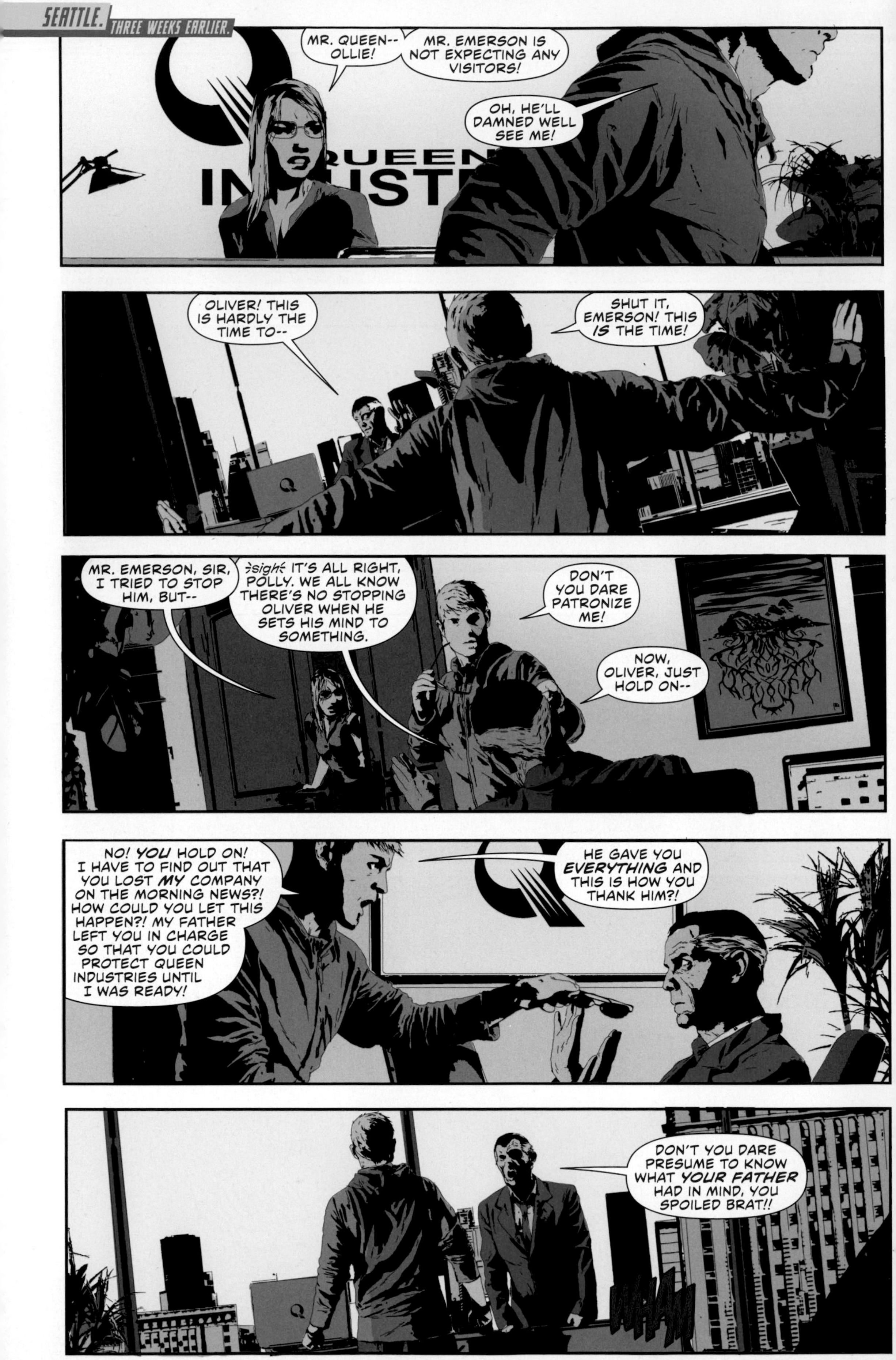
SEATTLE.
THREE WEEKS EARLIER.
MR. QUEEN-- OLLIE!
MR. EMERSON IS NOT EXPECTING ANY VISITORS!
OH, HE'LL DAMNED WELL SEE ME!
QUEEN INDUSTRIES
OLIVER! THIS IS HARDLY THE TIME TO--
SHUT IT, EMERSON! THIS IS THE TIME!
MR. EMERSON, SIR, I TRIED TO STOP HIM, BUT--
sigh IT'S ALL RIGHT, POLLY. WE ALL KNOW THERE'S NO STOPPING OLIVER WHEN HE SETS HIS MIND TO SOMETHING.
DON'T YOU DARE PATRONIZE ME!
NOW, OLIVER, JUST HOLD ON--
NO! YOU HOLD ON! I HAVE TO FIND OUT THAT YOU LOST MY COMPANY ON THE MORNING NEWS?! HOW COULD YOU LET THIS HAPPEN?! MY FATHER LEFT YOU IN CHARGE SO THAT YOU COULD PROTECT QUEEN INDUSTRIES UNTIL I WAS READY!
HE GAVE YOU EVERYTHING AND THIS IS HOW YOU THANK HIM?!
DON'T YOU DARE PRESUME TO KNOW WHAT YOUR FATHER HAD IN MIND, YOU SPOILED BRAT!!

YOUR FATHER WAS--

YOUR FATHER WAS A GREAT MAN, OLIVER. NOT JUST A GENIUS...BUT A *TRUE* VISIONARY. AND HE WAS ALSO *MY BEST FRIEND.*

AND IT'S TRUE, HE DID ENTRUST ME TO WATCH OVER QUEEN INDUSTRIES UNTIL YOU WERE READY.

AND I TRIED. I EVEN LET YOU HAVE Q-CORE, YOUR OWN LITTLE PET PROJECT, THINKING IT MIGHT HELP TO FOCUS YOU.

BUT YOU WERE ALWAYS RUNNING OFF TO GOD KNOWS WHERE, DOING GOD KNOWS WHAT. YOU SEE, THAT'S JUST IT, OLLIE...IT'S ALL JUST A GAME TO YOU.

BUT YOU'RE RIGHT, I DID FAIL. I WAS SO BUSY TRYING TO *TAKE CARE OF YOU* THAT I LOST TRACK OF QUEEN INDUSTRIES. I LEFT US *VULNERABLE.*

YOU SAY IT AS IF WE LOST A BASEBALL GAME, EMERSON. OUR DAMN COMPANY HAS BEEN STOLEN AWAY FROM US. STELLMOOR INTERNATIONAL OWNS US. YOU'VE *LOST EVERYTHING!*

YES. WELL, MAYBE THIS *HAD* TO HAPPEN.

I DON'T KNOW. MAYBE IT WILL FORCE YOU TO GROW UP...

...GIVE YOU A SECOND CHANCE. A CHANCE TO BECOME THE MAN YOU WERE *SUPPOSED* TO BE. *A GREAT MAN.*

YOU WERE BORN INTO PRIVILEGE. AND YES, YOU TOO ARE BRILLIANT, BUT ASIDE FROM YOUR ORDEAL ON *THE ISLAND,* YOU'VE NEVER HAD TO TRULY FIGHT FOR ANYTHING IN YOUR LIFE. AND IT'S MADE YOU IRRESPONSIBLE. WEAK.

BUT THE TIME FOR WEAKNESS IS OVER, OLLIE. THERE ARE THINGS ABOUT YOUR FATHER--THINGS WE DID...QUEEN INDUSTRIES IS NOT THE *ONLY LEGACY* HE LEFT YOU.

WHAT THE HELL ARE YOU TALKING ABOUT?

THAT'S JUST IT, OLIVER. YOU'RE *NOT READY* TO HEAR IT YET. BUT I DEARLY *NEED* YOU TO BE. AND IF THAT MEANS TAKING EVERYTHING AWAY...

SOMETIMES A MAN DOESN'T KNOW WHAT HE REALLY HAS UNTIL HE'S LOST IT ALL.

OH, PLEASE! SAVE THE SENTIMENTAL MUMBO-JUMBO, EMERSON! DON'T PRETEND THIS IS ALL PART OF SOME GRAND PLAN!

DON'T YOU UNDERSTAND...*NOTHING* THAT'S HAPPENED TO YOU HAS BEEN AN ACCIDENT. *NONE* OF IT!

WHAT'S *THAT* SUPPOSED TO MEAN?

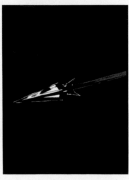

...

I'M TALKING ABOUT *THE TRUTH,* OLIVER... I'M TALKING ABOUT YOUR *TRUE BIRTHRIGHT.*

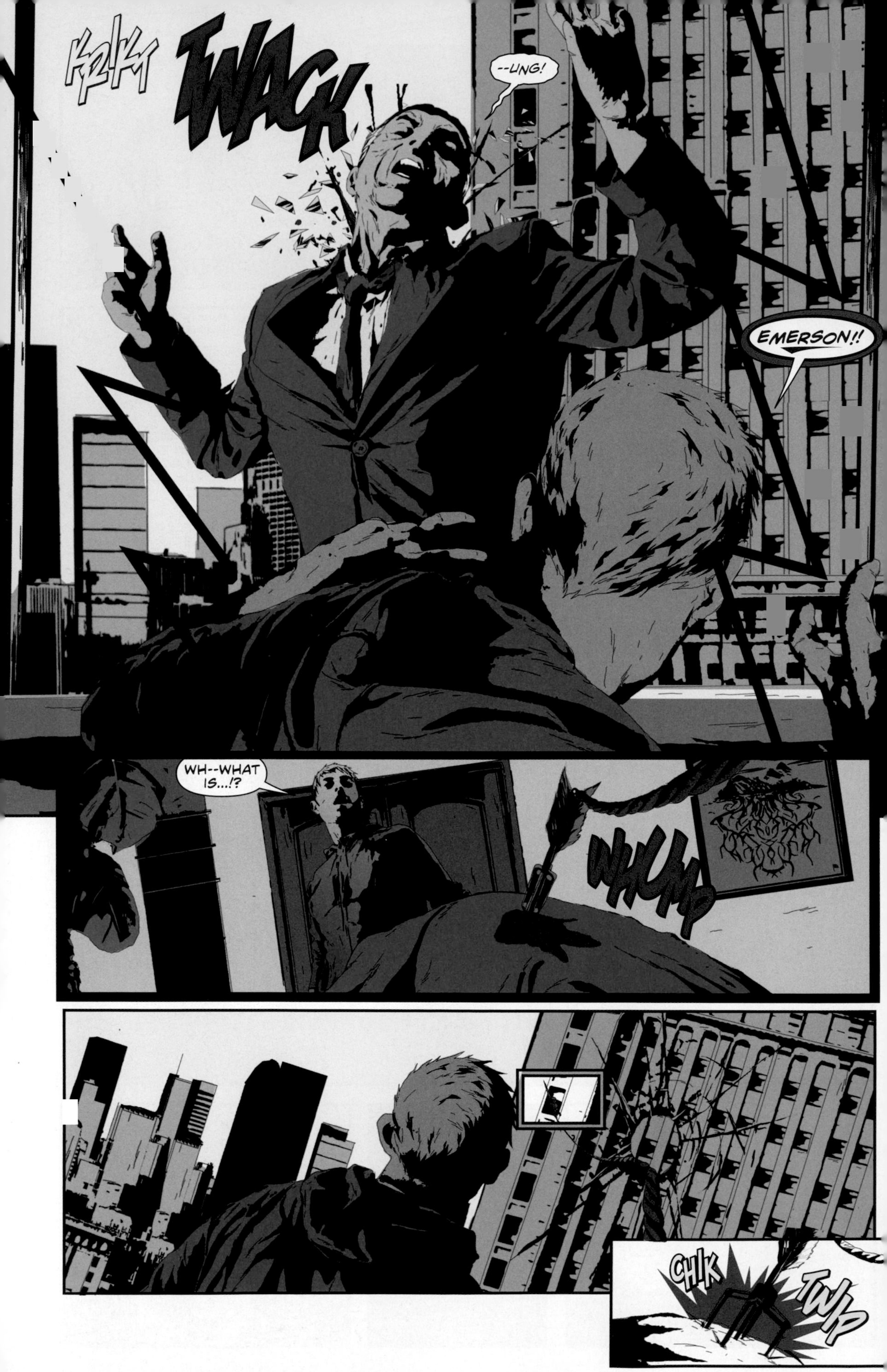
KRIKT
TWACK
--UNG!
EMERSON!!
WH--WHAT IS...!?
WHUMP
CHIK
TWIP

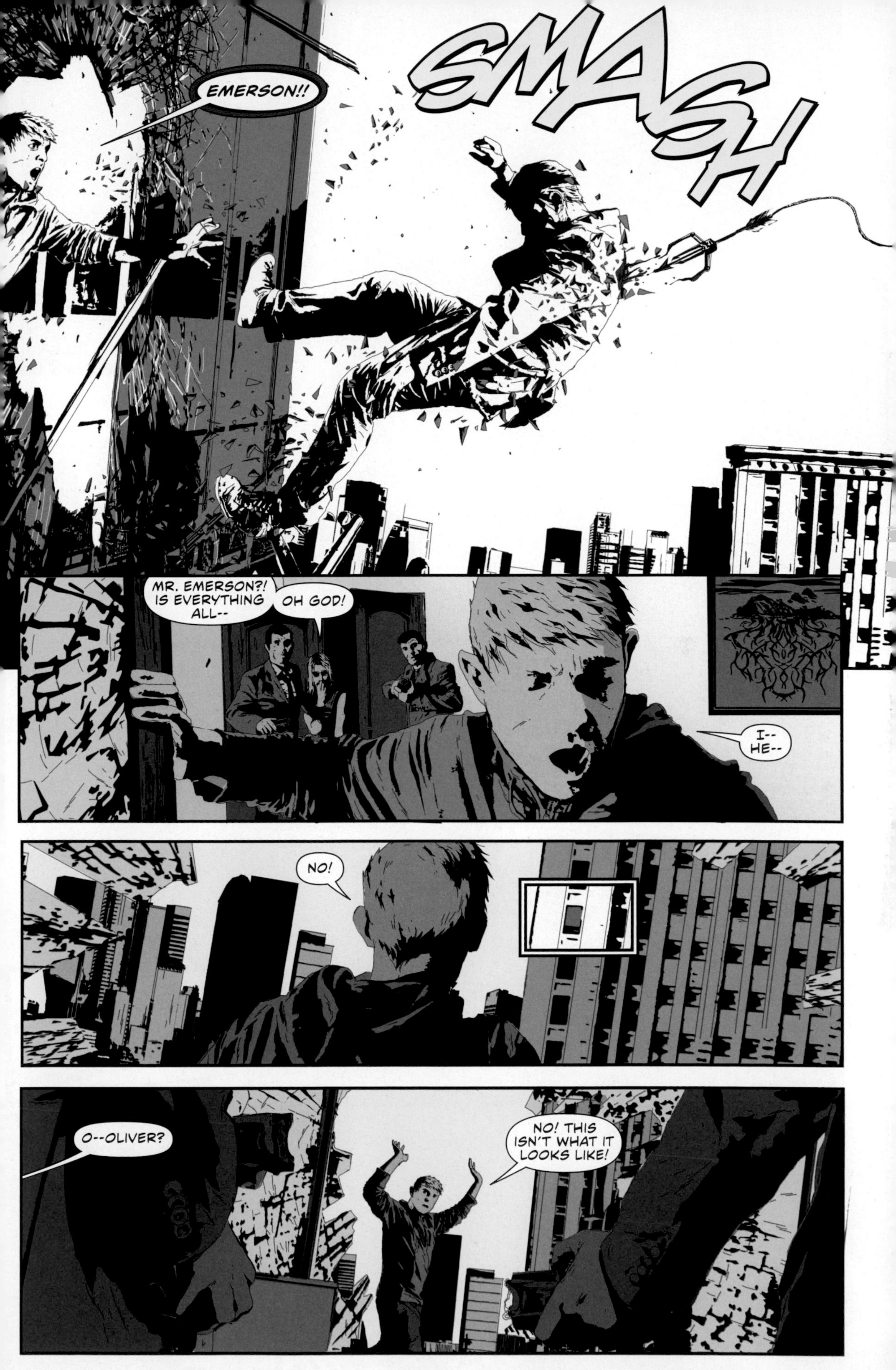
EMERSON!!
SMASH
MR. EMERSON?! IS EVERYTHING ALL--
OH GOD!
I-- HE--
NO!
O--OLIVER?
NO! THIS ISN'T WHAT IT LOOKS LIKE!

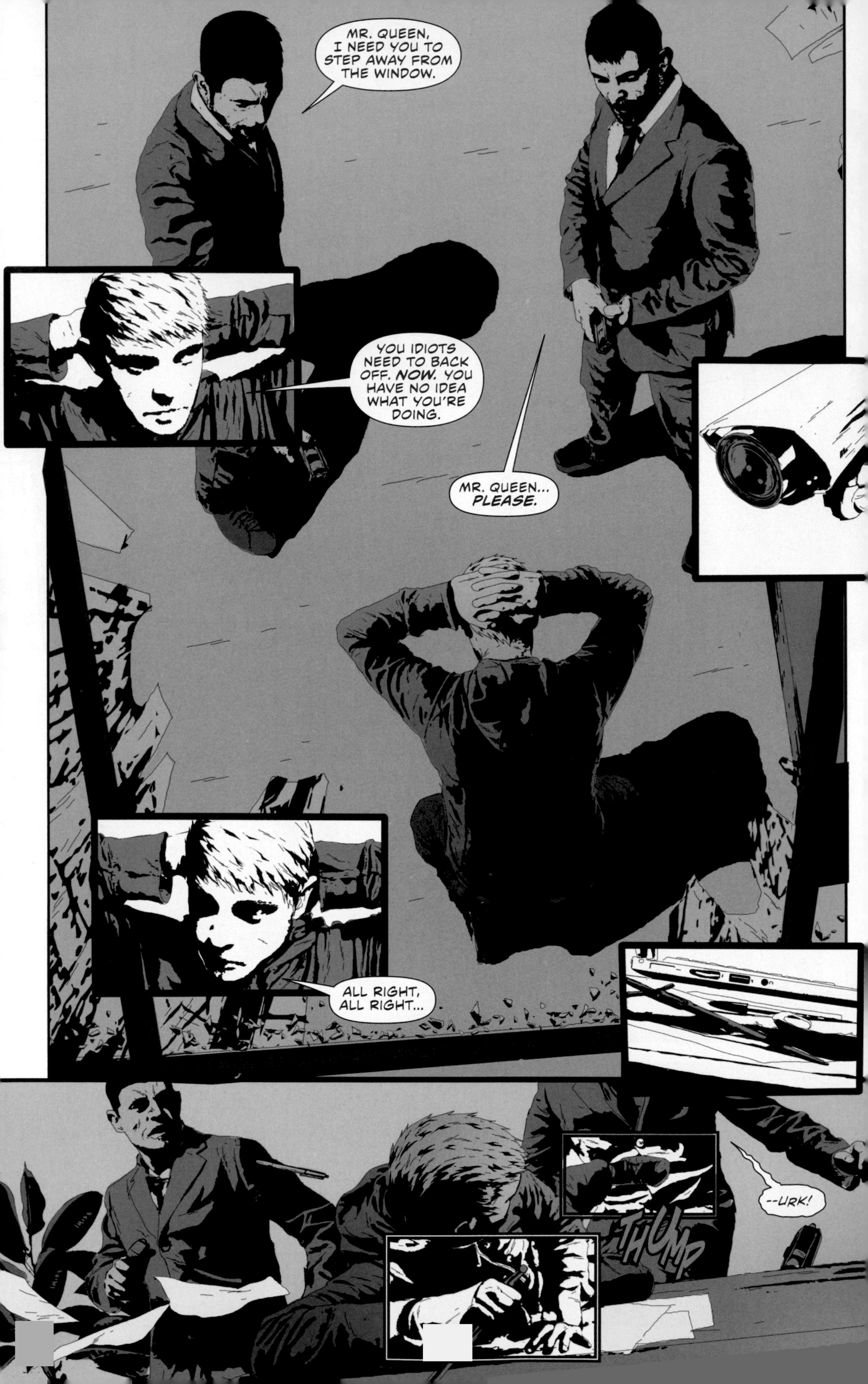
MR. QUEEN, I NEED YOU TO STEP AWAY FROM THE WINDOW.
YOU IDIOTS NEED TO BACK OFF. *NOW.* YOU HAVE NO IDEA WHAT YOU'RE DOING.
MR. QUEEN... *PLEASE.*
ALL RIGHT, ALL RIGHT...
THUMP
--URK!

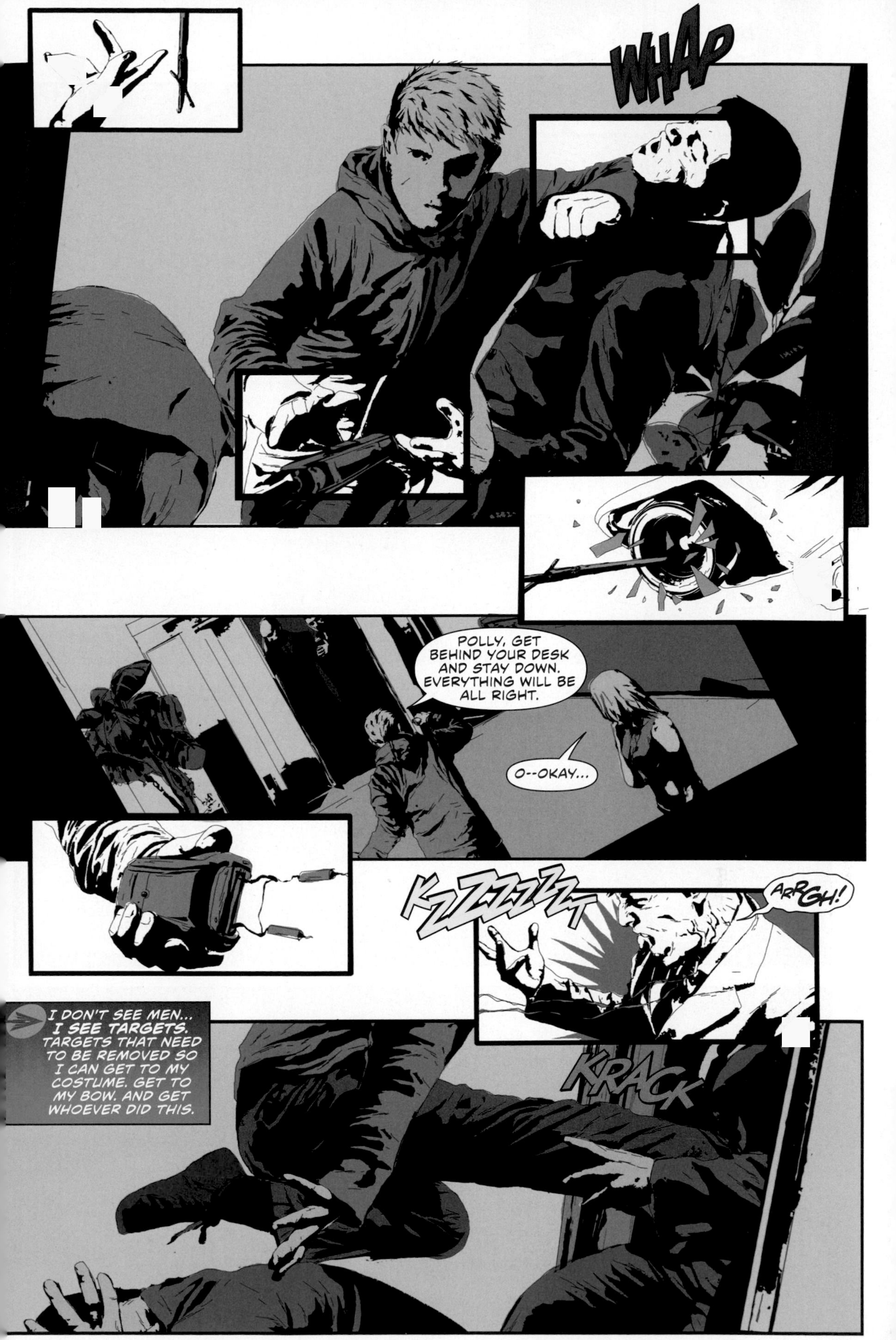
WHAP
POLLY, GET BEHIND YOUR DESK AND STAY DOWN. EVERYTHING WILL BE ALL RIGHT.
O--OKAY...
KZZZZZZT
ARRGH!
I DON'T SEE MEN... I SEE TARGETS. TARGETS THAT NEED TO BE REMOVED SO I CAN GET TO MY COSTUME. GET TO MY BOW. AND GET WHOEVER DID THIS.
KRACK

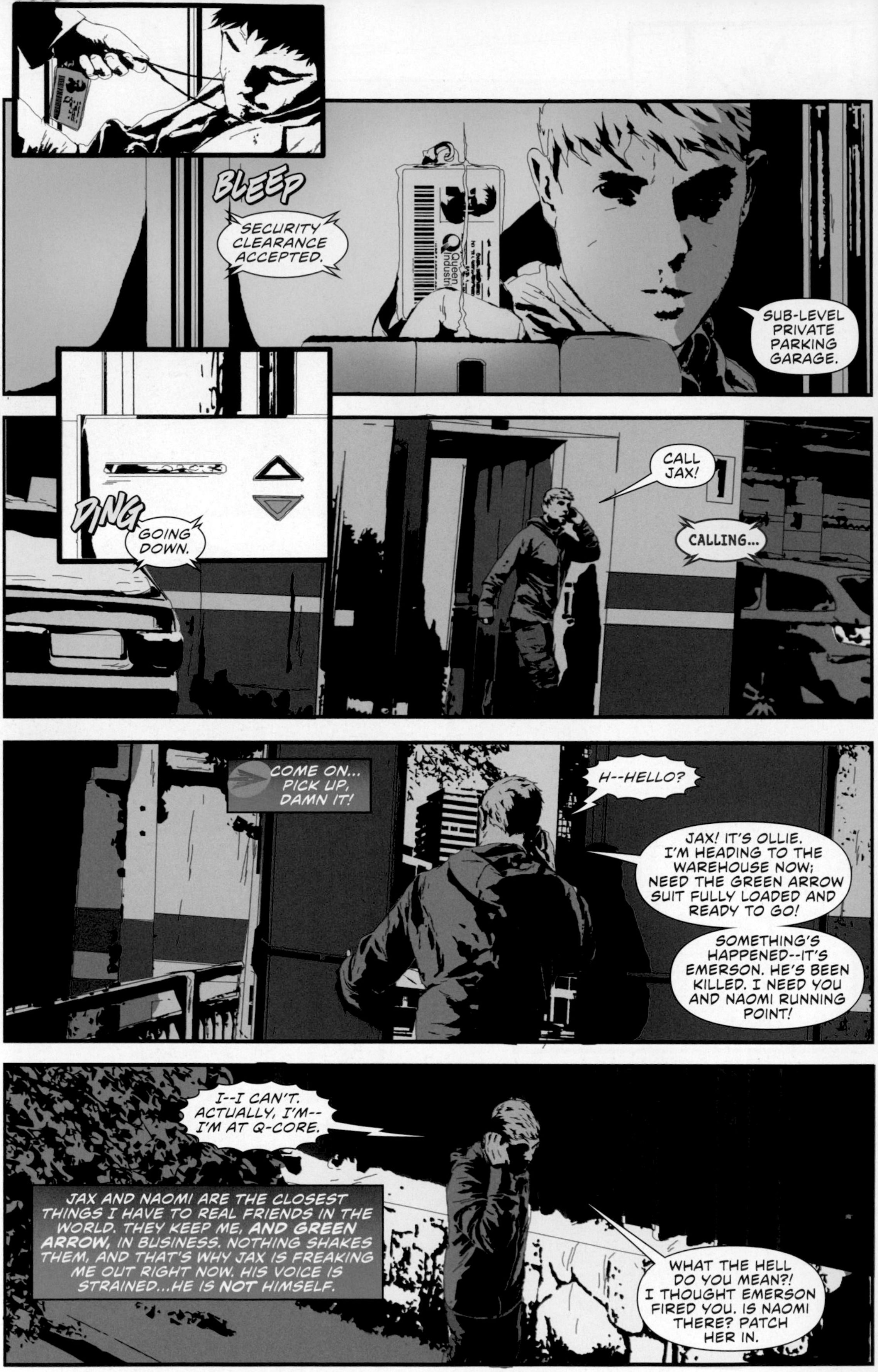
BLEEP
SECURITY CLEARANCE ACCEPTED.
SUB-LEVEL PRIVATE PARKING GARAGE.
DING
GOING DOWN.
CALL JAX!
CALLING...
COME ON... PICK UP, DAMN IT!
H--HELLO?
JAX! IT'S OLLIE. I'M HEADING TO THE WAREHOUSE NOW; NEED THE GREEN ARROW SUIT FULLY LOADED AND READY TO GO!
SOMETHING'S HAPPENED--IT'S EMERSON. HE'S BEEN KILLED. I NEED YOU AND NAOMI RUNNING POINT!
I--I CAN'T. ACTUALLY, I'M-- I'M AT Q-CORE.
JAX AND NAOMI ARE THE CLOSEST THINGS I HAVE TO REAL FRIENDS IN THE WORLD. THEY KEEP ME, AND GREEN ARROW, IN BUSINESS. NOTHING SHAKES THEM, AND THAT'S WHY JAX IS FREAKING ME OUT RIGHT NOW. HIS VOICE IS STRAINED...HE IS NOT HIMSELF.
WHAT THE HELL DO YOU MEAN?! I THOUGHT EMERSON FIRED YOU. IS NAOMI THERE? PATCH HER IN.

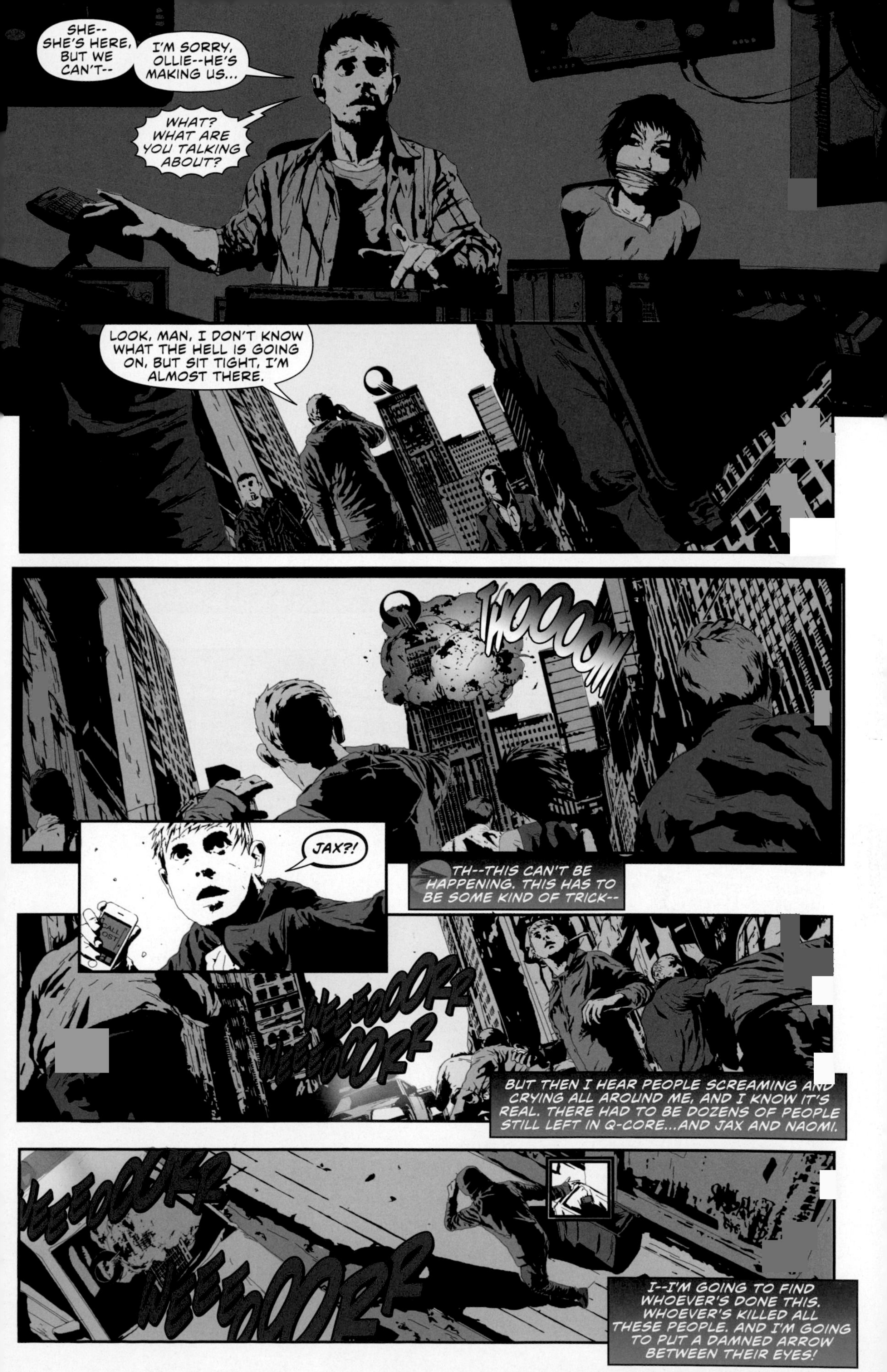
SHE-- SHE'S HERE, BUT WE CAN'T--
I'M SORRY, OLLIE--HE'S MAKING US...
WHAT? WHAT ARE YOU TALKING ABOUT?
LOOK, MAN, I DON'T KNOW WHAT THE HELL IS GOING ON, BUT SIT TIGHT, I'M ALMOST THERE.
THOOOOOM
JAX?!
CALL LOST
TH--THIS CAN'T BE HAPPENING. THIS HAS TO BE SOME KIND OF TRICK--
WEEEOOORRR
WEEEOOORRR
BUT THEN I HEAR PEOPLE SCREAMING AND CRYING ALL AROUND ME, AND I KNOW IT'S REAL. THERE HAD TO BE DOZENS OF PEOPLE STILL LEFT IN Q-CORE...AND JAX AND NAOMI.
WEEEOOORRR
WEEEOOORRR
I--I'M GOING TO FIND WHOEVER'S DONE THIS. WHOEVER'S KILLED ALL THESE PEOPLE. AND I'M GOING TO PUT A DAMNED ARROW BETWEEN THEIR EYES!

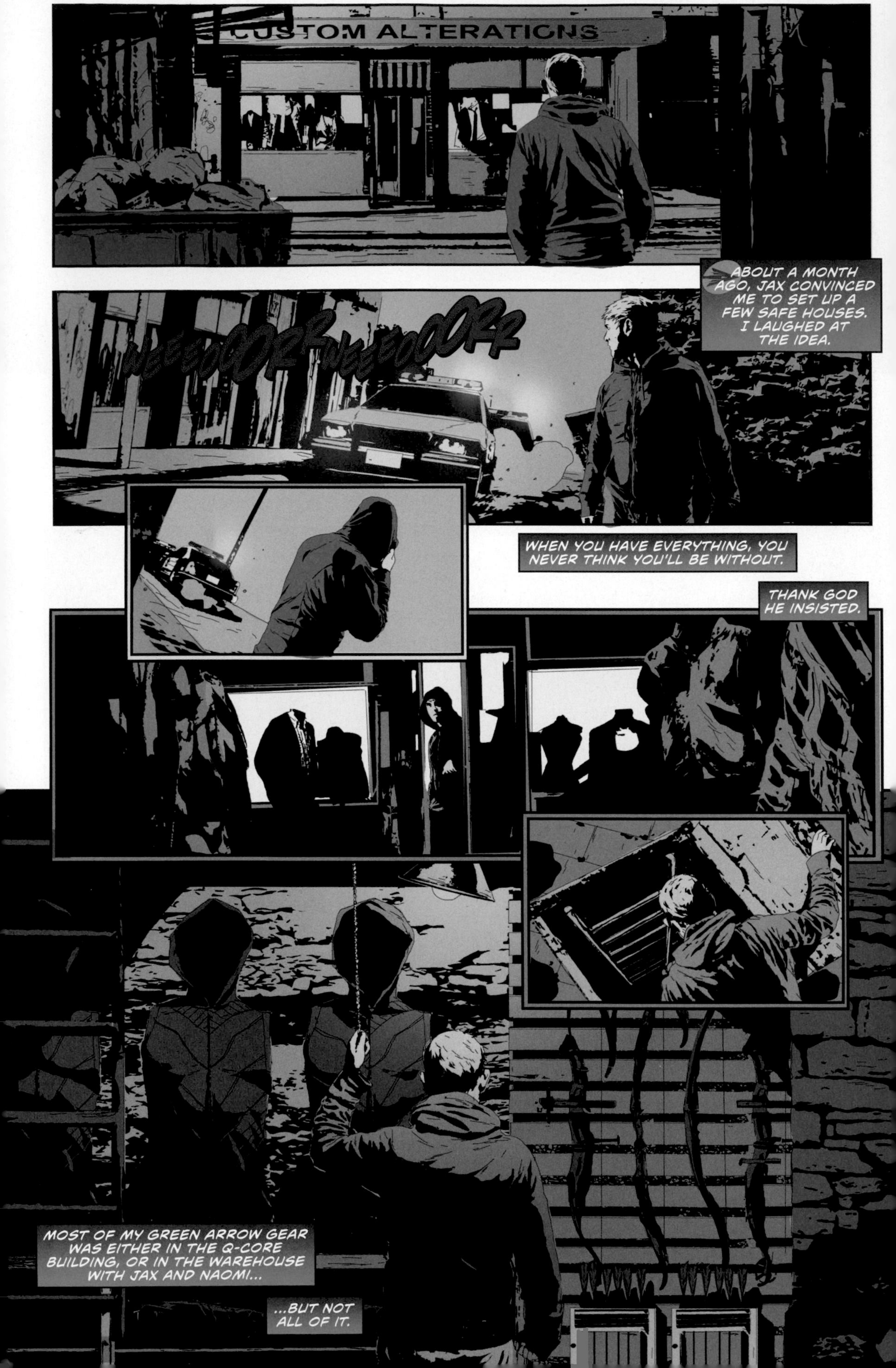
CUSTOM ALTERATIONS
ABOUT A MONTH AGO, JAX CONVINCED ME TO SET UP A FEW SAFE HOUSES. I LAUGHED AT THE IDEA.
WEEEOOOORR WEEEOOOORR
WHEN YOU HAVE EVERYTHING, YOU NEVER THINK YOU'LL BE WITHOUT.
THANK GOD HE INSISTED.
MOST OF MY GREEN ARROW GEAR WAS EITHER IN THE Q-CORE BUILDING, OR IN THE WAREHOUSE WITH JAX AND NAOMI...
...BUT NOT ALL OF IT.

EMERSON'S KILLER WAS AN ARCHER, AND A DAMN GOOD ONE, JUDGING BY THE SHOT HE MADE. IT CAN'T BE A COINCIDENCE. THE EXPLOSION AT Q-CORE--ALL THOSE PEOPLE WERE INNOCENT, BUT THIS IS CLEARLY A PERSONAL ATTACK.

HE'S HIT ME ON EVERY FRONT. SOMEHOW THIS GUY KNOWS OLIVER QUEEN IS GREEN ARROW. I HAVE NO IDEA HOW HE DID IT.

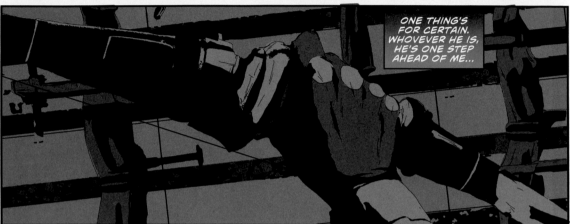

ONE THING'S FOR CERTAIN. WHOEVER HE IS, HE'S ONE STEP AHEAD OF ME...

I DON'T LIKE BEING A VICTIM...

I THINK IT'S TIME I DID THE HUNTING.

CREEEAK

EH?

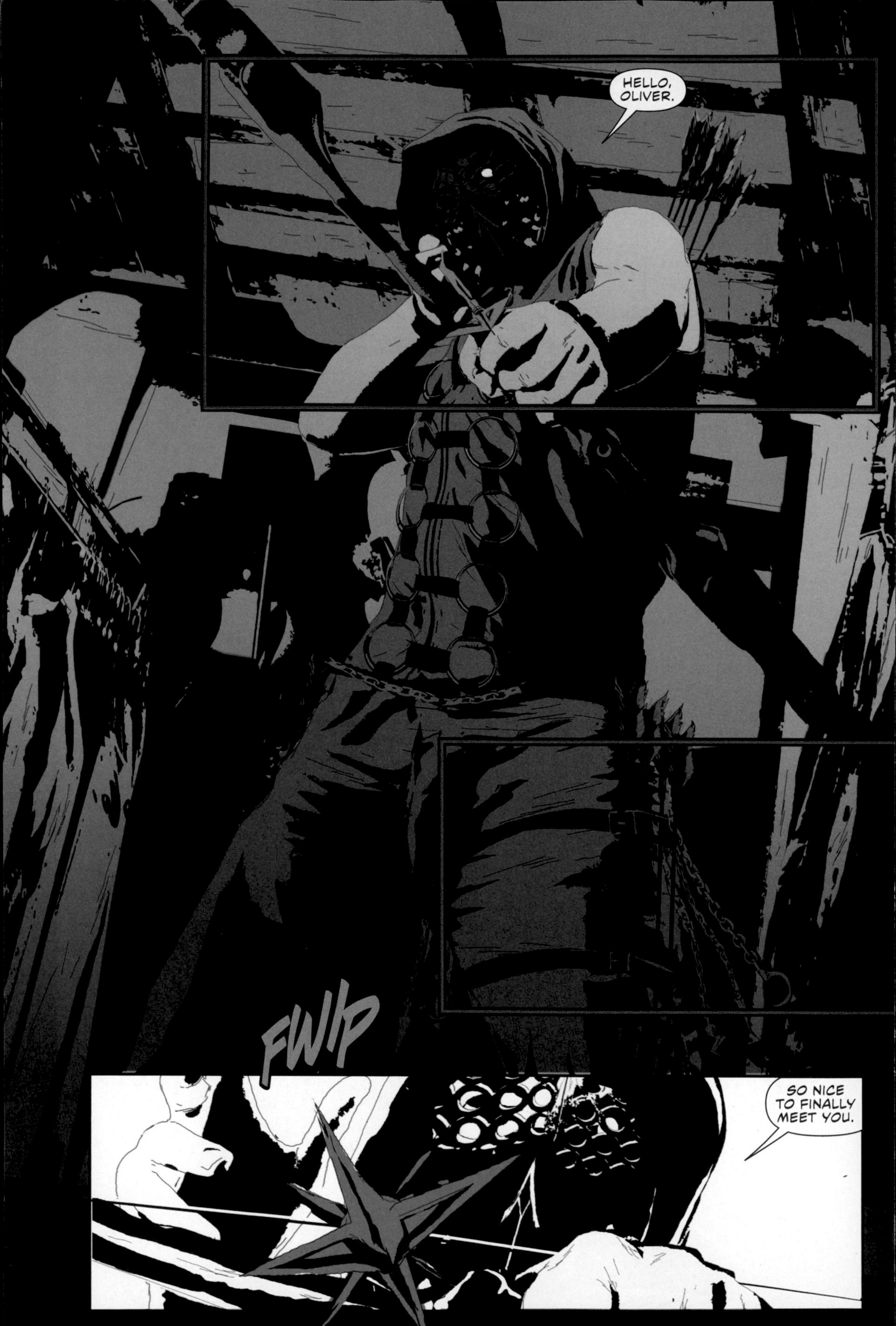
HELLO, OLIVER.
FWIP
SO NICE TO FINALLY MEET YOU.

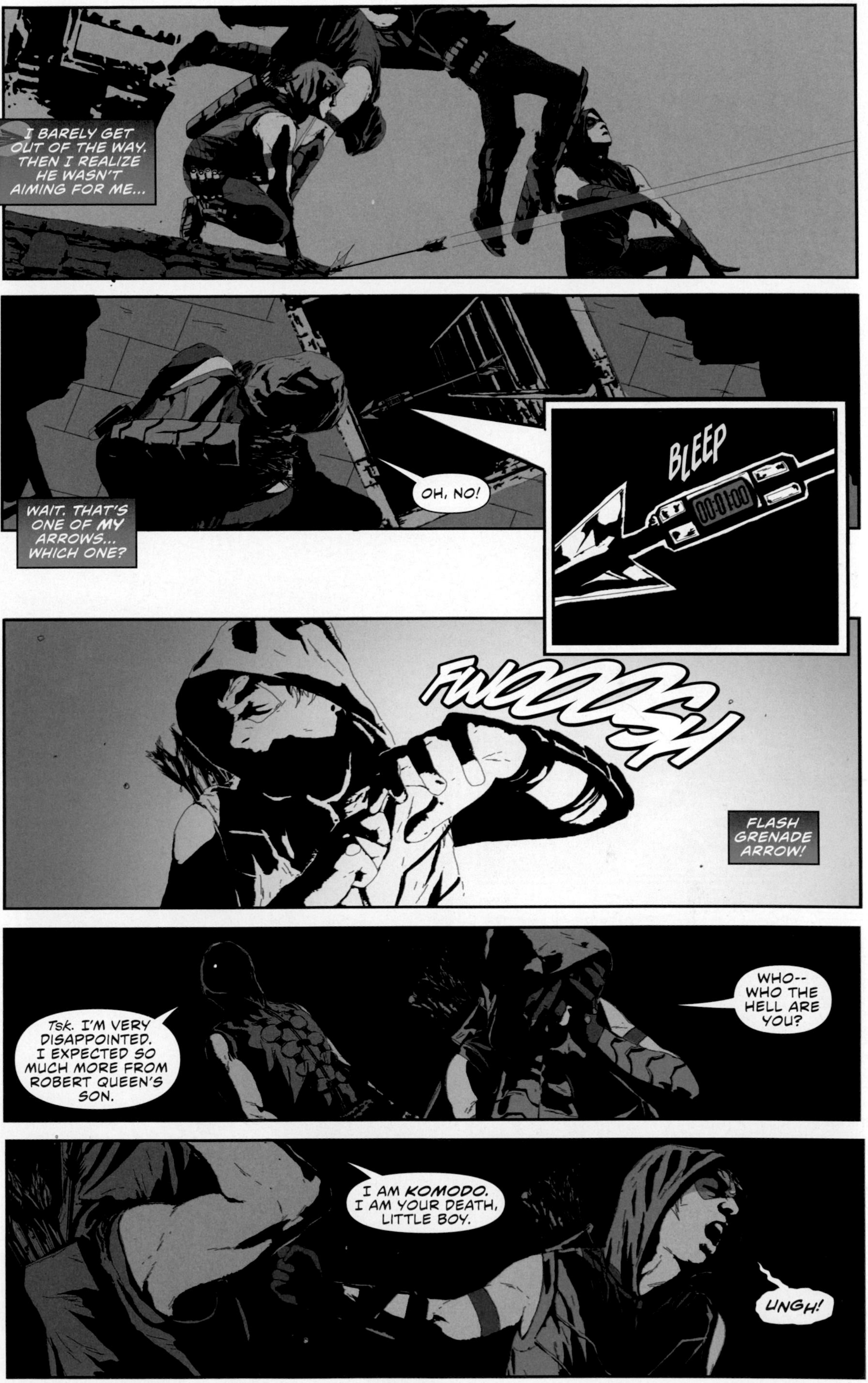
I BARELY GET OUT OF THE WAY. THEN I REALIZE HE WASN'T AIMING FOR ME...
WAIT. THAT'S ONE OF MY ARROWS... WHICH ONE?
OH, NO!
BLEEP
00:01:00
FWOOOSH
FLASH GRENADE ARROW!
Tsk. I'M VERY DISAPPOINTED. I EXPECTED SO MUCH MORE FROM ROBERT QUEEN'S SON.
WHO-- WHO THE HELL ARE YOU?
I AM KOMODO. I AM YOUR DEATH, LITTLE BOY.
UNGH!

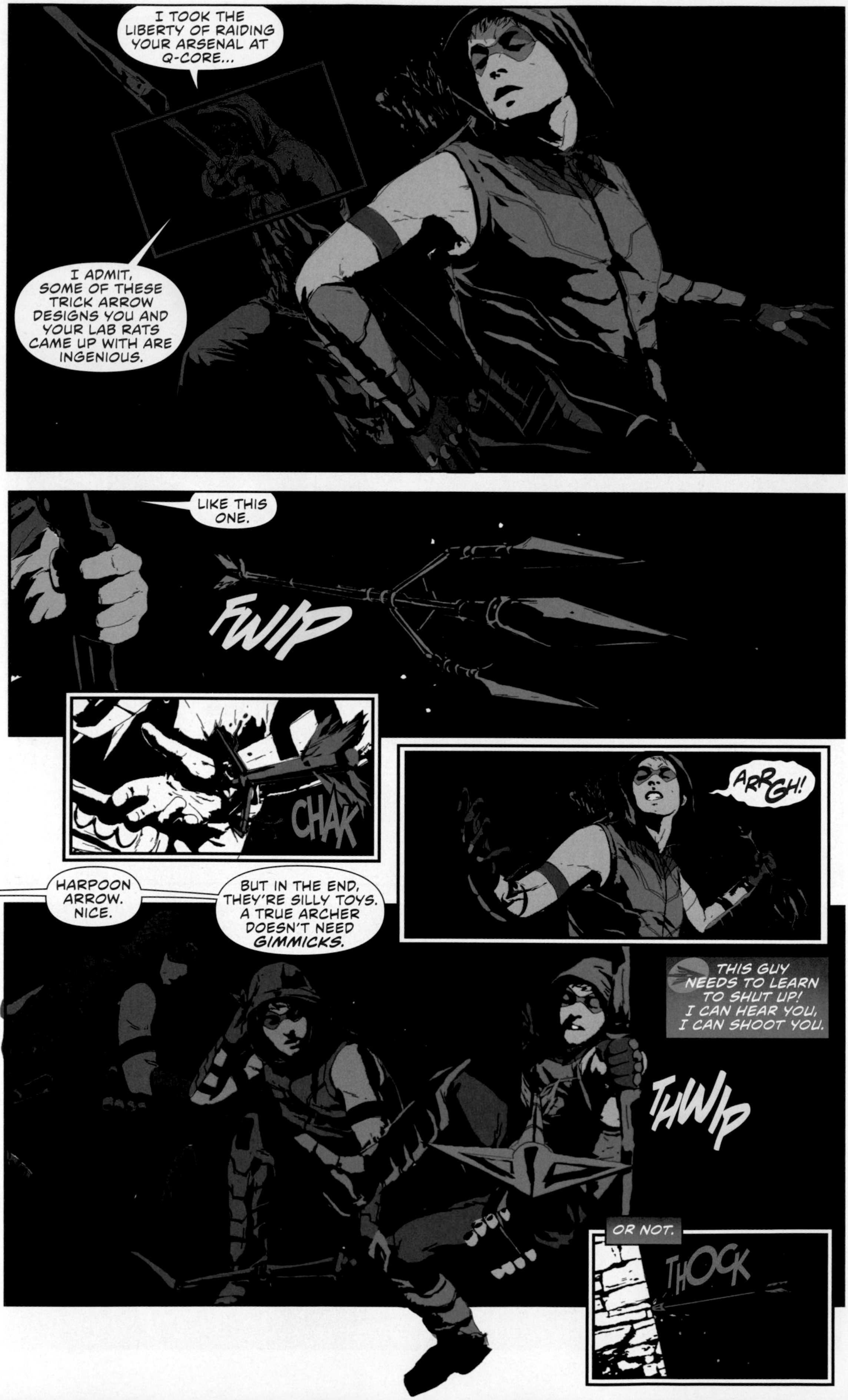

I TOOK THE LIBERTY OF RAIDING YOUR ARSENAL AT Q-CORE...
I ADMIT, SOME OF THESE TRICK ARROW DESIGNS YOU AND YOUR LAB RATS CAME UP WITH ARE INGENIOUS.
LIKE THIS ONE.
FWIP
CHAK
ARRGH!
HARPOON ARROW. NICE.
BUT IN THE END, THEY'RE SILLY TOYS. A TRUE ARCHER DOESN'T NEED GIMMICKS.
THIS GUY NEEDS TO LEARN TO SHUT UP! I CAN HEAR YOU, I CAN SHOOT YOU.
THWIP
OR NOT.
THOCK

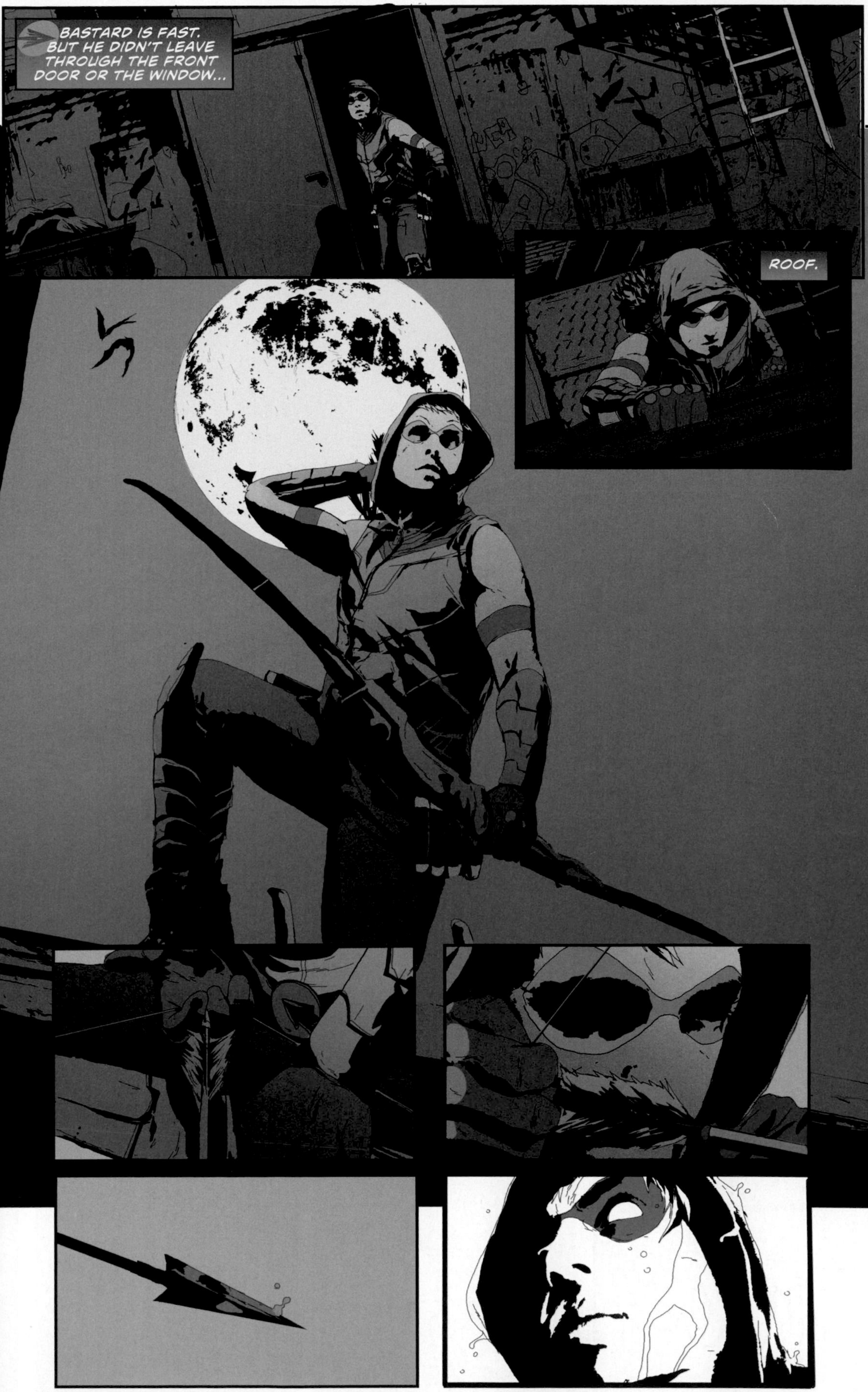
BASTARD IS FAST. BUT HE DIDN'T LEAVE THROUGH THE FRONT DOOR OR THE WINDOW...
ROOF.

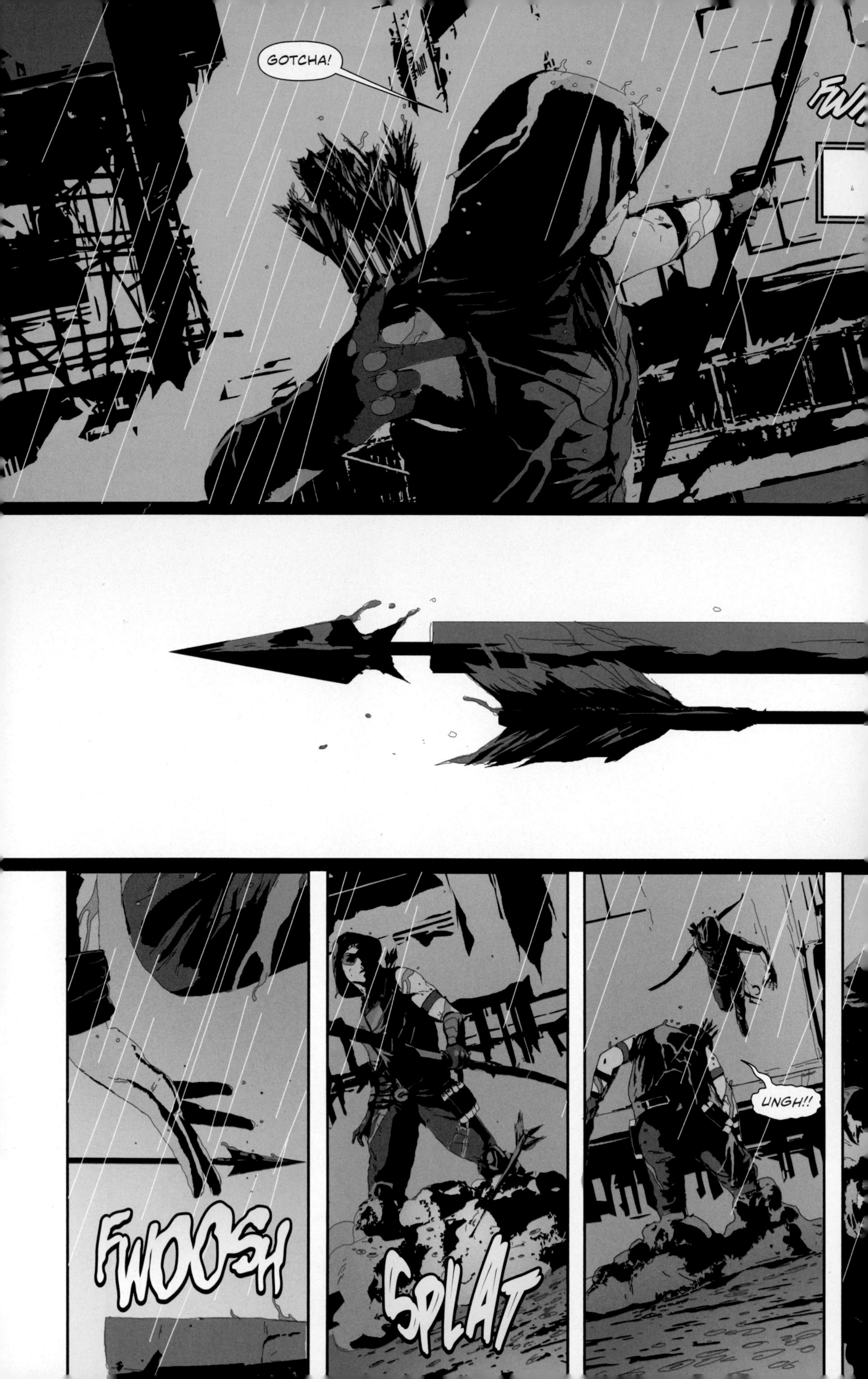
GOTCHA!
FWH
FWOOSH
SPLAT
UNGH!!

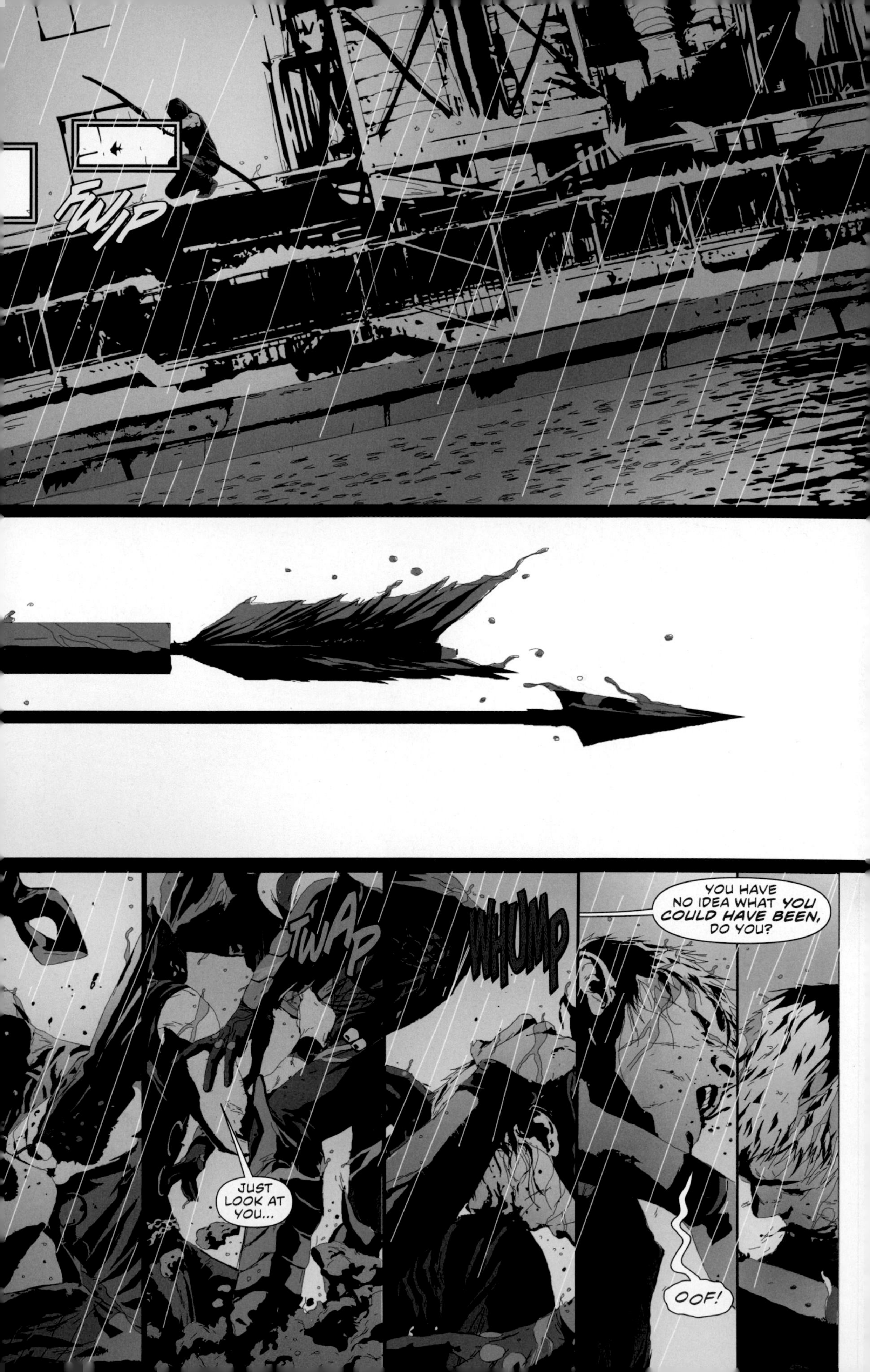
FWIP
TWAP
JUST LOOK AT YOU...
WHUMP
YOU HAVE NO IDEA WHAT YOU COULD HAVE BEEN, DO YOU?
OOF!

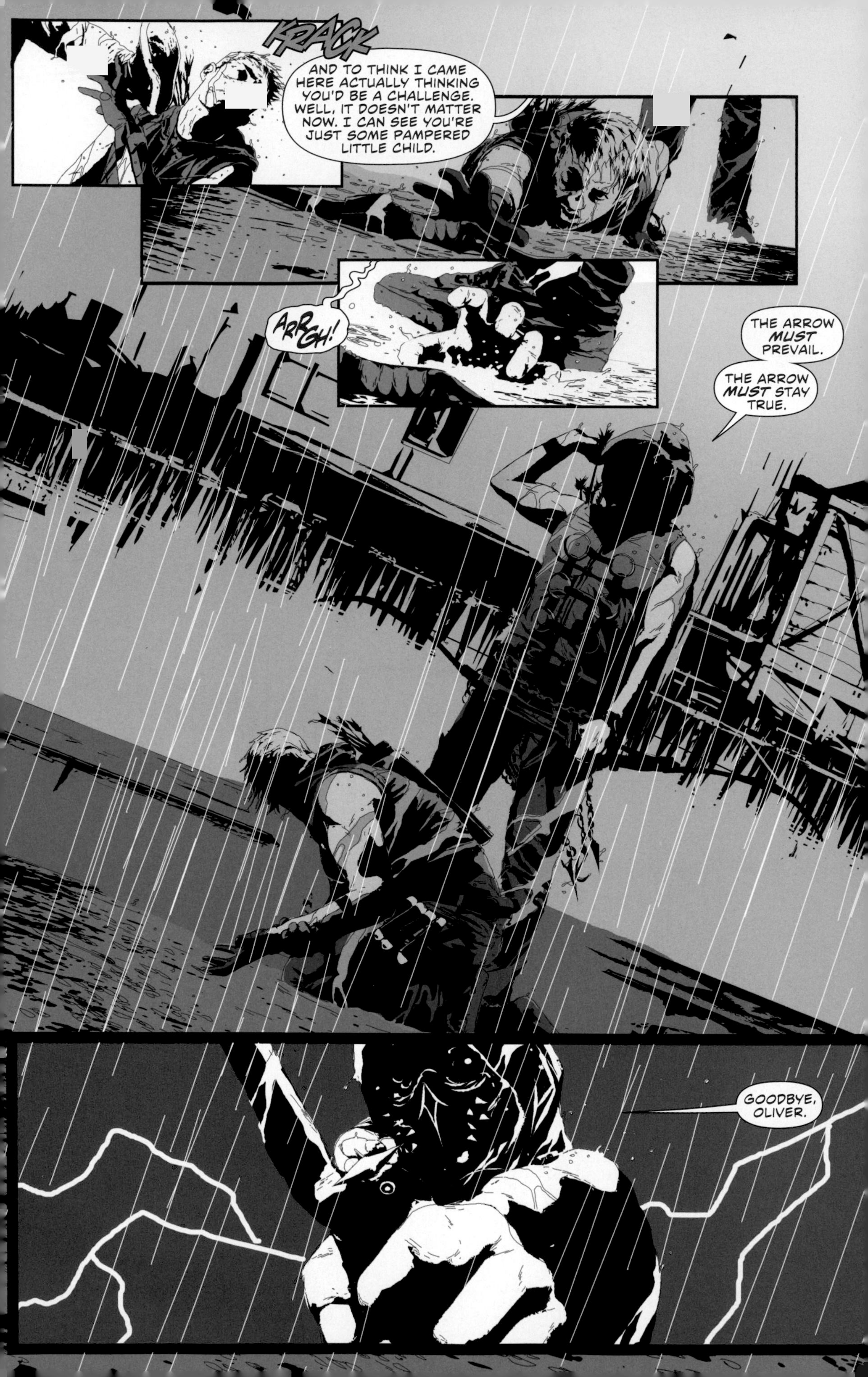
KRACK
AND TO THINK I CAME HERE ACTUALLY THINKING YOU'D BE A CHALLENGE. WELL, IT DOESN'T MATTER NOW. I CAN SEE YOU'RE JUST SOME PAMPERED LITTLE CHILD.
ARRGH!
THE ARROW MUST PREVAIL.
THE ARROW MUST STAY TRUE.
GOODBYE, OLIVER.

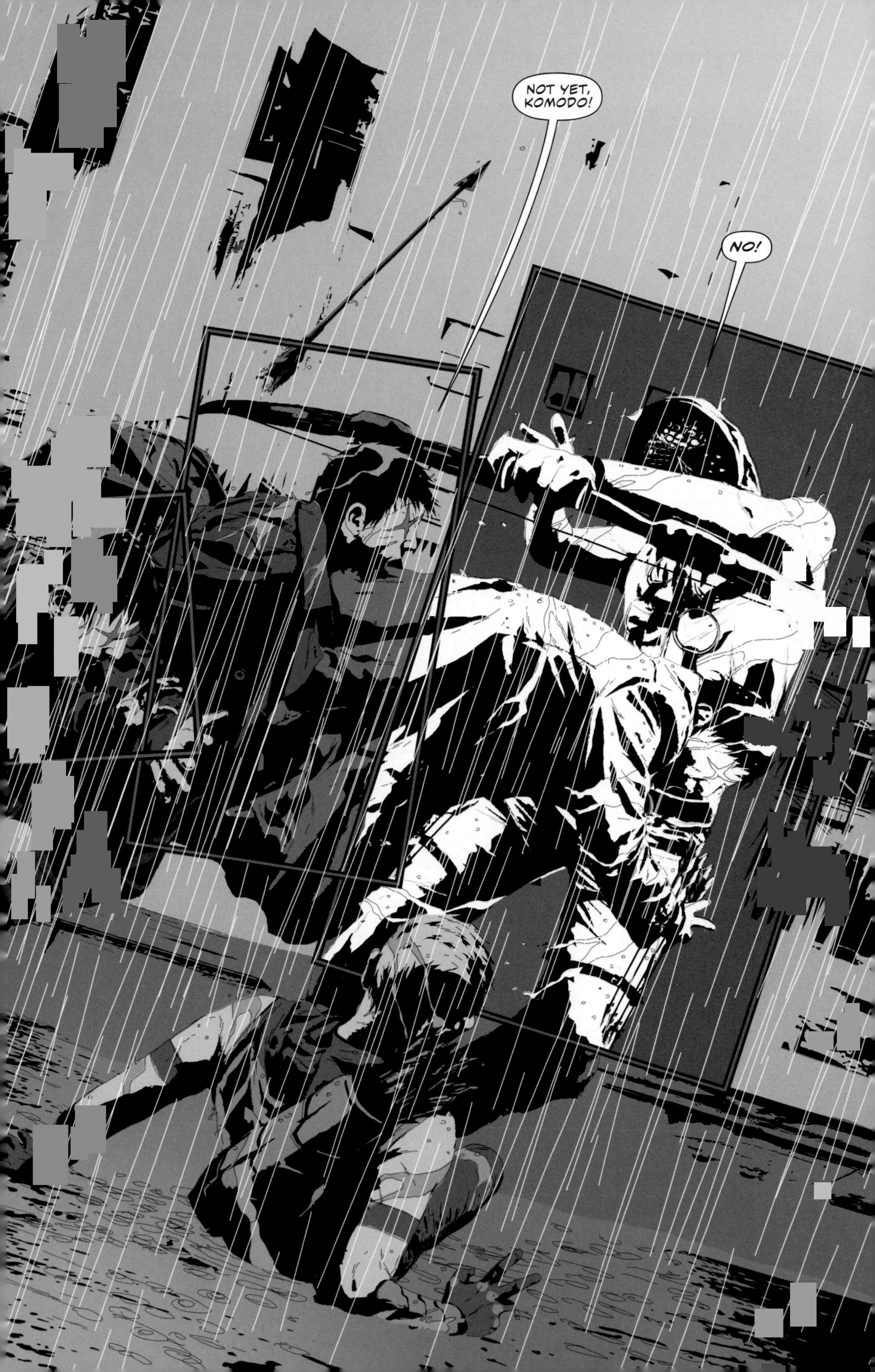
NOT YET, KOMODO!
NO!

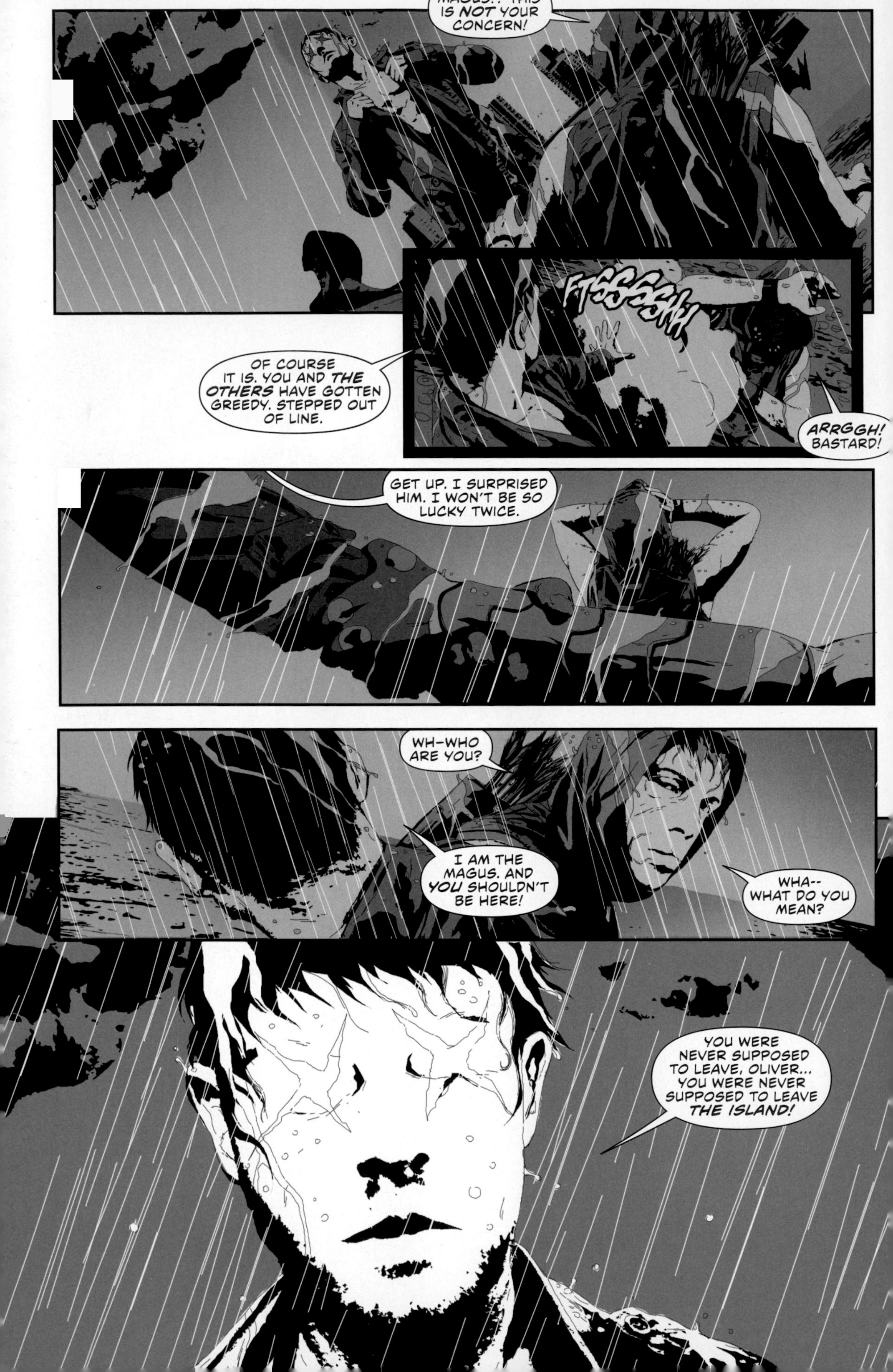
MAGUS!? THIS IS NOT YOUR CONCERN!
FTSSSSSHH
OF COURSE IT IS. YOU AND THE OTHERS HAVE GOTTEN GREEDY. STEPPED OUT OF LINE.
ARRGGH! BASTARD!
GET UP. I SURPRISED HIM. I WON'T BE SO LUCKY TWICE.
WH-WHO ARE YOU?
I AM THE MAGUS. AND YOU SHOULDN'T BE HERE!
WHA-- WHAT DO YOU MEAN?
YOU WERE NEVER SUPPOSED TO LEAVE, OLIVER... YOU WERE NEVER SUPPOSED TO LEAVE THE ISLAND!

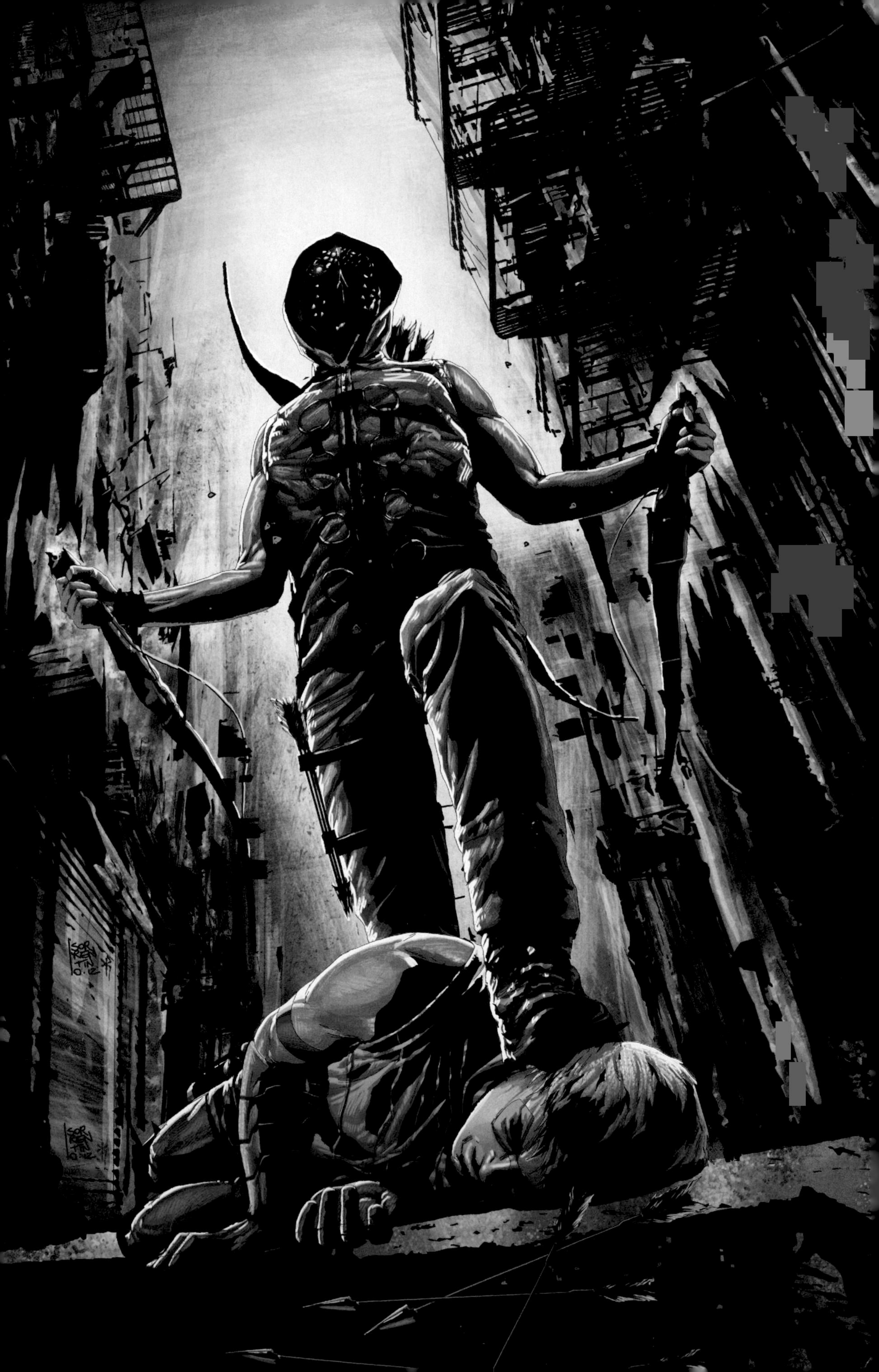

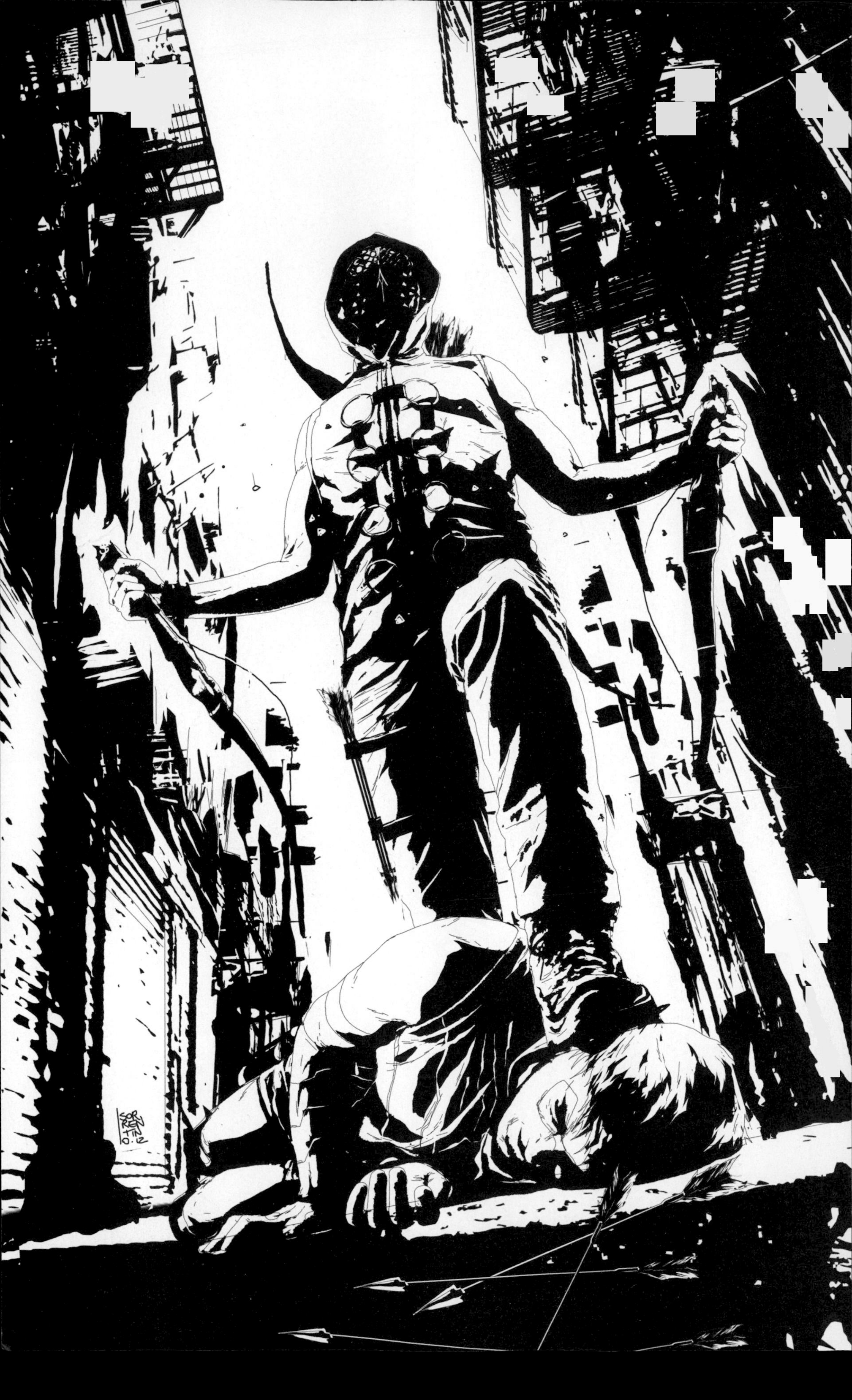

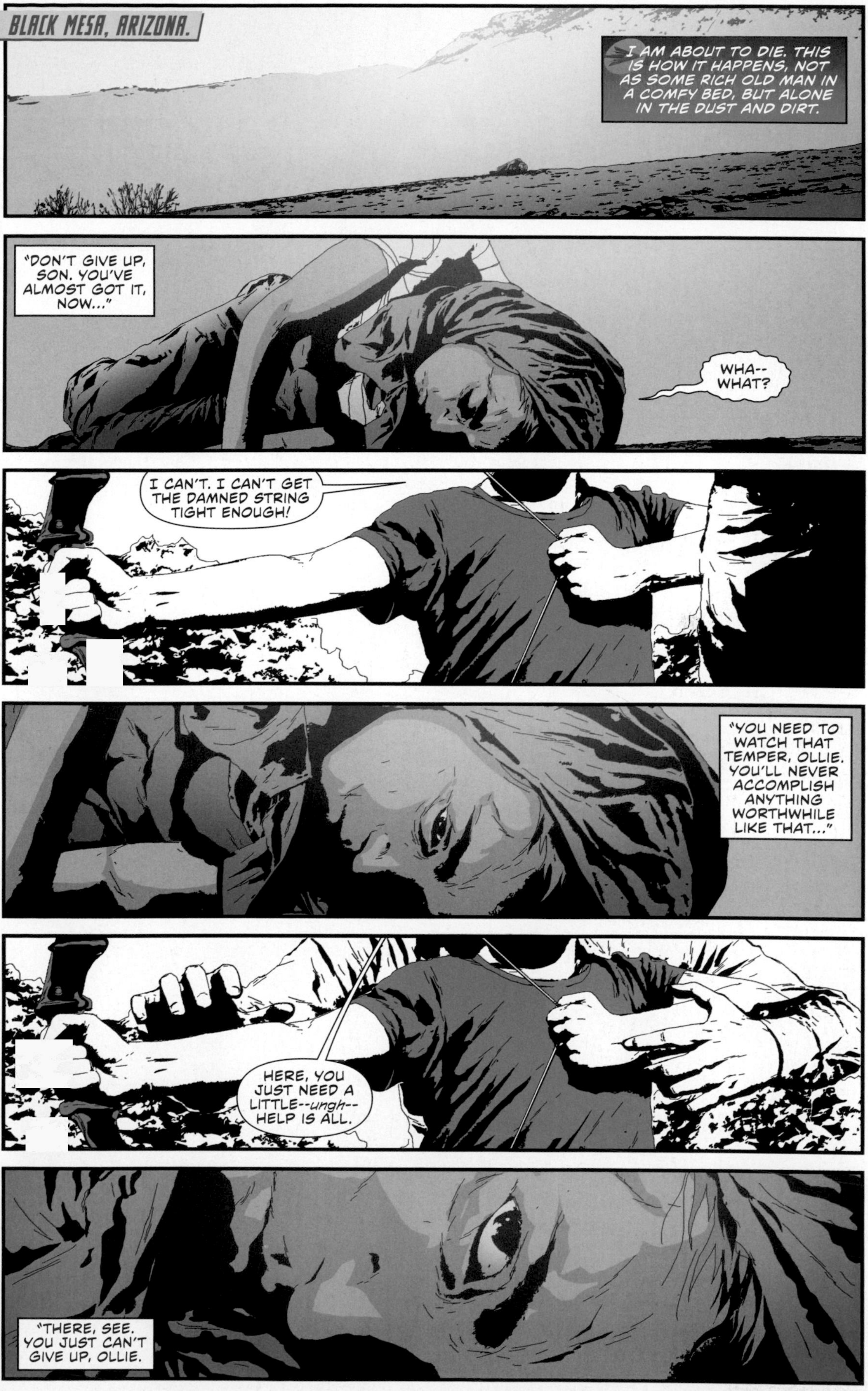
BLACK MESA, ARIZONA.
I AM ABOUT TO DIE. THIS IS HOW IT HAPPENS, NOT AS SOME RICH OLD MAN IN A COMFY BED, BUT ALONE IN THE DUST AND DIRT.
"DON'T GIVE UP, SON. YOU'VE ALMOST GOT IT, NOW..."
WHA-- WHAT?
I CAN'T. I CAN'T GET THE DAMNED STRING TIGHT ENOUGH!
"YOU NEED TO WATCH THAT TEMPER, OLLIE. YOU'LL NEVER ACCOMPLISH ANYTHING WORTHWHILE LIKE THAT..."
HERE, YOU JUST NEED A LITTLE--*ungh*-- HELP IS ALL.
"THERE, SEE. YOU JUST CAN'T GIVE UP, OLLIE.

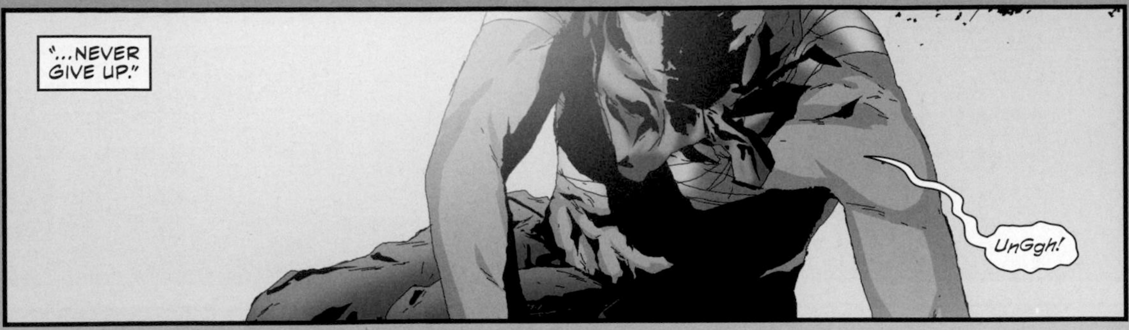
"...NEVER GIVE UP."
UnGgh!

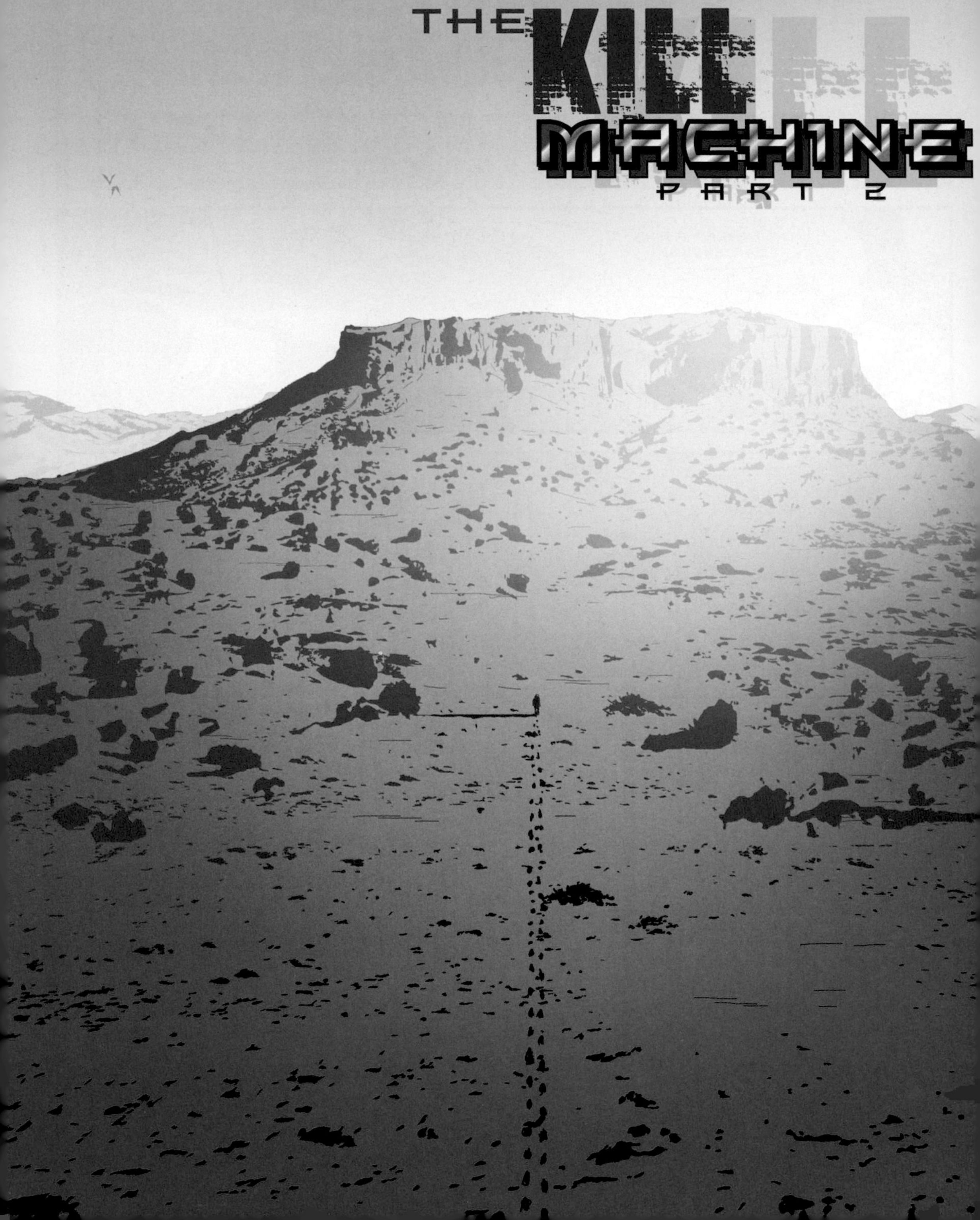
THE KILL MACHINE
PART 2

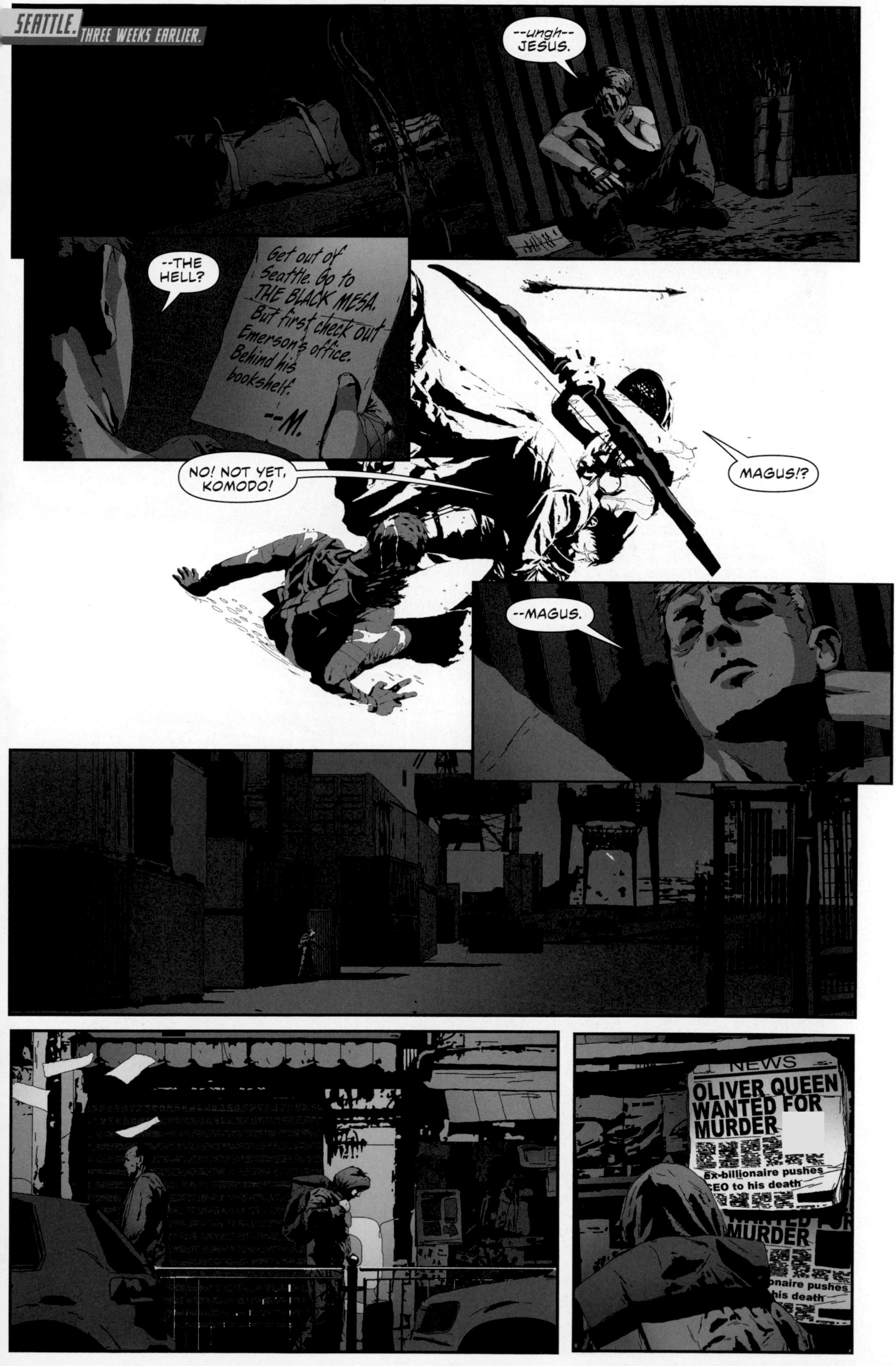
SEATTLE. THREE WEEKS EARLIER.
--ungh-- JESUS.
--THE HELL?
Get out of Seattle. Go to THE BLACK MESA. But first check out Emerson's office. Behind his bookshelf. --M.
MAGUS!?
NO! NOT YET, KOMODO!
--MAGUS.
NEWS
OLIVER QUEEN WANTED FOR MURDER
ex-billionaire pushes CEO to his death
WANTED FO
MURDER
onaire pushes
his death

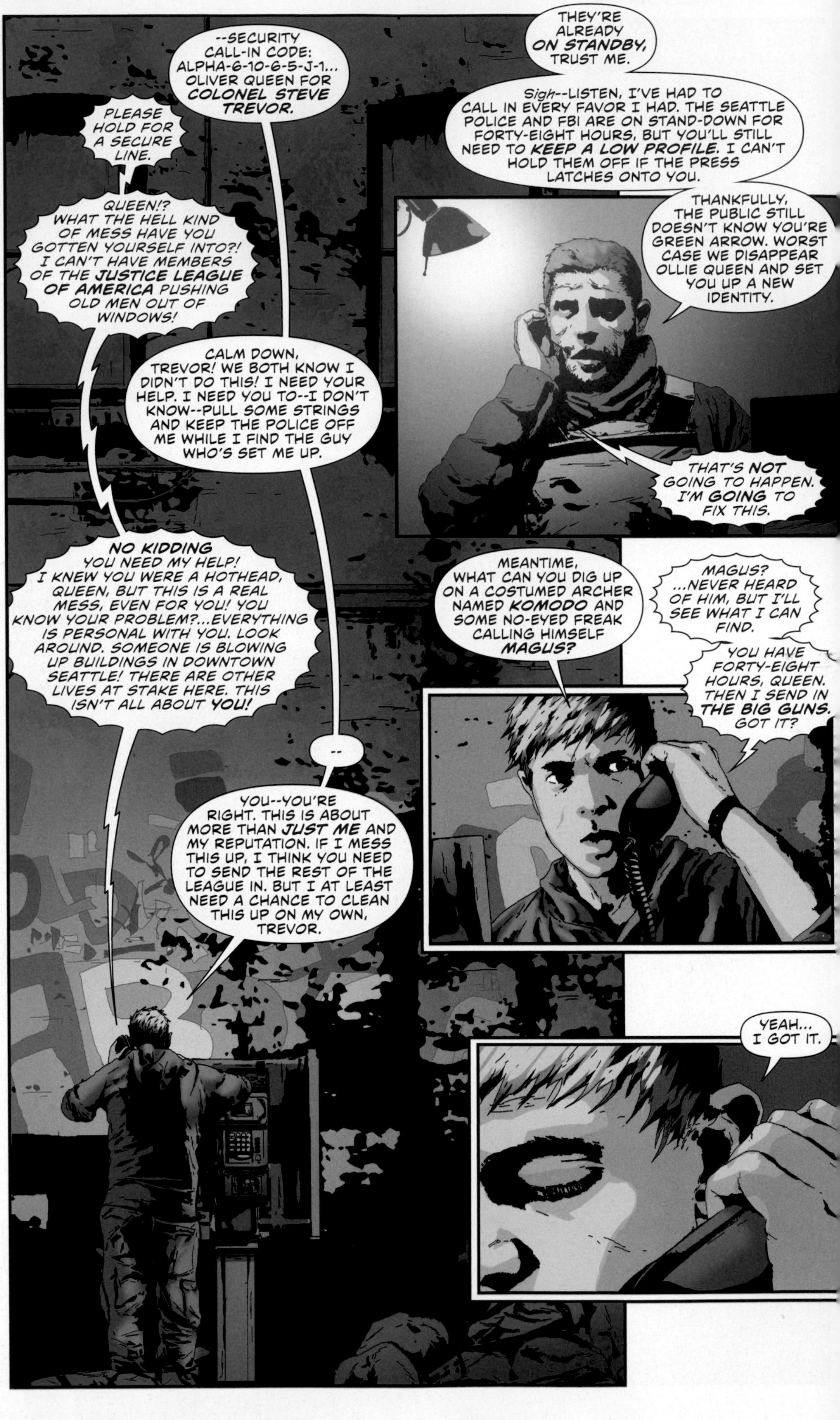
--SECURITY CALL-IN CODE: ALPHA-6-10-6-5-J-1... OLIVER QUEEN FOR COLONEL STEVE TREVOR.
PLEASE HOLD FOR A SECURE LINE.
QUEEN!? WHAT THE HELL KIND OF MESS HAVE YOU GOTTEN YOURSELF INTO?! I CAN'T HAVE MEMBERS OF THE JUSTICE LEAGUE OF AMERICA PUSHING OLD MEN OUT OF WINDOWS!
CALM DOWN, TREVOR! WE BOTH KNOW I DIDN'T DO THIS! I NEED YOUR HELP. I NEED YOU TO--I DON'T KNOW--PULL SOME STRINGS AND KEEP THE POLICE OFF ME WHILE I FIND THE GUY WHO'S SET ME UP.
NO KIDDING YOU NEED MY HELP! I KNEW YOU WERE A HOTHEAD, QUEEN, BUT THIS IS A REAL MESS, EVEN FOR YOU! YOU KNOW YOUR PROBLEM?...EVERYTHING IS PERSONAL WITH YOU. LOOK AROUND. SOMEONE IS BLOWING UP BUILDINGS IN DOWNTOWN SEATTLE! THERE ARE OTHER LIVES AT STAKE HERE. THIS ISN'T ALL ABOUT YOU!
--
YOU--YOU'RE RIGHT. THIS IS ABOUT MORE THAN JUST ME AND MY REPUTATION. IF I MESS THIS UP, I THINK YOU NEED TO SEND THE REST OF THE LEAGUE IN. BUT I AT LEAST NEED A CHANCE TO CLEAN THIS UP ON MY OWN, TREVOR.
THEY'RE ALREADY ON STANDBY, TRUST ME.
Sigh--LISTEN, I'VE HAD TO CALL IN EVERY FAVOR I HAD. THE SEATTLE POLICE AND FBI ARE ON STAND-DOWN FOR FORTY-EIGHT HOURS, BUT YOU'LL STILL NEED TO KEEP A LOW PROFILE. I CAN'T HOLD THEM OFF IF THE PRESS LATCHES ONTO YOU.
THANKFULLY, THE PUBLIC STILL DOESN'T KNOW YOU'RE GREEN ARROW. WORST CASE WE DISAPPEAR OLLIE QUEEN AND SET YOU UP A NEW IDENTITY.
THAT'S NOT GOING TO HAPPEN. I'M GOING TO FIX THIS.
MEANTIME, WHAT CAN YOU DIG UP ON A COSTUMED ARCHER NAMED KOMODO AND SOME NO-EYED FREAK CALLING HIMSELF MAGUS?
MAGUS? ...NEVER HEARD OF HIM, BUT I'LL SEE WHAT I CAN FIND.
YOU HAVE FORTY-EIGHT HOURS, QUEEN. THEN I SEND IN THE BIG GUNS. GOT IT?
YEAH... I GOT IT.

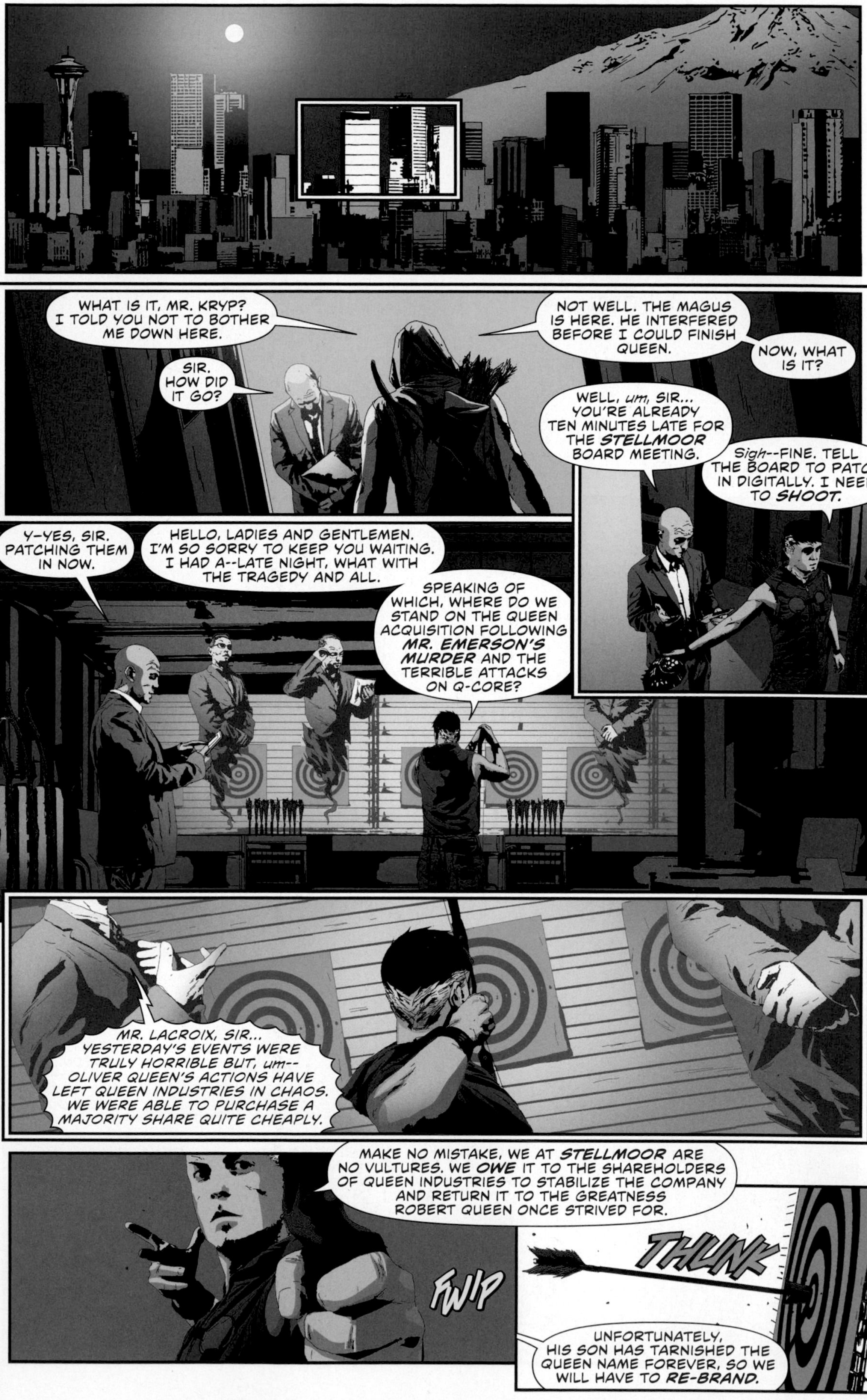
WHAT IS IT, MR. KRYP? I TOLD YOU NOT TO BOTHER ME DOWN HERE.
SIR. HOW DID IT GO?
NOT WELL. THE MAGUS IS HERE. HE INTERFERED BEFORE I COULD FINISH QUEEN.
NOW, WHAT IS IT?
WELL, *um,* SIR... YOU'RE ALREADY TEN MINUTES LATE FOR THE ***STELLMOOR*** BOARD MEETING.
Sigh--FINE. TELL THE BOARD TO PATCH IN DIGITALLY. I NEED TO ***SHOOT.***
Y-YES, SIR. PATCHING THEM IN NOW.
HELLO, LADIES AND GENTLEMEN. I'M SO SORRY TO KEEP YOU WAITING. I HAD A--LATE NIGHT, WHAT WITH THE TRAGEDY AND ALL.
SPEAKING OF WHICH, WHERE DO WE STAND ON THE QUEEN ACQUISITION FOLLOWING ***MR. EMERSON'S MURDER*** AND THE TERRIBLE ATTACKS ON Q-CORE?
MR. LACROIX, SIR... YESTERDAY'S EVENTS WERE TRULY HORRIBLE BUT, *um*-- OLIVER QUEEN'S ACTIONS HAVE LEFT QUEEN INDUSTRIES IN CHAOS. WE WERE ABLE TO PURCHASE A MAJORITY SHARE QUITE CHEAPLY.
MAKE NO MISTAKE, WE AT ***STELLMOOR*** ARE NO VULTURES. WE ***OWE*** IT TO THE SHAREHOLDERS OF QUEEN INDUSTRIES TO STABILIZE THE COMPANY AND RETURN IT TO THE GREATNESS ROBERT QUEEN ONCE STRIVED FOR.
FWIP
THUNK
UNFORTUNATELY, HIS SON HAS TARNISHED THE QUEEN NAME FOREVER, SO WE WILL HAVE TO ***RE-BRAND.***

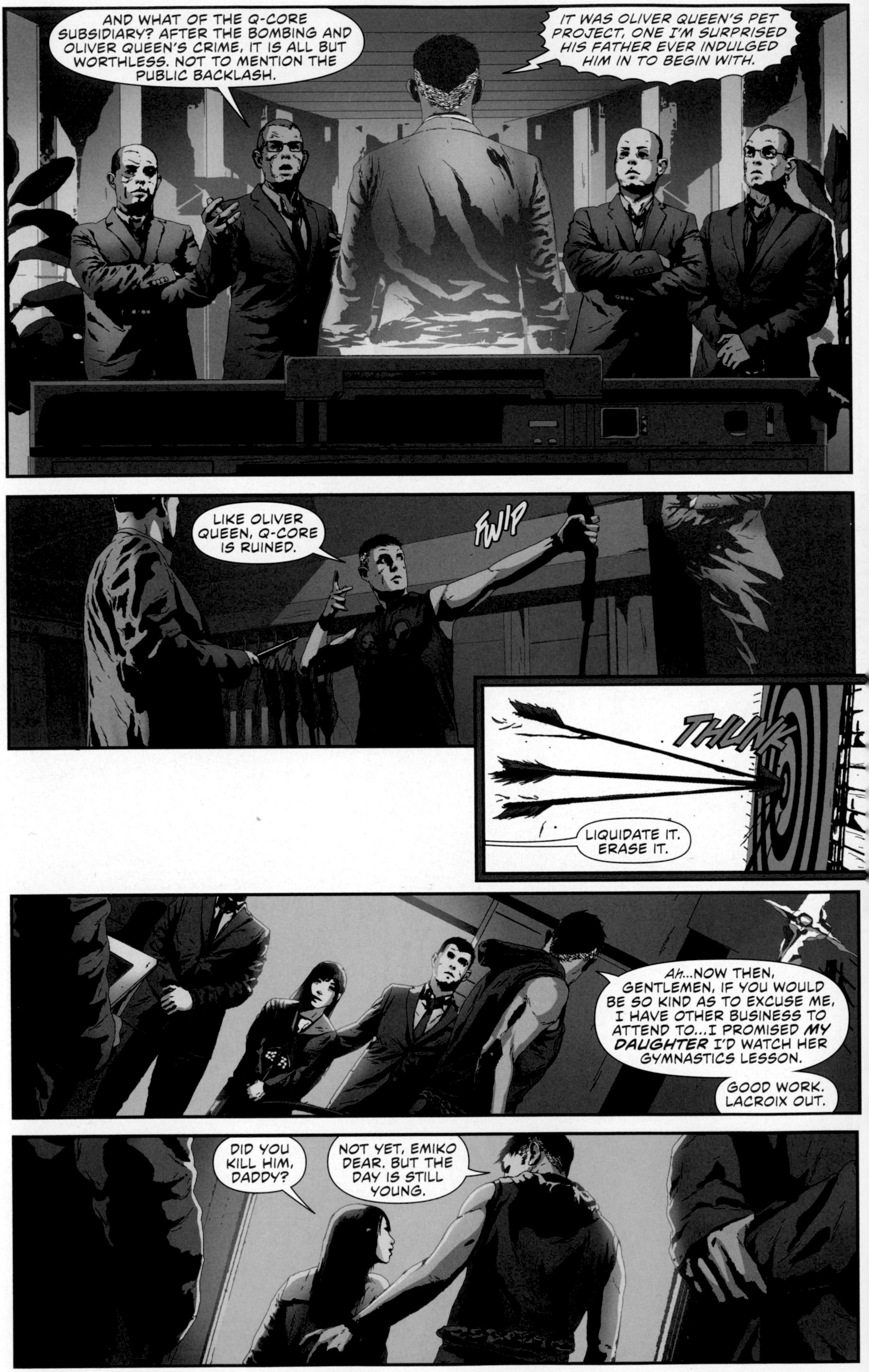
AND WHAT OF THE Q-CORE SUBSIDIARY? AFTER THE BOMBING AND OLIVER QUEEN'S CRIME, IT IS ALL BUT WORTHLESS. NOT TO MENTION THE PUBLIC BACKLASH.
IT WAS OLIVER QUEEN'S PET PROJECT, ONE I'M SURPRISED HIS FATHER EVER INDULGED HIM IN TO BEGIN WITH.
LIKE OLIVER QUEEN, Q-CORE IS RUINED.
FWIP
THUNK
LIQUIDATE IT. ERASE IT.
Ah...NOW THEN, GENTLEMEN, IF YOU WOULD BE SO KIND AS TO EXCUSE ME, I HAVE OTHER BUSINESS TO ATTEND TO...I PROMISED MY DAUGHTER I'D WATCH HER GYMNASTICS LESSON.
GOOD WORK. LACROIX OUT.
DID YOU KILL HIM, DADDY?
NOT YET, EMIKO DEAR. BUT THE DAY IS STILL YOUNG.

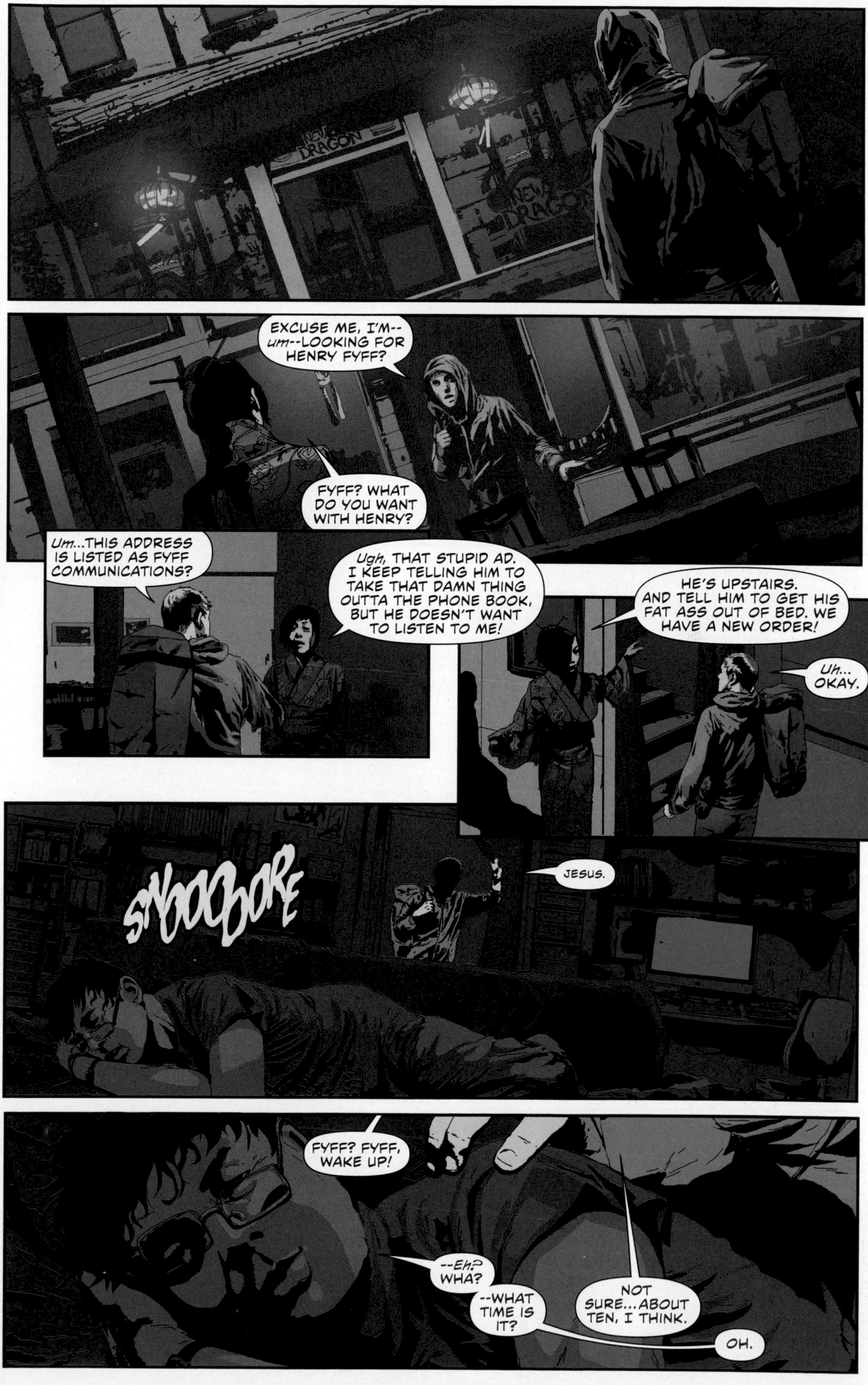
NEW DRAGON
NEW DRAGON
EXCUSE ME, I'M--*um*--LOOKING FOR HENRY FYFF?
FYFF? WHAT DO YOU WANT WITH HENRY?
Um...THIS ADDRESS IS LISTED AS FYFF COMMUNICATIONS?
Ugh, THAT STUPID AD. I KEEP TELLING HIM TO TAKE THAT DAMN THING OUTTA THE PHONE BOOK, BUT HE DOESN'T WANT TO LISTEN TO ME!
HE'S UPSTAIRS. AND TELL HIM TO GET HIS FAT ASS OUT OF BED. WE HAVE A NEW ORDER!
Uh... OKAY.
SNOOOORE
JESUS.
FYFF? FYFF, WAKE UP!
--*Eh*? WHA?
--WHAT TIME IS IT?
NOT SURE...ABOUT TEN, I THINK.
OH.

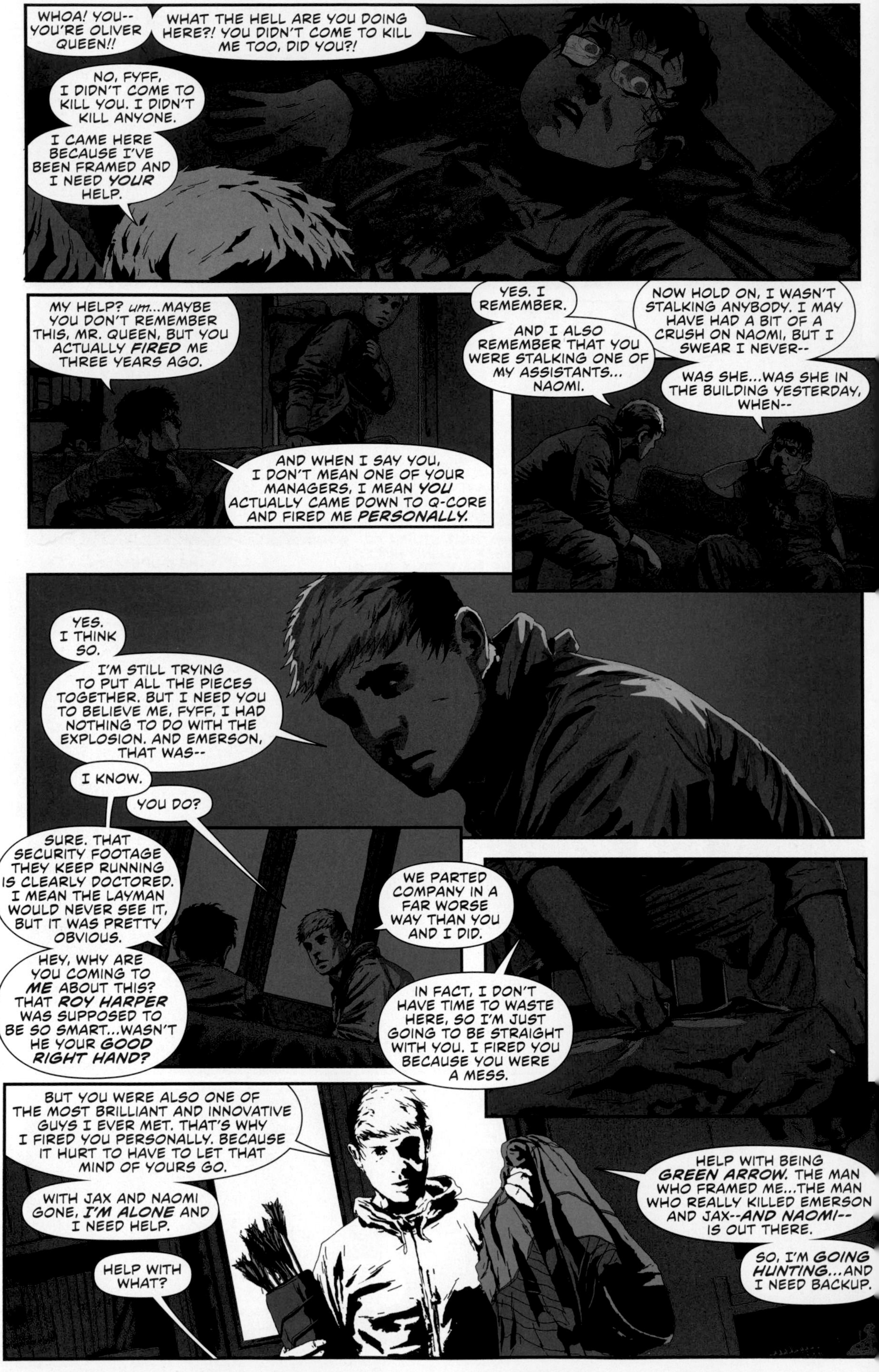
WHOA! YOU-- YOU'RE OLIVER QUEEN!!
WHAT THE HELL ARE YOU DOING HERE?! YOU DIDN'T COME TO KILL ME TOO, DID YOU?!
NO, FYFF, I DIDN'T COME TO KILL YOU. I DIDN'T KILL ANYONE.
I CAME HERE BECAUSE I'VE BEEN FRAMED AND I NEED YOUR HELP.
MY HELP? um...MAYBE YOU DON'T REMEMBER THIS, MR. QUEEN, BUT YOU ACTUALLY FIRED ME THREE YEARS AGO.
AND WHEN I SAY YOU, I DON'T MEAN ONE OF YOUR MANAGERS, I MEAN YOU ACTUALLY CAME DOWN TO Q-CORE AND FIRED ME PERSONALLY.
YES. I REMEMBER.
AND I ALSO REMEMBER THAT YOU WERE STALKING ONE OF MY ASSISTANTS... NAOMI.
NOW HOLD ON, I WASN'T STALKING ANYBODY. I MAY HAVE HAD A BIT OF A CRUSH ON NAOMI, BUT I SWEAR I NEVER--
WAS SHE...WAS SHE IN THE BUILDING YESTERDAY, WHEN--
YES. I THINK SO.
I'M STILL TRYING TO PUT ALL THE PIECES TOGETHER. BUT I NEED YOU TO BELIEVE ME, FYFF, I HAD NOTHING TO DO WITH THE EXPLOSION. AND EMERSON, THAT WAS--
I KNOW.
YOU DO?
SURE. THAT SECURITY FOOTAGE THEY KEEP RUNNING IS CLEARLY DOCTORED. I MEAN THE LAYMAN WOULD NEVER SEE IT, BUT IT WAS PRETTY OBVIOUS.
HEY, WHY ARE YOU COMING TO ME ABOUT THIS? THAT ROY HARPER WAS SUPPOSED TO BE SO SMART...WASN'T HE YOUR GOOD RIGHT HAND?
WE PARTED COMPANY IN A FAR WORSE WAY THAN YOU AND I DID.
IN FACT, I DON'T HAVE TIME TO WASTE HERE, SO I'M JUST GOING TO BE STRAIGHT WITH YOU. I FIRED YOU BECAUSE YOU WERE A MESS.
BUT YOU WERE ALSO ONE OF THE MOST BRILLIANT AND INNOVATIVE GUYS I EVER MET. THAT'S WHY I FIRED YOU PERSONALLY. BECAUSE IT HURT TO HAVE TO LET THAT MIND OF YOURS GO.
WITH JAX AND NAOMI GONE, I'M ALONE AND I NEED HELP.
HELP WITH WHAT?
HELP WITH BEING GREEN ARROW. THE MAN WHO FRAMED ME...THE MAN WHO REALLY KILLED EMERSON AND JAX--AND NAOMI-- IS OUT THERE.
SO, I'M GOING HUNTING...AND I NEED BACKUP.

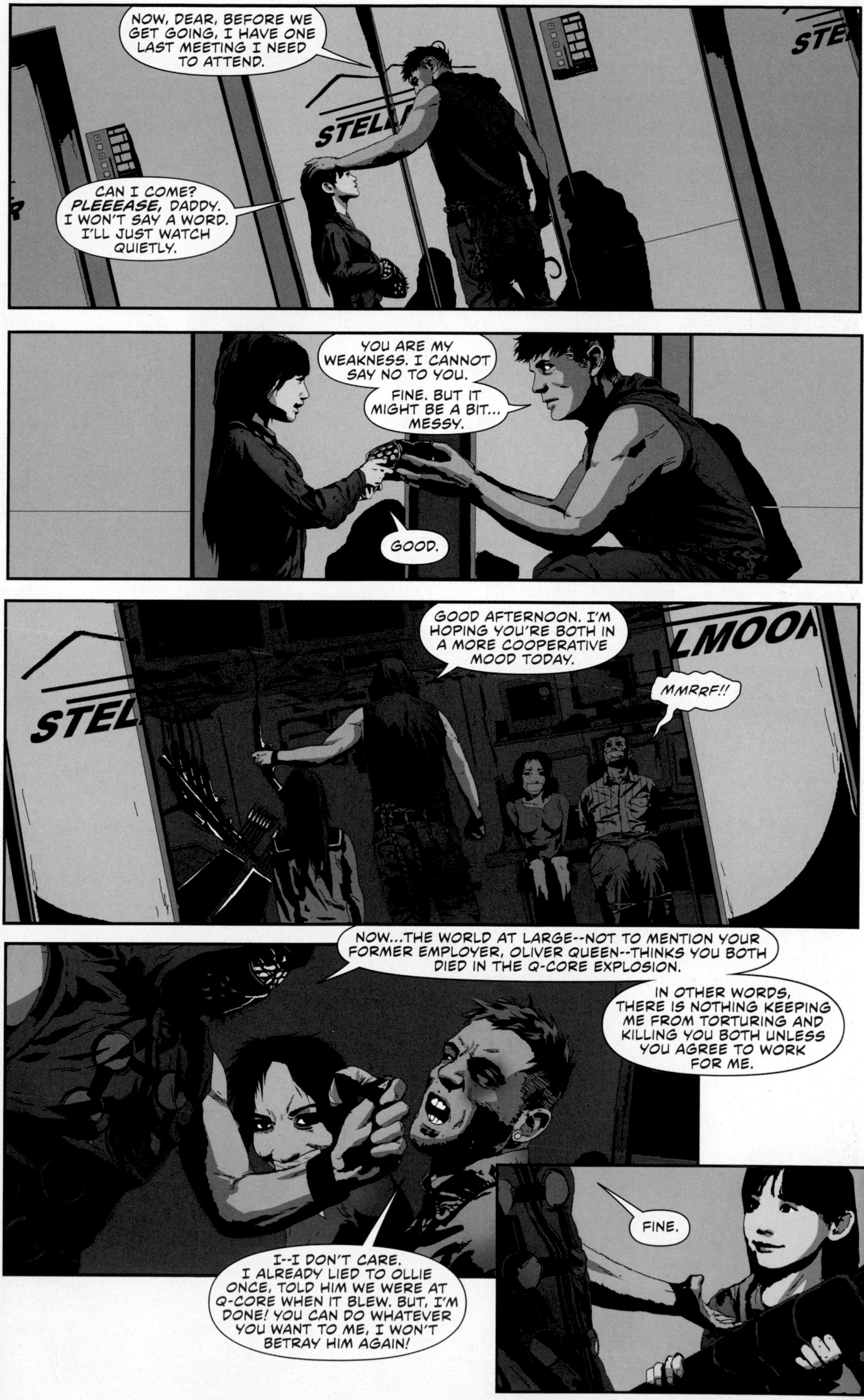
NOW, DEAR, BEFORE WE GET GOING, I HAVE ONE LAST MEETING I NEED TO ATTEND.
CAN I COME? *PLEEEASE,* DADDY. I WON'T SAY A WORD. I'LL JUST WATCH QUIETLY.
YOU ARE MY WEAKNESS. I CANNOT SAY NO TO YOU.
FINE. BUT IT MIGHT BE A BIT... MESSY.
GOOD.
STELLMOON
GOOD AFTERNOON. I'M HOPING YOU'RE BOTH IN A MORE COOPERATIVE MOOD TODAY.
MMRRF!!
NOW...THE WORLD AT LARGE--NOT TO MENTION YOUR FORMER EMPLOYER, OLIVER QUEEN--THINKS YOU BOTH DIED IN THE Q-CORE EXPLOSION.
IN OTHER WORDS, THERE IS NOTHING KEEPING ME FROM TORTURING AND KILLING YOU BOTH UNLESS YOU AGREE TO WORK FOR ME.
I--I DON'T CARE. I ALREADY LIED TO OLLIE ONCE, TOLD HIM WE WERE AT Q-CORE WHEN IT BLEW. BUT, I'M DONE! YOU CAN DO WHATEVER YOU WANT TO ME, I WON'T BETRAY HIM AGAIN!
FINE.

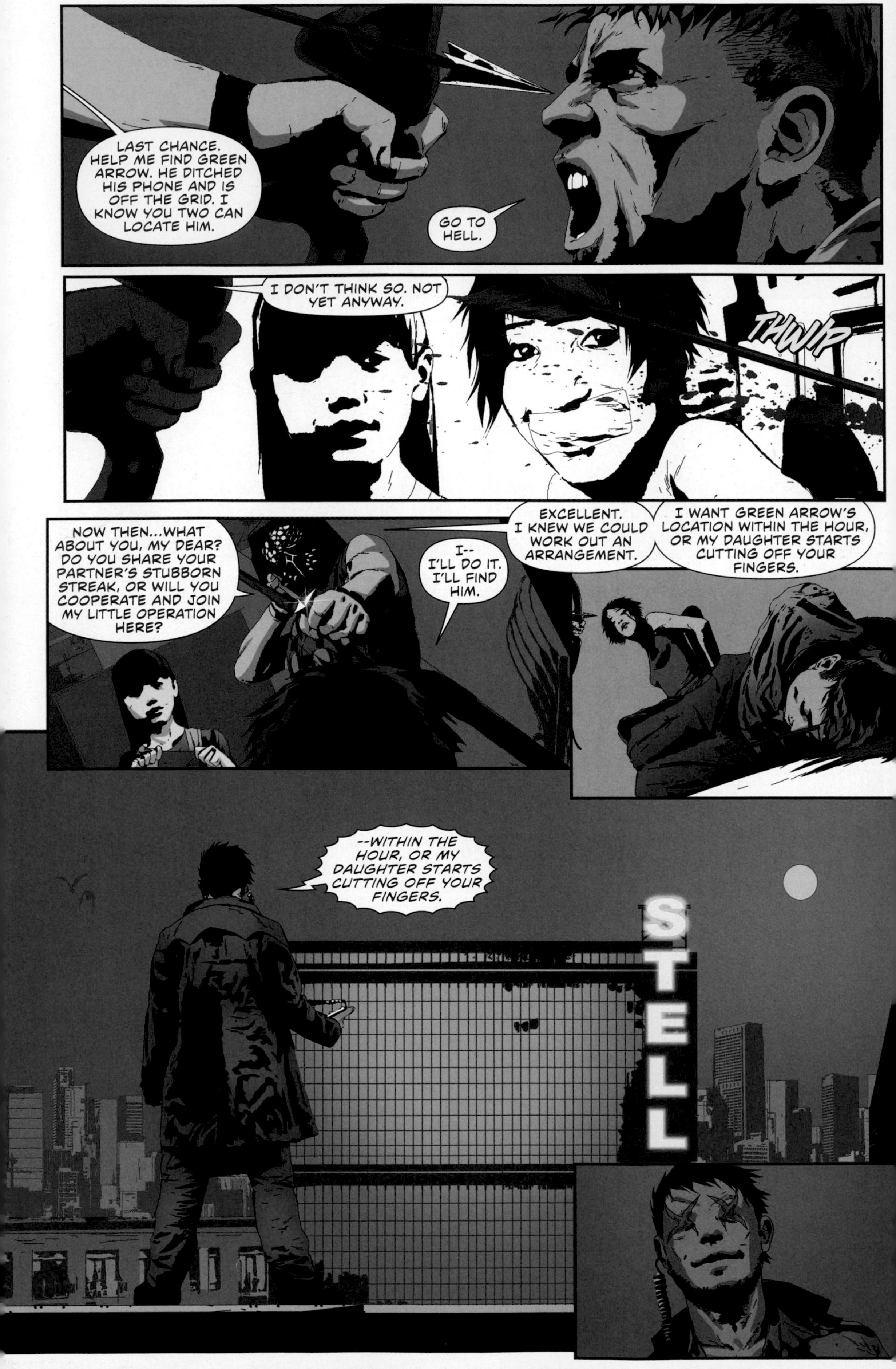
LAST CHANCE. HELP ME FIND GREEN ARROW. HE DITCHED HIS PHONE AND IS OFF THE GRID. I KNOW YOU TWO CAN LOCATE HIM.
GO TO HELL.
I DON'T THINK SO. NOT YET ANYWAY.
THWIP
NOW THEN...WHAT ABOUT YOU, MY DEAR? DO YOU SHARE YOUR PARTNER'S STUBBORN STREAK, OR WILL YOU COOPERATE AND JOIN MY LITTLE OPERATION HERE?
I-- I'LL DO IT. I'LL FIND HIM.
EXCELLENT. I KNEW WE COULD WORK OUT AN ARRANGEMENT.
I WANT GREEN ARROW'S LOCATION WITHIN THE HOUR, OR MY DAUGHTER STARTS CUTTING OFF YOUR FINGERS.
--WITHIN THE HOUR, OR MY DAUGHTER STARTS CUTTING OFF YOUR FINGERS.
STELL

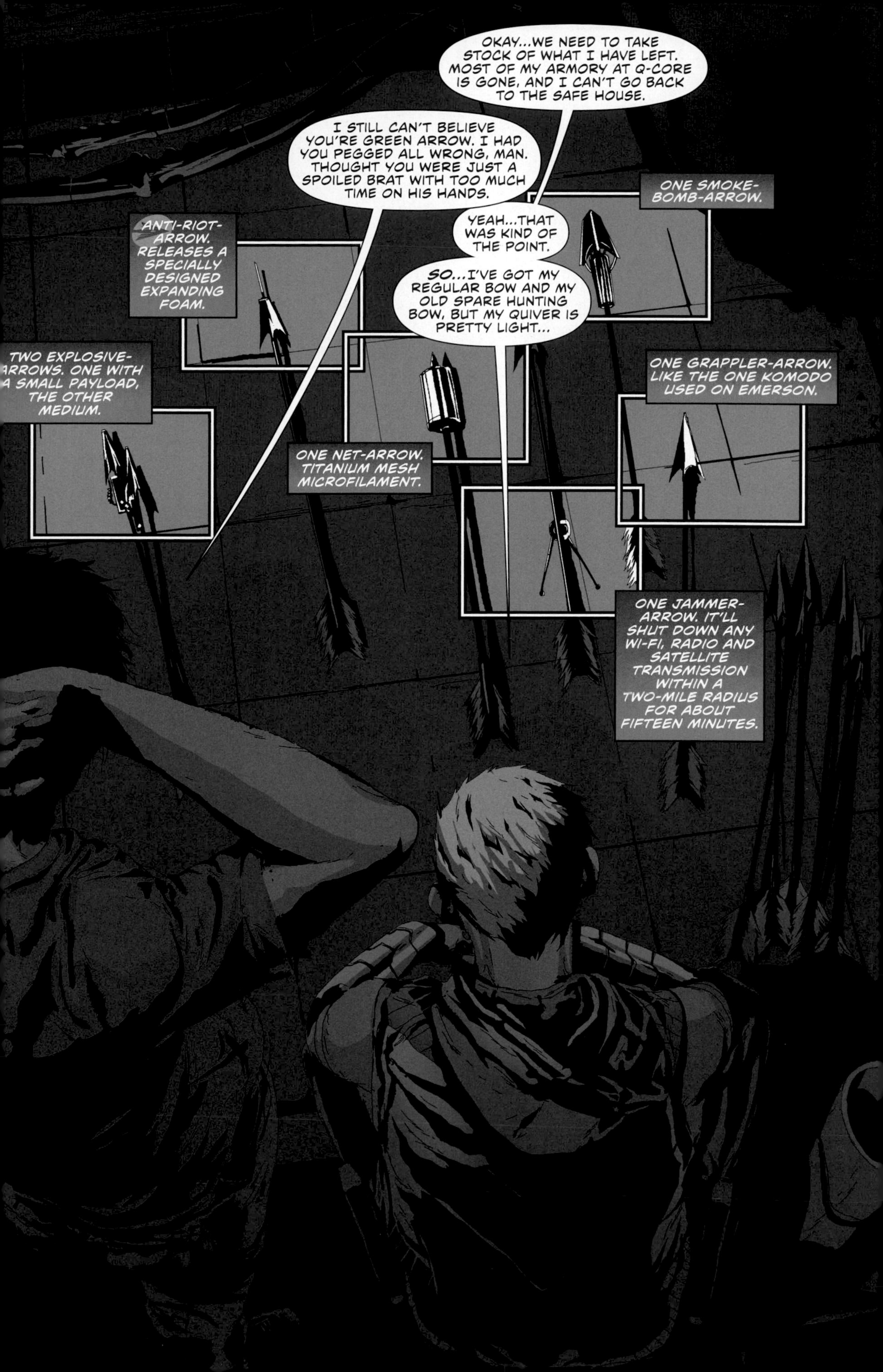
OKAY...WE NEED TO TAKE STOCK OF WHAT I HAVE LEFT. MOST OF MY ARMORY AT Q-CORE IS GONE, AND I CAN'T GO BACK TO THE SAFE HOUSE.
I STILL CAN'T BELIEVE YOU'RE GREEN ARROW. I HAD YOU PEGGED ALL WRONG, MAN. THOUGHT YOU WERE JUST A SPOILED BRAT WITH TOO MUCH TIME ON HIS HANDS.
YEAH...THAT WAS KIND OF THE POINT.
SO...I'VE GOT MY REGULAR BOW AND MY OLD SPARE HUNTING BOW, BUT MY QUIVER IS PRETTY LIGHT...
ANTI-RIOT-ARROW. RELEASES A SPECIALLY DESIGNED EXPANDING FOAM.
ONE SMOKE-BOMB-ARROW.
TWO EXPLOSIVE-ARROWS. ONE WITH A SMALL PAYLOAD, THE OTHER MEDIUM.
ONE NET-ARROW. TITANIUM MESH MICROFILAMENT.
ONE GRAPPLER-ARROW. LIKE THE ONE KOMODO USED ON EMERSON.
ONE JAMMER-ARROW. IT'LL SHUT DOWN ANY WI-FI, RADIO AND SATELLITE TRANSMISSION WITHIN A TWO-MILE RADIUS FOR ABOUT FIFTEEN MINUTES.

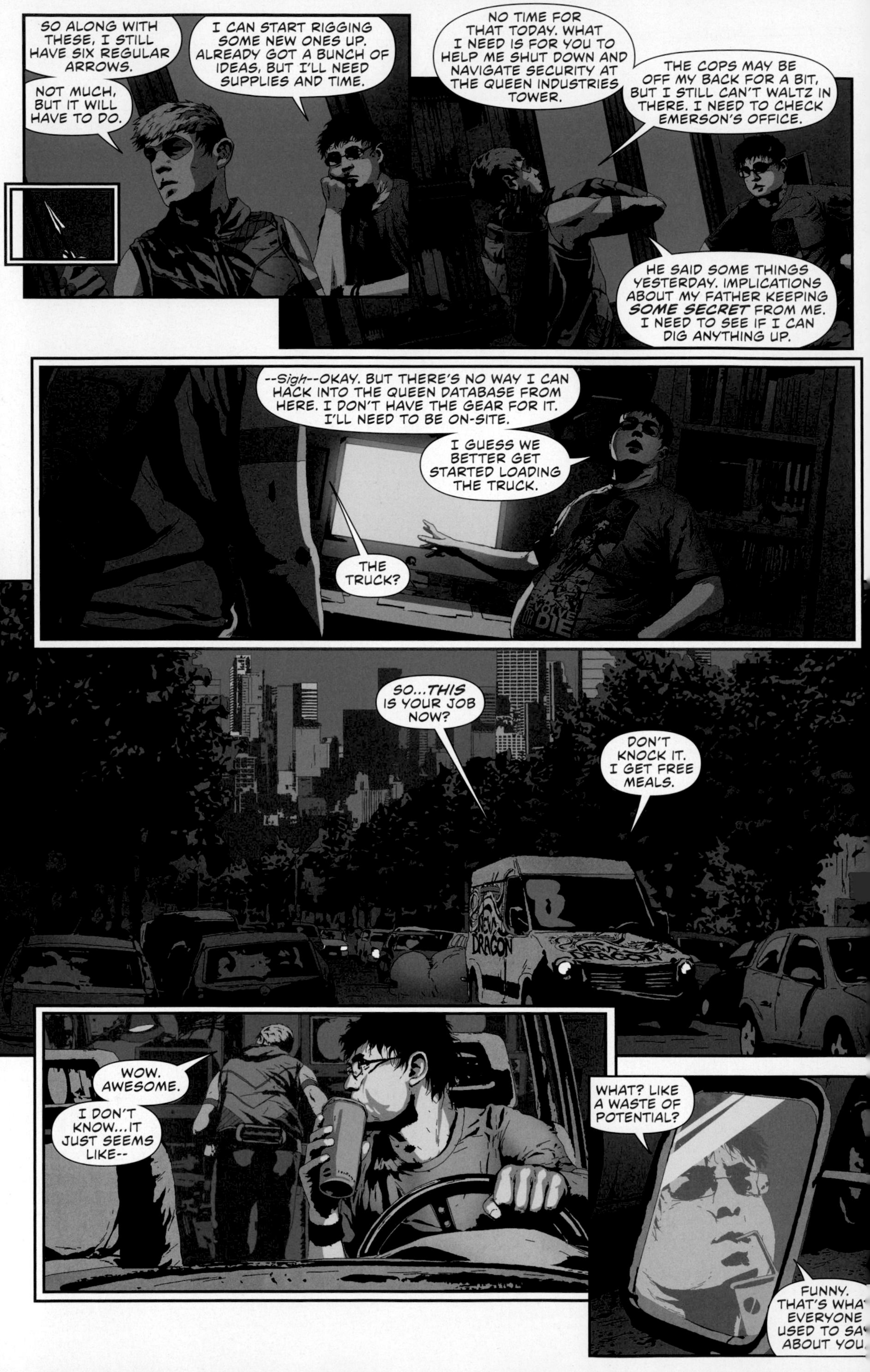
SO ALONG WITH THESE, I STILL HAVE SIX REGULAR ARROWS.
NOT MUCH, BUT IT WILL HAVE TO DO.
I CAN START RIGGING SOME NEW ONES UP. ALREADY GOT A BUNCH OF IDEAS, BUT I'LL NEED SUPPLIES AND TIME.
NO TIME FOR THAT TODAY. WHAT I NEED IS FOR YOU TO HELP ME SHUT DOWN AND NAVIGATE SECURITY AT THE QUEEN INDUSTRIES TOWER.
THE COPS MAY BE OFF MY BACK FOR A BIT, BUT I STILL CAN'T WALTZ IN THERE. I NEED TO CHECK EMERSON'S OFFICE.
HE SAID SOME THINGS YESTERDAY. IMPLICATIONS ABOUT MY FATHER KEEPING SOME SECRET FROM ME. I NEED TO SEE IF I CAN DIG ANYTHING UP.
--Sigh--OKAY. BUT THERE'S NO WAY I CAN HACK INTO THE QUEEN DATABASE FROM HERE. I DON'T HAVE THE GEAR FOR IT. I'LL NEED TO BE ON-SITE.
I GUESS WE BETTER GET STARTED LOADING THE TRUCK.
THE TRUCK?
EVOLVE OR DIE
SO...THIS IS YOUR JOB NOW?
DON'T KNOCK IT. I GET FREE MEALS.
NEW DRAGON
WOW. AWESOME.
I DON'T KNOW...IT JUST SEEMS LIKE--
WHAT? LIKE A WASTE OF POTENTIAL?
FUNNY. THAT'S WHAT EVERYONE USED TO SAY ABOUT YOU.

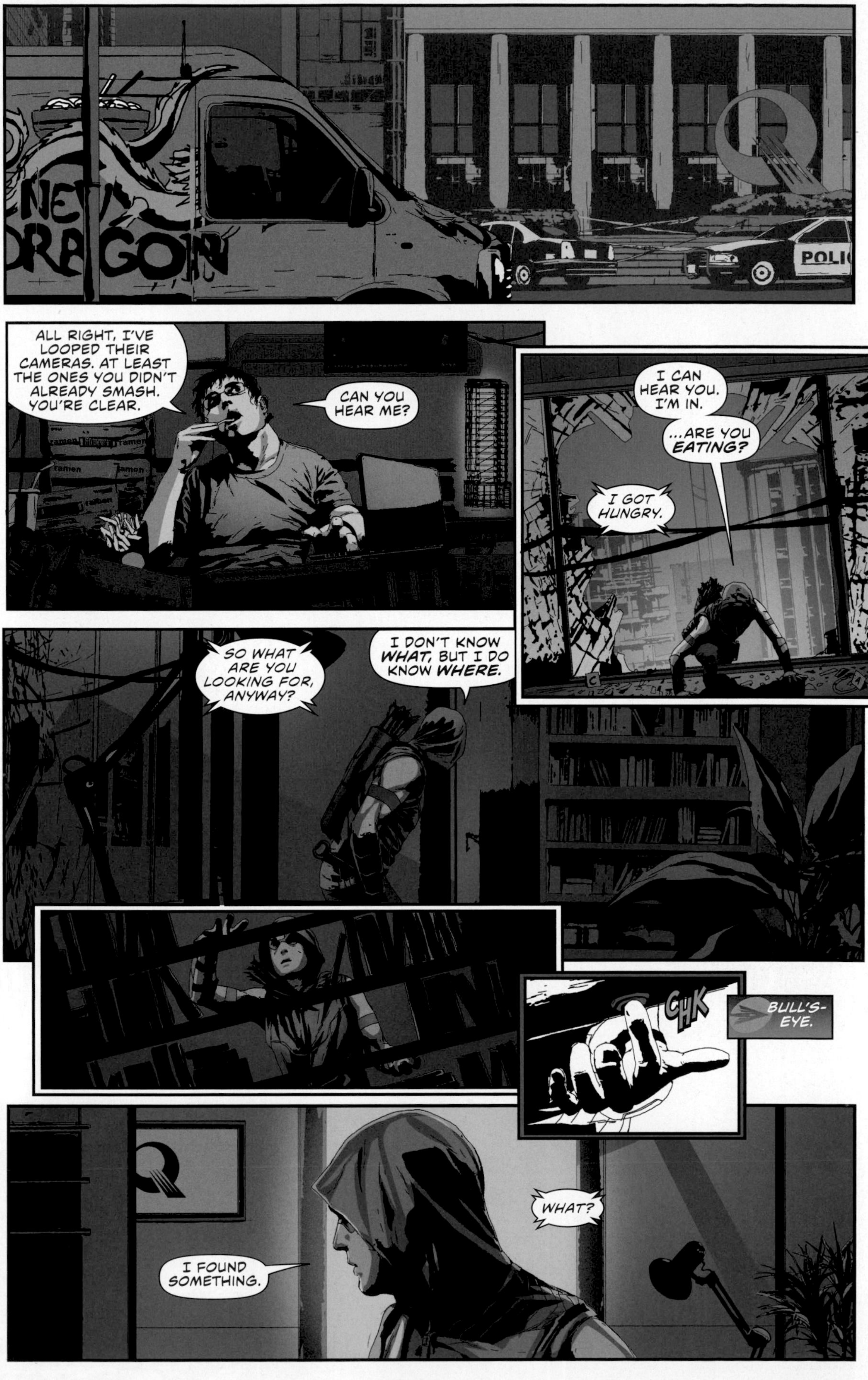
NEW DRAGON
POLIC
ramen
ALL RIGHT, I'VE LOOPED THEIR CAMERAS. AT LEAST THE ONES YOU DIDN'T ALREADY SMASH. YOU'RE CLEAR.
CAN YOU HEAR ME?
I CAN HEAR YOU. I'M IN.
...ARE YOU *EATING?*
I GOT HUNGRY.
SO WHAT ARE YOU LOOKING FOR, ANYWAY?
I DON'T KNOW *WHAT,* BUT I DO KNOW *WHERE.*
CHK
BULL'S-EYE.
WHAT?
I FOUND SOMETHING.

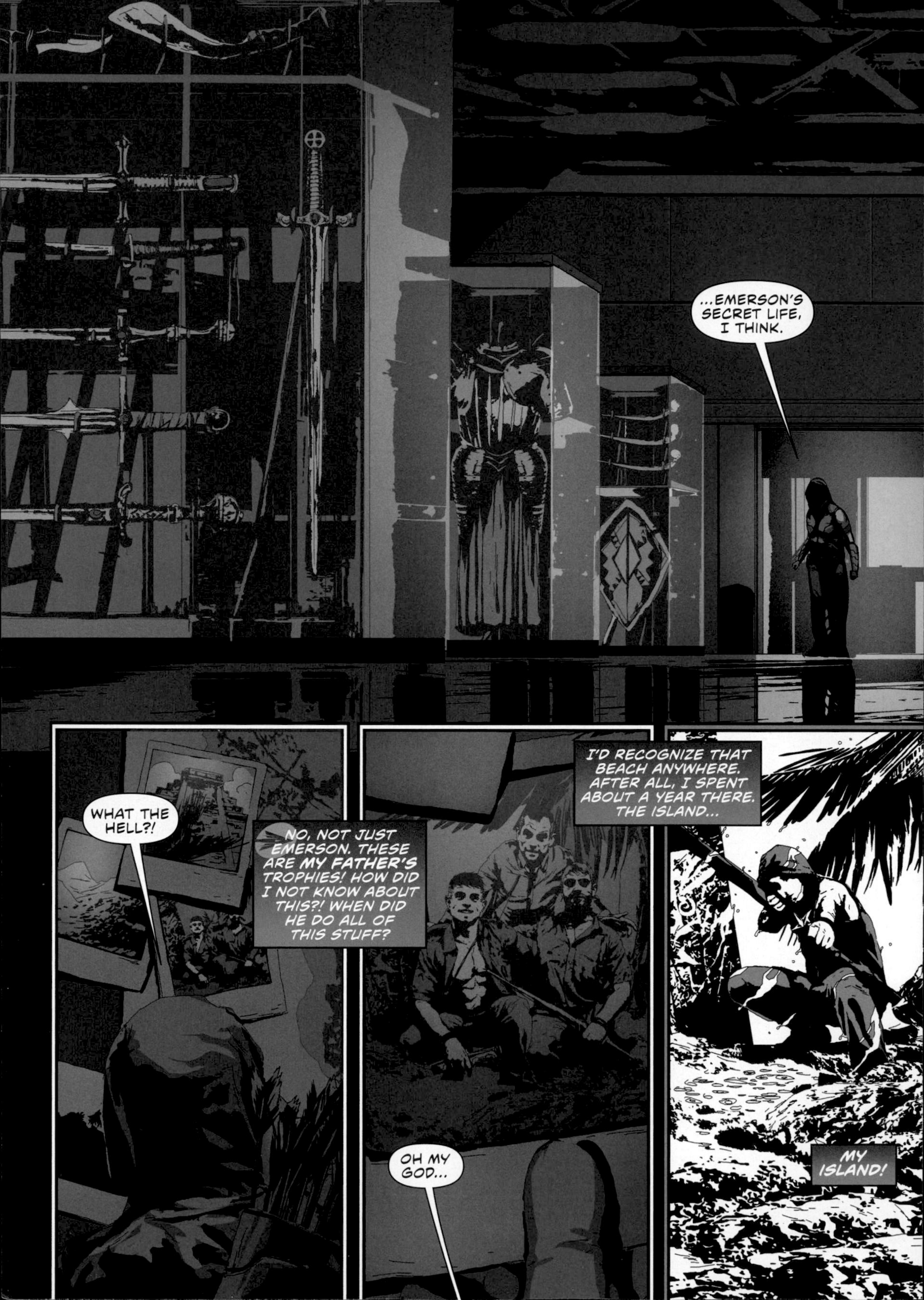
...EMERSON'S SECRET LIFE, I THINK.
WHAT THE HELL?!
NO, NOT JUST EMERSON. THESE ARE MY FATHER'S TROPHIES! HOW DID I NOT KNOW ABOUT THIS?! WHEN DID HE DO ALL OF THIS STUFF?
OH MY GOD...
I'D RECOGNIZE THAT BEACH ANYWHERE. AFTER ALL, I SPENT ABOUT A YEAR THERE. THE ISLAND...
MY ISLAND!

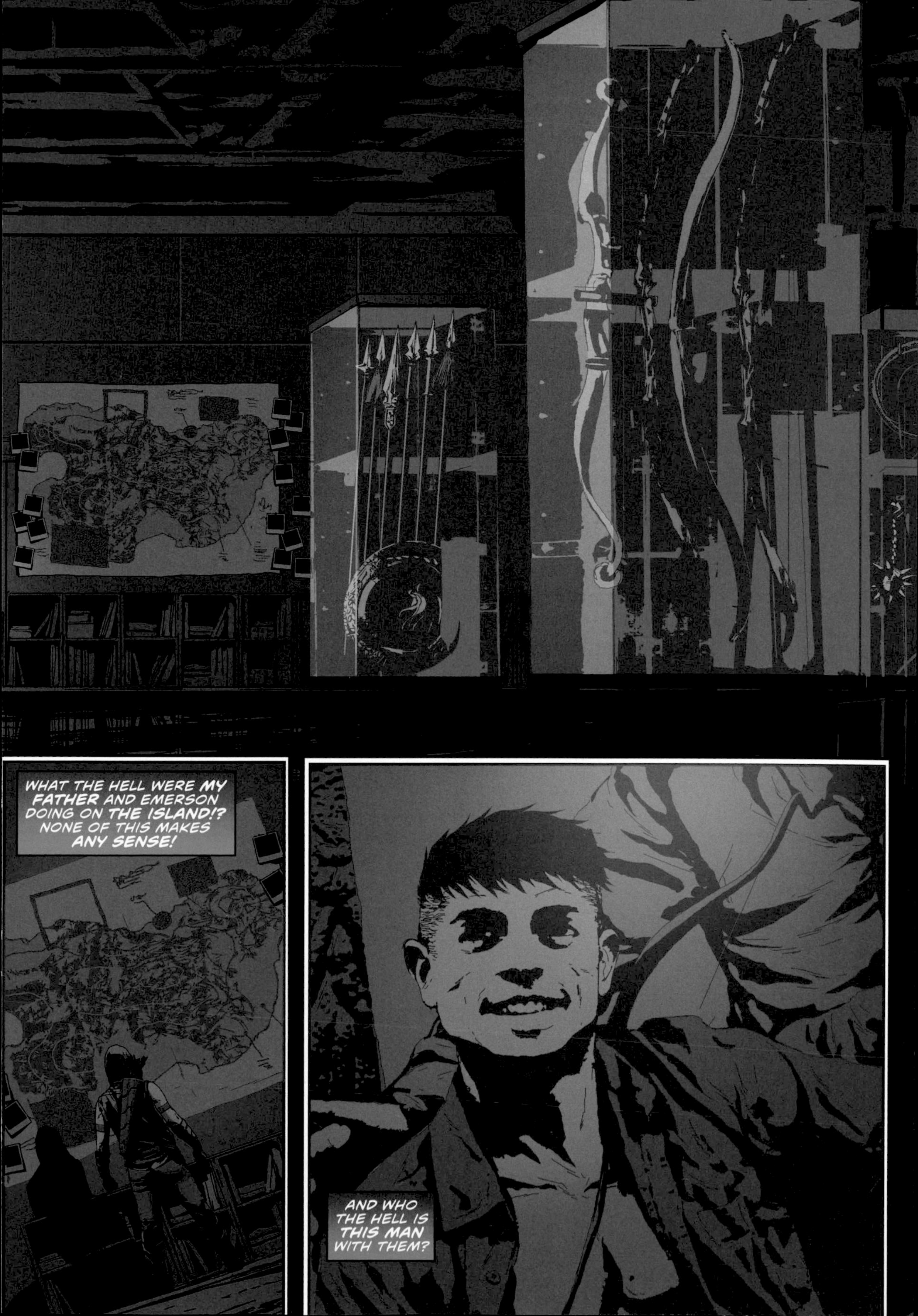
WHAT THE HELL WERE MY FATHER AND EMERSON DOING ON THE ISLAND!? NONE OF THIS MAKES ANY SENSE!
AND WHO THE HELL IS THIS MAN WITH THEM?

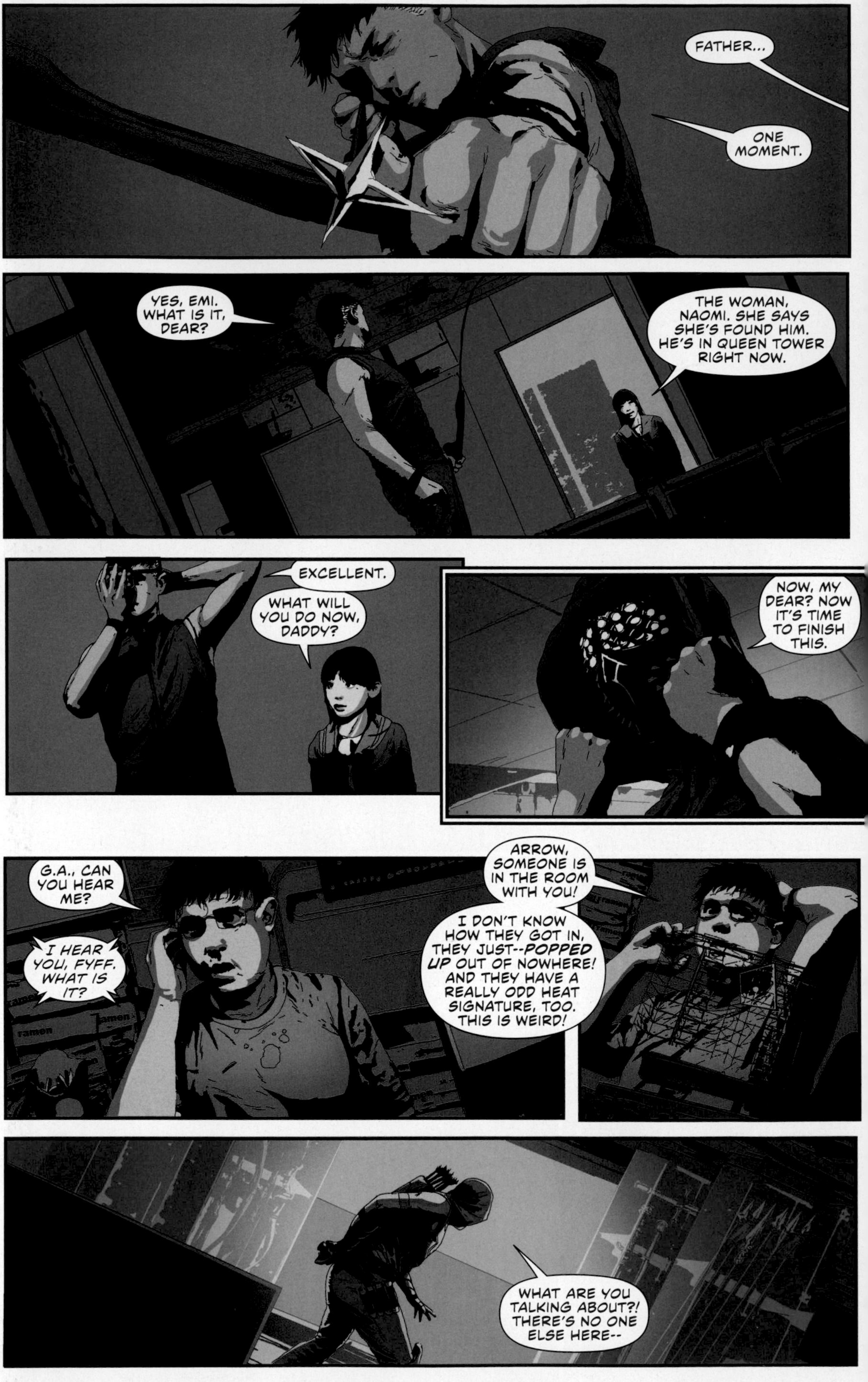
FATHER...
ONE MOMENT.
YES, EMI. WHAT IS IT, DEAR?
THE WOMAN, NAOMI. SHE SAYS SHE'S FOUND HIM. HE'S IN QUEEN TOWER RIGHT NOW.
EXCELLENT.
WHAT WILL YOU DO NOW, DADDY?
NOW, MY DEAR? NOW IT'S TIME TO FINISH THIS.
G.A., CAN YOU HEAR ME?
I HEAR YOU, FYFF. WHAT IS IT?
ARROW, SOMEONE IS IN THE ROOM WITH YOU!
I DON'T KNOW HOW THEY GOT IN, THEY JUST--POPPED UP OUT OF NOWHERE! AND THEY HAVE A REALLY ODD HEAT SIGNATURE, TOO. THIS IS WEIRD!
WHAT ARE YOU TALKING ABOUT?! THERE'S NO ONE ELSE HERE--

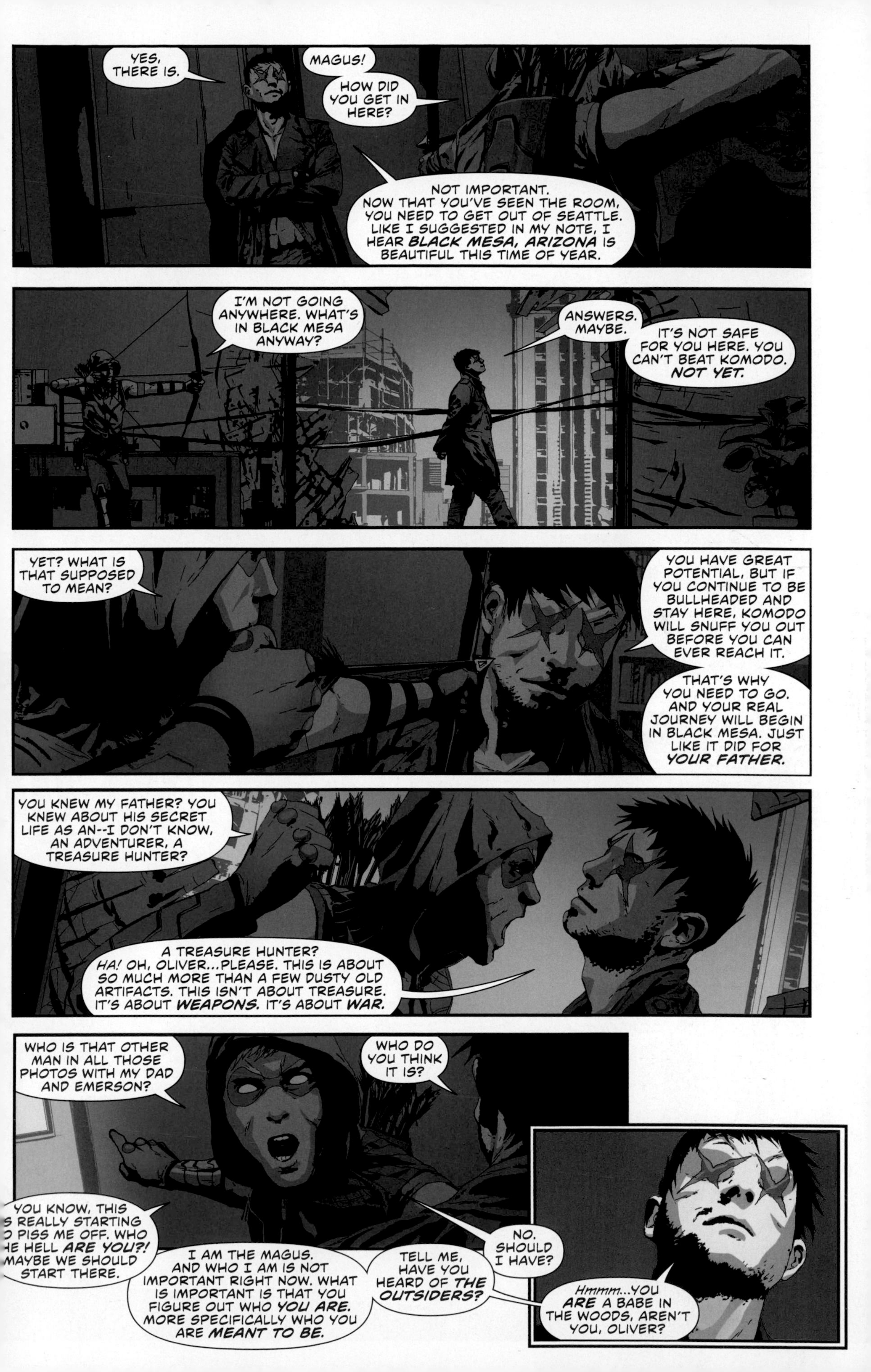
YES, THERE IS.
MAGUS!
HOW DID YOU GET IN HERE?
NOT IMPORTANT. NOW THAT YOU'VE SEEN THE ROOM, YOU NEED TO GET OUT OF SEATTLE. LIKE I SUGGESTED IN MY NOTE, I HEAR BLACK MESA, ARIZONA IS BEAUTIFUL THIS TIME OF YEAR.
I'M NOT GOING ANYWHERE. WHAT'S IN BLACK MESA ANYWAY?
ANSWERS. MAYBE.
IT'S NOT SAFE FOR YOU HERE. YOU CAN'T BEAT KOMODO. NOT YET.
YET? WHAT IS THAT SUPPOSED TO MEAN?
YOU HAVE GREAT POTENTIAL, BUT IF YOU CONTINUE TO BE BULLHEADED AND STAY HERE, KOMODO WILL SNUFF YOU OUT BEFORE YOU CAN EVER REACH IT.
THAT'S WHY YOU NEED TO GO. AND YOUR REAL JOURNEY WILL BEGIN IN BLACK MESA. JUST LIKE IT DID FOR YOUR FATHER.
YOU KNEW MY FATHER? YOU KNEW ABOUT HIS SECRET LIFE AS AN--I DON'T KNOW, AN ADVENTURER, A TREASURE HUNTER?
A TREASURE HUNTER? HA! OH, OLIVER...PLEASE. THIS IS ABOUT SO MUCH MORE THAN A FEW DUSTY OLD ARTIFACTS. THIS ISN'T ABOUT TREASURE. IT'S ABOUT WEAPONS. IT'S ABOUT WAR.
WHO IS THAT OTHER MAN IN ALL THOSE PHOTOS WITH MY DAD AND EMERSON?
WHO DO YOU THINK IT IS?
YOU KNOW, THIS S REALLY STARTING O PISS ME OFF. WHO HE HELL ARE YOU?! MAYBE WE SHOULD START THERE.
I AM THE MAGUS. AND WHO I AM IS NOT IMPORTANT RIGHT NOW. WHAT IS IMPORTANT IS THAT YOU FIGURE OUT WHO YOU ARE. MORE SPECIFICALLY WHO YOU ARE MEANT TO BE.
TELL ME, HAVE YOU HEARD OF THE OUTSIDERS?
NO. SHOULD I HAVE?
Hmmm...YOU ARE A BABE IN THE WOODS, AREN'T YOU, OLIVER?

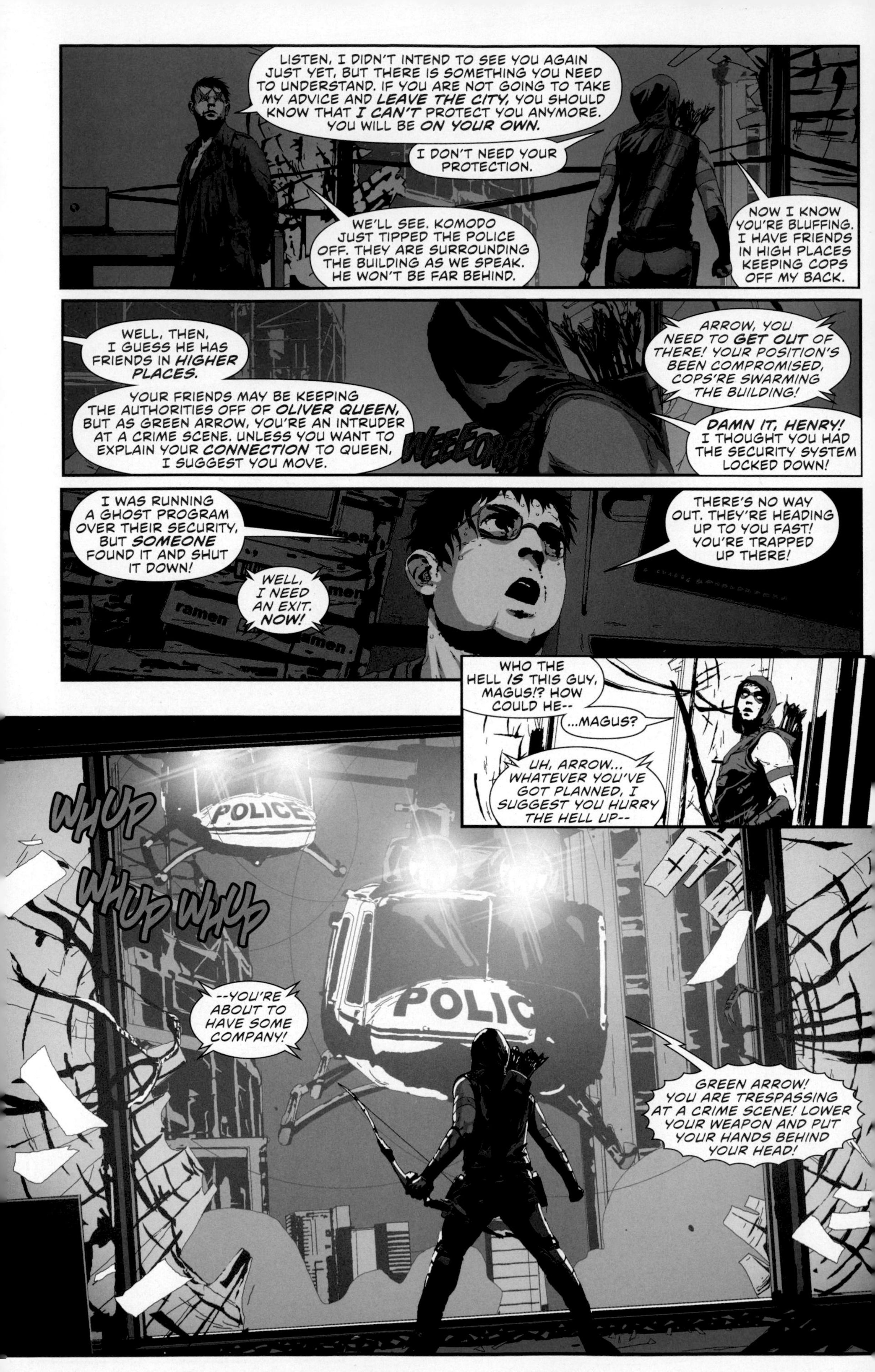
LISTEN, I DIDN'T INTEND TO SEE YOU AGAIN JUST YET, BUT THERE IS SOMETHING YOU NEED TO UNDERSTAND. IF YOU ARE NOT GOING TO TAKE MY ADVICE AND LEAVE THE CITY, YOU SHOULD KNOW THAT I CAN'T PROTECT YOU ANYMORE. YOU WILL BE ON YOUR OWN.
I DON'T NEED YOUR PROTECTION.
WE'LL SEE. KOMODO JUST TIPPED THE POLICE OFF. THEY ARE SURROUNDING THE BUILDING AS WE SPEAK. HE WON'T BE FAR BEHIND.
NOW I KNOW YOU'RE BLUFFING. I HAVE FRIENDS IN HIGH PLACES KEEPING COPS OFF MY BACK.
WELL, THEN, I GUESS HE HAS FRIENDS IN HIGHER PLACES.
YOUR FRIENDS MAY BE KEEPING THE AUTHORITIES OFF OF OLIVER QUEEN, BUT AS GREEN ARROW, YOU'RE AN INTRUDER AT A CRIME SCENE. UNLESS YOU WANT TO EXPLAIN YOUR CONNECTION TO QUEEN, I SUGGEST YOU MOVE.
WEEEORRR
ARROW, YOU NEED TO GET OUT OF THERE! YOUR POSITION'S BEEN COMPROMISED, COPS'RE SWARMING THE BUILDING!
DAMN IT, HENRY! I THOUGHT YOU HAD THE SECURITY SYSTEM LOCKED DOWN!
I WAS RUNNING A GHOST PROGRAM OVER THEIR SECURITY, BUT SOMEONE FOUND IT AND SHUT IT DOWN!
WELL, I NEED AN EXIT. NOW!
THERE'S NO WAY OUT. THEY'RE HEADING UP TO YOU FAST! YOU'RE TRAPPED UP THERE!
WHO THE HELL IS THIS GUY, MAGUS!? HOW COULD HE--
...MAGUS?
UH, ARROW... WHATEVER YOU'VE GOT PLANNED, I SUGGEST YOU HURRY THE HELL UP--
WHUP
WHUP WHUP WHUP
POLICE
--YOU'RE ABOUT TO HAVE SOME COMPANY!
POLIC
GREEN ARROW! YOU ARE TRESPASSING AT A CRIME SCENE! LOWER YOUR WEAPON AND PUT YOUR HANDS BEHIND YOUR HEAD!

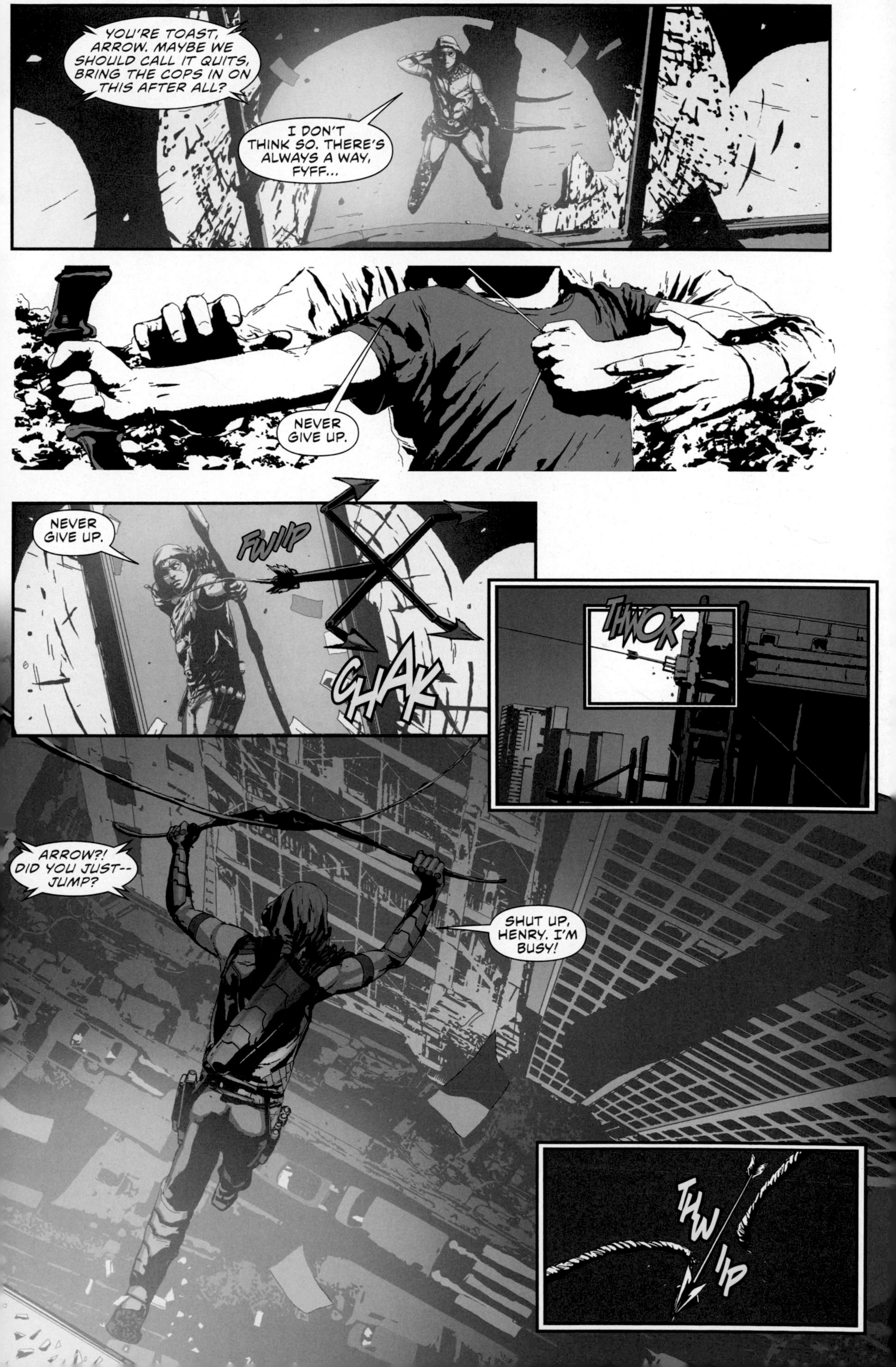
YOU'RE TOAST, ARROW. MAYBE WE SHOULD CALL IT QUITS, BRING THE COPS IN ON THIS AFTER ALL?
I DON'T THINK SO. THERE'S ALWAYS A WAY, FYFF...
NEVER GIVE UP.
NEVER GIVE UP.
FWIIP
CHAK
THWOK
ARROW?! DID YOU JUST-- JUMP?
SHUT UP, HENRY. I'M BUSY!
THWIIP

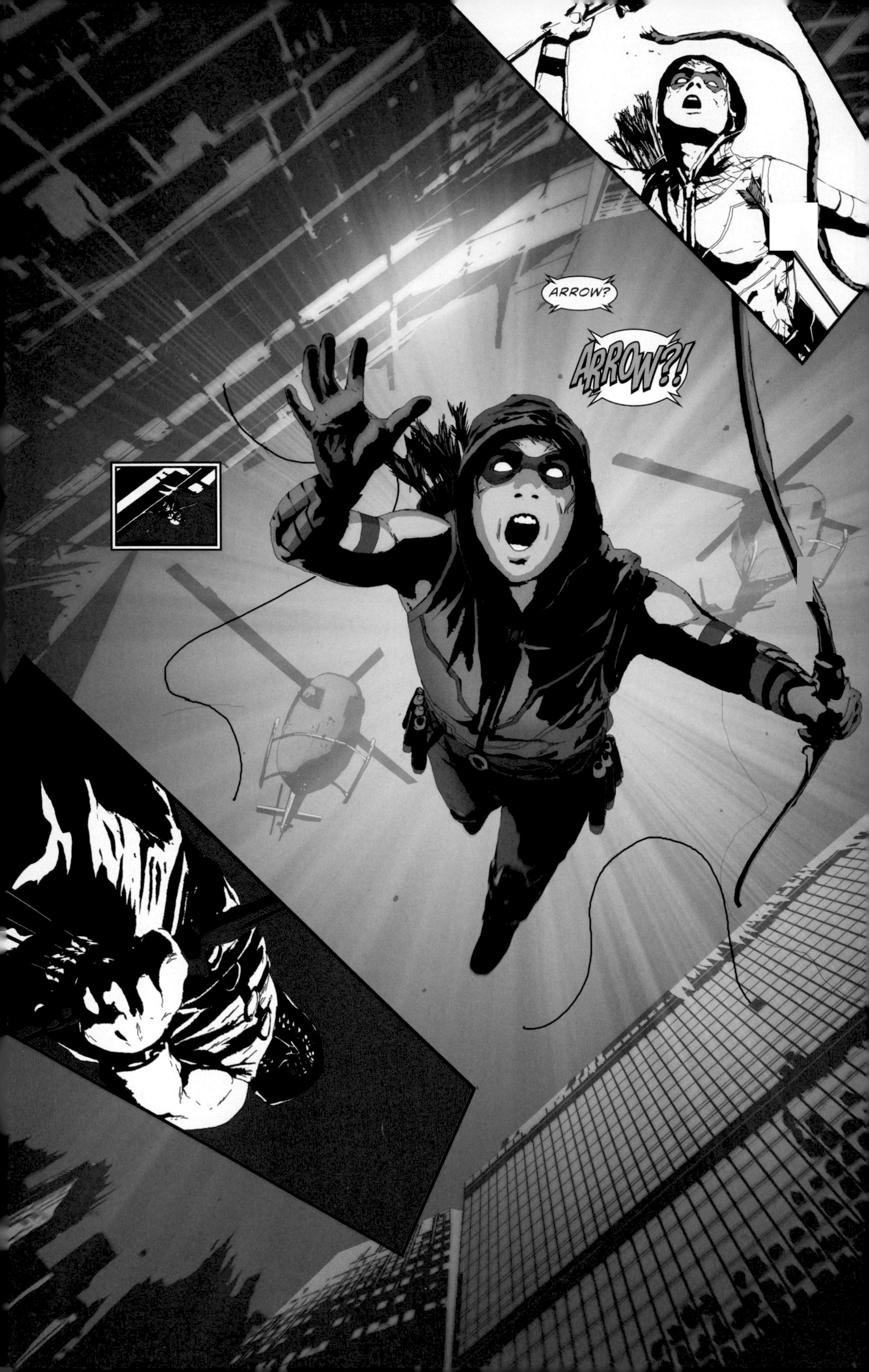
ARROW?
ARROW?!

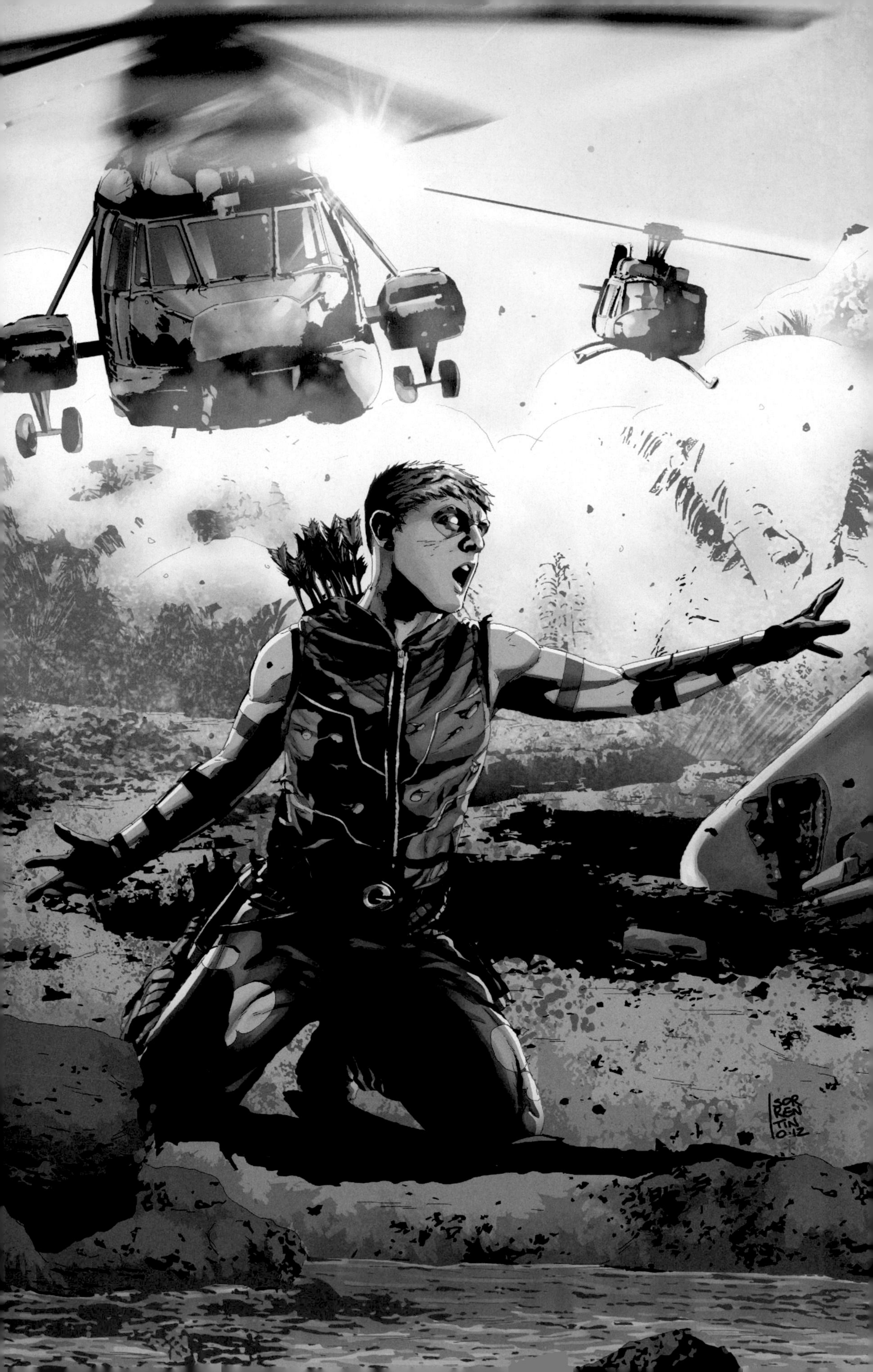
SOR
REN
TIN
O·12

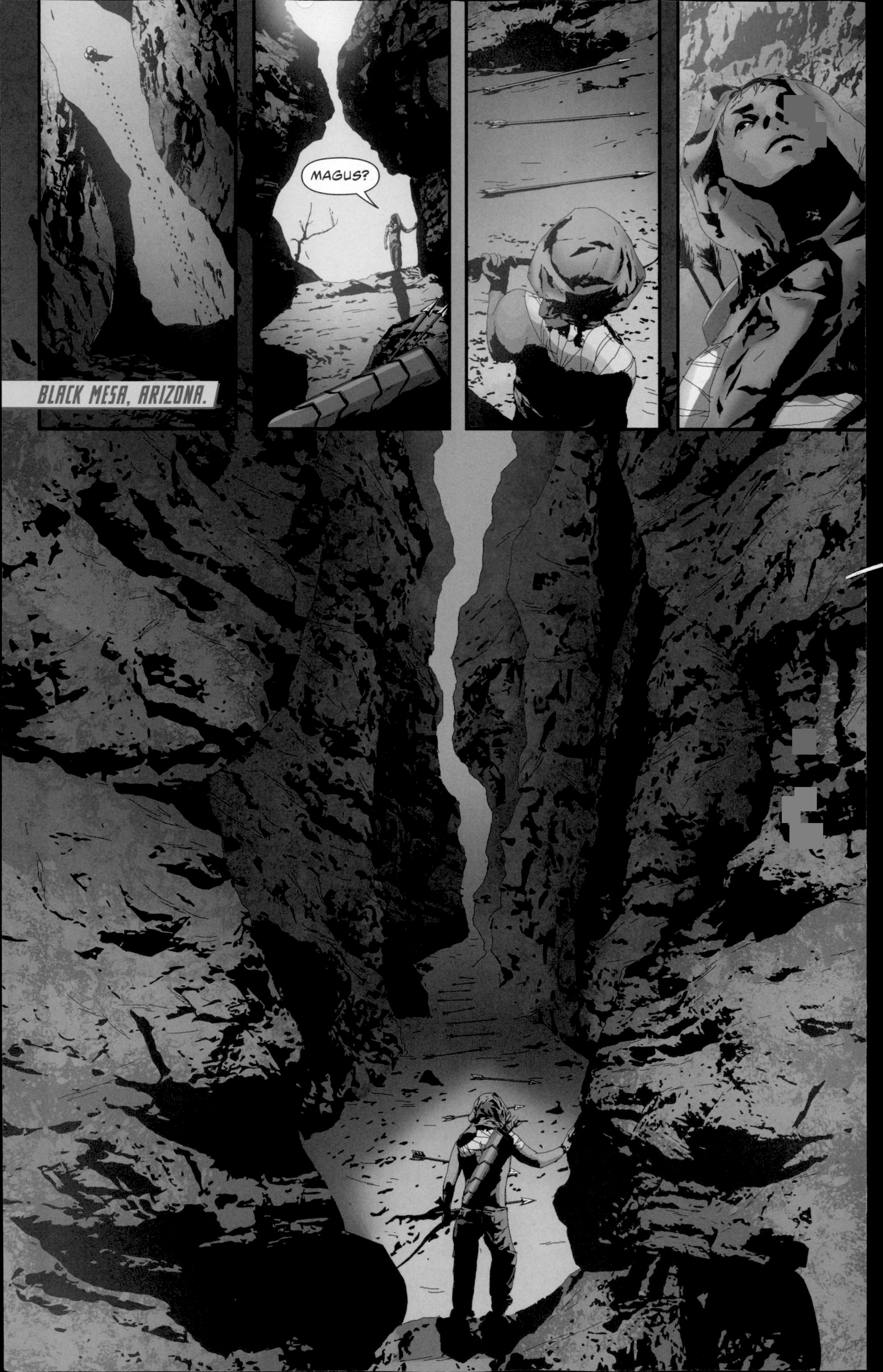
BLACK MESA, ARIZONA.
MAGUS?

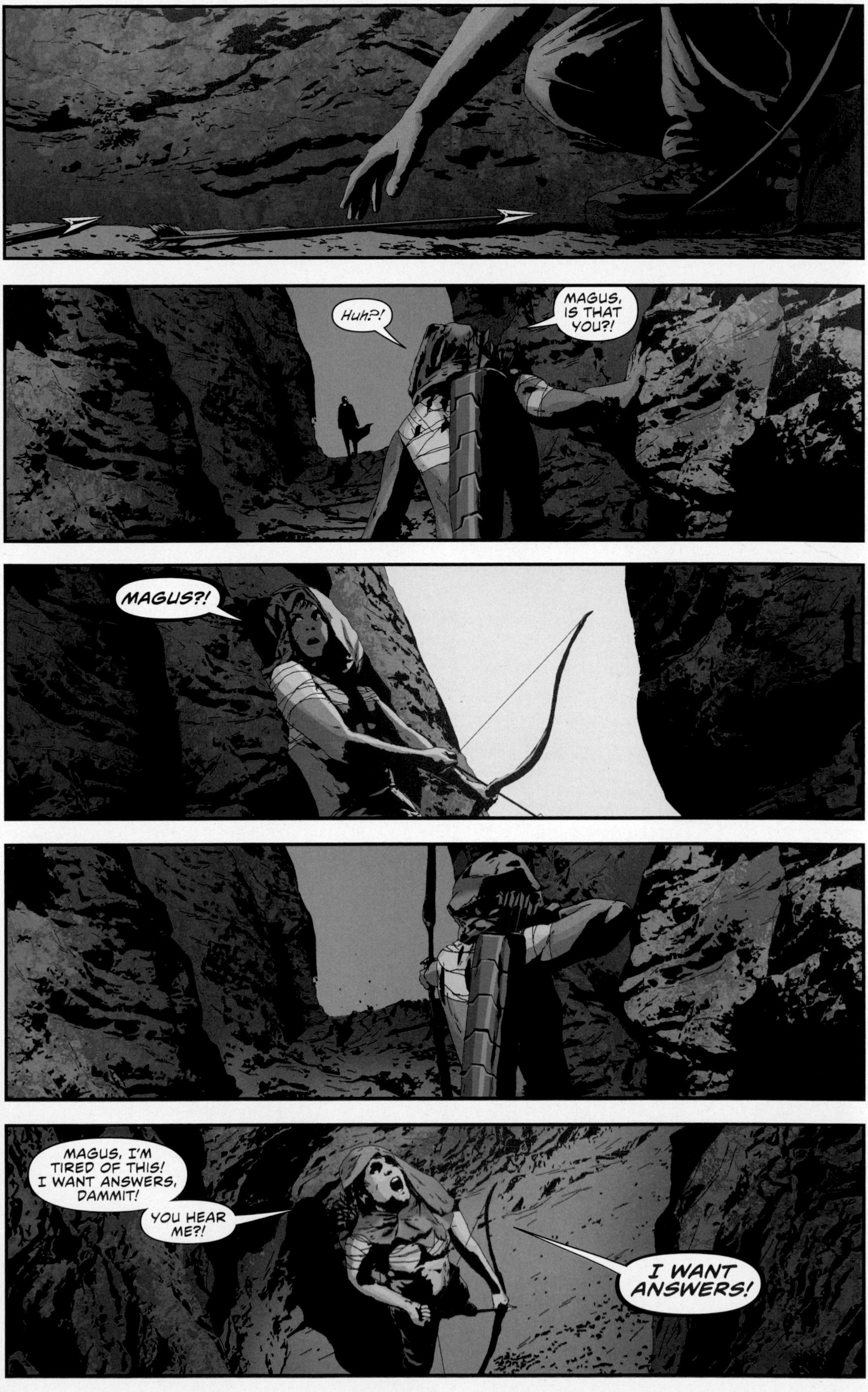
Huh?!
MAGUS, IS THAT YOU?!
MAGUS?!
MAGUS, I'M TIRED OF THIS! I WANT ANSWERS, DAMMIT!
YOU HEAR ME?!
I WANT ANSWERS!

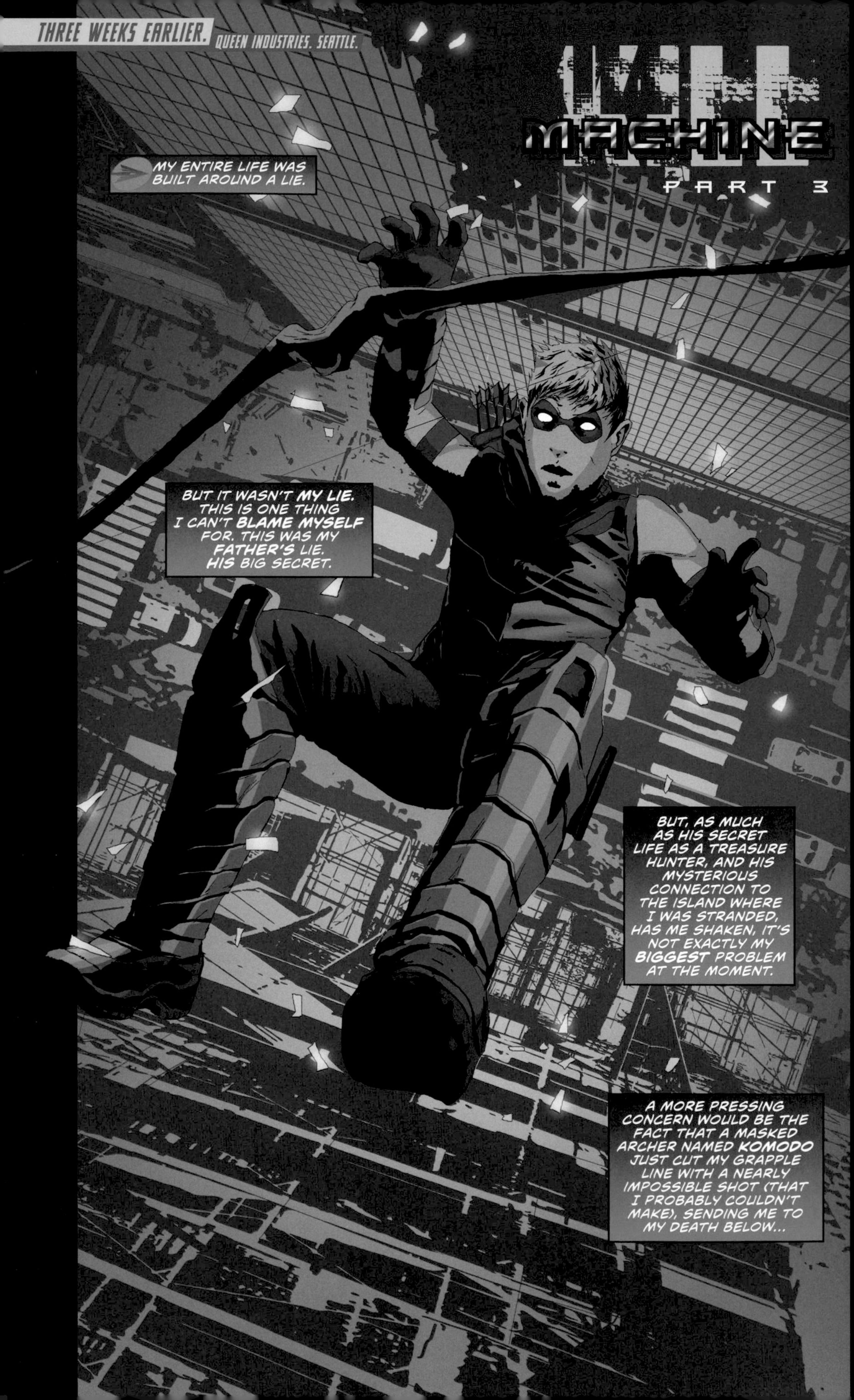
THREE WEEKS EARLIER.
QUEEN INDUSTRIES. SEATTLE.
MACHINE
PART 3
MY ENTIRE LIFE WAS BUILT AROUND A LIE.
BUT IT WASN'T MY LIE. THIS IS ONE THING I CAN'T BLAME MYSELF FOR. THIS WAS MY FATHER'S LIE. HIS BIG SECRET.
BUT, AS MUCH AS HIS SECRET LIFE AS A TREASURE HUNTER, AND HIS MYSTERIOUS CONNECTION TO THE ISLAND WHERE I WAS STRANDED, HAS ME SHAKEN, IT'S NOT EXACTLY MY BIGGEST PROBLEM AT THE MOMENT.
A MORE PRESSING CONCERN WOULD BE THE FACT THAT A MASKED ARCHER NAMED KOMODO JUST CUT MY GRAPPLE LINE WITH A NEARLY IMPOSSIBLE SHOT (THAT I PROBABLY COULDN'T MAKE), SENDING ME TO MY DEATH BELOW...

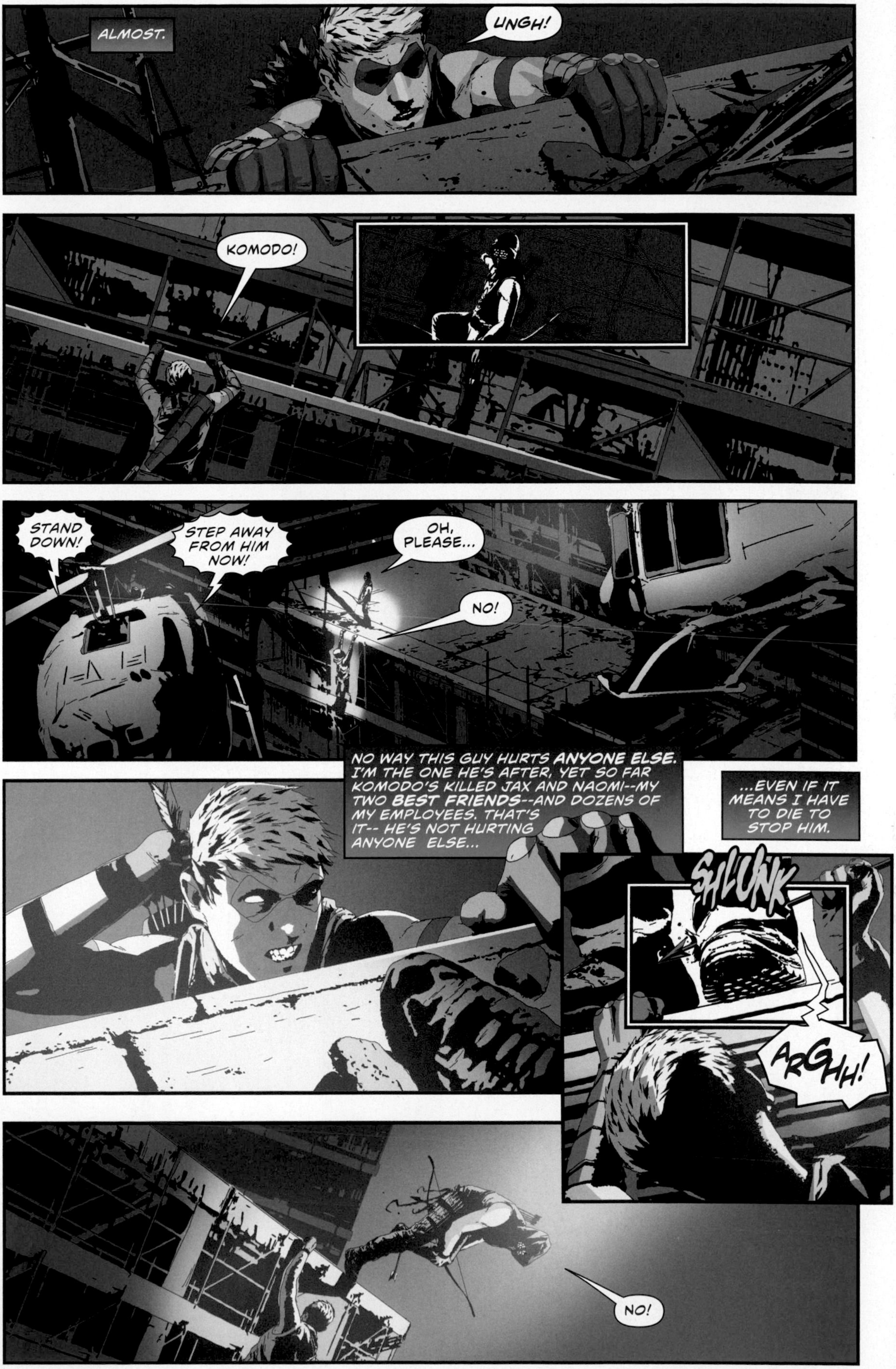
ALMOST.
UNGH!
KOMODO!
STAND DOWN!
STEP AWAY FROM HIM NOW!
OH, PLEASE...
NO!
NO WAY THIS GUY HURTS ANYONE ELSE. I'M THE ONE HE'S AFTER, YET SO FAR KOMODO'S KILLED JAX AND NAOMI--MY TWO BEST FRIENDS--AND DOZENS OF MY EMPLOYEES. THAT'S IT-- HE'S NOT HURTING ANYONE ELSE...
...EVEN IF IT MEANS I HAVE TO DIE TO STOP HIM.
SHLUNK
ARGHH!
NO!

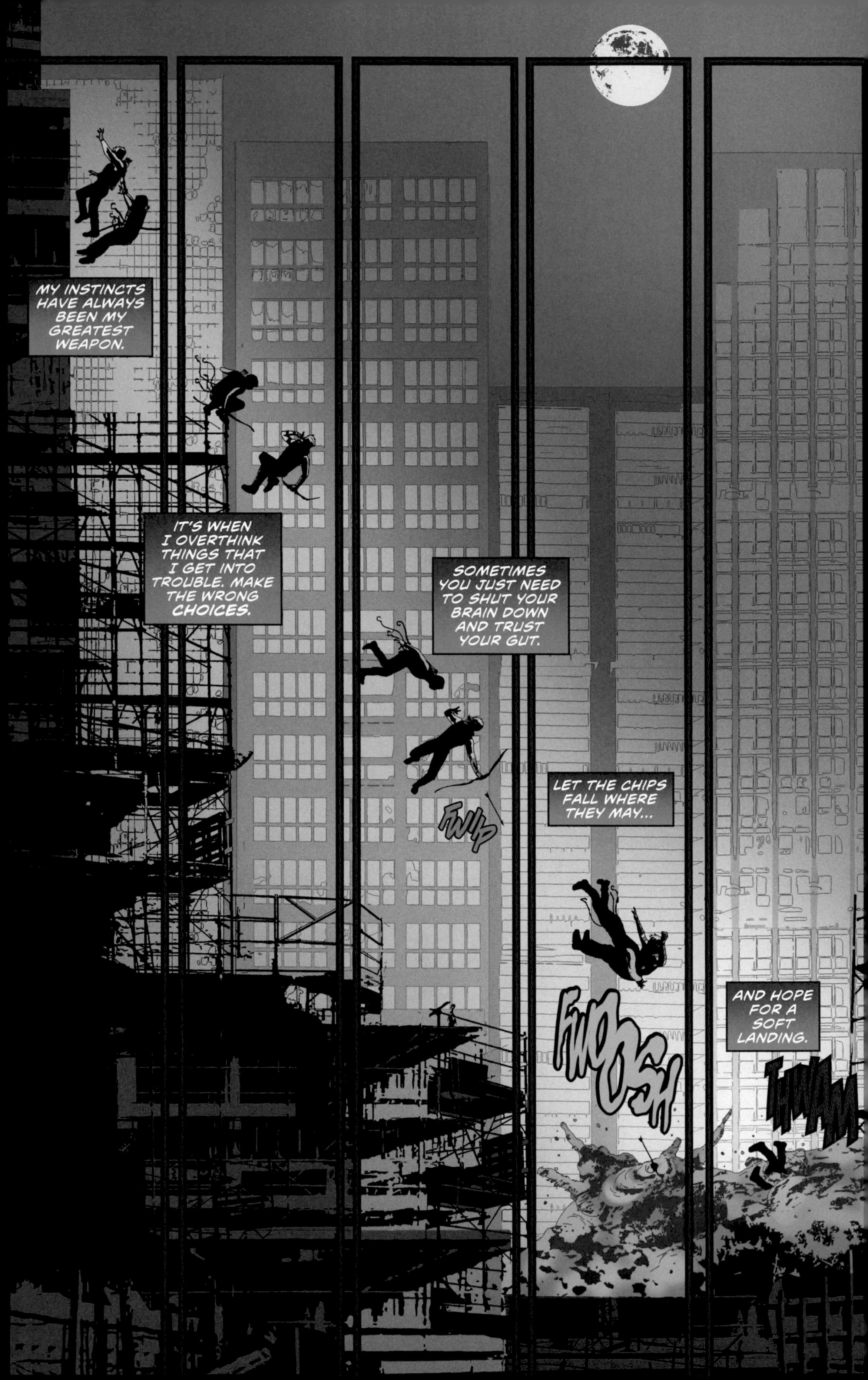

MY INSTINCTS HAVE ALWAYS BEEN MY GREATEST WEAPON.
IT'S WHEN I OVERTHINK THINGS THAT I GET INTO TROUBLE. MAKE THE WRONG CHOICES.
SOMETIMES YOU JUST NEED TO SHUT YOUR BRAIN DOWN AND TRUST YOUR GUT.
FWIP
LET THE CHIPS FALL WHERE THEY MAY...
FWOOSH
AND HOPE FOR A SOFT LANDING.

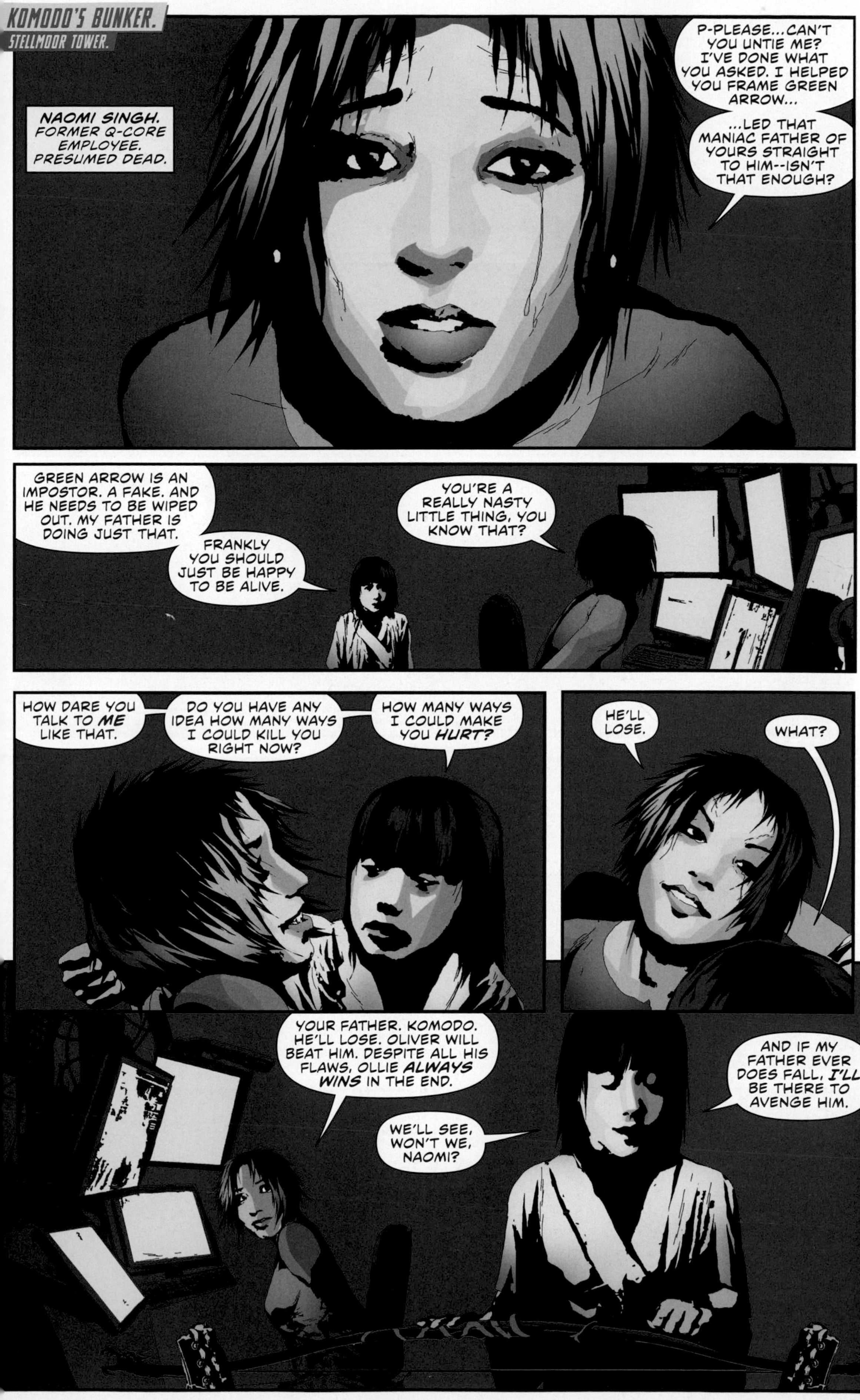
KOMODO'S BUNKER.
STELLMOOR TOWER.
NAOMI SINGH. FORMER Q-CORE EMPLOYEE. PRESUMED DEAD.
P-PLEASE...CAN'T YOU UNTIE ME? I'VE DONE WHAT YOU ASKED. I HELPED YOU FRAME GREEN ARROW...
...LED THAT MANIAC FATHER OF YOURS STRAIGHT TO HIM--ISN'T THAT ENOUGH?
GREEN ARROW IS AN IMPOSTOR. A FAKE. AND HE NEEDS TO BE WIPED OUT. MY FATHER IS DOING JUST THAT.
FRANKLY YOU SHOULD JUST BE HAPPY TO BE ALIVE.
YOU'RE A REALLY NASTY LITTLE THING, YOU KNOW THAT?
HOW DARE YOU TALK TO *ME* LIKE THAT.
DO YOU HAVE ANY IDEA HOW MANY WAYS I COULD KILL YOU RIGHT NOW?
HOW MANY WAYS I COULD MAKE YOU *HURT?*
HE'LL LOSE.
WHAT?
YOUR FATHER. KOMODO. HE'LL LOSE. OLIVER WILL BEAT HIM. DESPITE ALL HIS FLAWS, OLLIE *ALWAYS WINS* IN THE END.
AND IF MY FATHER EVER DOES FALL, *I'LL* BE THERE TO AVENGE HIM.
WE'LL SEE, WON'T WE, NAOMI?

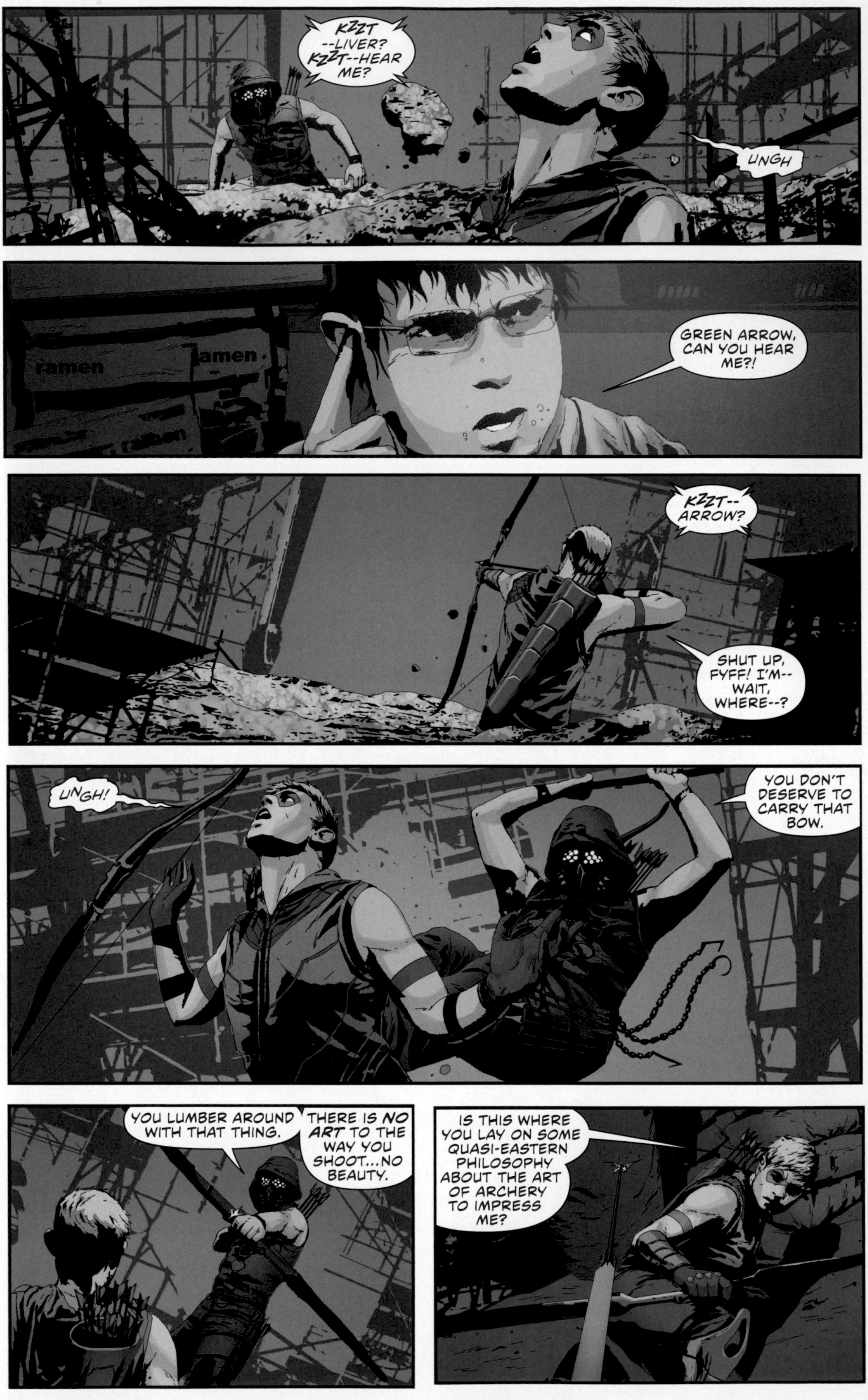
KZZT --LIVER? KZZT--HEAR ME?
UNGH
GREEN ARROW, CAN YOU HEAR ME?!
ramen
KZZT-- ARROW?
SHUT UP, FYFF! I'M-- WAIT, WHERE--?
UNGH!
YOU DON'T DESERVE TO CARRY THAT BOW.
YOU LUMBER AROUND WITH THAT THING.
THERE IS NO ART TO THE WAY YOU SHOOT...NO BEAUTY.
IS THIS WHERE YOU LAY ON SOME QUASI-EASTERN PHILOSOPHY ABOUT THE ART OF ARCHERY TO IMPRESS ME?

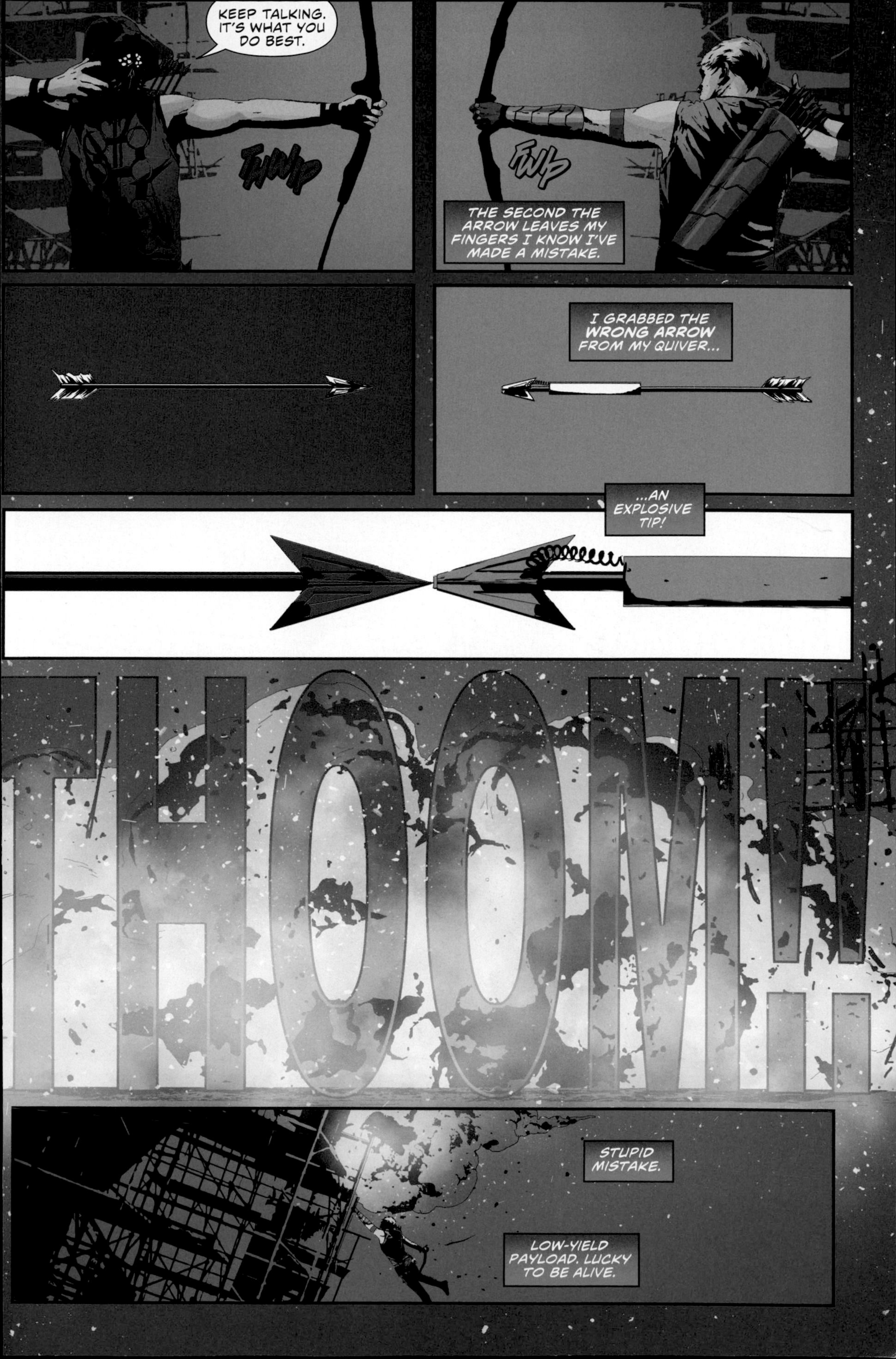
KEEP TALKING. IT'S WHAT YOU DO BEST.
THWIP
FWIP
THE SECOND THE ARROW LEAVES MY FINGERS I KNOW I'VE MADE A MISTAKE.
I GRABBED THE WRONG ARROW FROM MY QUIVER...
...AN EXPLOSIVE TIP!
THOOM!
STUPID MISTAKE.
LOW-YIELD PAYLOAD. LUCKY TO BE ALIVE.

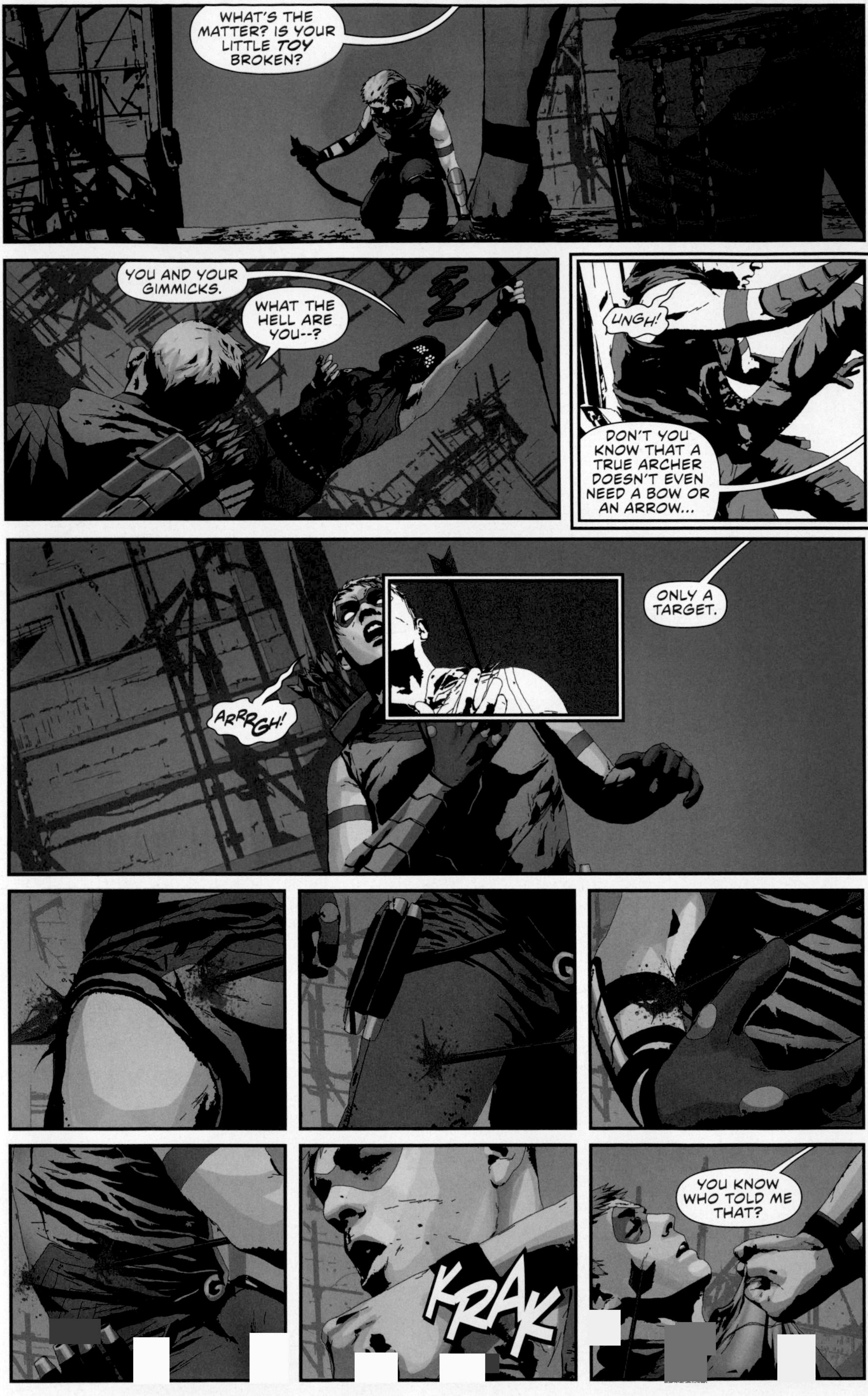
WHAT'S THE MATTER? IS YOUR LITTLE TOY BROKEN?
YOU AND YOUR GIMMICKS.
WHAT THE HELL ARE YOU--?
UNGH!
DON'T YOU KNOW THAT A TRUE ARCHER DOESN'T EVEN NEED A BOW OR AN ARROW...
ONLY A TARGET.
ARRRGH!
KRAK
YOU KNOW WHO TOLD ME THAT?

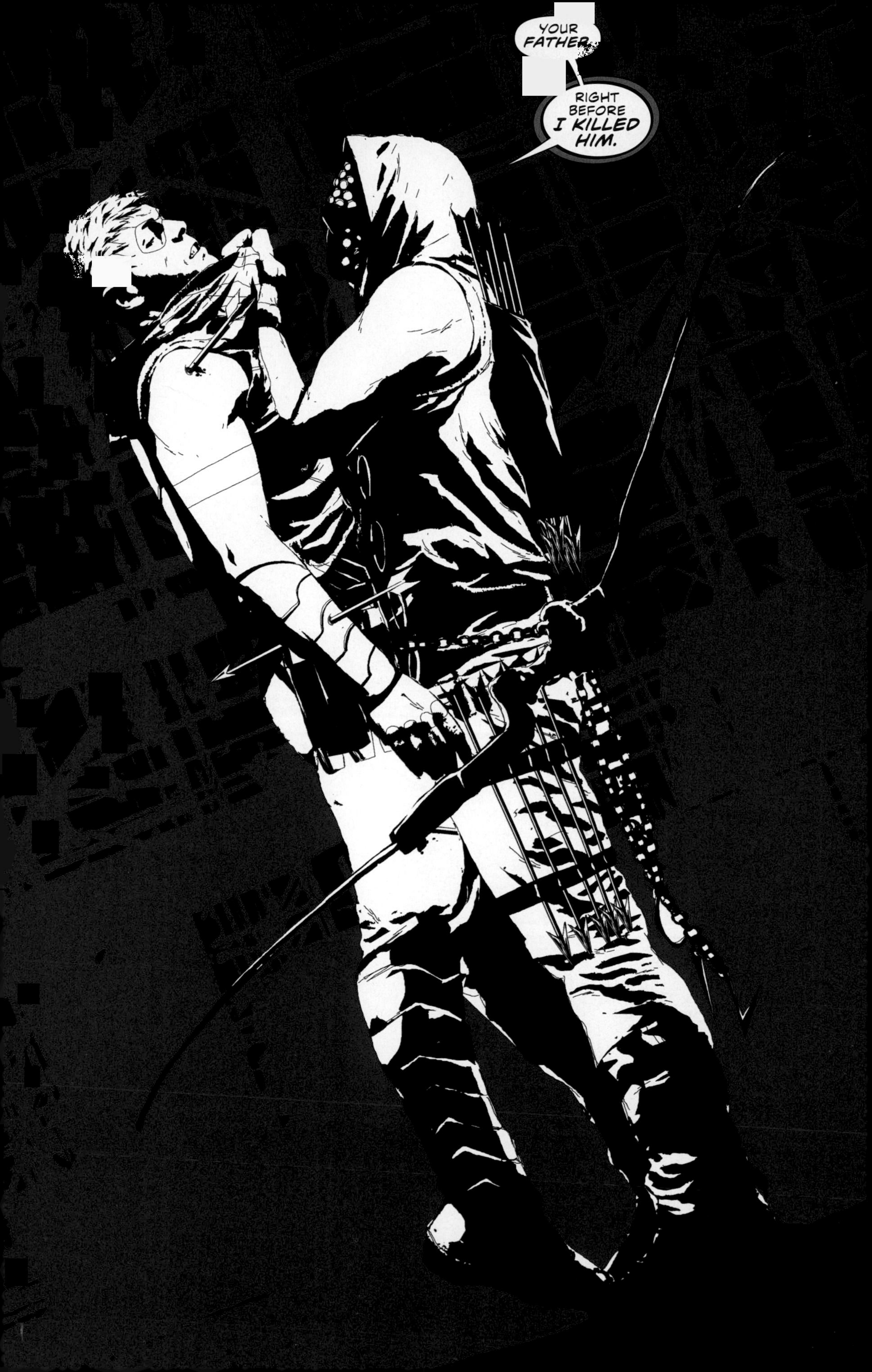
YOUR FATHER...
RIGHT BEFORE I KILLED HIM.

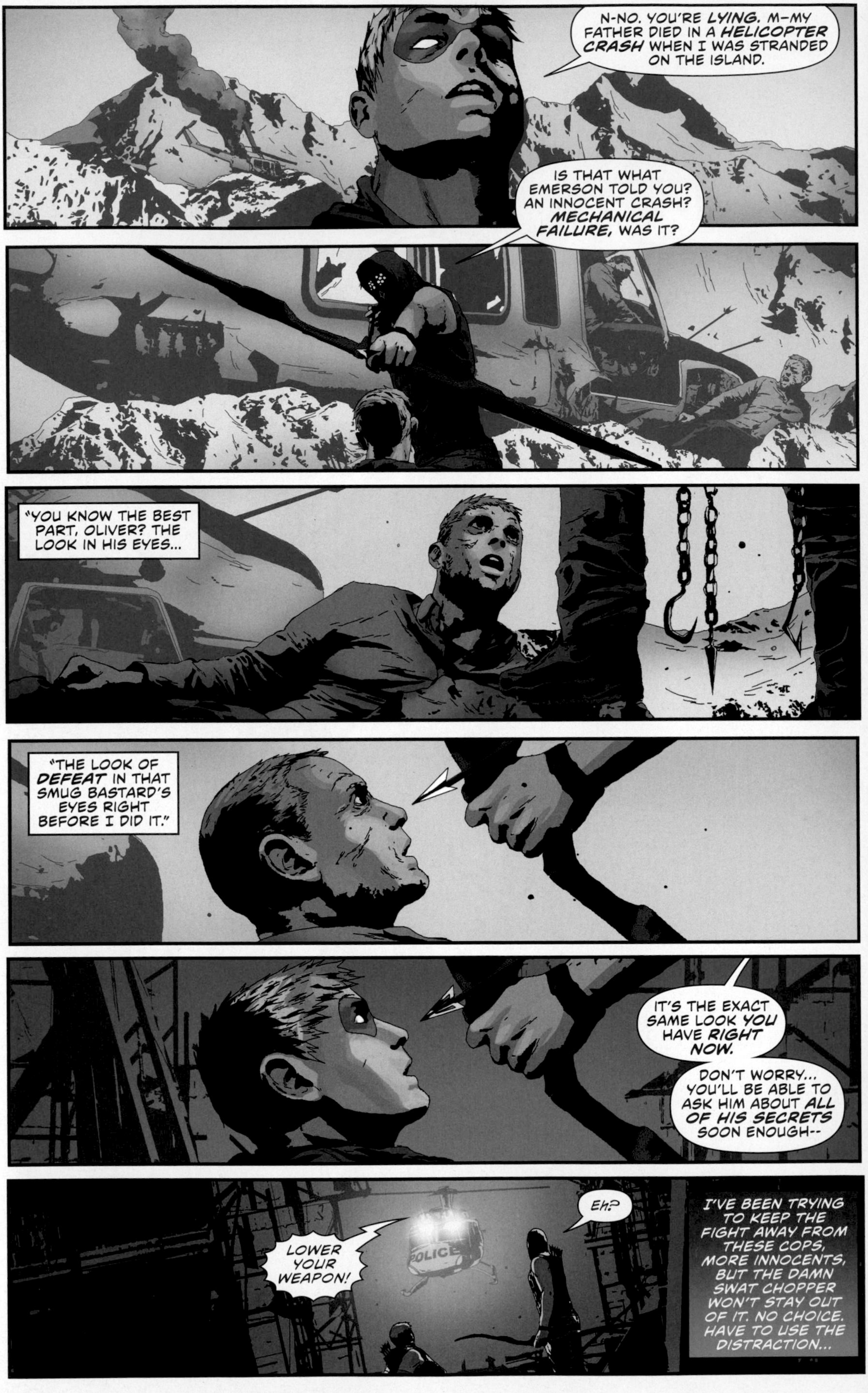
N-NO. YOU'RE LYING. M-MY FATHER DIED IN A HELICOPTER CRASH WHEN I WAS STRANDED ON THE ISLAND.
IS THAT WHAT EMERSON TOLD YOU? AN INNOCENT CRASH? MECHANICAL FAILURE, WAS IT?
"YOU KNOW THE BEST PART, OLIVER? THE LOOK IN HIS EYES...
"THE LOOK OF DEFEAT IN THAT SMUG BASTARD'S EYES RIGHT BEFORE I DID IT."
IT'S THE EXACT SAME LOOK YOU HAVE RIGHT NOW.
DON'T WORRY... YOU'LL BE ABLE TO ASK HIM ABOUT ALL OF HIS SECRETS SOON ENOUGH--
LOWER YOUR WEAPON!
POLICE
Eh?
I'VE BEEN TRYING TO KEEP THE FIGHT AWAY FROM THESE COPS, MORE INNOCENTS, BUT THE DAMN SWAT CHOPPER WON'T STAY OUT OF IT. NO CHOICE. HAVE TO USE THE DISTRACTION...

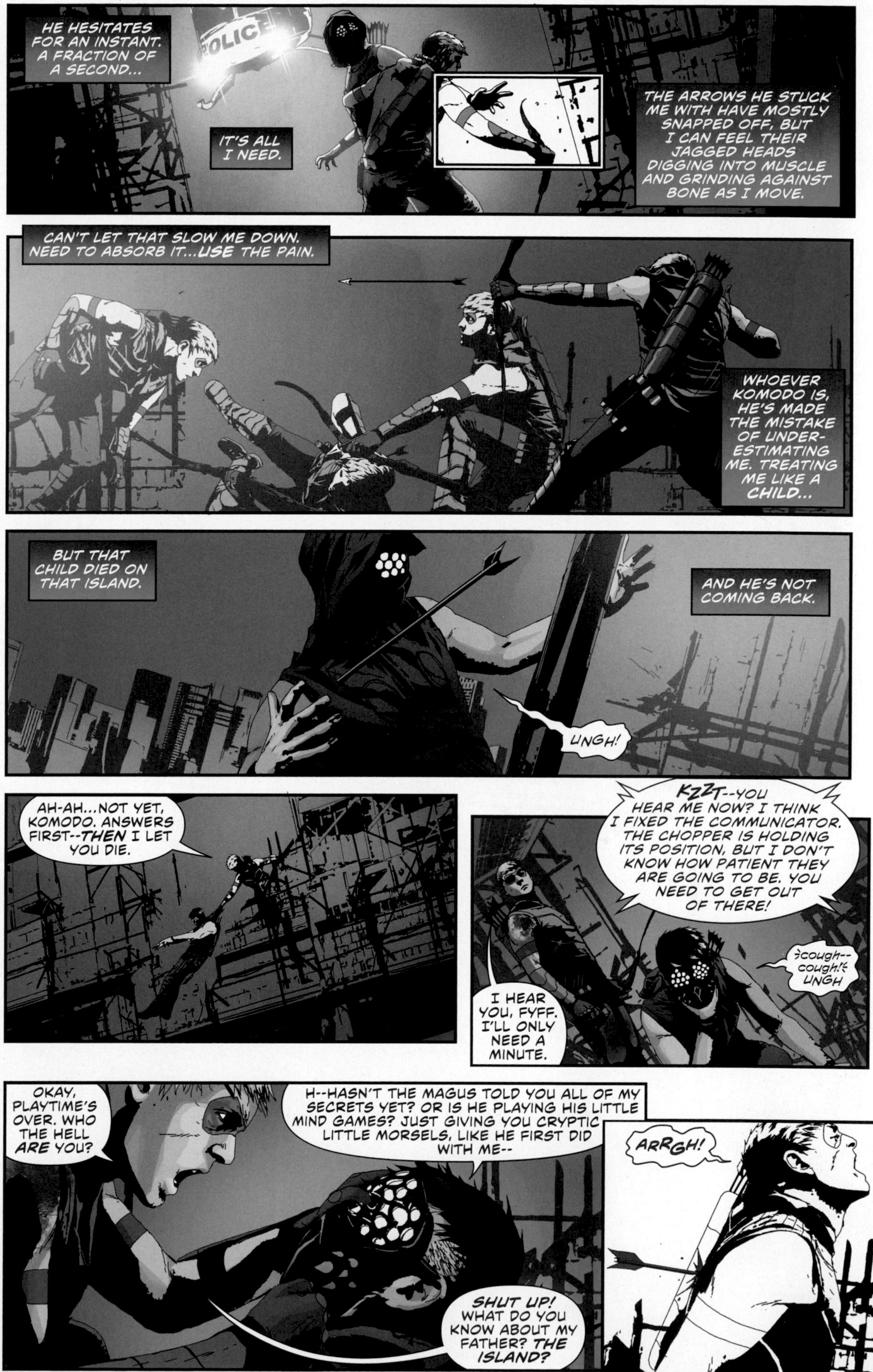
HE HESITATES FOR AN INSTANT. A FRACTION OF A SECOND...
POLICE
IT'S ALL I NEED.
THE ARROWS HE STUCK ME WITH HAVE MOSTLY SNAPPED OFF, BUT I CAN FEEL THEIR JAGGED HEADS DIGGING INTO MUSCLE AND GRINDING AGAINST BONE AS I MOVE.
CAN'T LET THAT SLOW ME DOWN. NEED TO ABSORB IT...USE THE PAIN.
WHOEVER KOMODO IS, HE'S MADE THE MISTAKE OF UNDER-ESTIMATING ME. TREATING ME LIKE A CHILD...
BUT THAT CHILD DIED ON THAT ISLAND.
AND HE'S NOT COMING BACK.
UNGH!
AH-AH...NOT YET, KOMODO. ANSWERS FIRST--THEN I LET YOU DIE.
KZZT--YOU HEAR ME NOW? I THINK I FIXED THE COMMUNICATOR. THE CHOPPER IS HOLDING ITS POSITION, BUT I DON'T KNOW HOW PATIENT THEY ARE GOING TO BE. YOU NEED TO GET OUT OF THERE!
cough-- cough! UNGH
I HEAR YOU, FYFF. I'LL ONLY NEED A MINUTE.
OKAY, PLAYTIME'S OVER. WHO THE HELL ARE YOU?
H--HASN'T THE MAGUS TOLD YOU ALL OF MY SECRETS YET? OR IS HE PLAYING HIS LITTLE MIND GAMES? JUST GIVING YOU CRYPTIC LITTLE MORSELS, LIKE HE FIRST DID WITH ME--
SHUT UP! WHAT DO YOU KNOW ABOUT MY FATHER? THE ISLAND?
ARRGH!

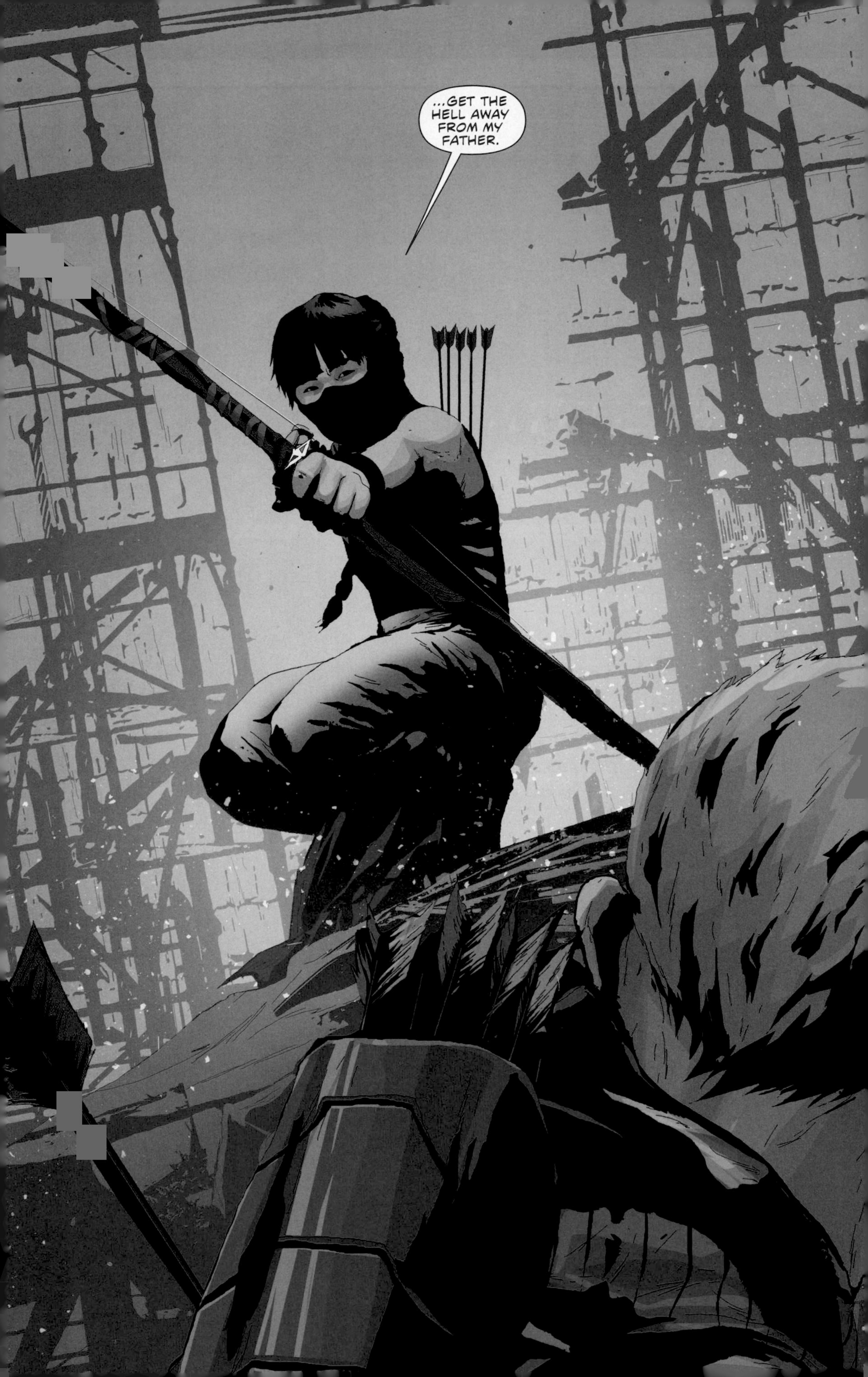
...GET THE HELL AWAY FROM MY FATHER.

CHILD, WHAT DO YOU THINK YOU'RE *DOING?* YOU'LL GET YOURSELF KILLED!

QUIET, DADDY. I HAVE THIS UNDER CONTROL.

"DADDY"?!

WHOEVER SHE IS, THE GIRL KNOWS HOW TO HANDLE A BOW... I CAN TELL BY THE WAY HER SHOULDERS RELAX UNDER ITS TENSION. BY THE WAY HER BREATH IS CALM AND STEADY.

I'VE TOLD YOU, YOU'RE NOT READY! *GET AWAY FROM HERE!*

AND LEAVE YOU TO *THIS IDIOT?* I DON'T THINK SO! I CAN DO THIS!

NOW!

ALL OF YOU--DROP YOUR WEAPONS AND GET DOWN!

THE COPS, ON THE OTHER HAND, ARE GETTING EDGY. I'M WORRIED THEY'RE GOING TO START SHOOTING SOON. THEN THIS MESS WILL TURN *REAL BAD.*

ALL OF YOU, BACK AWAY!

NO MORE THINKING. I NEED TO TAKE ACTION.

THIS TIME I GRAB THE *RIGHT* ARROW... THE NET ARROW.

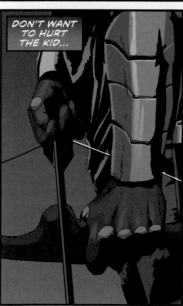

DON'T WANT TO HURT THE KID...

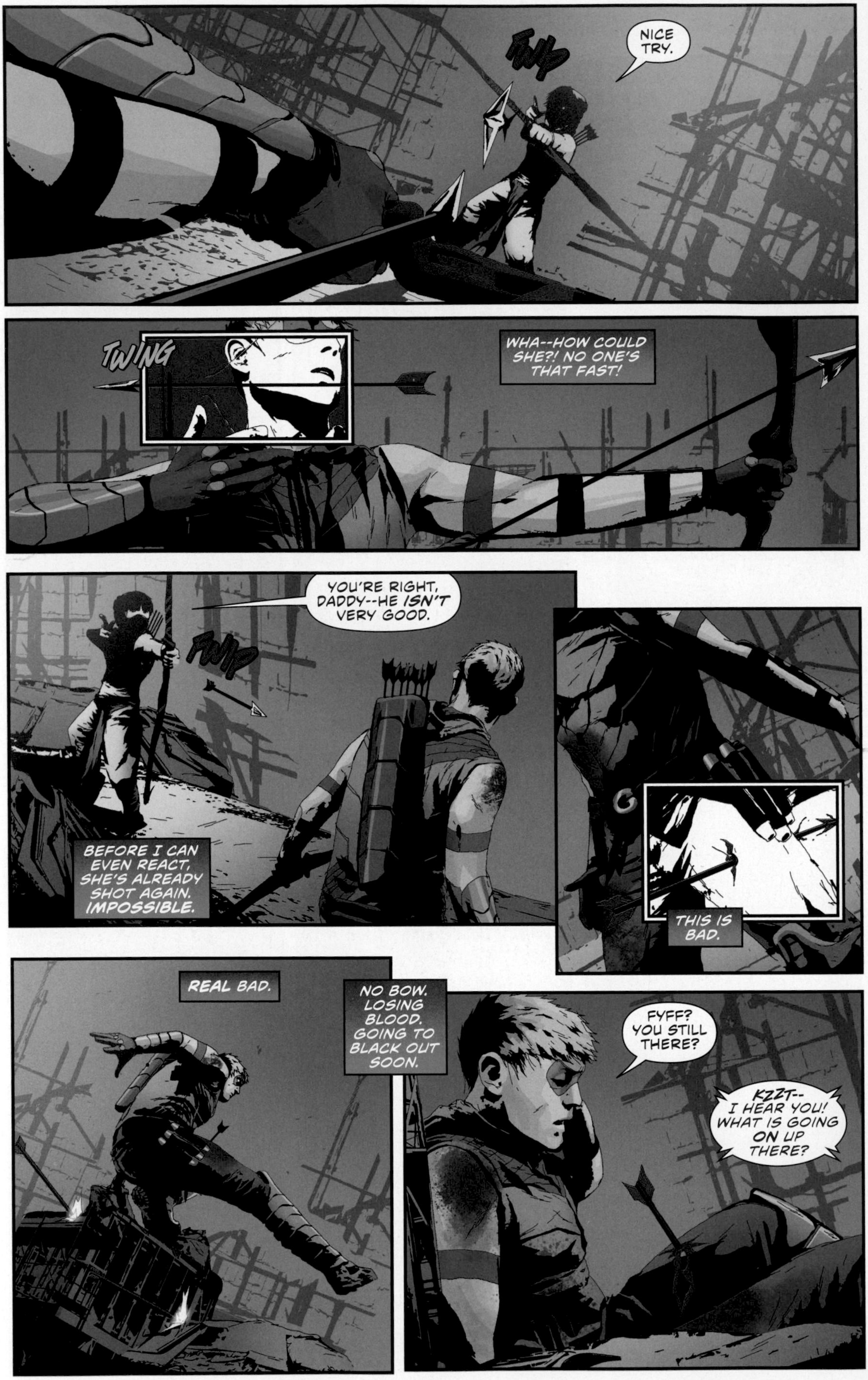
FWIP
NICE TRY.
TWING
WHA--HOW COULD SHE?! NO ONE'S THAT FAST!
YOU'RE RIGHT, DADDY--HE ISN'T VERY GOOD.
FWIP
BEFORE I CAN EVEN REACT, SHE'S ALREADY SHOT AGAIN. IMPOSSIBLE.
THIS IS BAD.
REAL BAD.
NO BOW. LOSING BLOOD. GOING TO BLACK OUT SOON.
FYFF? YOU STILL THERE?
KZZT-- I HEAR YOU! WHAT IS GOING ON UP THERE?

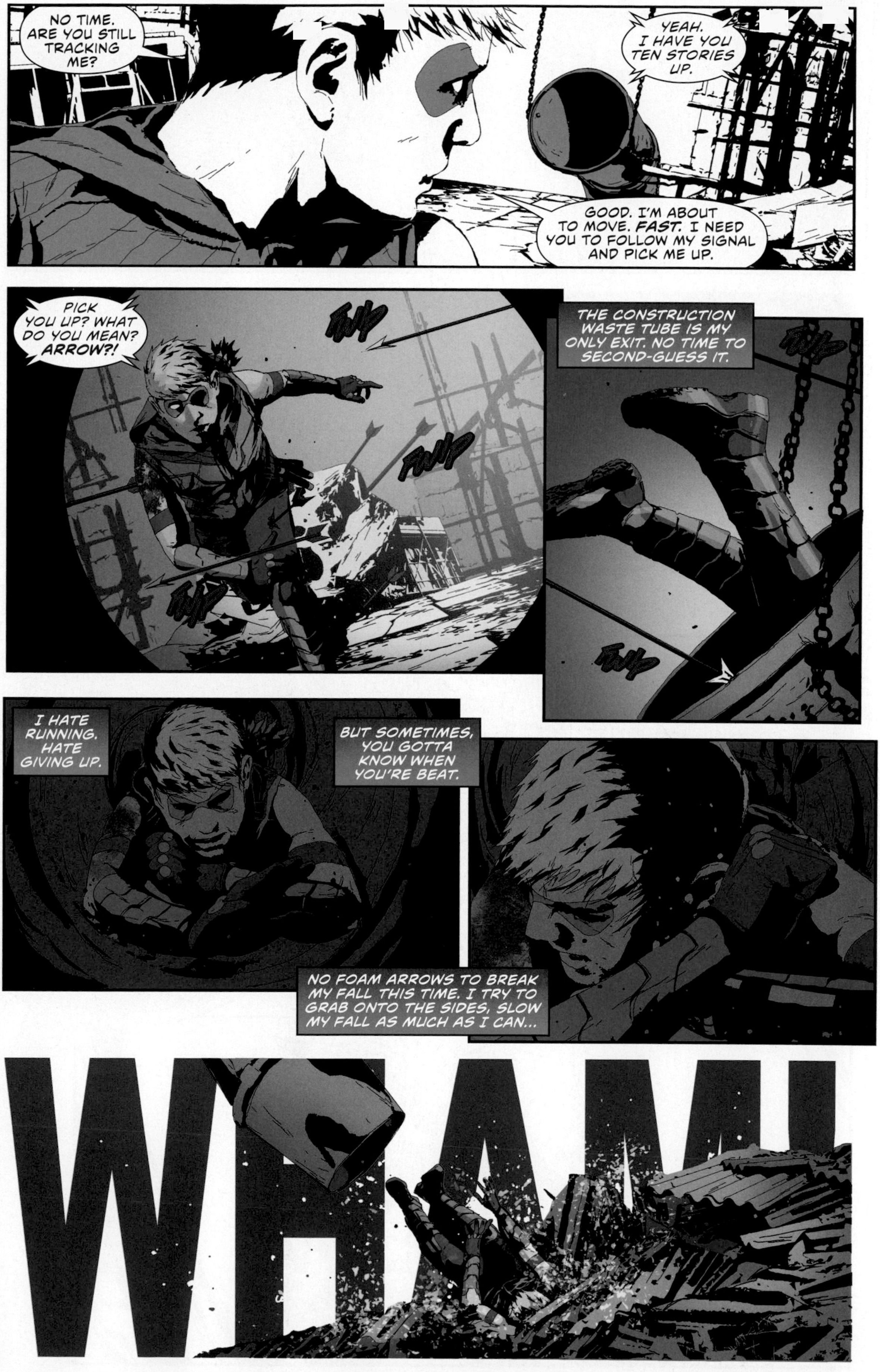
NO TIME. ARE YOU STILL TRACKING ME?
YEAH. I HAVE YOU TEN STORIES UP.
GOOD. I'M ABOUT TO MOVE. FAST. I NEED YOU TO FOLLOW MY SIGNAL AND PICK ME UP.
PICK YOU UP? WHAT DO YOU MEAN? ARROW?!
FWIP
FWIP
FWIP
THE CONSTRUCTION WASTE TUBE IS MY ONLY EXIT. NO TIME TO SECOND-GUESS IT.
FWIP
FWIP
I HATE RUNNING. HATE GIVING UP.
BUT SOMETIMES, YOU GOTTA KNOW WHEN YOU'RE BEAT.
NO FOAM ARROWS TO BREAK MY FALL THIS TIME. I TRY TO GRAB ONTO THE SIDES, SLOW MY FALL AS MUCH AS I CAN...
WHAM

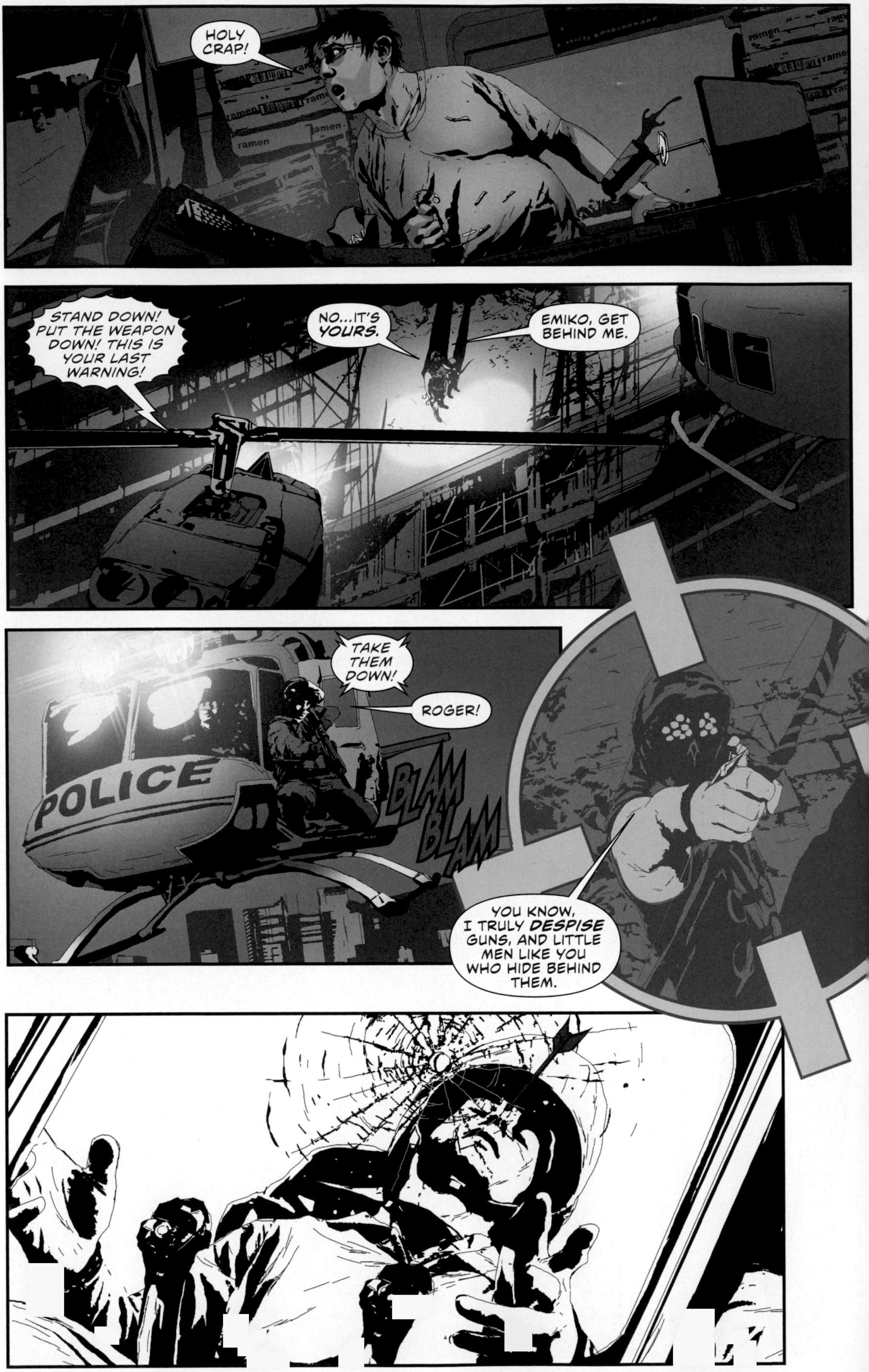
HOLY CRAP!
STAND DOWN! PUT THE WEAPON DOWN! THIS IS YOUR LAST WARNING!
NO...IT'S YOURS.
EMIKO, GET BEHIND ME.
TAKE THEM DOWN!
ROGER!
POLICE
BLAM BLAM BLAM
YOU KNOW, I TRULY DESPISE GUNS, AND LITTLE MEN LIKE YOU WHO HIDE BEHIND THEM.

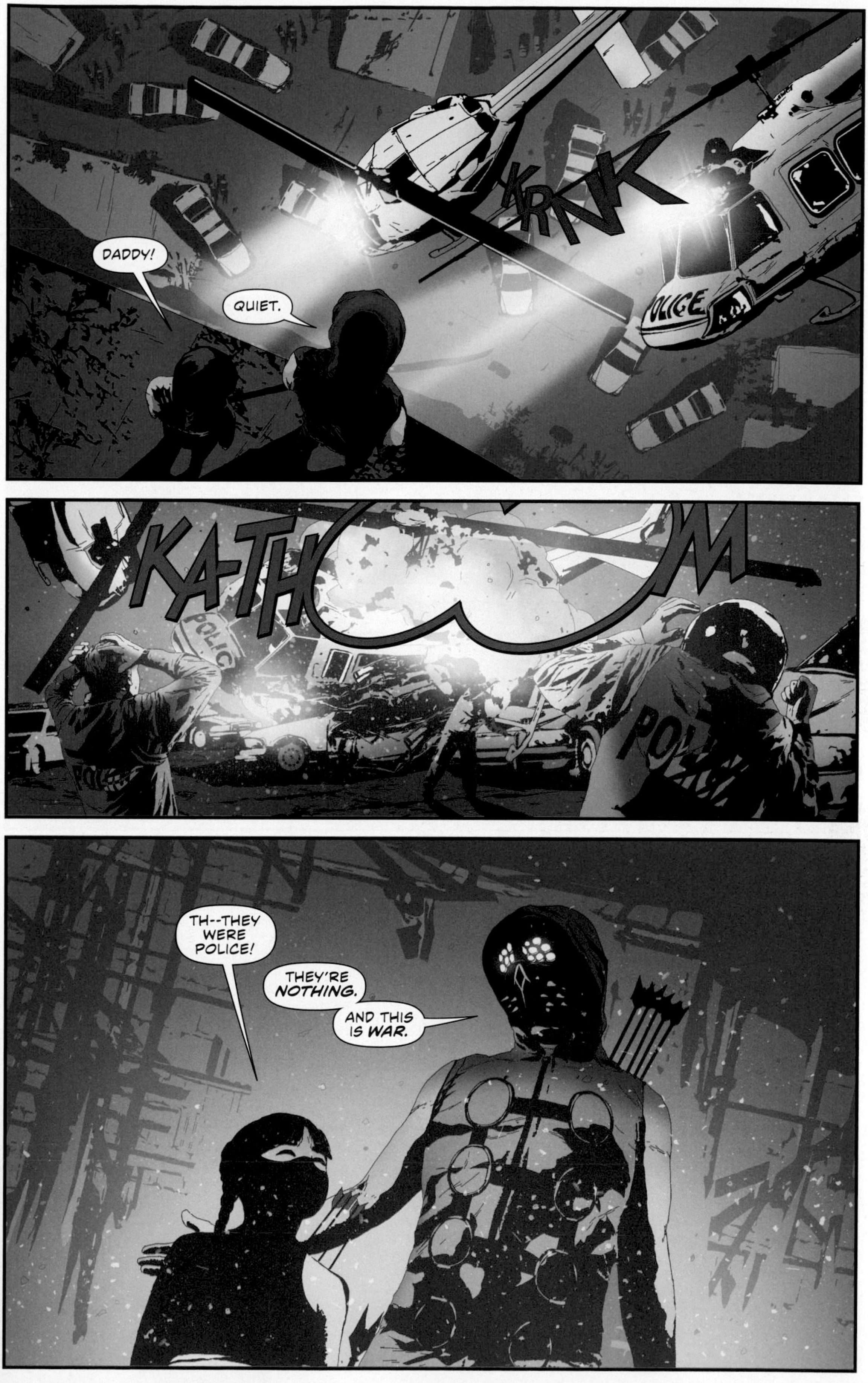
KRNK
DADDY!
QUIET.
KATHOOM
TH--THEY WERE POLICE!
THEY'RE *NOTHING.*
AND THIS IS *WAR.*

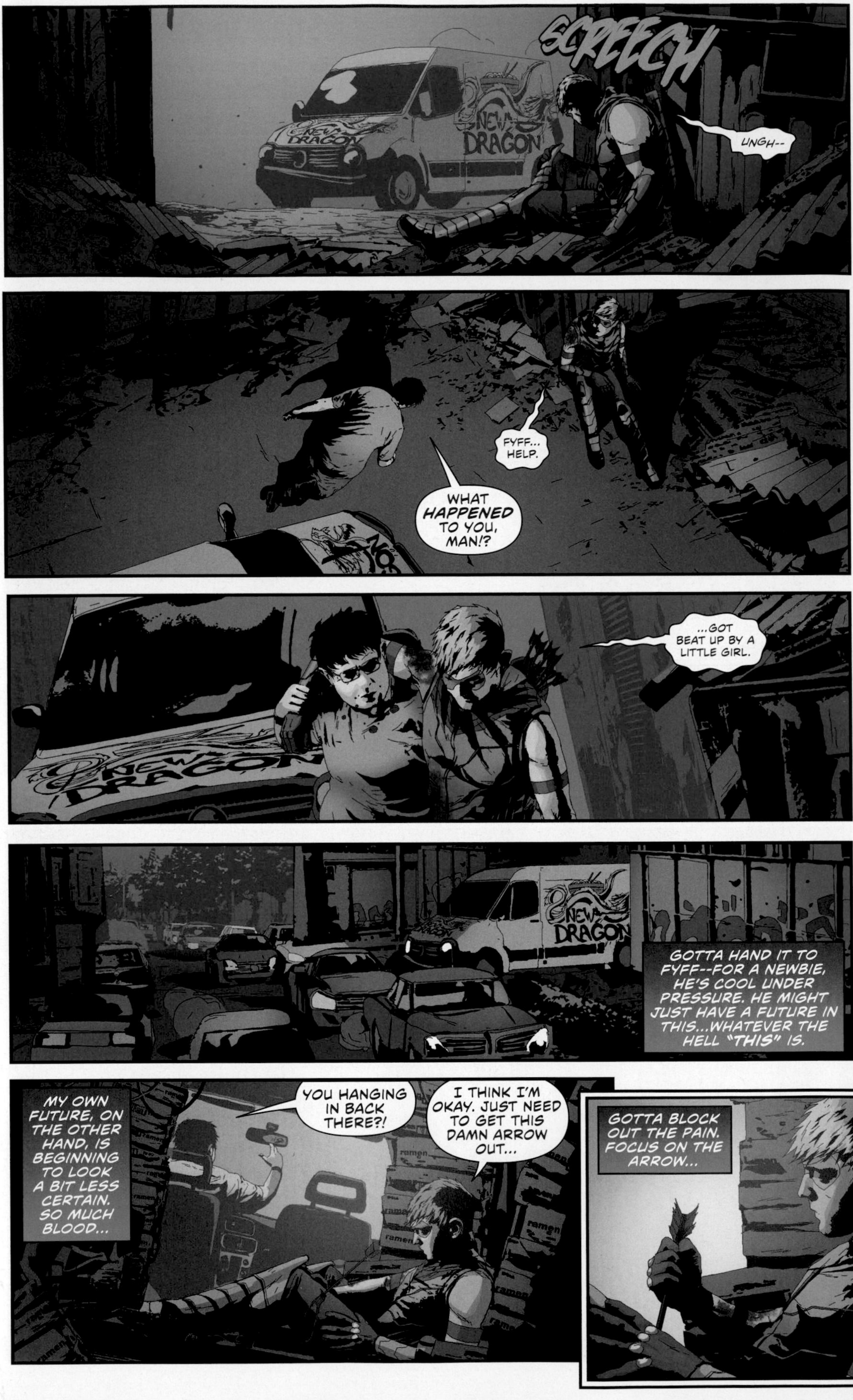
SCREECH
UNGH--
WHAT HAPPENED TO YOU, MAN!?
FYFF... HELP.
...GOT BEAT UP BY A LITTLE GIRL.
GOTTA HAND IT TO FYFF--FOR A NEWBIE, HE'S COOL UNDER PRESSURE. HE MIGHT JUST HAVE A FUTURE IN THIS...WHATEVER THE HELL "THIS" IS.
MY OWN FUTURE, ON THE OTHER HAND, IS BEGINNING TO LOOK A BIT LESS CERTAIN. SO MUCH BLOOD...
YOU HANGING IN BACK THERE?!
I THINK I'M OKAY. JUST NEED TO GET THIS DAMN ARROW OUT...
GOTTA BLOCK OUT THE PAIN. FOCUS ON THE ARROW...

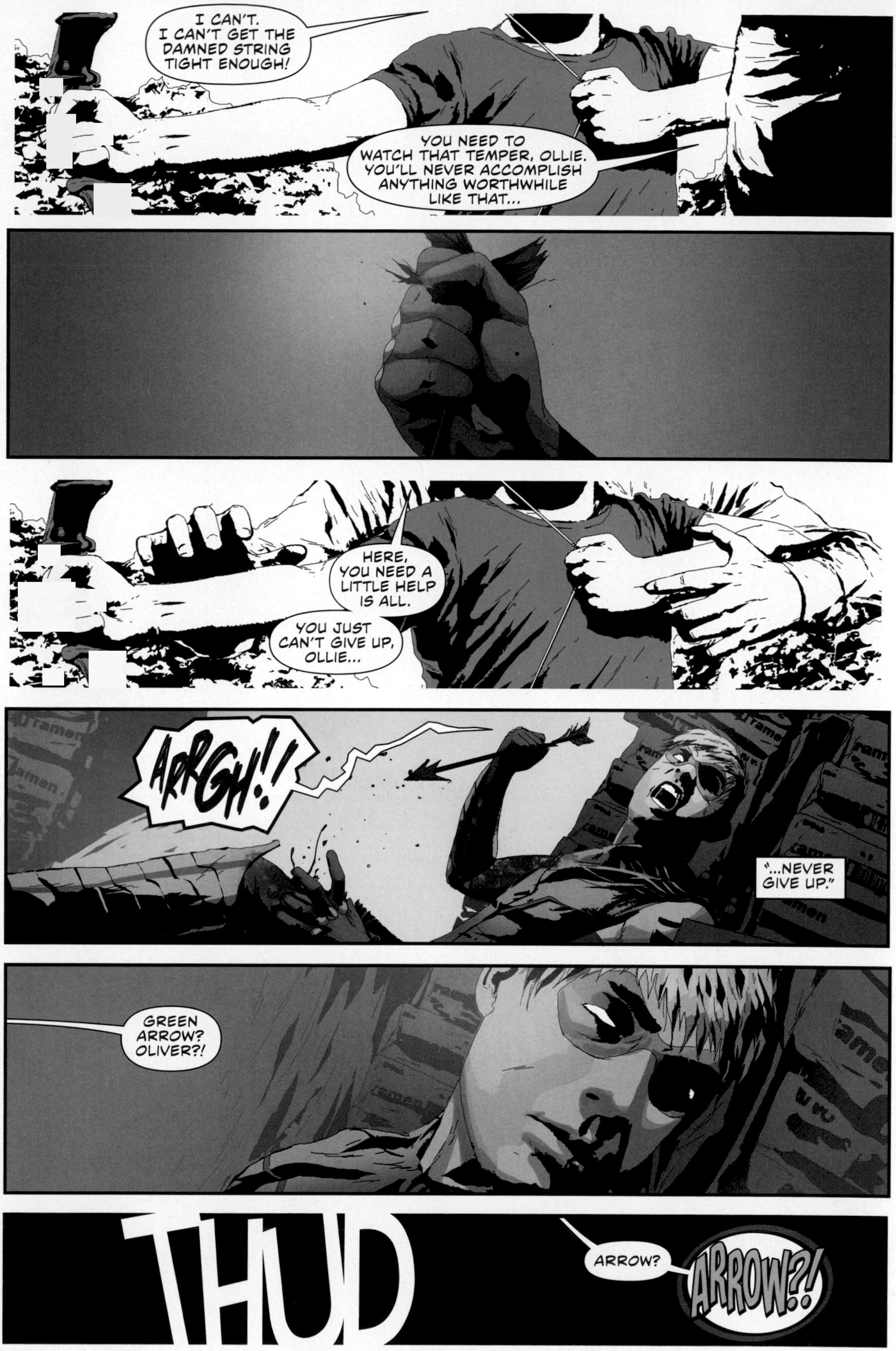
I CAN'T. I CAN'T GET THE DAMNED STRING TIGHT ENOUGH!
YOU NEED TO WATCH THAT TEMPER, OLLIE. YOU'LL NEVER ACCOMPLISH ANYTHING WORTHWHILE LIKE THAT...
HERE, YOU NEED A LITTLE HELP IS ALL.
YOU JUST CAN'T GIVE UP, OLLIE...
ARRGH!!
"...NEVER GIVE UP."
GREEN ARROW? OLIVER?!
THUD
ARROW?
ARROW?!

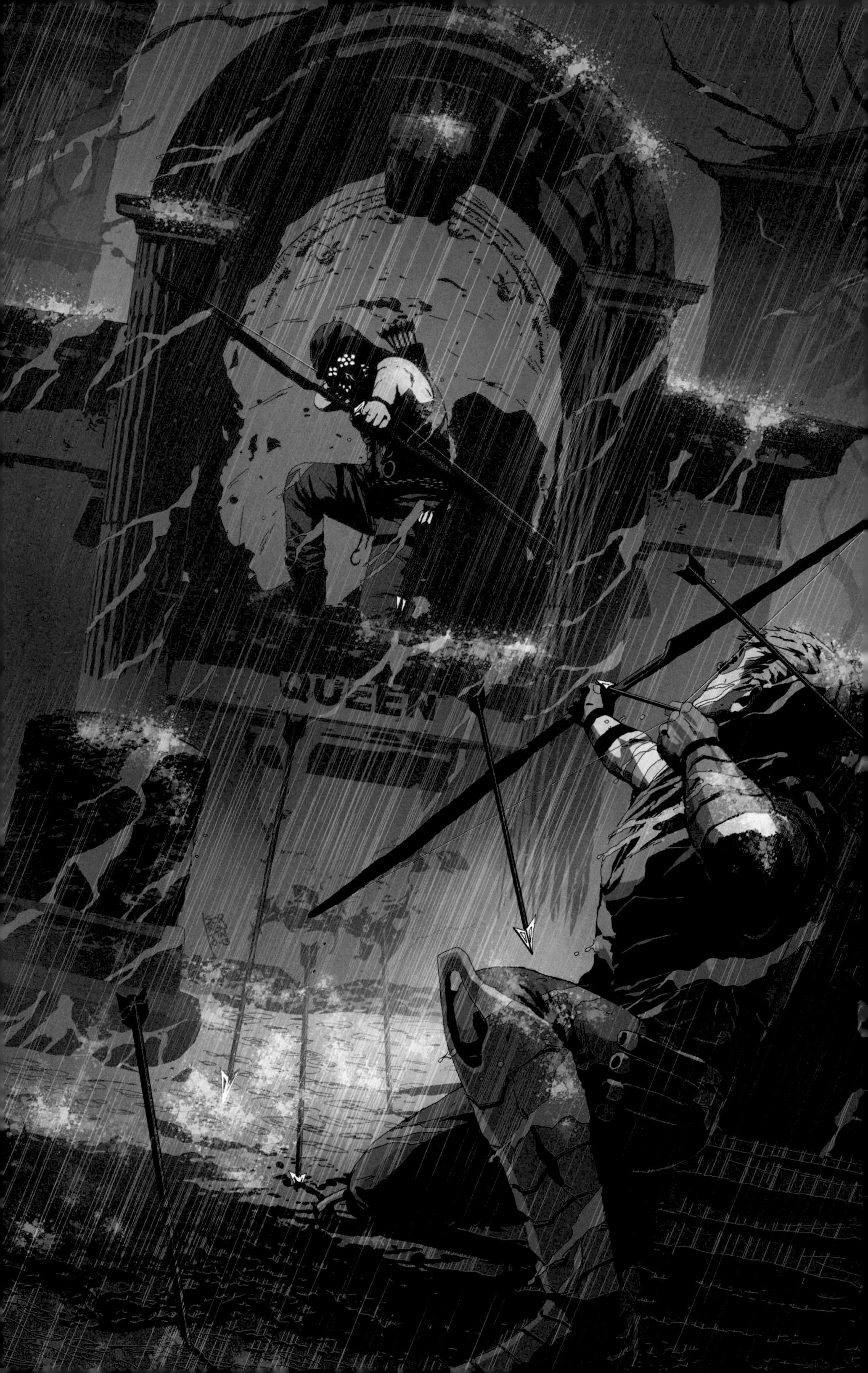
QUEEN

BLACK MESA, ARIZONA.

IT WOULD BE SO EASY.

SO EASY TO JUST STOP. TO LIE DOWN AND LET THE SUN FINISH ME OFF.

NO MORE GREEN ARROW. NO MORE OLIVER QUEEN. NO MORE PRESSURE. NO MORE RESPONSIBILITY.

I COULD JUST DRIFT AWAY.

I COULD JUST LET MYSELF BECOME THAT SHALLOW, PAMPERED RICH KID I ALWAYS PRETENDED TO BE. JUST GIVE UP.

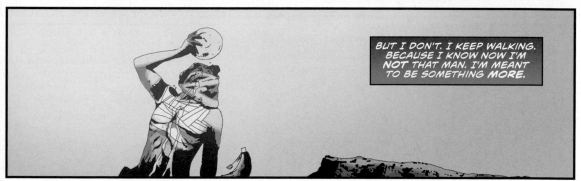

BUT I DON'T. I KEEP WALKING. BECAUSE I KNOW NOW I'M NOT THAT MAN. I'M MEANT TO BE SOMETHING MORE.

MAGUS?

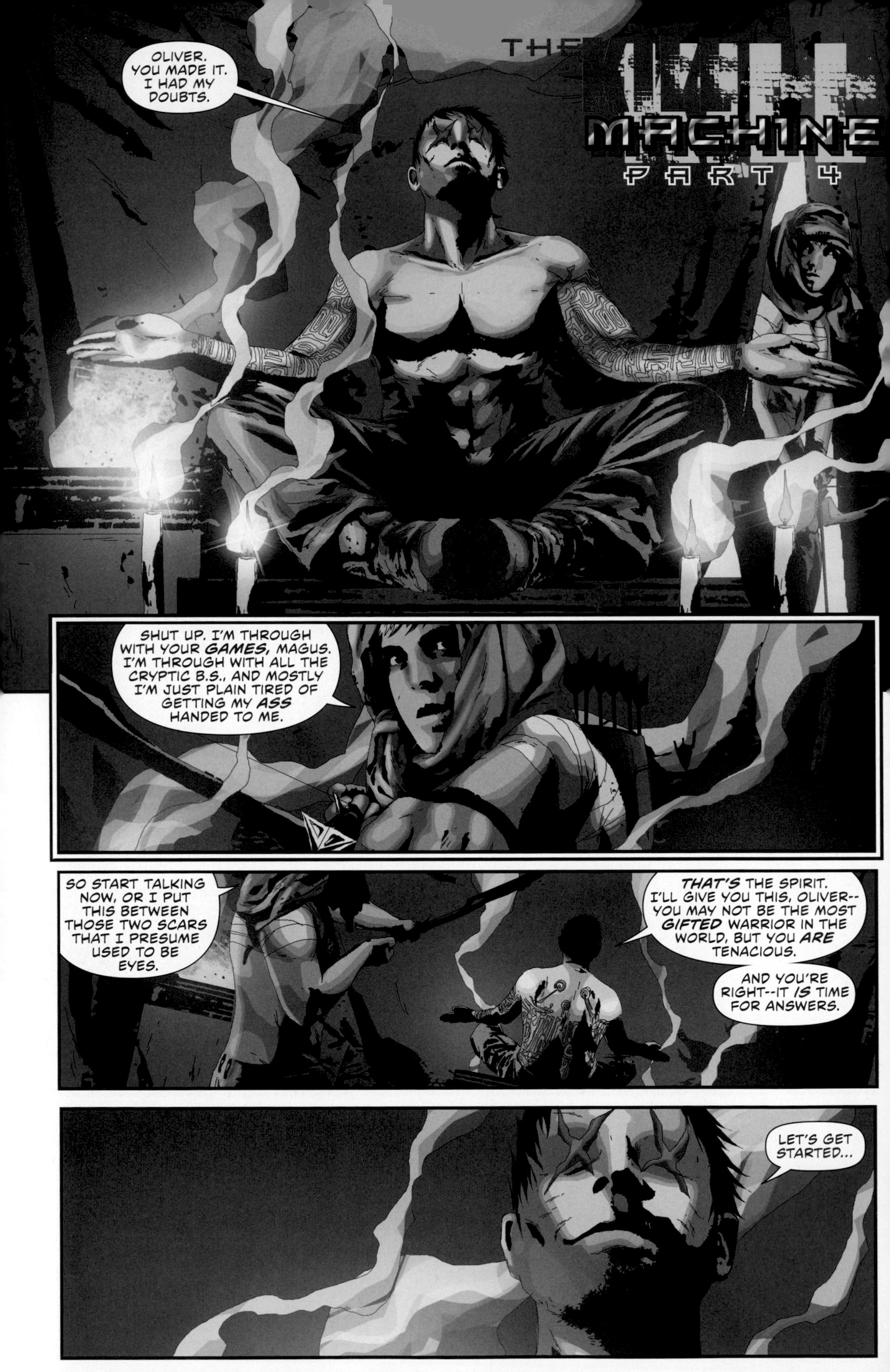
THE KILL MACHINE
PART 4
OLIVER. YOU MADE IT. I HAD MY DOUBTS.
SHUT UP. I'M THROUGH WITH YOUR GAMES, MAGUS. I'M THROUGH WITH ALL THE CRYPTIC B.S., AND MOSTLY I'M JUST PLAIN TIRED OF GETTING MY ASS HANDED TO ME.
SO START TALKING NOW, OR I PUT THIS BETWEEN THOSE TWO SCARS THAT I PRESUME USED TO BE EYES.
THAT'S THE SPIRIT. I'LL GIVE YOU THIS, OLIVER--YOU MAY NOT BE THE MOST GIFTED WARRIOR IN THE WORLD, BUT YOU ARE TENACIOUS.
AND YOU'RE RIGHT--IT IS TIME FOR ANSWERS.
LET'S GET STARTED...

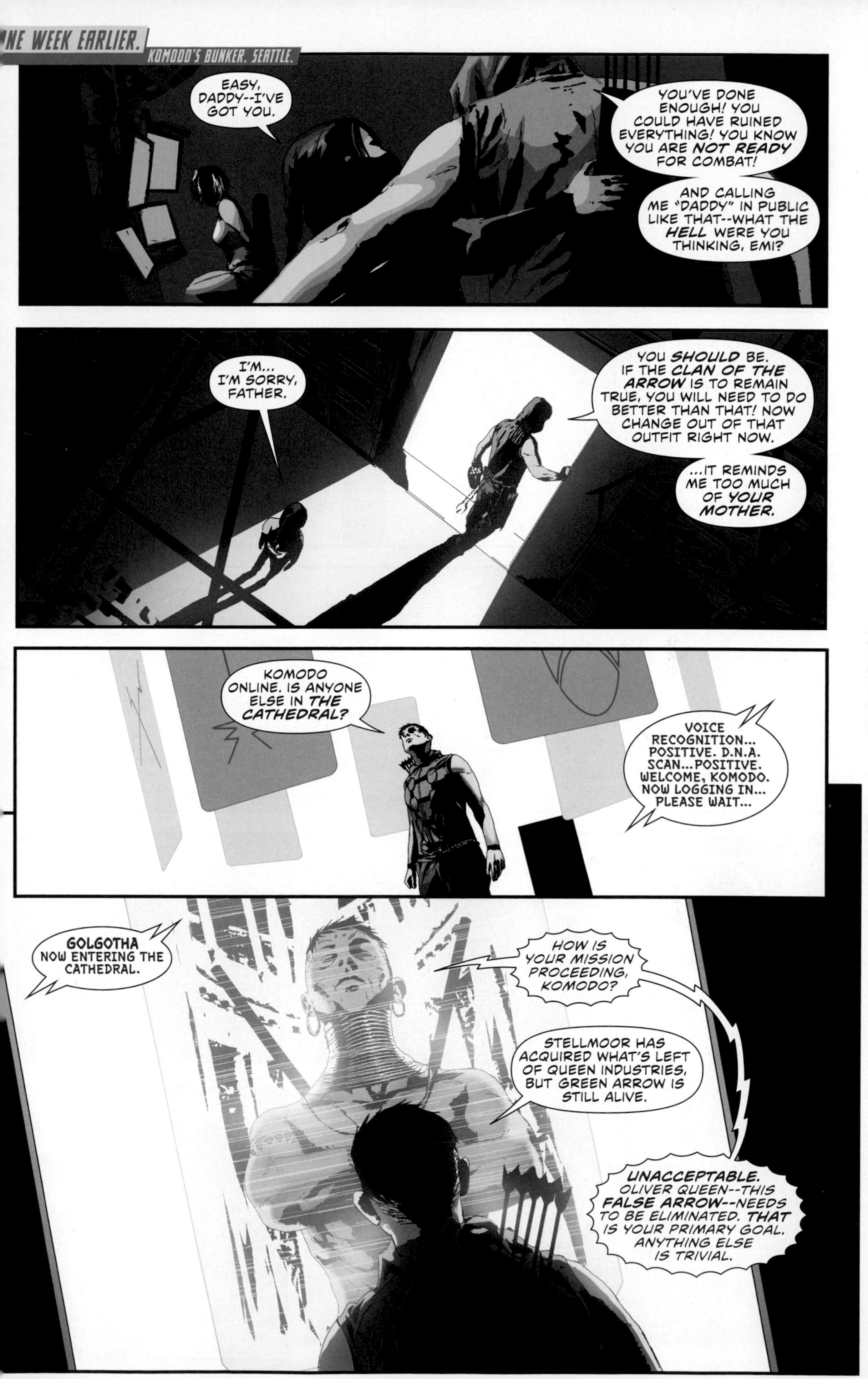
NE WEEK EARLIER.
KOMODO'S BUNKER. SEATTLE.
EASY, DADDY--I'VE GOT YOU.
YOU'VE DONE ENOUGH! YOU COULD HAVE RUINED EVERYTHING! YOU KNOW YOU ARE NOT READY FOR COMBAT!
AND CALLING ME "DADDY" IN PUBLIC LIKE THAT--WHAT THE HELL WERE YOU THINKING, EMI?
I'M... I'M SORRY, FATHER.
YOU SHOULD BE. IF THE CLAN OF THE ARROW IS TO REMAIN TRUE, YOU WILL NEED TO DO BETTER THAN THAT! NOW CHANGE OUT OF THAT OUTFIT RIGHT NOW.
...IT REMINDS ME TOO MUCH OF YOUR MOTHER.
KOMODO ONLINE. IS ANYONE ELSE IN THE CATHEDRAL?
VOICE RECOGNITION... POSITIVE. D.N.A. SCAN...POSITIVE. WELCOME, KOMODO. NOW LOGGING IN... PLEASE WAIT...
GOLGOTHA NOW ENTERING THE CATHEDRAL.
HOW IS YOUR MISSION PROCEEDING, KOMODO?
STELLMOOR HAS ACQUIRED WHAT'S LEFT OF QUEEN INDUSTRIES, BUT GREEN ARROW IS STILL ALIVE.
UNACCEPTABLE. OLIVER QUEEN--THIS FALSE ARROW--NEEDS TO BE ELIMINATED. THAT IS YOUR PRIMARY GOAL. ANYTHING ELSE IS TRIVIAL.

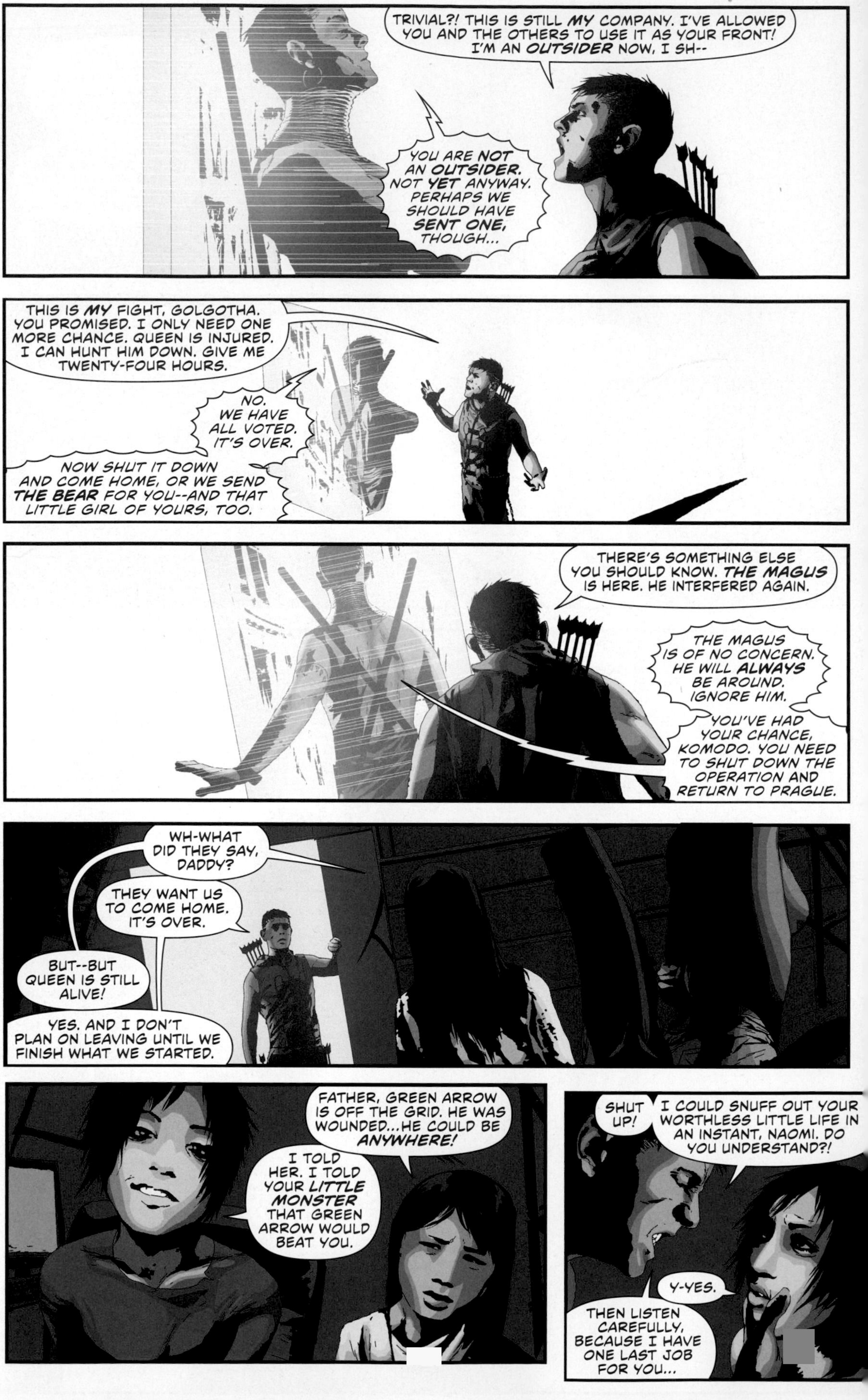
TRIVIAL?! THIS IS STILL MY COMPANY. I'VE ALLOWED YOU AND THE OTHERS TO USE IT AS YOUR FRONT! I'M AN OUTSIDER NOW, I SH--
YOU ARE NOT AN OUTSIDER. NOT YET ANYWAY. PERHAPS WE SHOULD HAVE SENT ONE, THOUGH...
THIS IS MY FIGHT, GOLGOTHA. YOU PROMISED. I ONLY NEED ONE MORE CHANCE. QUEEN IS INJURED. I CAN HUNT HIM DOWN. GIVE ME TWENTY-FOUR HOURS.
NO. WE HAVE ALL VOTED. IT'S OVER.
NOW SHUT IT DOWN AND COME HOME, OR WE SEND THE BEAR FOR YOU--AND THAT LITTLE GIRL OF YOURS, TOO.
THERE'S SOMETHING ELSE YOU SHOULD KNOW. THE MAGUS IS HERE. HE INTERFERED AGAIN.
THE MAGUS IS OF NO CONCERN. HE WILL ALWAYS BE AROUND. IGNORE HIM.
YOU'VE HAD YOUR CHANCE, KOMODO. YOU NEED TO SHUT DOWN THE OPERATION AND RETURN TO PRAGUE.
WH-WHAT DID THEY SAY, DADDY?
THEY WANT US TO COME HOME. IT'S OVER.
BUT--BUT QUEEN IS STILL ALIVE!
YES. AND I DON'T PLAN ON LEAVING UNTIL WE FINISH WHAT WE STARTED.
FATHER, GREEN ARROW IS OFF THE GRID. HE WAS WOUNDED...HE COULD BE ANYWHERE!
I TOLD HER. I TOLD YOUR LITTLE MONSTER THAT GREEN ARROW WOULD BEAT YOU.
SHUT UP!
I COULD SNUFF OUT YOUR WORTHLESS LITTLE LIFE IN AN INSTANT, NAOMI. DO YOU UNDERSTAND?!
Y-YES.
THEN LISTEN CAREFULLY, BECAUSE I HAVE ONE LAST JOB FOR YOU...

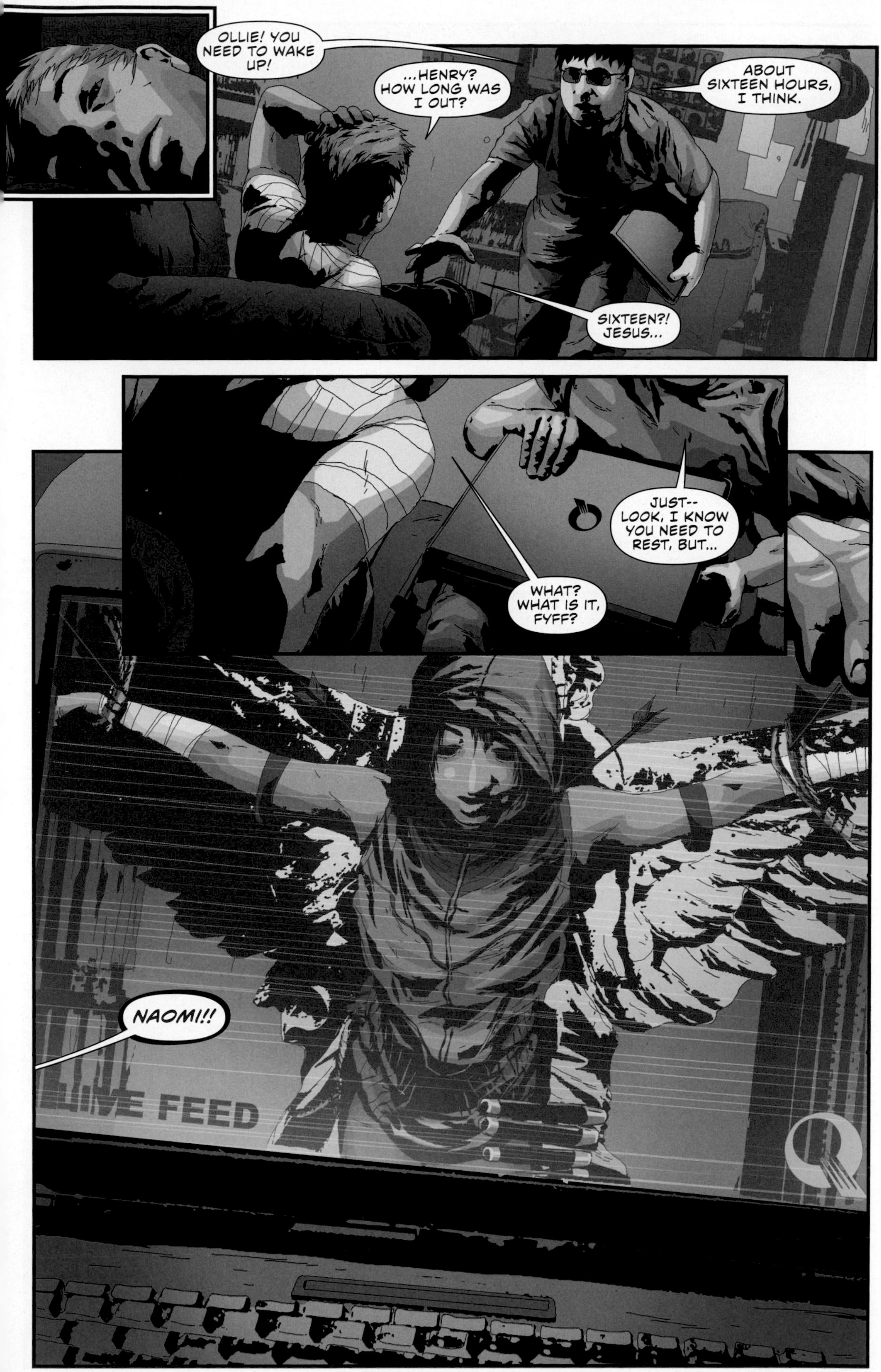
OLLIE! YOU NEED TO WAKE UP!
...HENRY? HOW LONG WAS I OUT?
ABOUT SIXTEEN HOURS, I THINK.
SIXTEEN?! JESUS...
JUST-- LOOK, I KNOW YOU NEED TO REST, BUT...
WHAT? WHAT IS IT, FYFF?
NAOMI!!
LIVE FEED

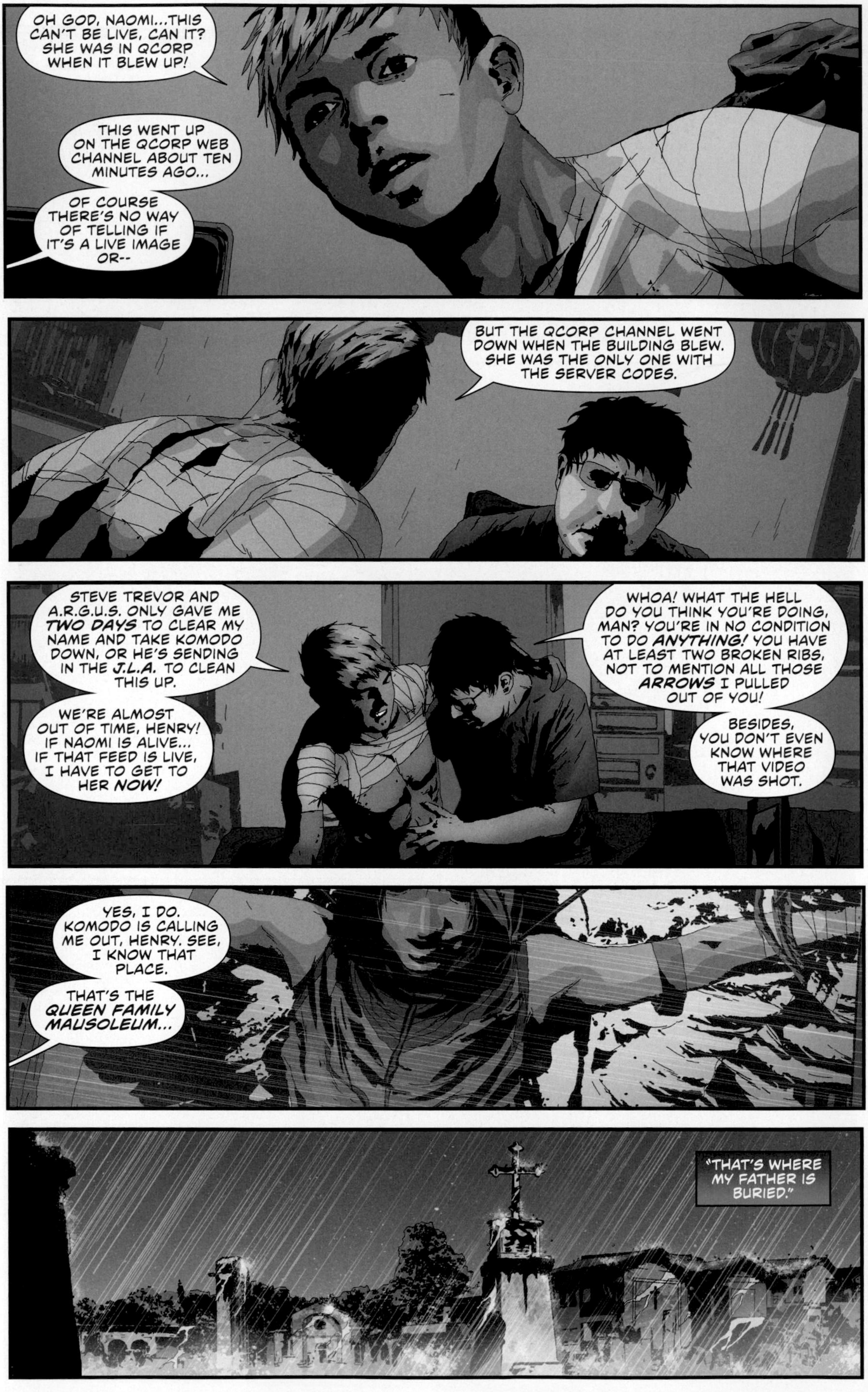
OH GOD, NAOMI...THIS CAN'T BE LIVE, CAN IT? SHE WAS IN QCORP WHEN IT BLEW UP!
THIS WENT UP ON THE QCORP WEB CHANNEL ABOUT TEN MINUTES AGO...
OF COURSE THERE'S NO WAY OF TELLING IF IT'S A LIVE IMAGE OR--
BUT THE QCORP CHANNEL WENT DOWN WHEN THE BUILDING BLEW. SHE WAS THE ONLY ONE WITH THE SERVER CODES.
STEVE TREVOR AND A.R.G.U.S. ONLY GAVE ME TWO DAYS TO CLEAR MY NAME AND TAKE KOMODO DOWN, OR HE'S SENDING IN THE J.L.A. TO CLEAN THIS UP.
WE'RE ALMOST OUT OF TIME, HENRY! IF NAOMI IS ALIVE... IF THAT FEED IS LIVE, I HAVE TO GET TO HER NOW!
WHOA! WHAT THE HELL DO YOU THINK YOU'RE DOING, MAN? YOU'RE IN NO CONDITION TO DO ANYTHING! YOU HAVE AT LEAST TWO BROKEN RIBS, NOT TO MENTION ALL THOSE ARROWS I PULLED OUT OF YOU!
BESIDES, YOU DON'T EVEN KNOW WHERE THAT VIDEO WAS SHOT.
YES, I DO. KOMODO IS CALLING ME OUT, HENRY. SEE, I KNOW THAT PLACE.
THAT'S THE QUEEN FAMILY MAUSOLEUM...
"THAT'S WHERE MY FATHER IS BURIED."

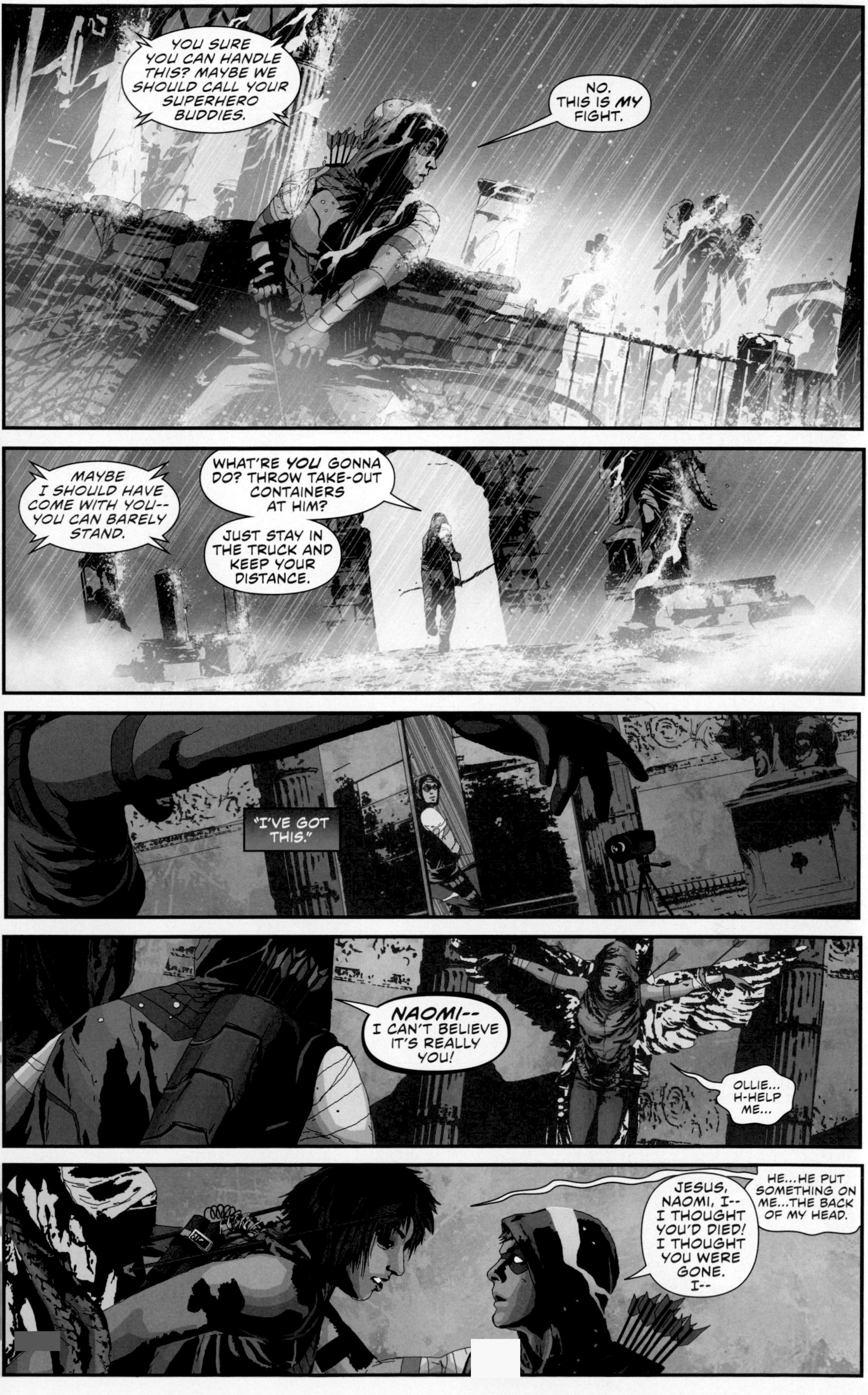
YOU SURE YOU CAN HANDLE THIS? MAYBE WE SHOULD CALL YOUR SUPERHERO BUDDIES.
NO. THIS IS MY FIGHT.
MAYBE I SHOULD HAVE COME WITH YOU-- YOU CAN BARELY STAND.
WHAT'RE YOU GONNA DO? THROW TAKE-OUT CONTAINERS AT HIM?
JUST STAY IN THE TRUCK AND KEEP YOUR DISTANCE.
"I'VE GOT THIS."
NAOMI-- I CAN'T BELIEVE IT'S REALLY YOU!
OLLIE... H-HELP ME...
JESUS, NAOMI, I-- I THOUGHT YOU'D DIED! I THOUGHT YOU WERE GONE. I--
HE...HE PUT SOMETHING ON ME...THE BACK OF MY HEAD.

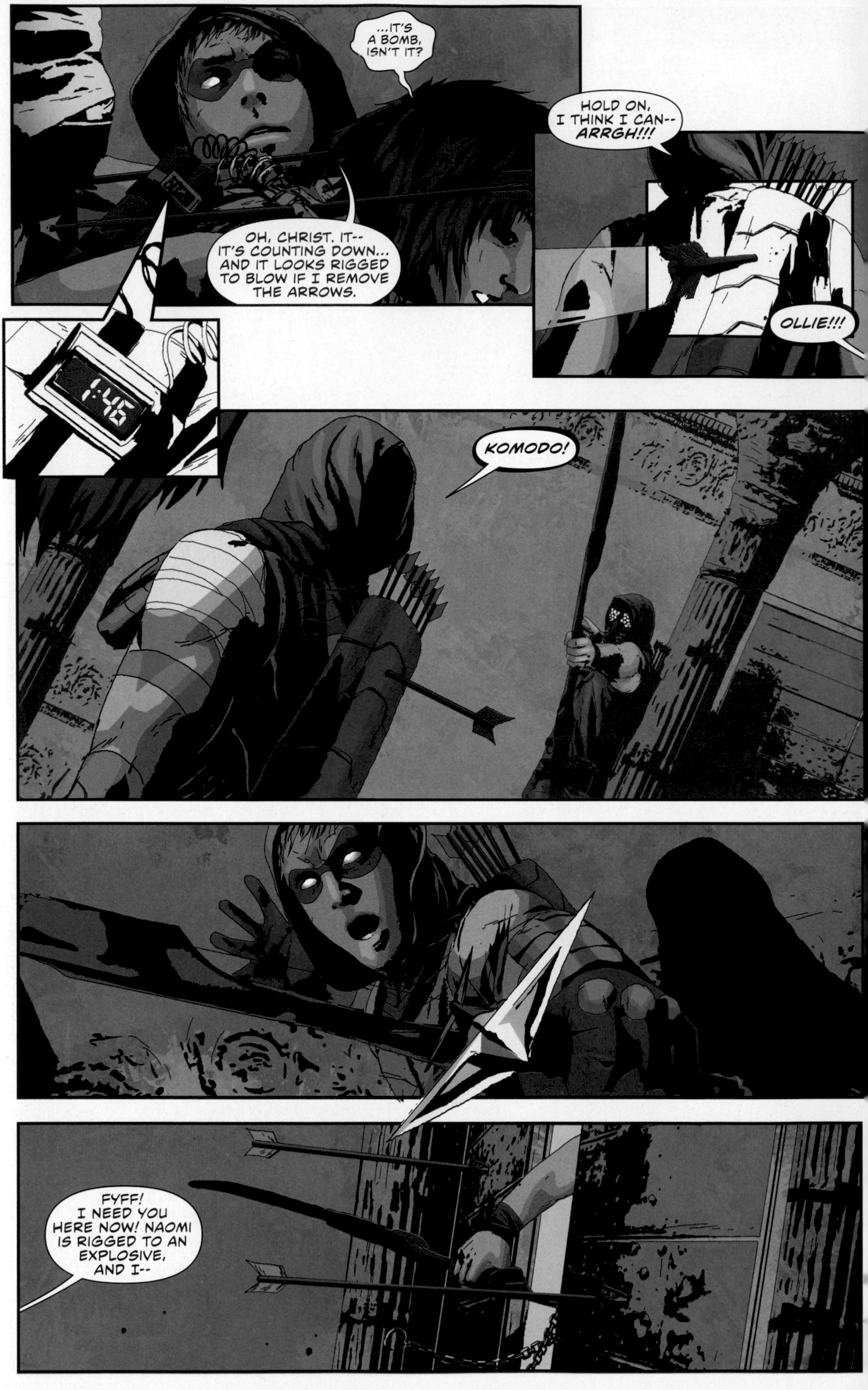
...IT'S A BOMB, ISN'T IT?
OH, CHRIST. IT-- IT'S COUNTING DOWN... AND IT LOOKS RIGGED TO BLOW IF I REMOVE THE ARROWS.
1:46
HOLD ON, I THINK I CAN-- ARRGH!!!
OLLIE!!!
KOMODO!
FYFF! I NEED YOU HERE NOW! NAOMI IS RIGGED TO AN EXPLOSIVE, AND I--

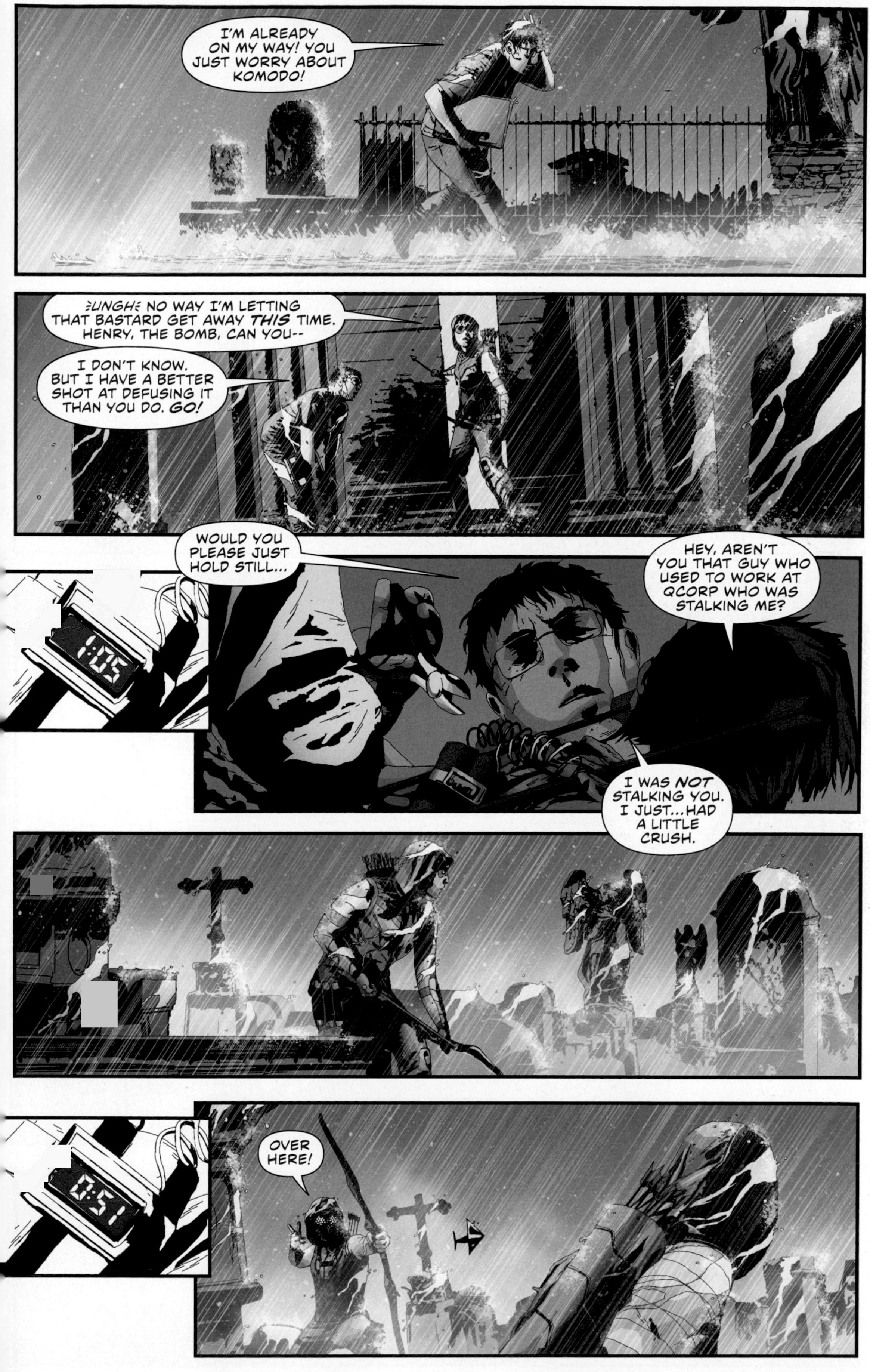
I'M ALREADY ON MY WAY! YOU JUST WORRY ABOUT KOMODO!
UNGH NO WAY I'M LETTING THAT BASTARD GET AWAY THIS TIME. HENRY, THE BOMB, CAN YOU--
I DON'T KNOW. BUT I HAVE A BETTER SHOT AT DEFUSING IT THAN YOU DO. GO!
1:05
WOULD YOU PLEASE JUST HOLD STILL...
HEY, AREN'T YOU THAT GUY WHO USED TO WORK AT QCORP WHO WAS STALKING ME?
I WAS NOT STALKING YOU. I JUST...HAD A LITTLE CRUSH.
0:51
OVER HERE!

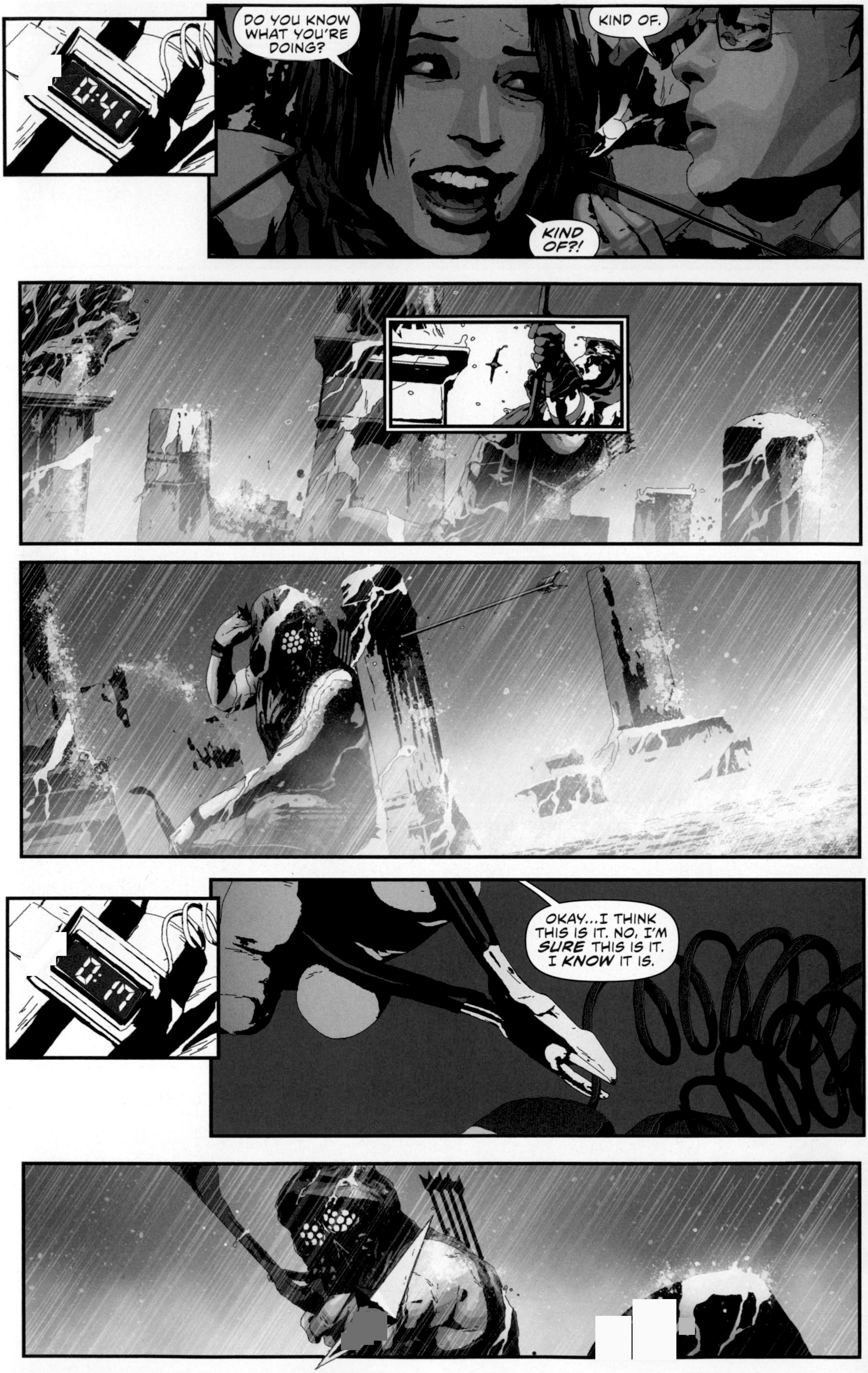
0:41
DO YOU KNOW WHAT YOU'RE DOING?
KIND OF.
KIND OF?!
0:17
OKAY...I THINK THIS IS IT. NO, I'M *SURE* THIS IS IT. I *KNOW* IT IS.

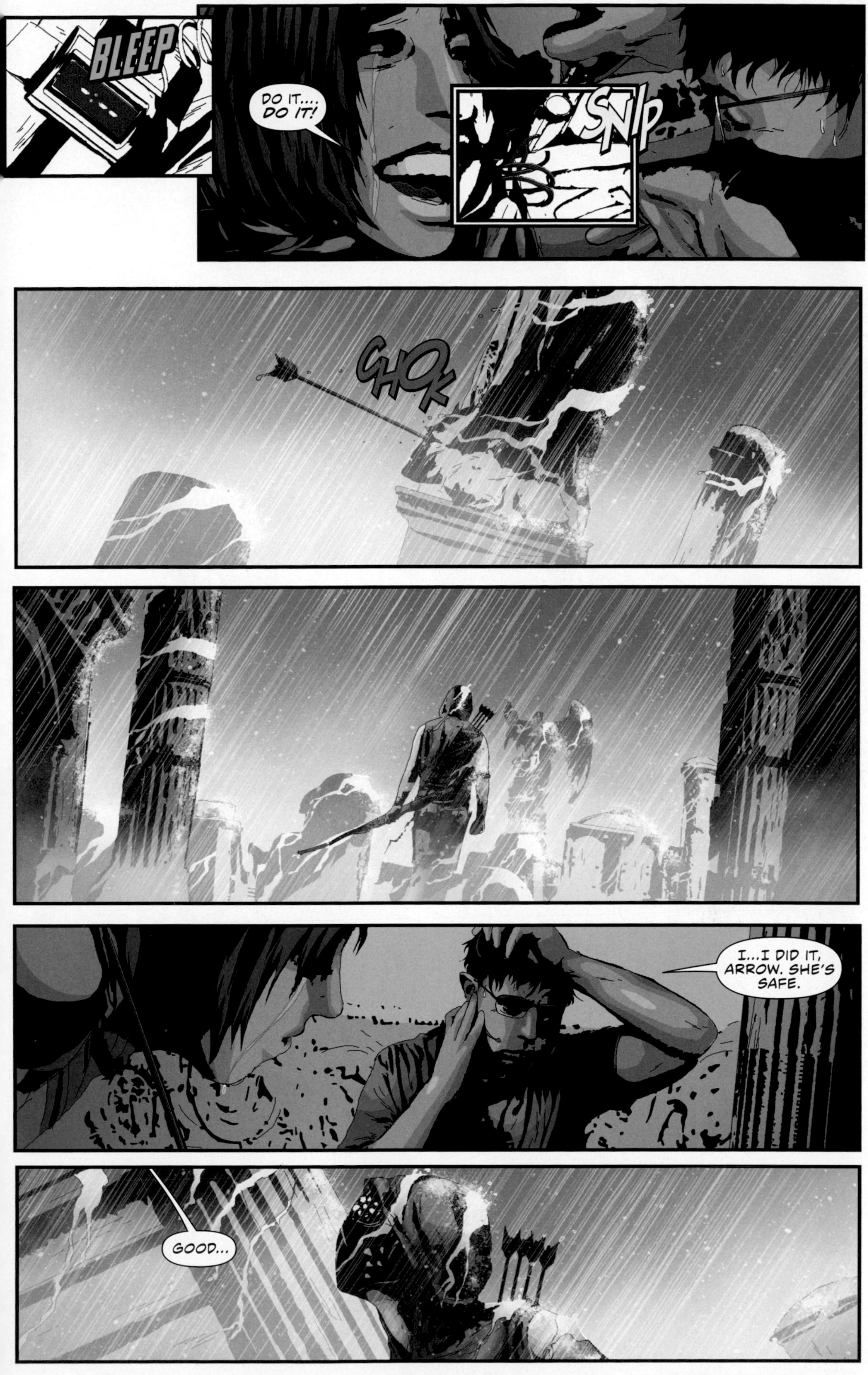
BLEEP
DO IT.... DO IT!
SNIP
CHOK
I...I DID IT, ARROW. SHE'S SAFE.
GOOD...

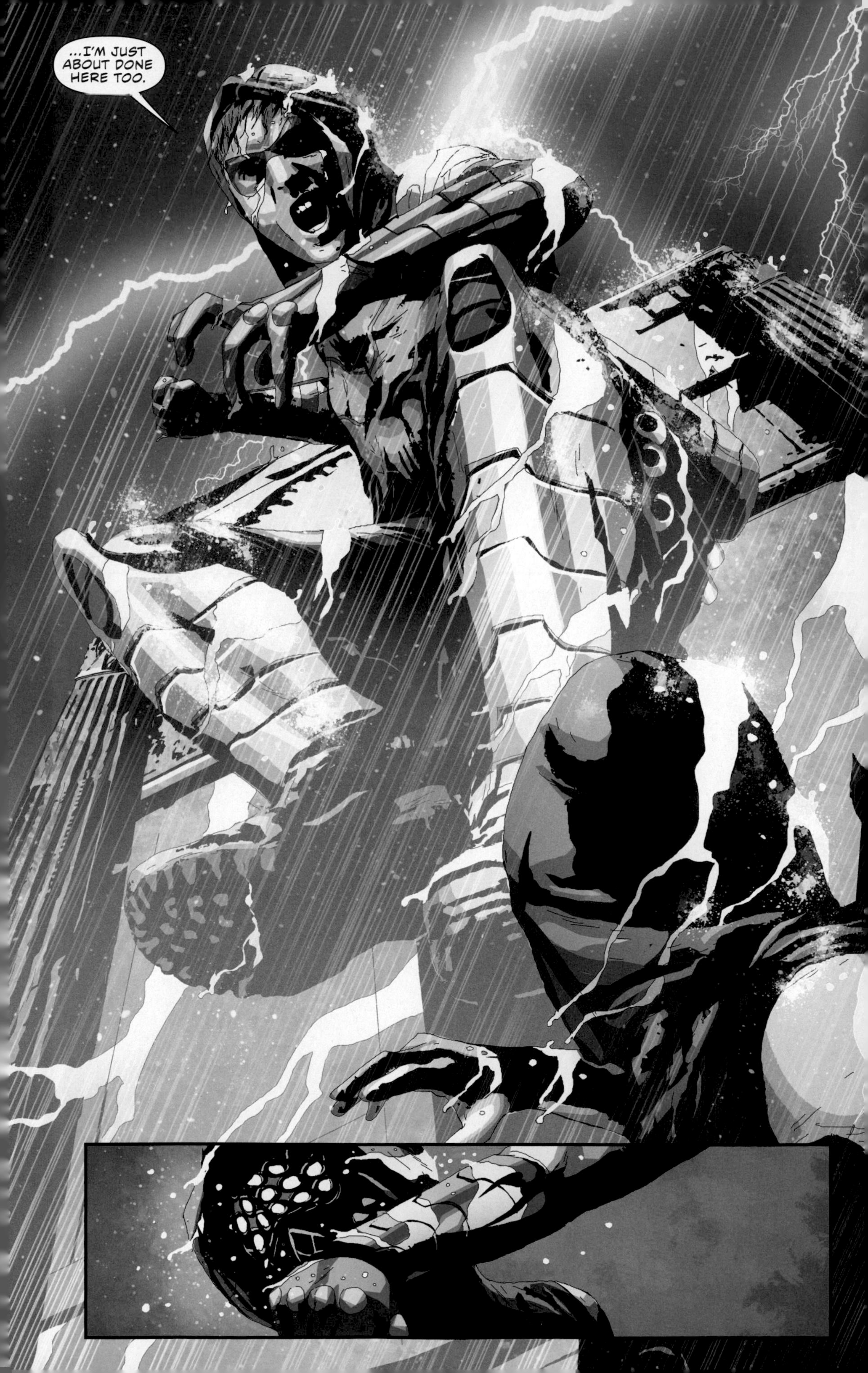
...I'M JUST ABOUT DONE HERE TOO.

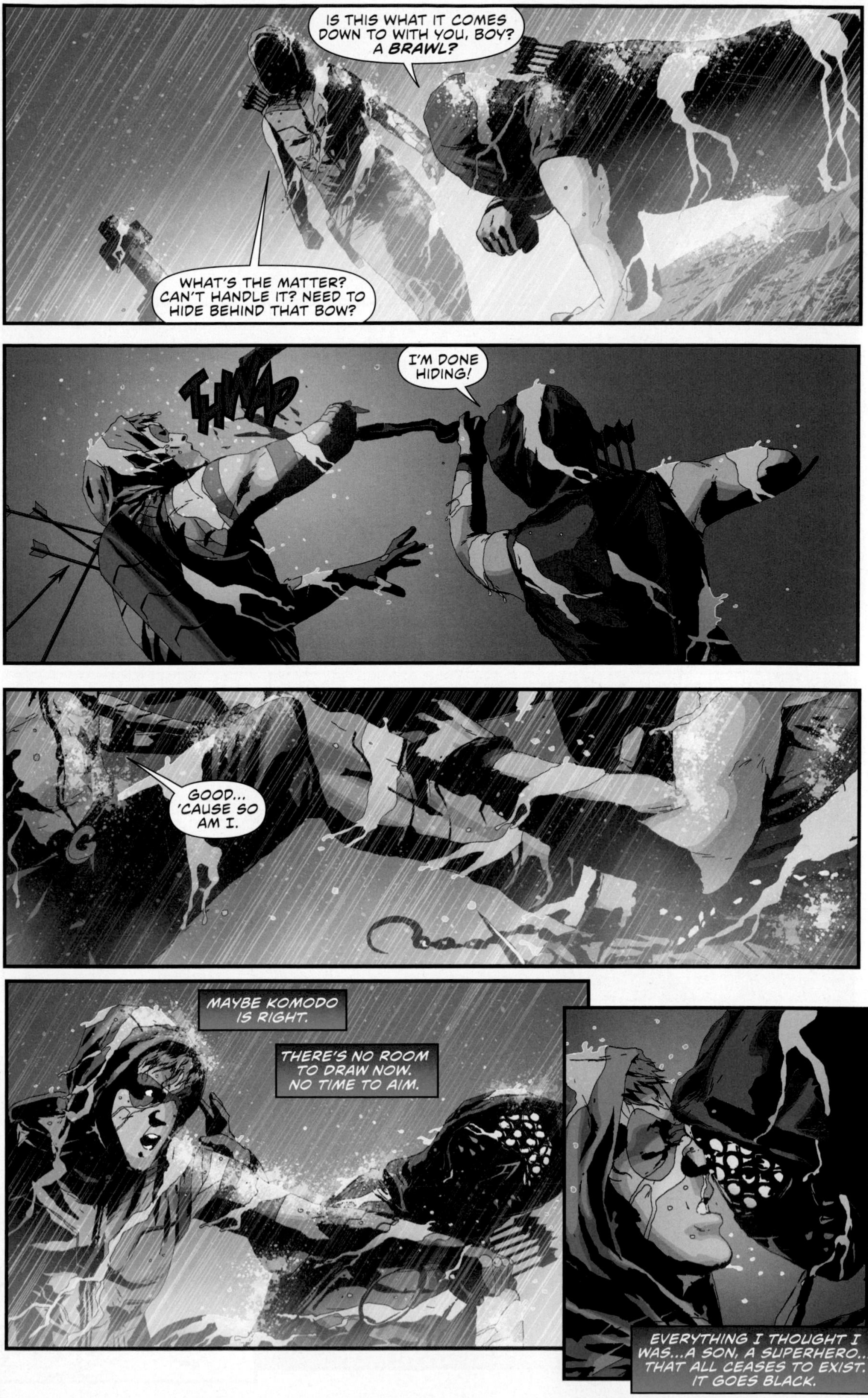
IS THIS WHAT IT COMES DOWN TO WITH YOU, BOY? A BRAWL?
WHAT'S THE MATTER? CAN'T HANDLE IT? NEED TO HIDE BEHIND THAT BOW?
I'M DONE HIDING!
THWAP
GOOD... 'CAUSE SO AM I.
MAYBE KOMODO IS RIGHT.
THERE'S NO ROOM TO DRAW NOW. NO TIME TO AIM.
EVERYTHING I THOUGHT I WAS...A SON, A SUPERHERO... THAT ALL CEASES TO EXIST. IT GOES BLACK.

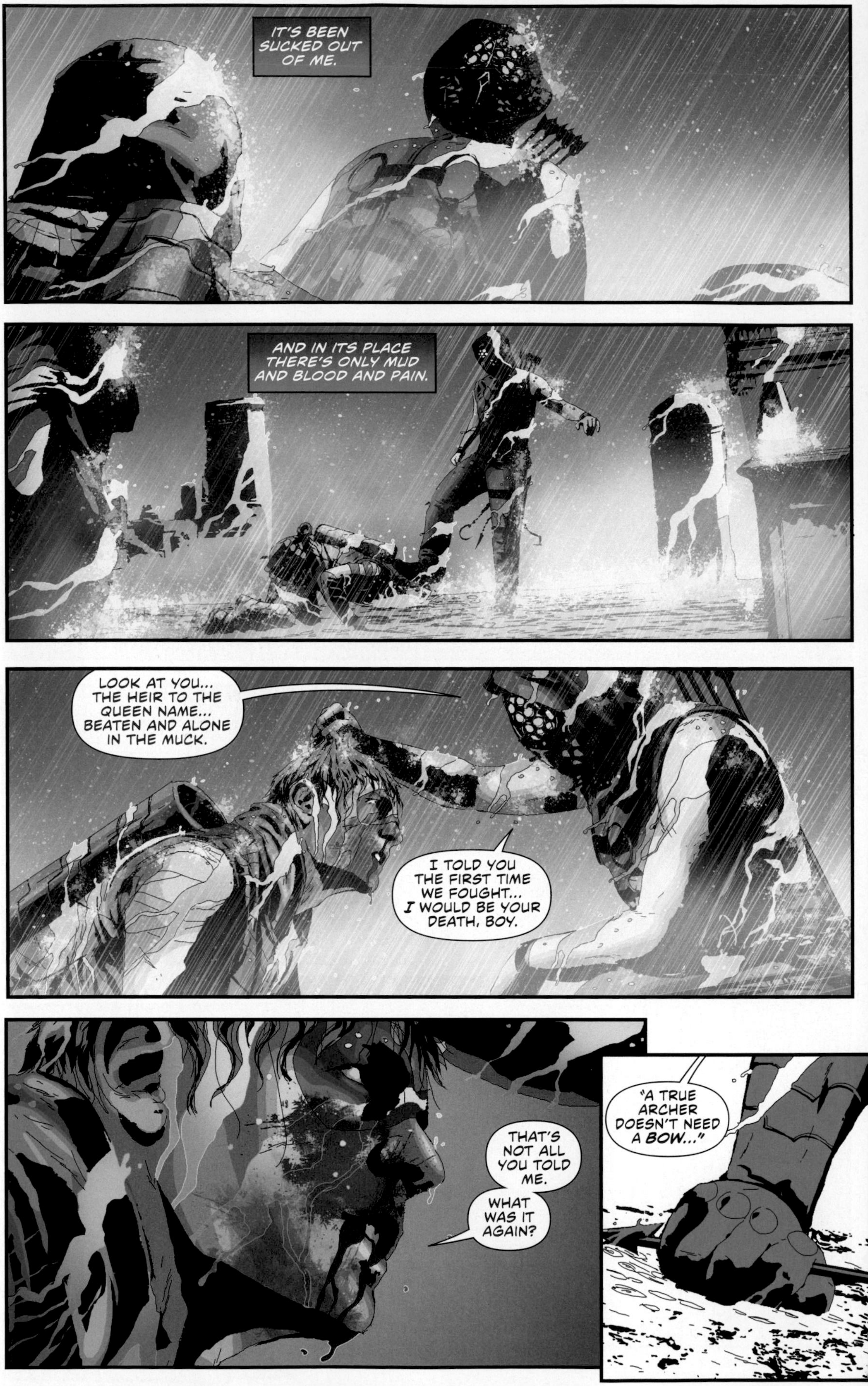
IT'S BEEN SUCKED OUT OF ME.
AND IN ITS PLACE THERE'S ONLY MUD AND BLOOD AND PAIN.
LOOK AT YOU... THE HEIR TO THE QUEEN NAME... BEATEN AND ALONE IN THE MUCK.
I TOLD YOU THE FIRST TIME WE FOUGHT... I WOULD BE YOUR DEATH, BOY.
THAT'S NOT ALL YOU TOLD ME.
WHAT WAS IT AGAIN?
"A TRUE ARCHER DOESN'T NEED A BOW..."

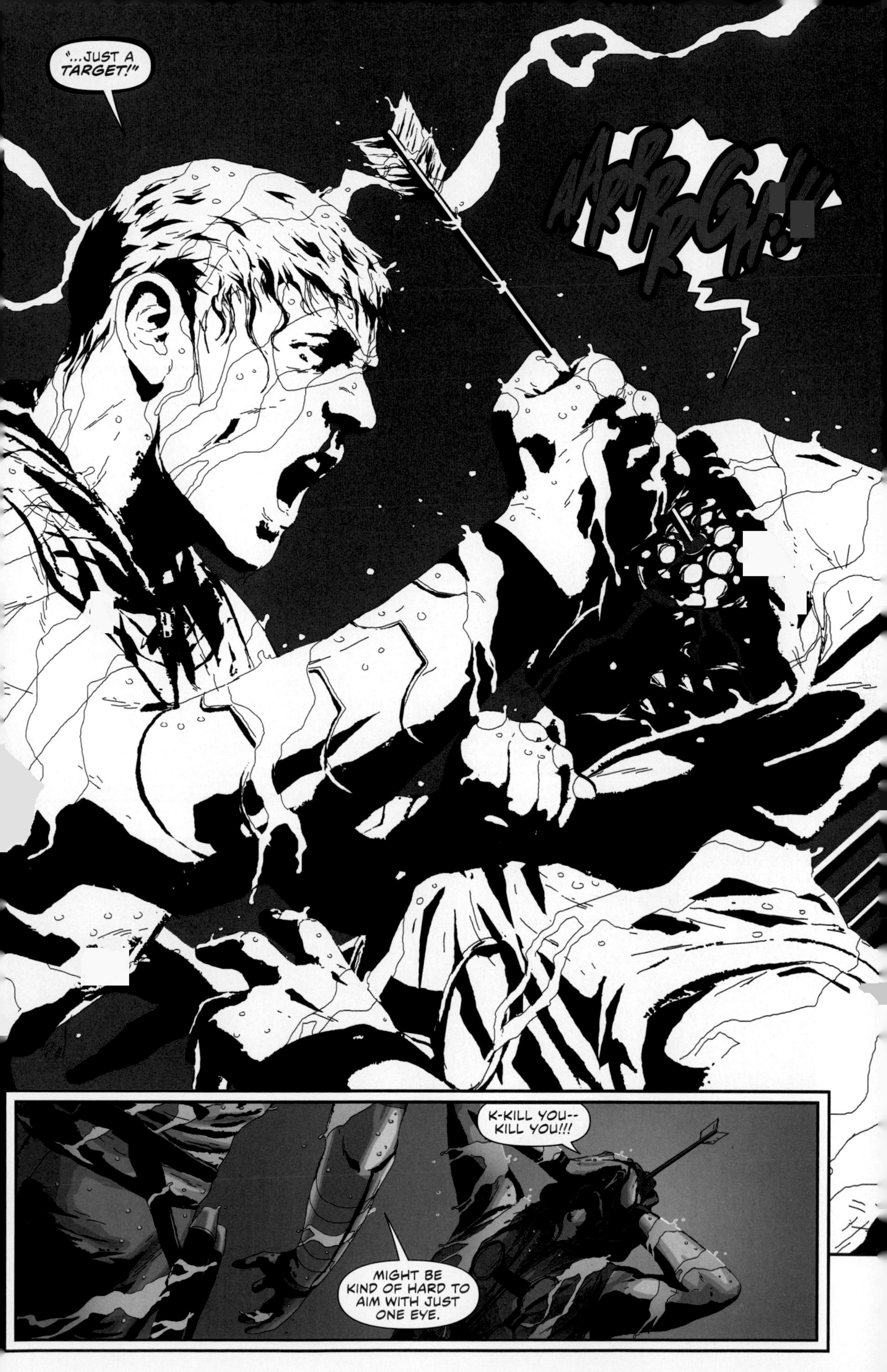
"...JUST A TARGET!"
AARRRGH!!
K-KILL YOU-- KILL YOU!!!
MIGHT BE KIND OF HARD TO AIM WITH JUST ONE EYE.

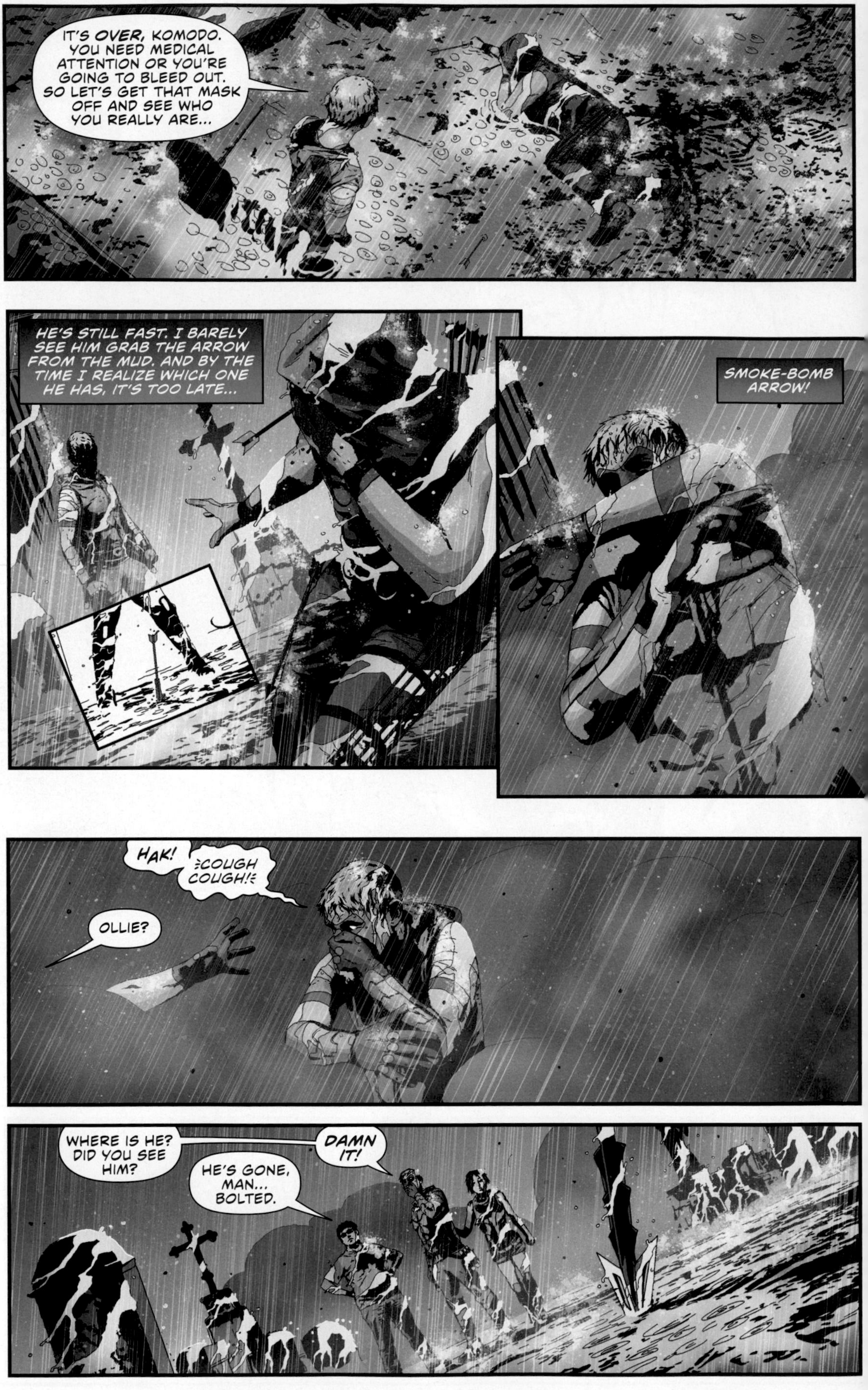

IT'S OVER, KOMODO. YOU NEED MEDICAL ATTENTION OR YOU'RE GOING TO BLEED OUT. SO LET'S GET THAT MASK OFF AND SEE WHO YOU REALLY ARE...
HE'S STILL FAST. I BARELY SEE HIM GRAB THE ARROW FROM THE MUD. AND BY THE TIME I REALIZE WHICH ONE HE HAS, IT'S TOO LATE...
SMOKE-BOMB ARROW!
HAK!
COUGH COUGH!
OLLIE?
WHERE IS HE? DID YOU SEE HIM?
HE'S GONE, MAN... BOLTED.
DAMN IT!

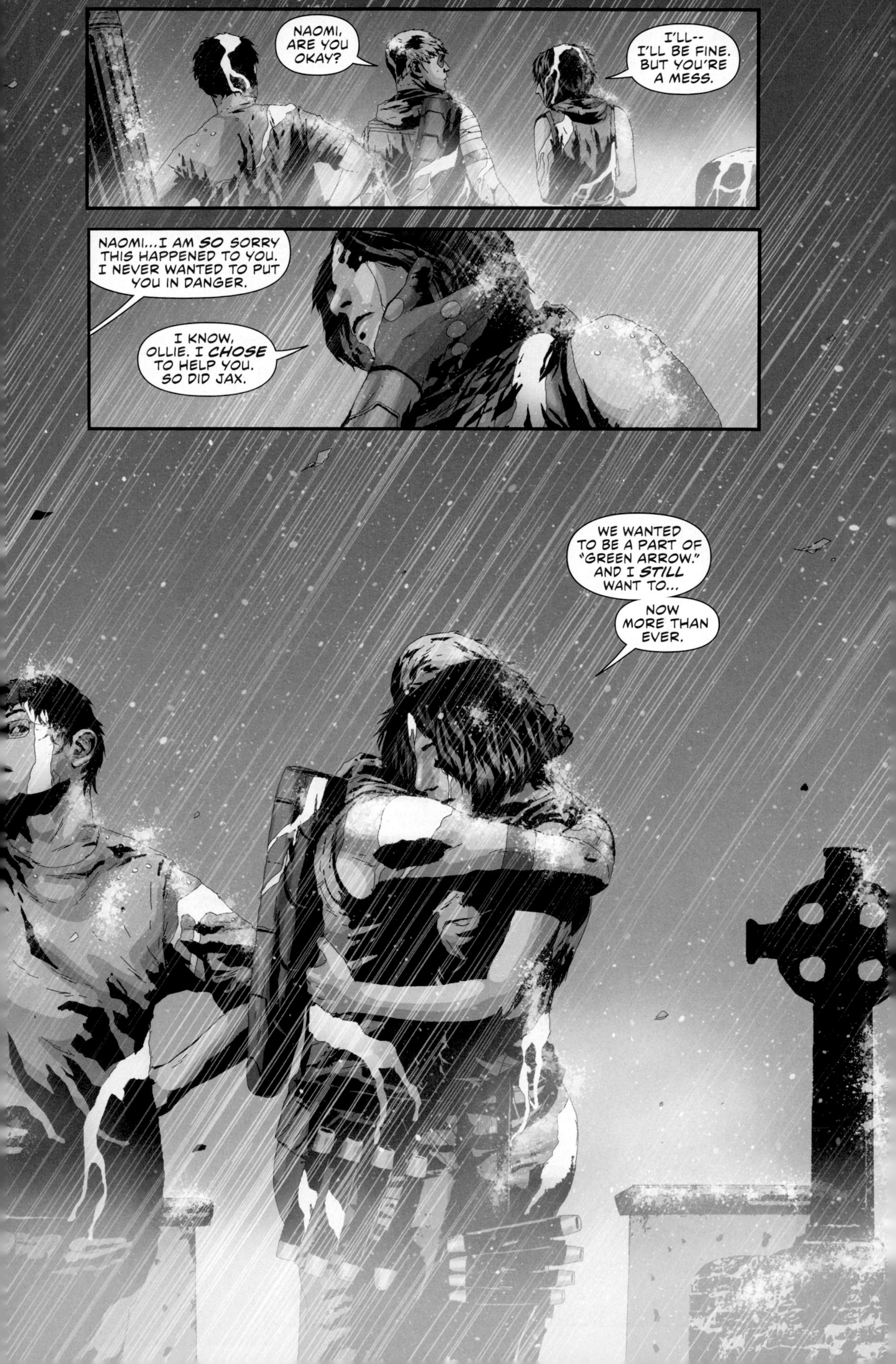
NAOMI, ARE YOU OKAY?
I'LL-- I'LL BE FINE. BUT YOU'RE A MESS.
NAOMI...I AM *SO* SORRY THIS HAPPENED TO YOU. I NEVER WANTED TO PUT YOU IN DANGER.
I KNOW, OLLIE. I *CHOSE* TO HELP YOU. SO DID JAX.
WE WANTED TO BE A PART OF "GREEN ARROW." AND I *STILL* WANT TO...
NOW MORE THAN EVER.

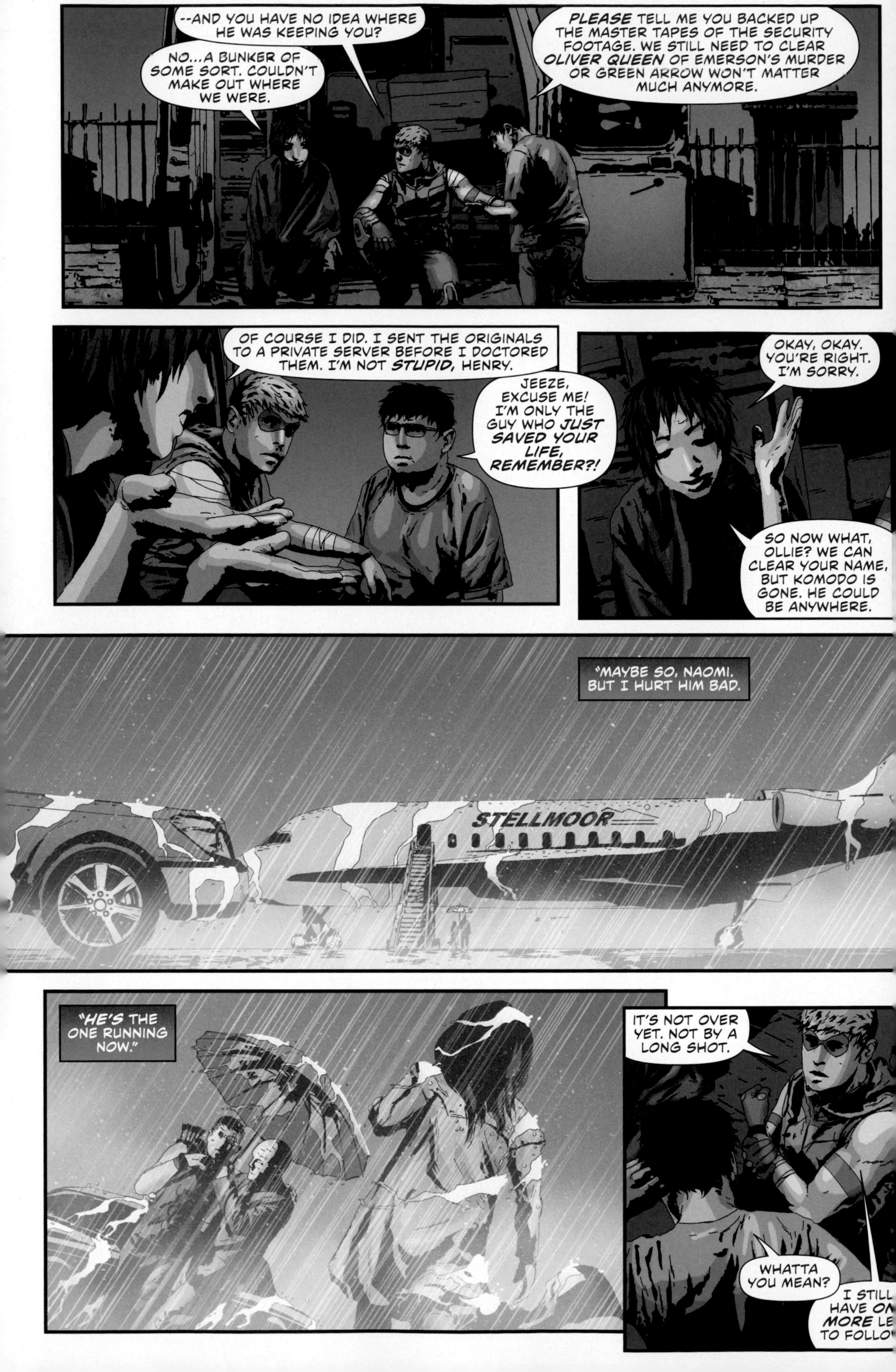
--AND YOU HAVE NO IDEA WHERE HE WAS KEEPING YOU?
NO...A BUNKER OF SOME SORT. COULDN'T MAKE OUT WHERE WE WERE.
PLEASE TELL ME YOU BACKED UP THE MASTER TAPES OF THE SECURITY FOOTAGE. WE STILL NEED TO CLEAR OLIVER QUEEN OF EMERSON'S MURDER OR GREEN ARROW WON'T MATTER MUCH ANYMORE.
OF COURSE I DID. I SENT THE ORIGINALS TO A PRIVATE SERVER BEFORE I DOCTORED THEM. I'M NOT STUPID, HENRY.
JEEZE, EXCUSE ME! I'M ONLY THE GUY WHO JUST SAVED YOUR LIFE, REMEMBER?!
OKAY, OKAY. YOU'RE RIGHT. I'M SORRY.
SO NOW WHAT, OLLIE? WE CAN CLEAR YOUR NAME, BUT KOMODO IS GONE. HE COULD BE ANYWHERE.
"MAYBE SO, NAOMI. BUT I HURT HIM BAD.
STELLMOOR
"HE'S THE ONE RUNNING NOW."
IT'S NOT OVER YET. NOT BY A LONG SHOT.
WHATTA YOU MEAN?
I STILL HAVE ON MORE LE TO FOLLO

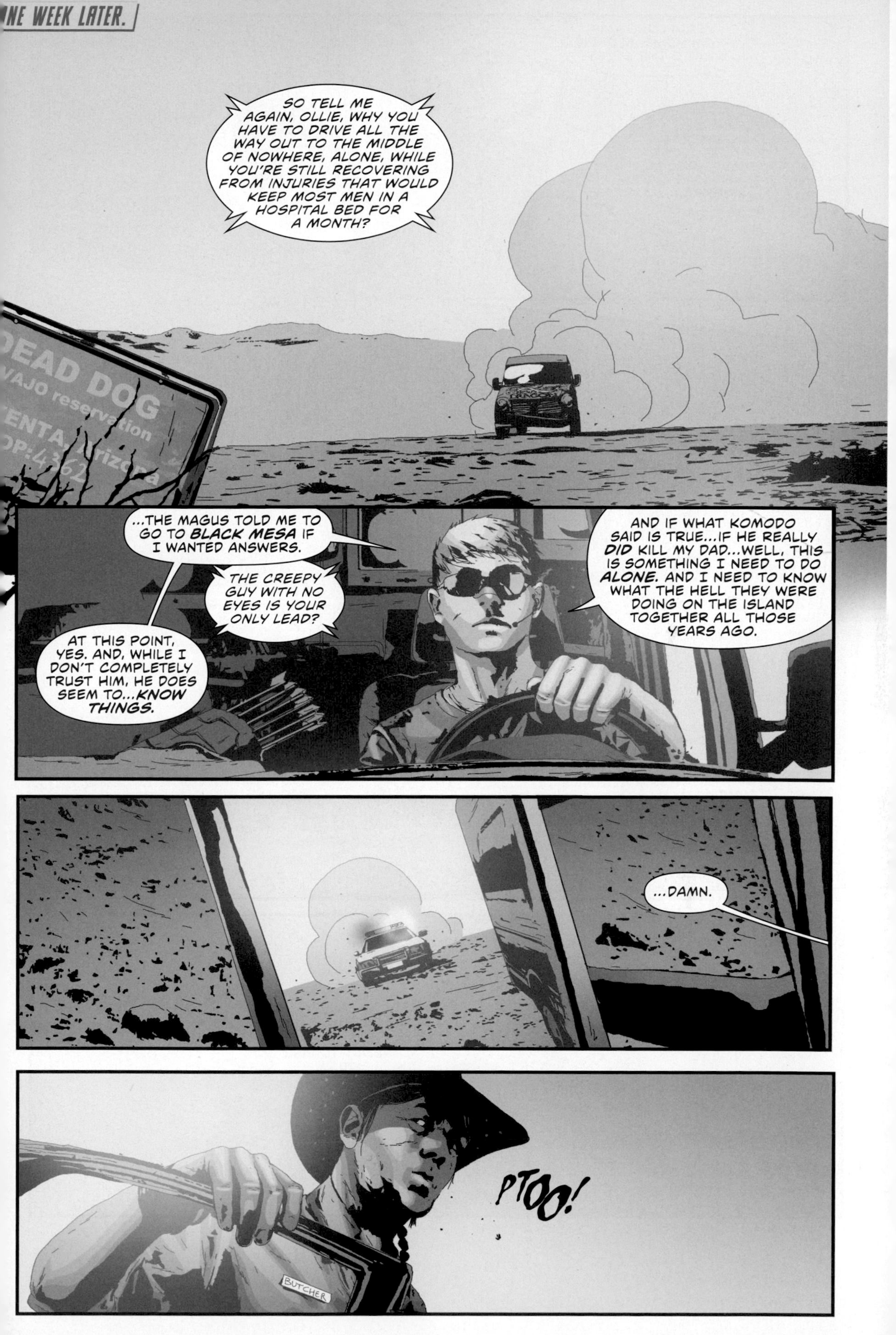
NE WEEK LATER.
SO TELL ME AGAIN, OLLIE, WHY YOU HAVE TO DRIVE ALL THE WAY OUT TO THE MIDDLE OF NOWHERE, ALONE, WHILE YOU'RE STILL RECOVERING FROM INJURIES THAT WOULD KEEP MOST MEN IN A HOSPITAL BED FOR A MONTH?
DEAD DOG
VAJO reservation
ENTA, Arizona
OP:4362
...THE MAGUS TOLD ME TO GO TO BLACK MESA IF I WANTED ANSWERS.
THE CREEPY GUY WITH NO EYES IS YOUR ONLY LEAD?
AT THIS POINT, YES. AND, WHILE I DON'T COMPLETELY TRUST HIM, HE DOES SEEM TO...KNOW THINGS.
AND IF WHAT KOMODO SAID IS TRUE...IF HE REALLY DID KILL MY DAD...WELL, THIS IS SOMETHING I NEED TO DO ALONE. AND I NEED TO KNOW WHAT THE HELL THEY WERE DOING ON THE ISLAND TOGETHER ALL THOSE YEARS AGO.
...DAMN.
PTOO!
BUTCHER

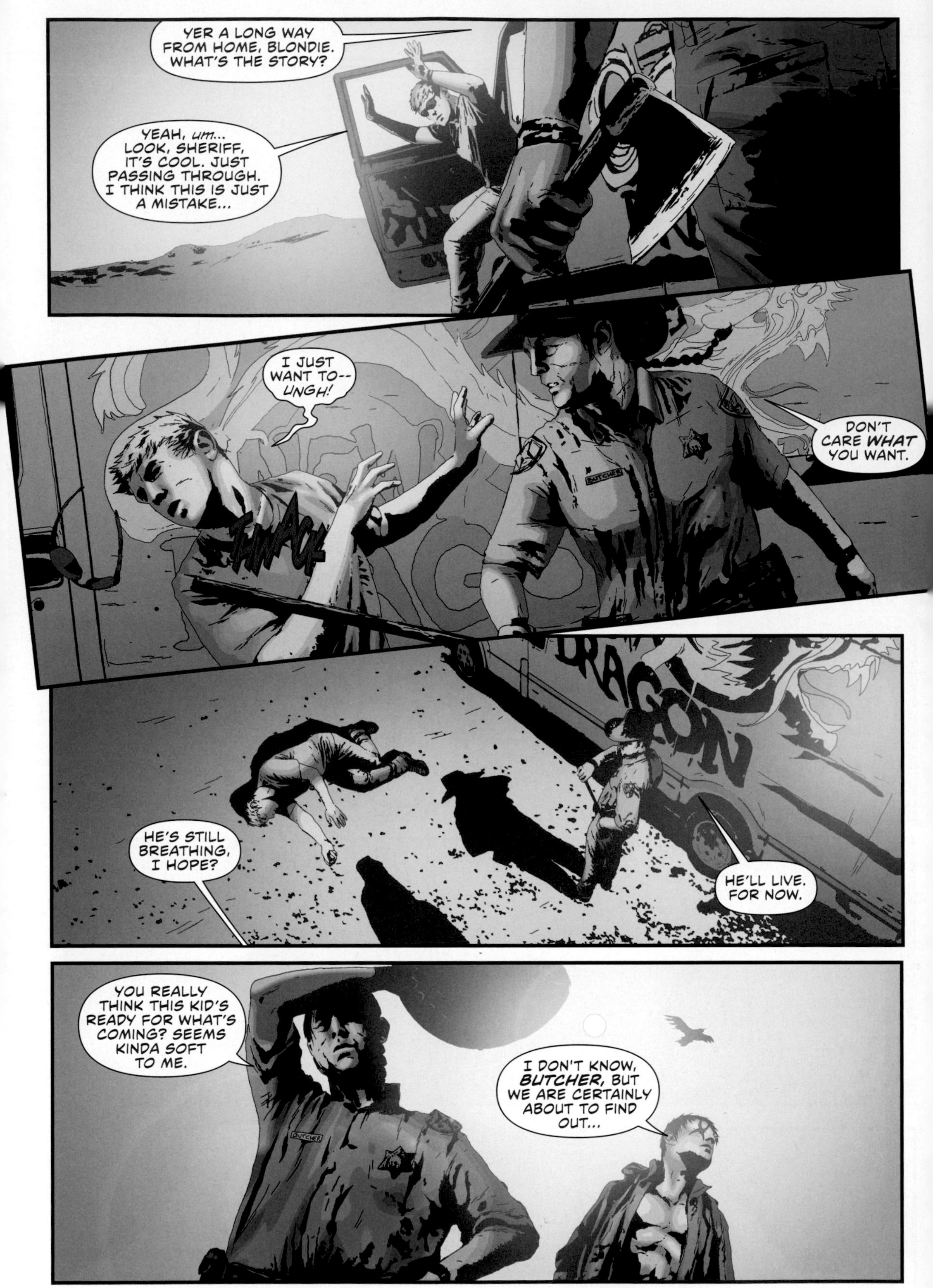
YER A LONG WAY FROM HOME, BLONDIE. WHAT'S THE STORY?
YEAH, *um*... LOOK, SHERIFF, IT'S COOL. JUST PASSING THROUGH. I THINK THIS IS JUST A MISTAKE...
I JUST WANT TO-- *UNGH!*
DON'T CARE ***WHAT*** YOU WANT.
HE'S STILL BREATHING, I HOPE?
HE'LL LIVE. FOR NOW.
YOU REALLY THINK THIS KID'S READY FOR WHAT'S COMING? SEEMS KINDA SOFT TO ME.
I DON'T KNOW, ***BUTCHER,*** BUT WE ARE CERTAINLY ABOUT TO FIND OUT...

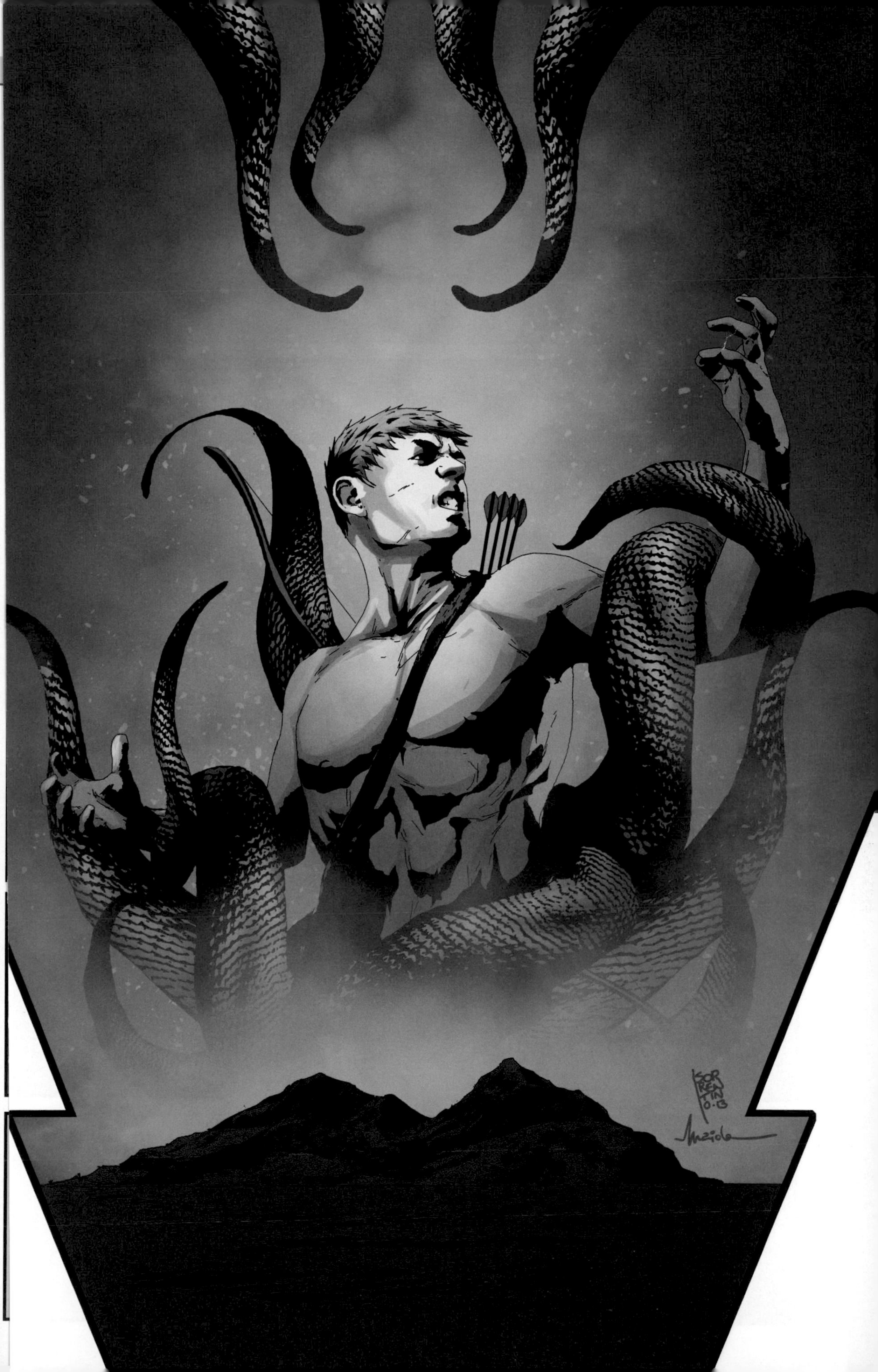

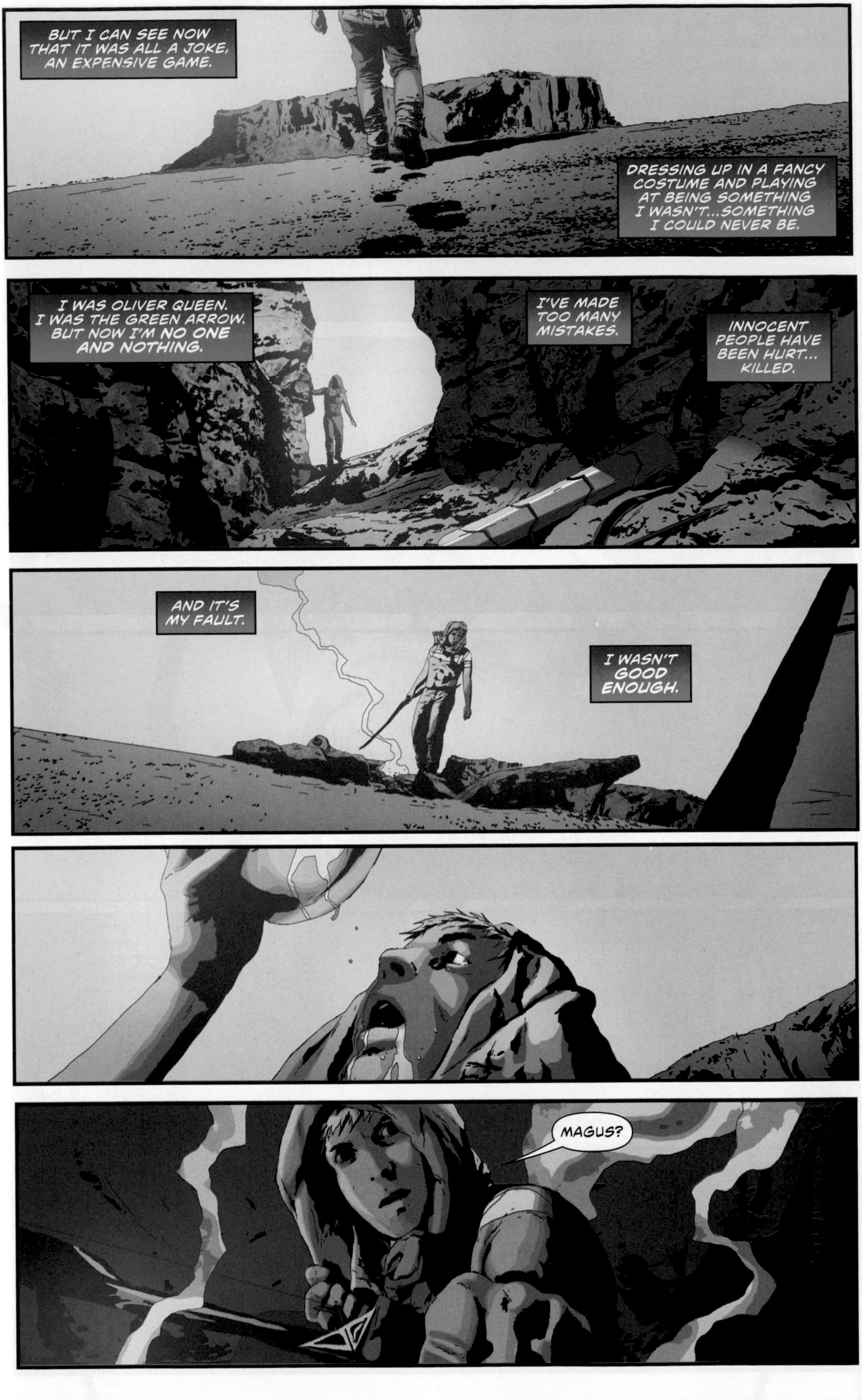
BUT I CAN SEE NOW THAT IT WAS ALL A JOKE, AN EXPENSIVE GAME.
DRESSING UP IN A FANCY COSTUME AND PLAYING AT BEING SOMETHING I WASN'T...SOMETHING I COULD NEVER BE.
I WAS OLIVER QUEEN. I WAS THE GREEN ARROW. BUT NOW I'M NO ONE AND NOTHING.
I'VE MADE TOO MANY MISTAKES.
INNOCENT PEOPLE HAVE BEEN HURT... KILLED.
AND IT'S MY FAULT.
I WASN'T GOOD ENOUGH.
MAGUS?

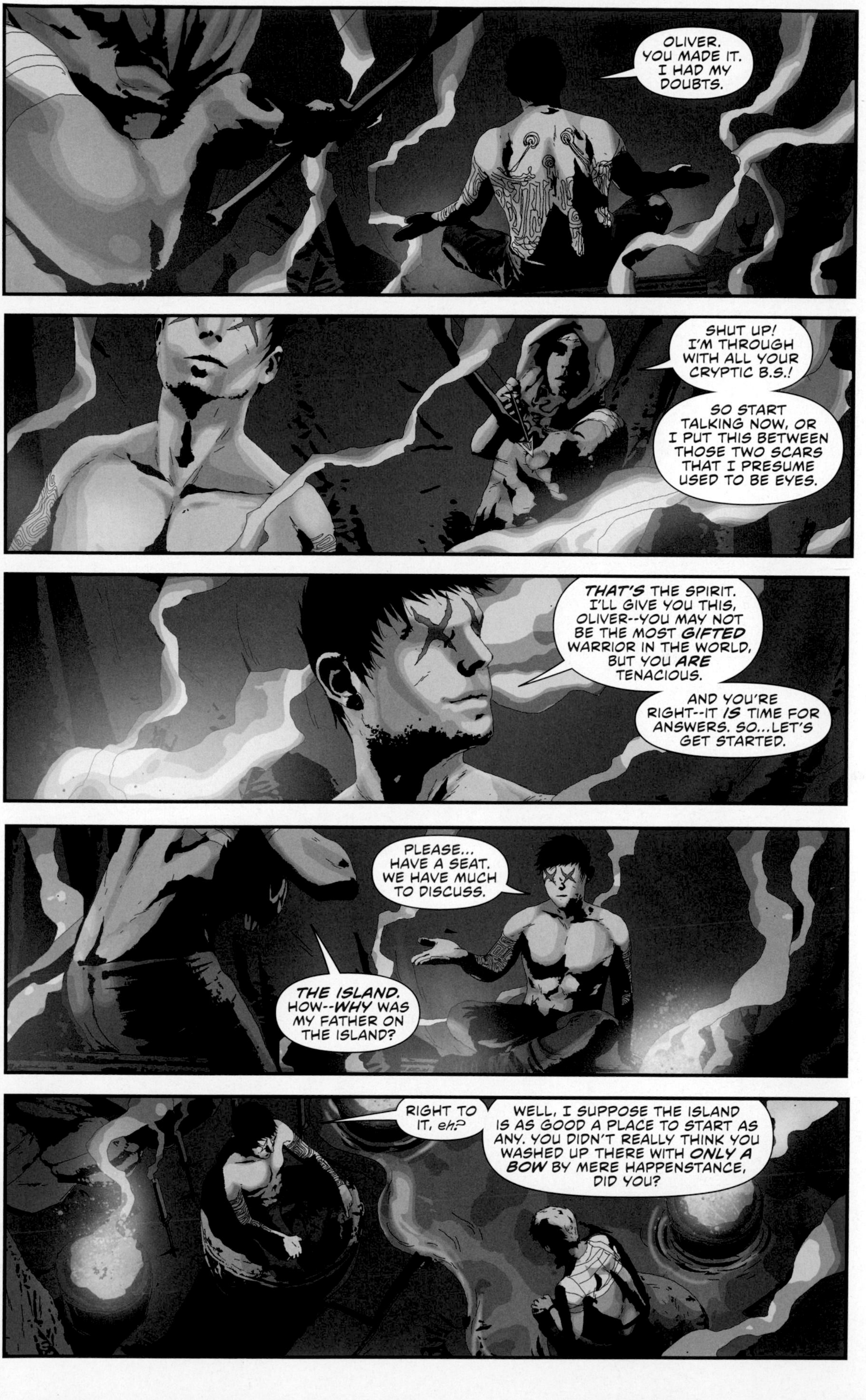
OLIVER. YOU MADE IT. I HAD MY DOUBTS.
SHUT UP! I'M THROUGH WITH ALL YOUR CRYPTIC B.S.!
SO START TALKING NOW, OR I PUT THIS BETWEEN THOSE TWO SCARS THAT I PRESUME USED TO BE EYES.
THAT'S THE SPIRIT. I'LL GIVE YOU THIS, OLIVER--YOU MAY NOT BE THE MOST GIFTED WARRIOR IN THE WORLD, BUT YOU ARE TENACIOUS.
AND YOU'RE RIGHT--IT IS TIME FOR ANSWERS. SO...LET'S GET STARTED.
PLEASE... HAVE A SEAT. WE HAVE MUCH TO DISCUSS.
THE ISLAND. HOW--WHY WAS MY FATHER ON THE ISLAND?
RIGHT TO IT, eh?
WELL, I SUPPOSE THE ISLAND IS AS GOOD A PLACE TO START AS ANY. YOU DIDN'T REALLY THINK YOU WASHED UP THERE WITH ONLY A BOW BY MERE HAPPENSTANCE, DID YOU?

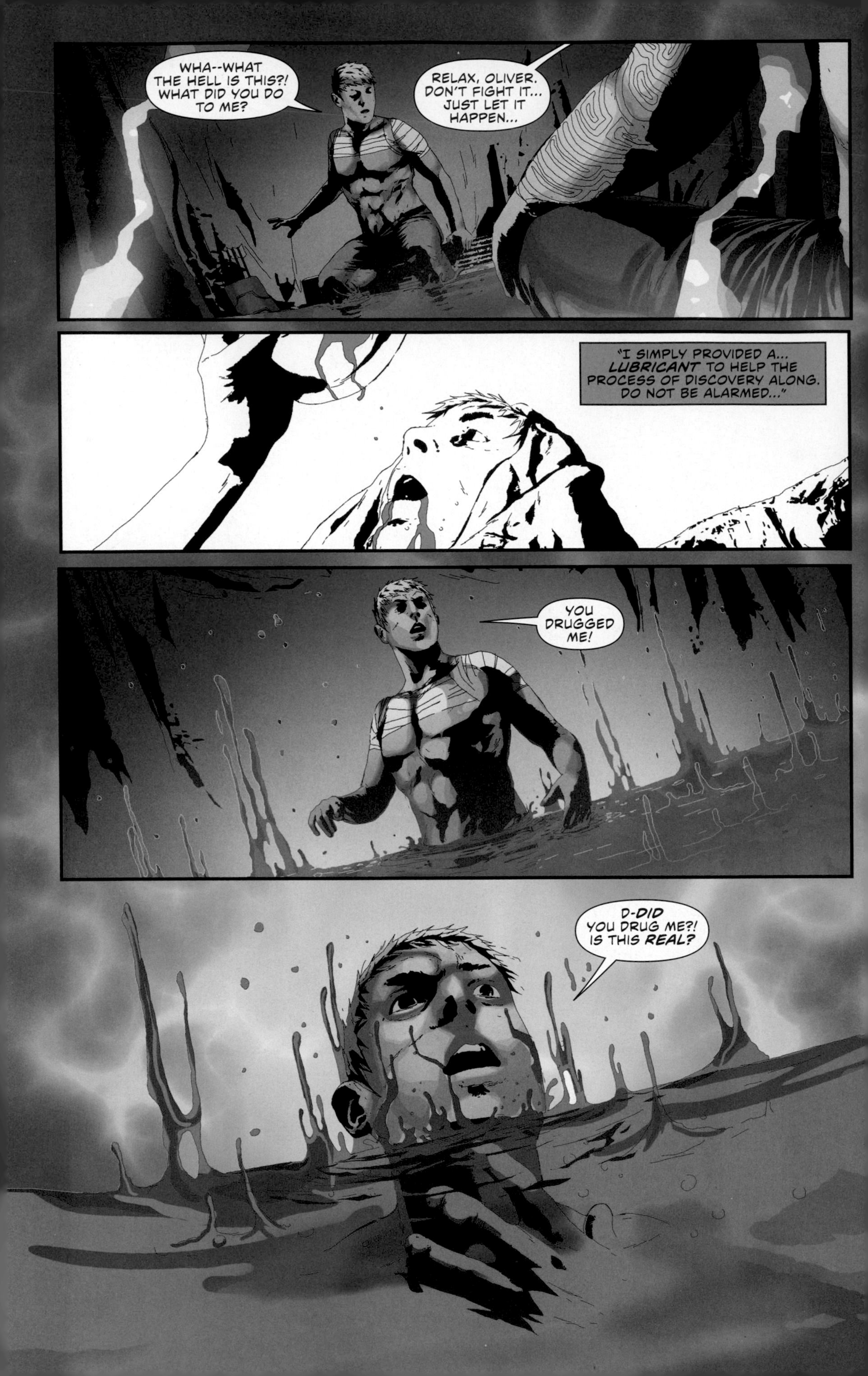
WHA--WHAT THE HELL IS THIS?! WHAT DID YOU DO TO ME?
RELAX, OLIVER. DON'T FIGHT IT... JUST LET IT HAPPEN...
"I SIMPLY PROVIDED A... LUBRICANT TO HELP THE PROCESS OF DISCOVERY ALONG. DO NOT BE ALARMED..."
YOU DRUGGED ME!
D-DID YOU DRUG ME?! IS THIS REAL?

M-MAGUS?!

CONCLUSION

THE KILL MACHINE

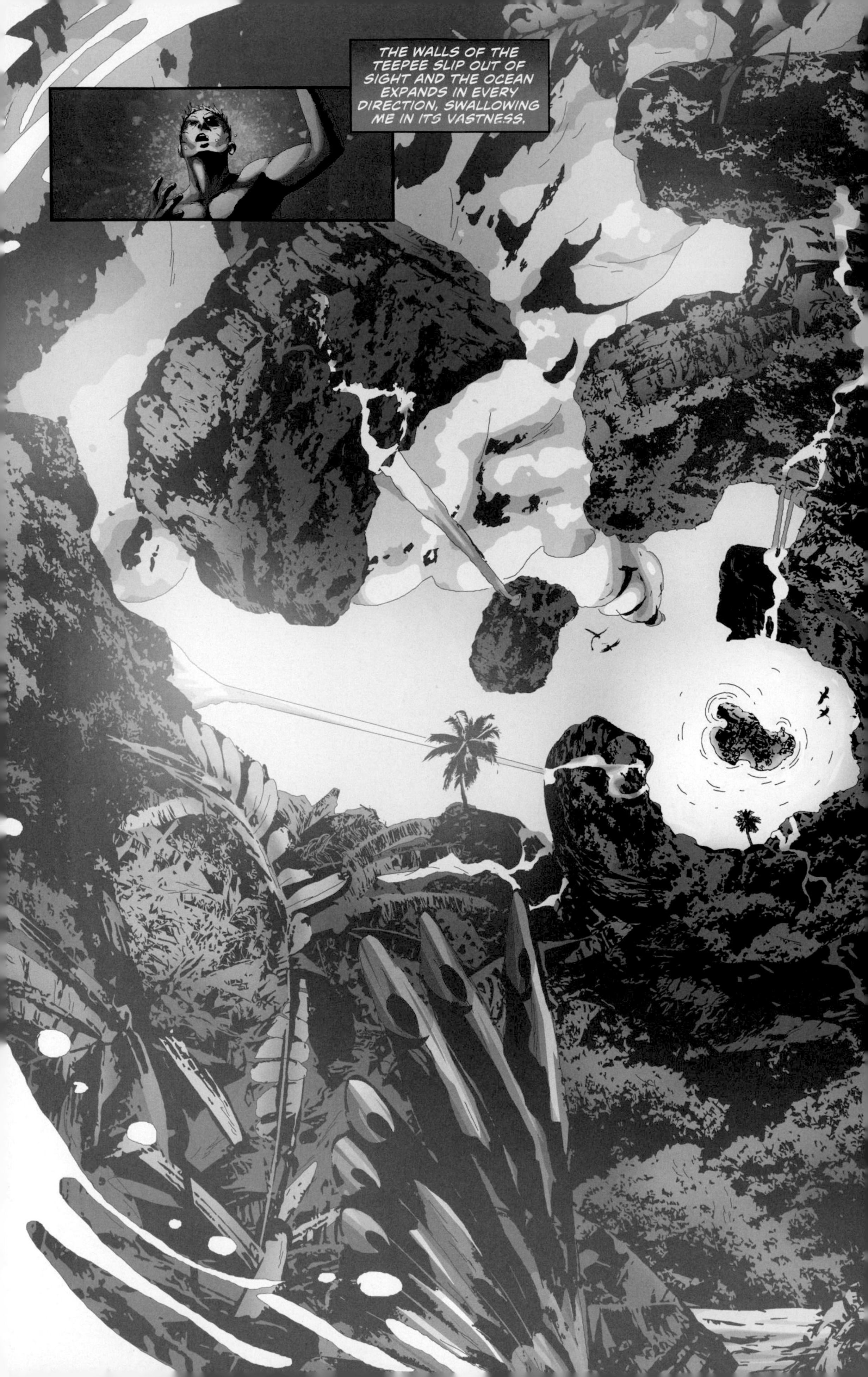
THE WALLS OF THE TEEPEE SLIP OUT OF SIGHT AND THE OCEAN EXPANDS IN EVERY DIRECTION, SWALLOWING ME IN ITS VASTNESS.

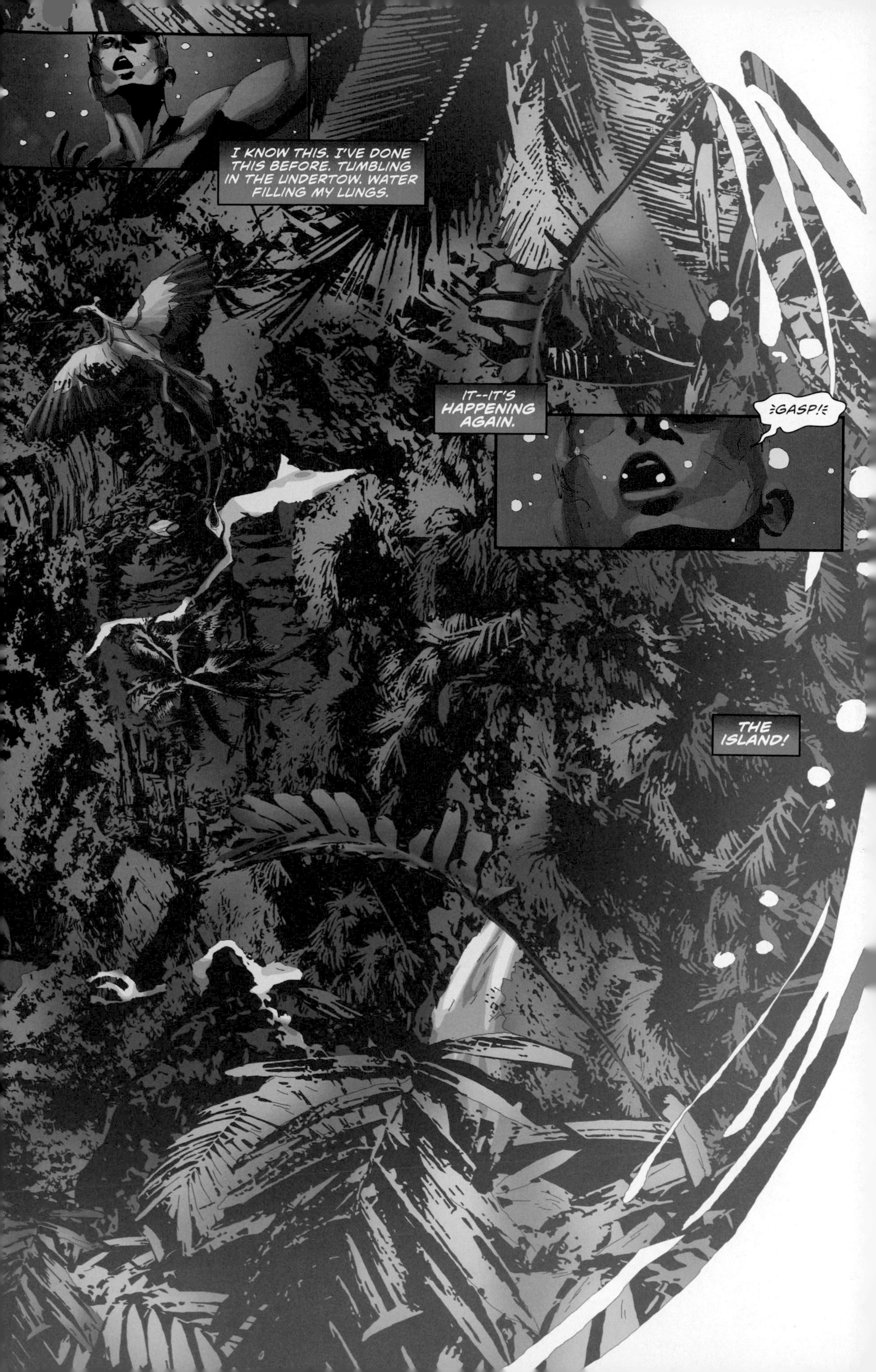
I KNOW THIS. I'VE DONE THIS BEFORE. TUMBLING IN THE UNDERTOW. WATER FILLING MY LUNGS.
IT--IT'S HAPPENING AGAIN.
GASP!
THE ISLAND!

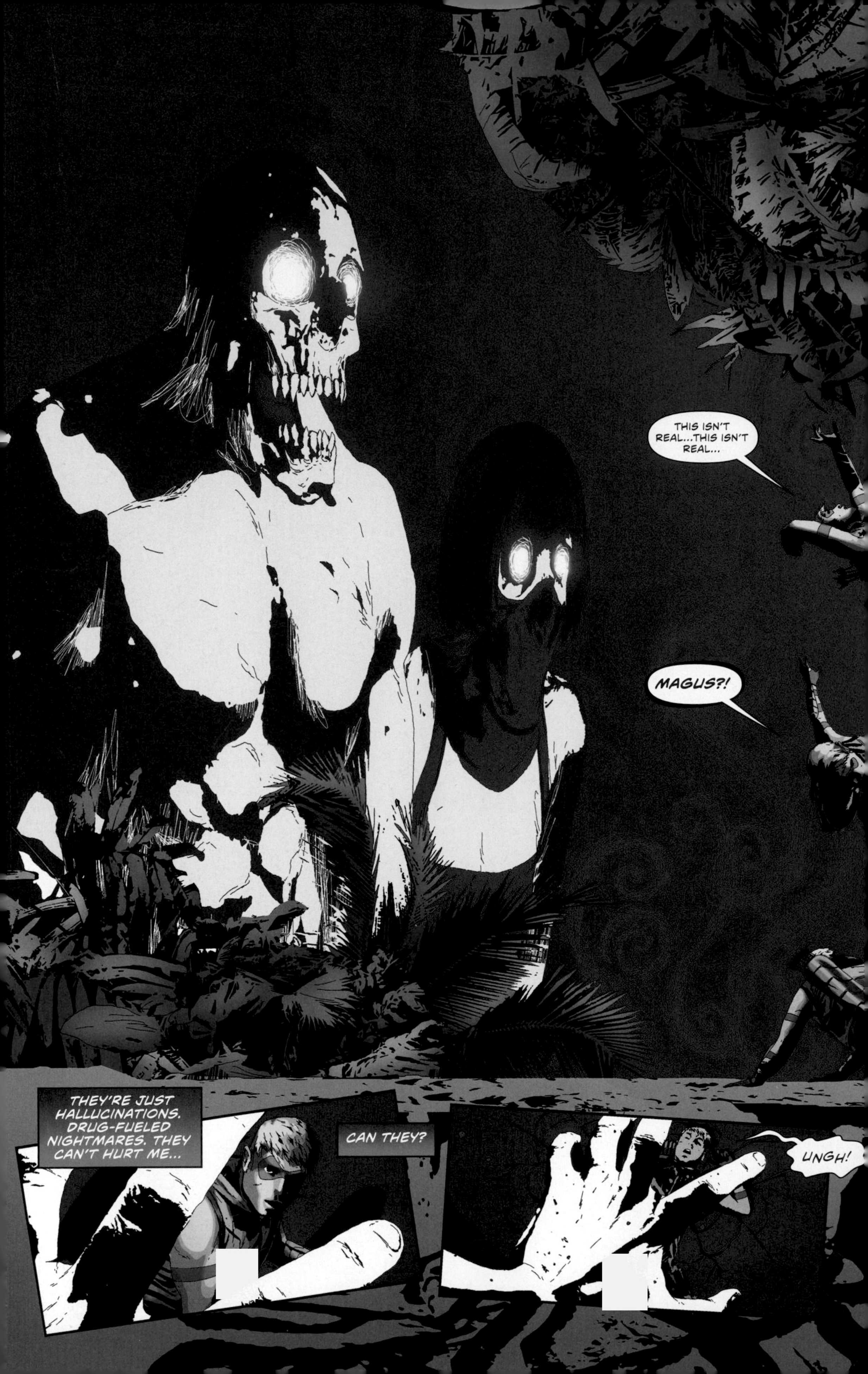

THIS ISN'T REAL...THIS ISN'T REAL...
MAGUS?!
THEY'RE JUST HALLUCINATIONS. DRUG-FUELED NIGHTMARES. THEY CAN'T HURT ME...
CAN THEY?
UNGH!

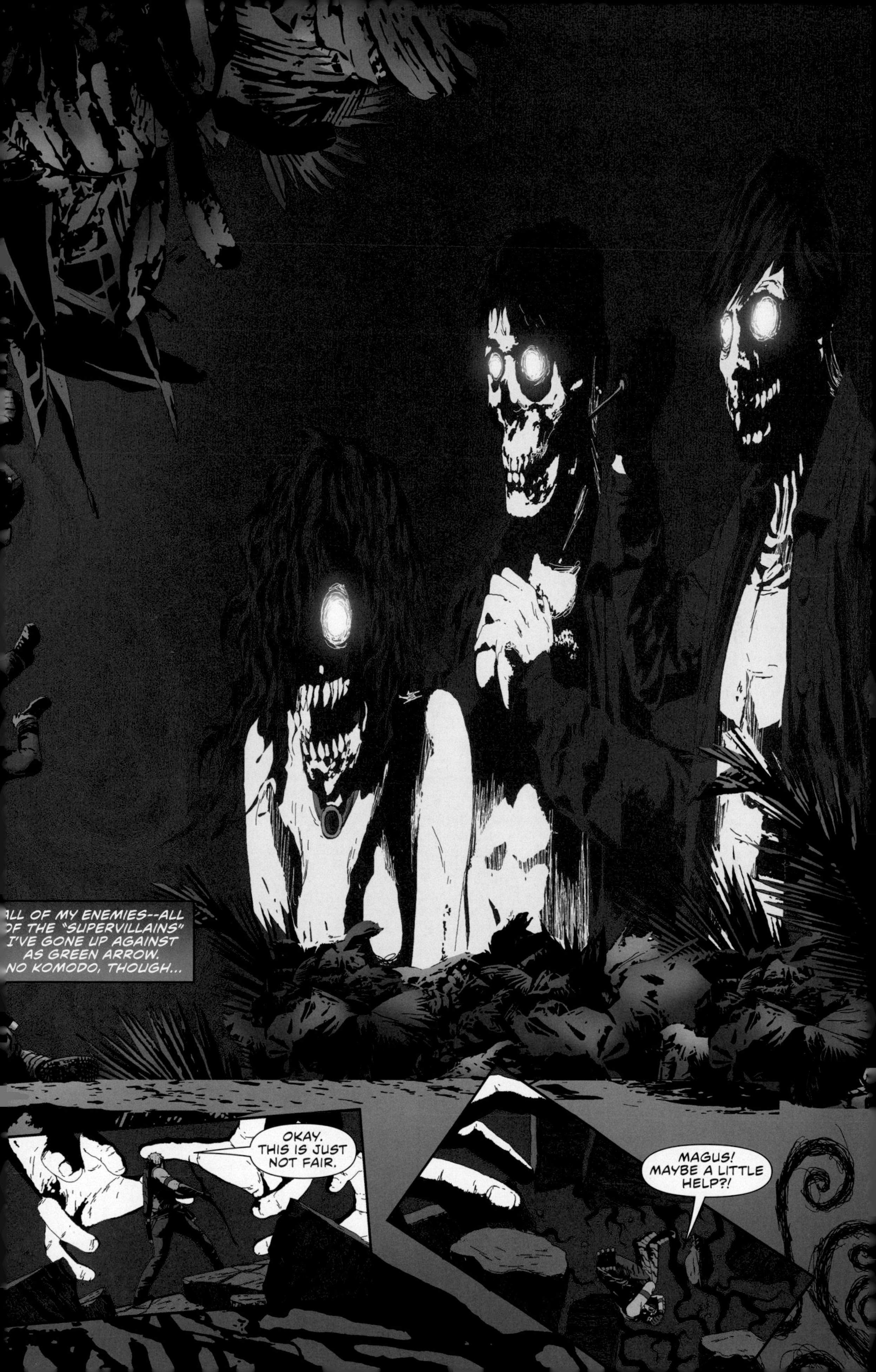
ALL OF MY ENEMIES--ALL OF THE "SUPERVILLAINS" I'VE GONE UP AGAINST AS GREEN ARROW. NO KOMODO, THOUGH...
OKAY. THIS IS JUST NOT FAIR.
MAGUS! MAYBE A LITTLE HELP?!

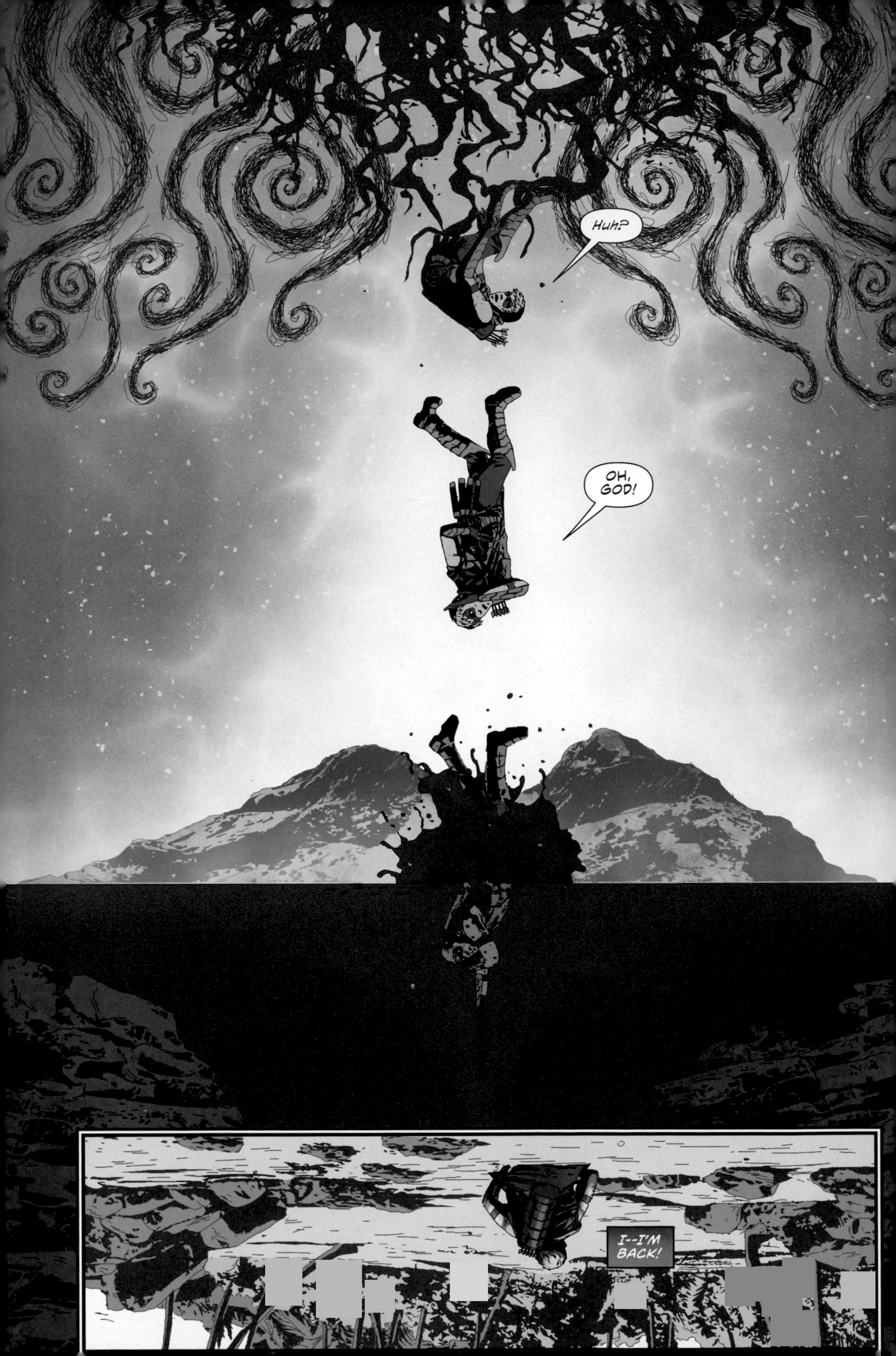
Huh?
OH, GOD!
I--I'M BACK!

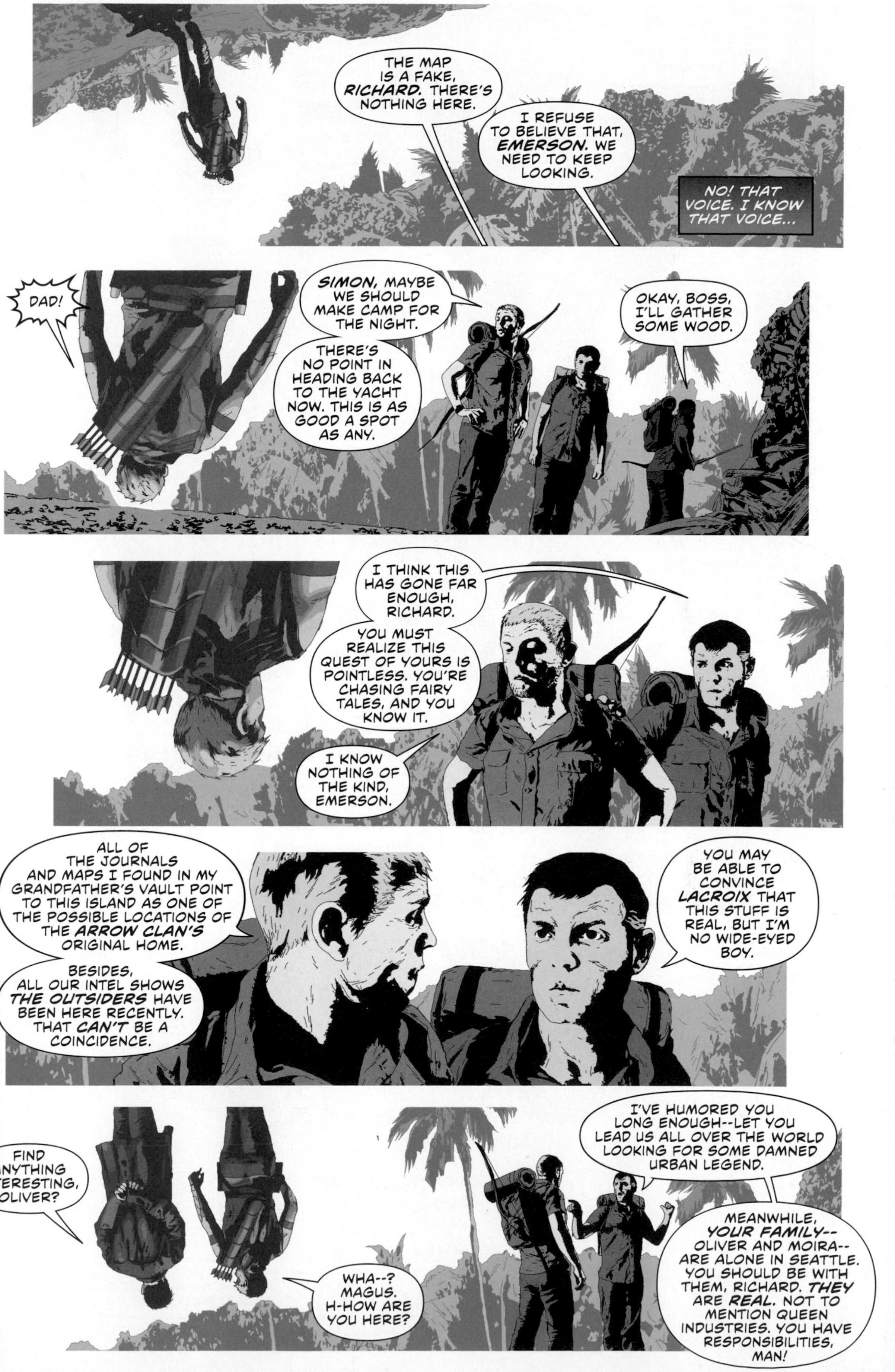

THE MAP IS A FAKE, RICHARD. THERE'S NOTHING HERE.
I REFUSE TO BELIEVE THAT, EMERSON. WE NEED TO KEEP LOOKING.
NO! THAT VOICE. I KNOW THAT VOICE...
DAD!
SIMON, MAYBE WE SHOULD MAKE CAMP FOR THE NIGHT.
THERE'S NO POINT IN HEADING BACK TO THE YACHT NOW. THIS IS AS GOOD A SPOT AS ANY.
OKAY, BOSS, I'LL GATHER SOME WOOD.
I THINK THIS HAS GONE FAR ENOUGH, RICHARD.
YOU MUST REALIZE THIS QUEST OF YOURS IS POINTLESS. YOU'RE CHASING FAIRY TALES, AND YOU KNOW IT.
I KNOW NOTHING OF THE KIND, EMERSON.
ALL OF THE JOURNALS AND MAPS I FOUND IN MY GRANDFATHER'S VAULT POINT TO THIS ISLAND AS ONE OF THE POSSIBLE LOCATIONS OF THE ARROW CLAN'S ORIGINAL HOME.
BESIDES, ALL OUR INTEL SHOWS THE OUTSIDERS HAVE BEEN HERE RECENTLY. THAT CAN'T BE A COINCIDENCE.
YOU MAY BE ABLE TO CONVINCE LACROIX THAT THIS STUFF IS REAL, BUT I'M NO WIDE-EYED BOY.
FIND ANYTHING TERESTING, OLIVER?
WHA--? MAGUS. H-HOW ARE YOU HERE?
I'VE HUMORED YOU LONG ENOUGH--LET YOU LEAD US ALL OVER THE WORLD LOOKING FOR SOME DAMNED URBAN LEGEND.
MEANWHILE, YOUR FAMILY-- OLIVER AND MOIRA-- ARE ALONE IN SEATTLE. YOU SHOULD BE WITH THEM, RICHARD. THEY ARE REAL. NOT TO MENTION QUEEN INDUSTRIES. YOU HAVE RESPONSIBILITIES, MAN!

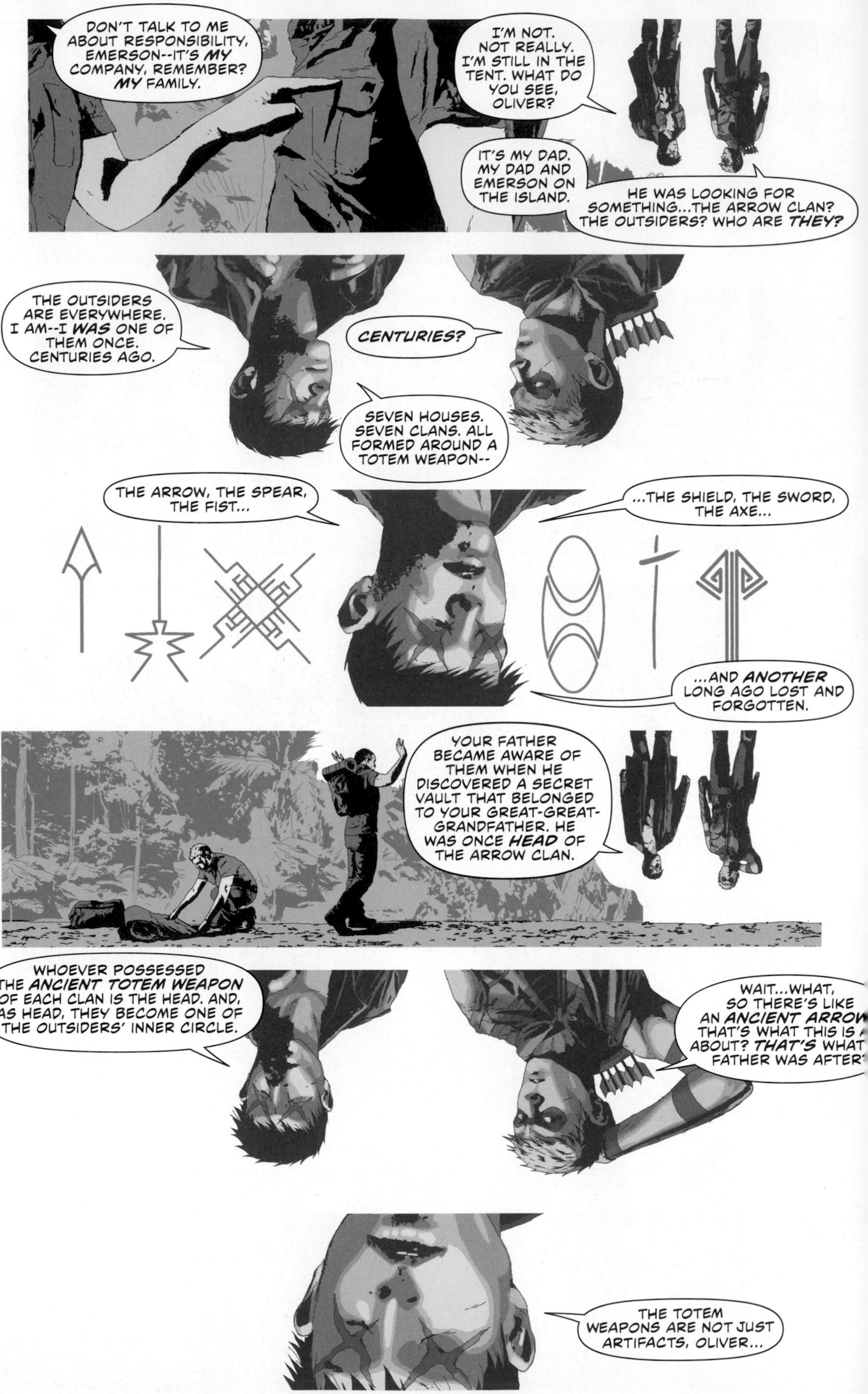
DON'T TALK TO ME ABOUT RESPONSIBILITY, EMERSON--IT'S MY COMPANY, REMEMBER? MY FAMILY.
I'M NOT. NOT REALLY. I'M STILL IN THE TENT. WHAT DO YOU SEE, OLIVER?
IT'S MY DAD. MY DAD AND EMERSON ON THE ISLAND.
HE WAS LOOKING FOR SOMETHING...THE ARROW CLAN? THE OUTSIDERS? WHO ARE THEY?
THE OUTSIDERS ARE EVERYWHERE. I AM--I WAS ONE OF THEM ONCE. CENTURIES AGO.
CENTURIES?
SEVEN HOUSES. SEVEN CLANS. ALL FORMED AROUND A TOTEM WEAPON--
THE ARROW, THE SPEAR, THE FIST...
...THE SHIELD, THE SWORD, THE AXE...
...AND ANOTHER LONG AGO LOST AND FORGOTTEN.
YOUR FATHER BECAME AWARE OF THEM WHEN HE DISCOVERED A SECRET VAULT THAT BELONGED TO YOUR GREAT-GREAT-GRANDFATHER. HE WAS ONCE HEAD OF THE ARROW CLAN.
WHOEVER POSSESSED THE ANCIENT TOTEM WEAPON OF EACH CLAN IS THE HEAD. AND, AS HEAD, THEY BECOME ONE OF THE OUTSIDERS' INNER CIRCLE.
WAIT...WHAT, SO THERE'S LIKE AN ANCIENT THAT'S WHAT THIS IS ABOUT? THAT'S WHAT FATHER WAS AFTER
THE TOTEM WEAPONS ARE NOT JUST ARTIFACTS, OLIVER...

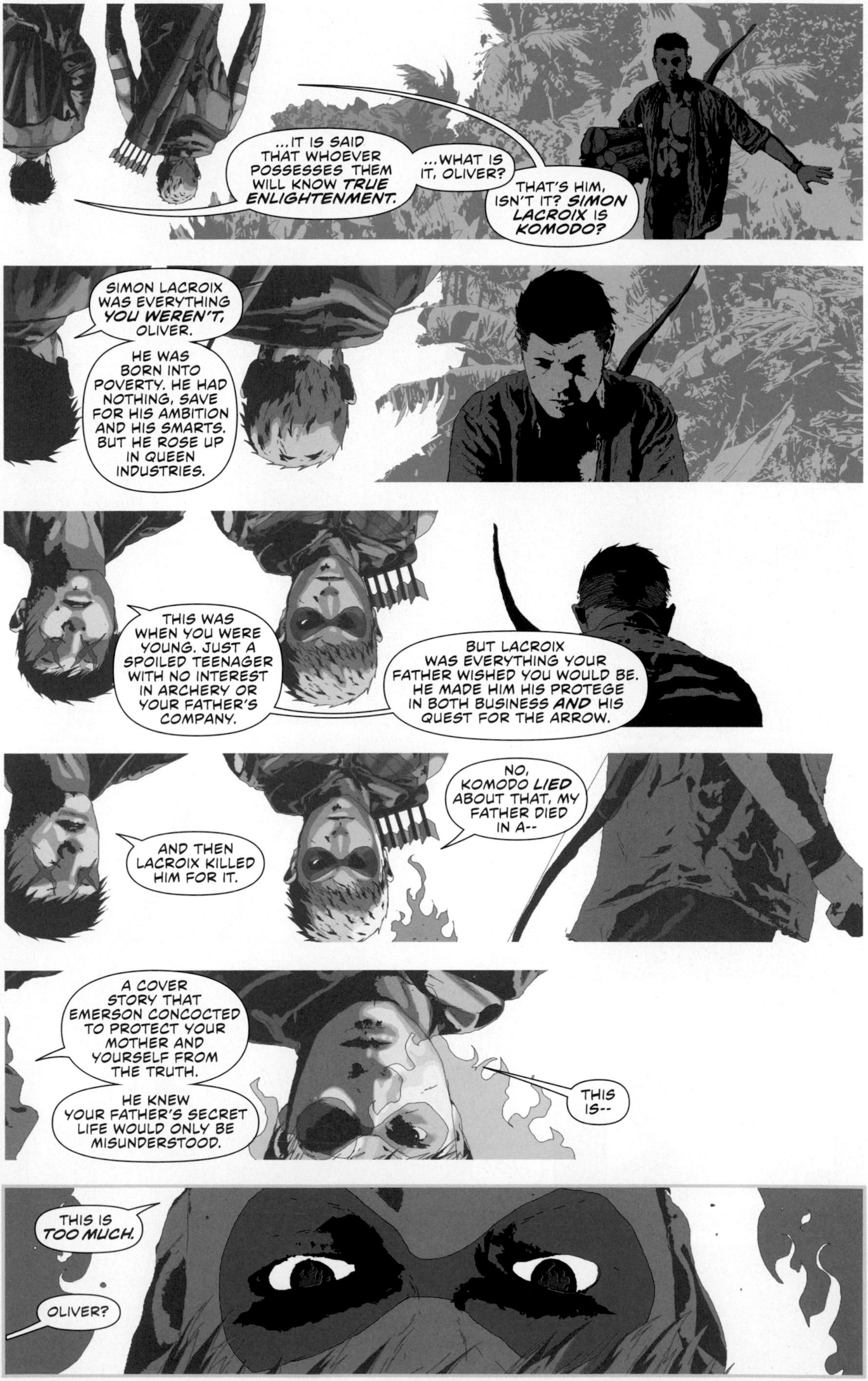
...IT IS SAID THAT WHOEVER POSSESSES THEM WILL KNOW TRUE ENLIGHTENMENT.
...WHAT IS IT, OLIVER?
THAT'S HIM, ISN'T IT? SIMON LACROIX IS KOMODO?
SIMON LACROIX WAS EVERYTHING YOU WEREN'T, OLIVER.
HE WAS BORN INTO POVERTY. HE HAD NOTHING, SAVE FOR HIS AMBITION AND HIS SMARTS. BUT HE ROSE UP IN QUEEN INDUSTRIES.
THIS WAS WHEN YOU WERE YOUNG. JUST A SPOILED TEENAGER WITH NO INTEREST IN ARCHERY OR YOUR FATHER'S COMPANY.
BUT LACROIX WAS EVERYTHING YOUR FATHER WISHED YOU WOULD BE. HE MADE HIM HIS PROTEGE IN BOTH BUSINESS AND HIS QUEST FOR THE ARROW.
AND THEN LACROIX KILLED HIM FOR IT.
NO, KOMODO LIED ABOUT THAT, MY FATHER DIED IN A--
A COVER STORY THAT EMERSON CONCOCTED TO PROTECT YOUR MOTHER AND YOURSELF FROM THE TRUTH.
HE KNEW YOUR FATHER'S SECRET LIFE WOULD ONLY BE MISUNDERSTOOD.
THIS IS--
THIS IS TOO MUCH.
OLIVER?

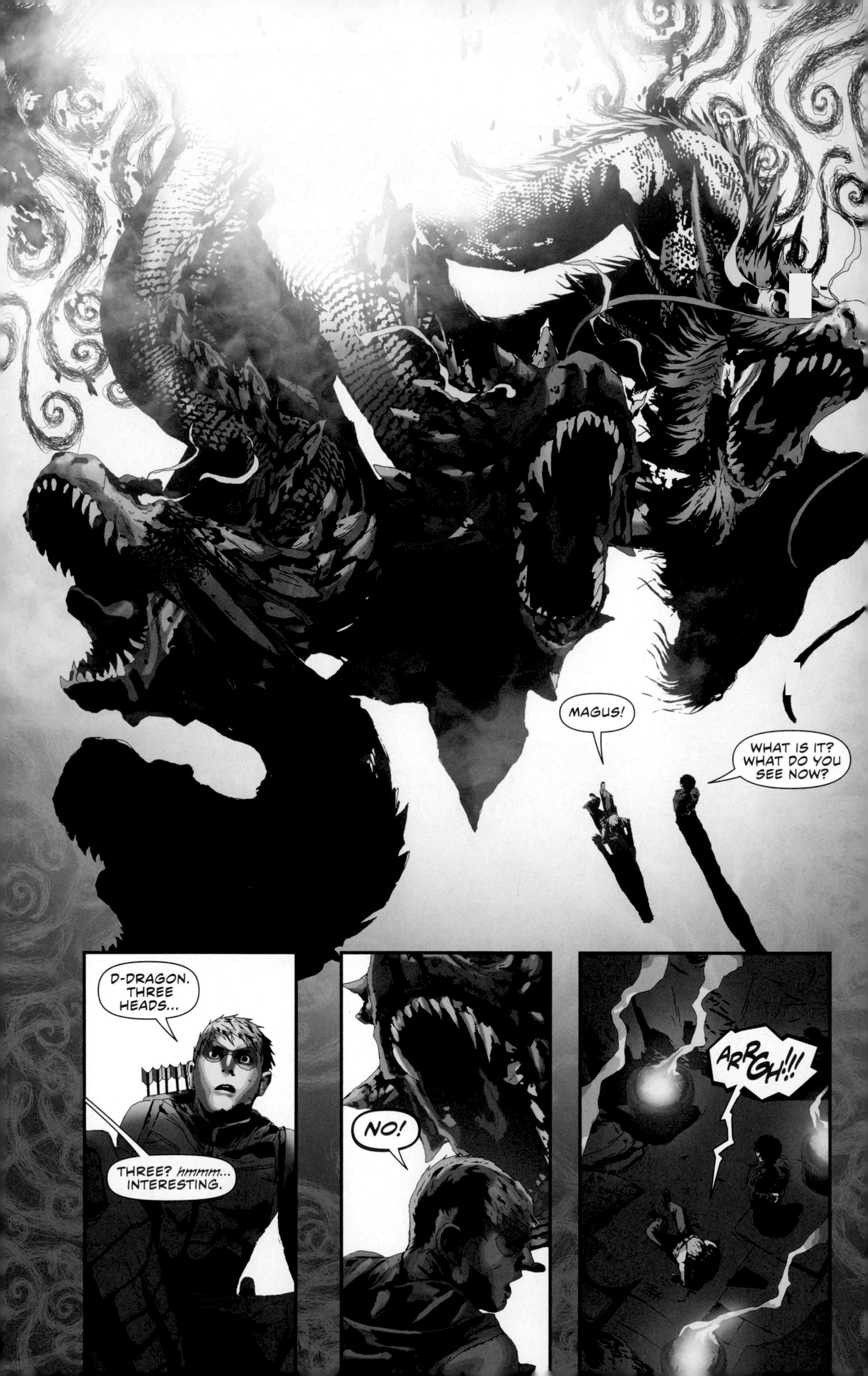
MAGUS!
WHAT IS IT? WHAT DO YOU SEE NOW?
D-DRAGON. THREE HEADS...
THREE? hmmm... INTERESTING.
NO!
ARRGH!!!

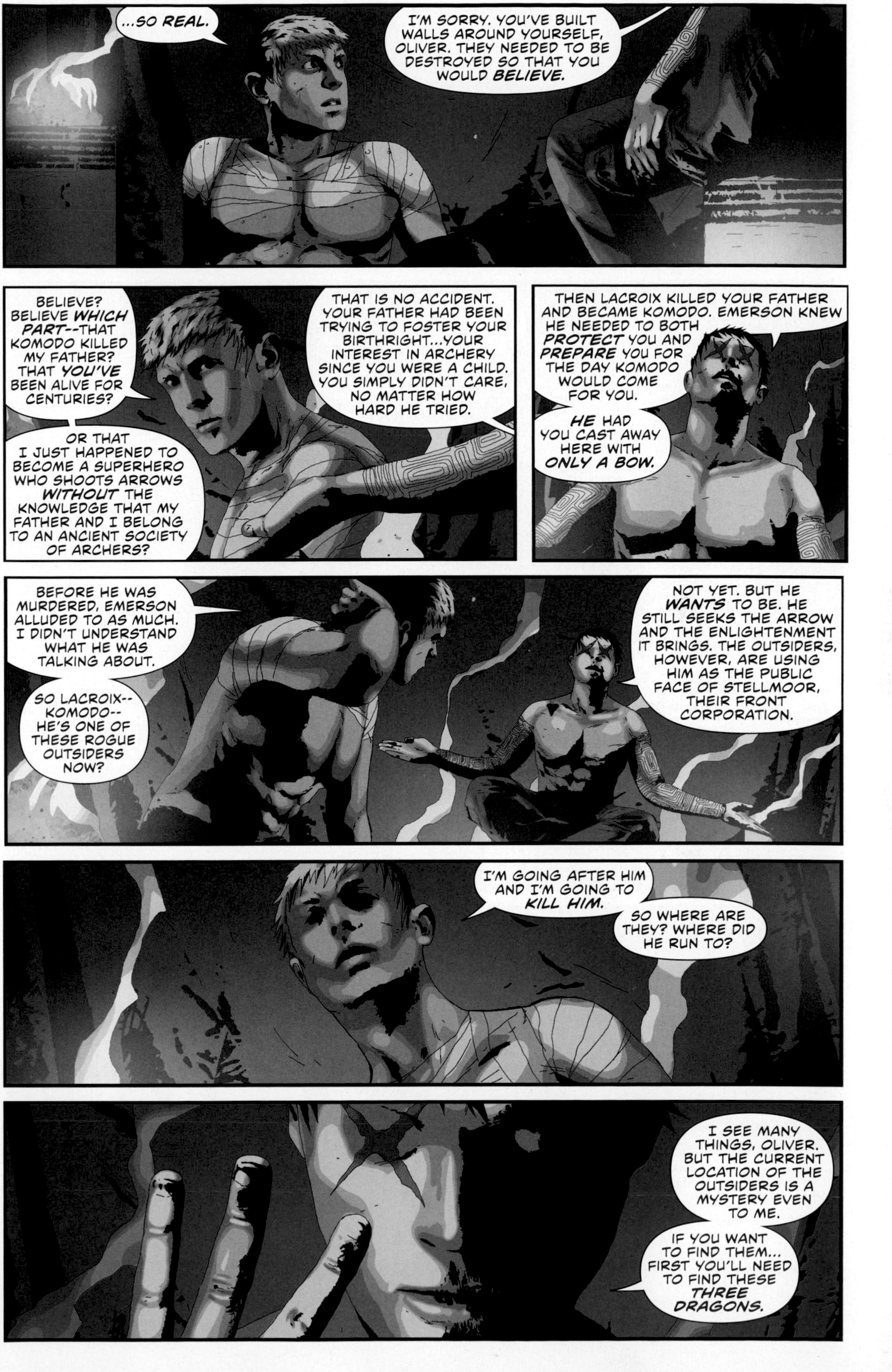
...SO REAL.
I'M SORRY. YOU'VE BUILT WALLS AROUND YOURSELF, OLIVER. THEY NEEDED TO BE DESTROYED SO THAT YOU WOULD BELIEVE.
BELIEVE? BELIEVE WHICH PART--THAT KOMODO KILLED MY FATHER? THAT YOU'VE BEEN ALIVE FOR CENTURIES?
OR THAT I JUST HAPPENED TO BECOME A SUPERHERO WHO SHOOTS ARROWS WITHOUT THE KNOWLEDGE THAT MY FATHER AND I BELONG TO AN ANCIENT SOCIETY OF ARCHERS?
THAT IS NO ACCIDENT. YOUR FATHER HAD BEEN TRYING TO FOSTER YOUR BIRTHRIGHT...YOUR INTEREST IN ARCHERY SINCE YOU WERE A CHILD. YOU SIMPLY DIDN'T CARE, NO MATTER HOW HARD HE TRIED.
THEN LACROIX KILLED YOUR FATHER AND BECAME KOMODO. EMERSON KNEW HE NEEDED TO BOTH PROTECT YOU AND PREPARE YOU FOR THE DAY KOMODO WOULD COME FOR YOU.
HE HAD YOU CAST AWAY HERE WITH ONLY A BOW.
BEFORE HE WAS MURDERED, EMERSON ALLUDED TO AS MUCH. I DIDN'T UNDERSTAND WHAT HE WAS TALKING ABOUT.
SO LACROIX--KOMODO--HE'S ONE OF THESE ROGUE OUTSIDERS NOW?
NOT YET. BUT HE WANTS TO BE. HE STILL SEEKS THE ARROW AND THE ENLIGHTENMENT IT BRINGS. THE OUTSIDERS, HOWEVER, ARE USING HIM AS THE PUBLIC FACE OF STELLMOOR, THEIR FRONT CORPORATION.
I'M GOING AFTER HIM AND I'M GOING TO KILL HIM.
SO WHERE ARE THEY? WHERE DID HE RUN TO?
I SEE MANY THINGS, OLIVER. BUT THE CURRENT LOCATION OF THE OUTSIDERS IS A MYSTERY EVEN TO ME.
IF YOU WANT TO FIND THEM... FIRST YOU'LL NEED TO FIND THESE THREE DRAGONS.

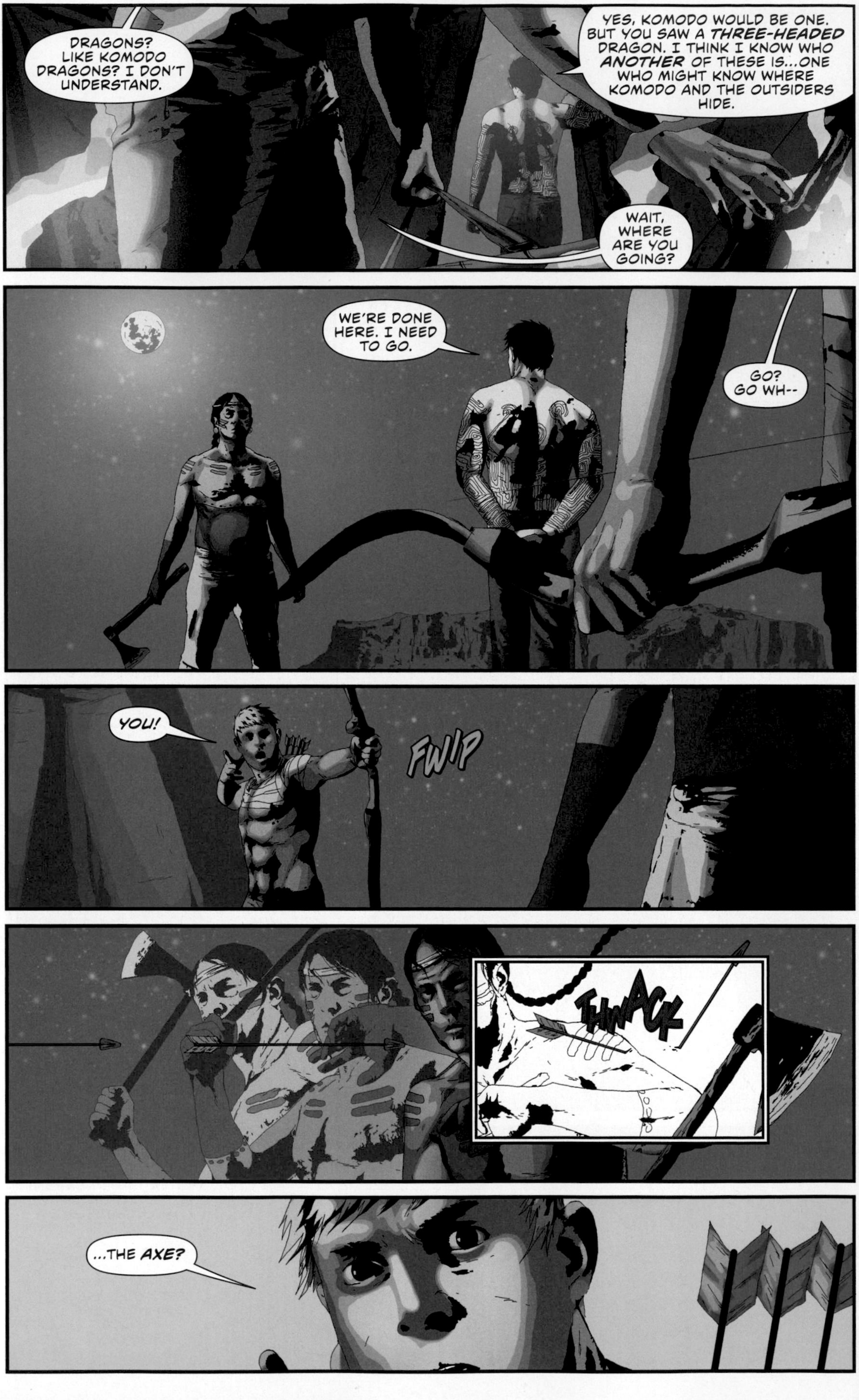
DRAGONS? LIKE KOMODO DRAGONS? I DON'T UNDERSTAND.
YES, KOMODO WOULD BE ONE. BUT YOU SAW A *THREE-HEADED* DRAGON. I THINK I KNOW WHO *ANOTHER* OF THESE IS...ONE WHO MIGHT KNOW WHERE KOMODO AND THE OUTSIDERS HIDE.
WAIT, WHERE ARE YOU GOING?
WE'RE DONE HERE. I NEED TO GO.
GO? GO WH--
YOU!
FWIP
THWACK
...THE *AXE?*

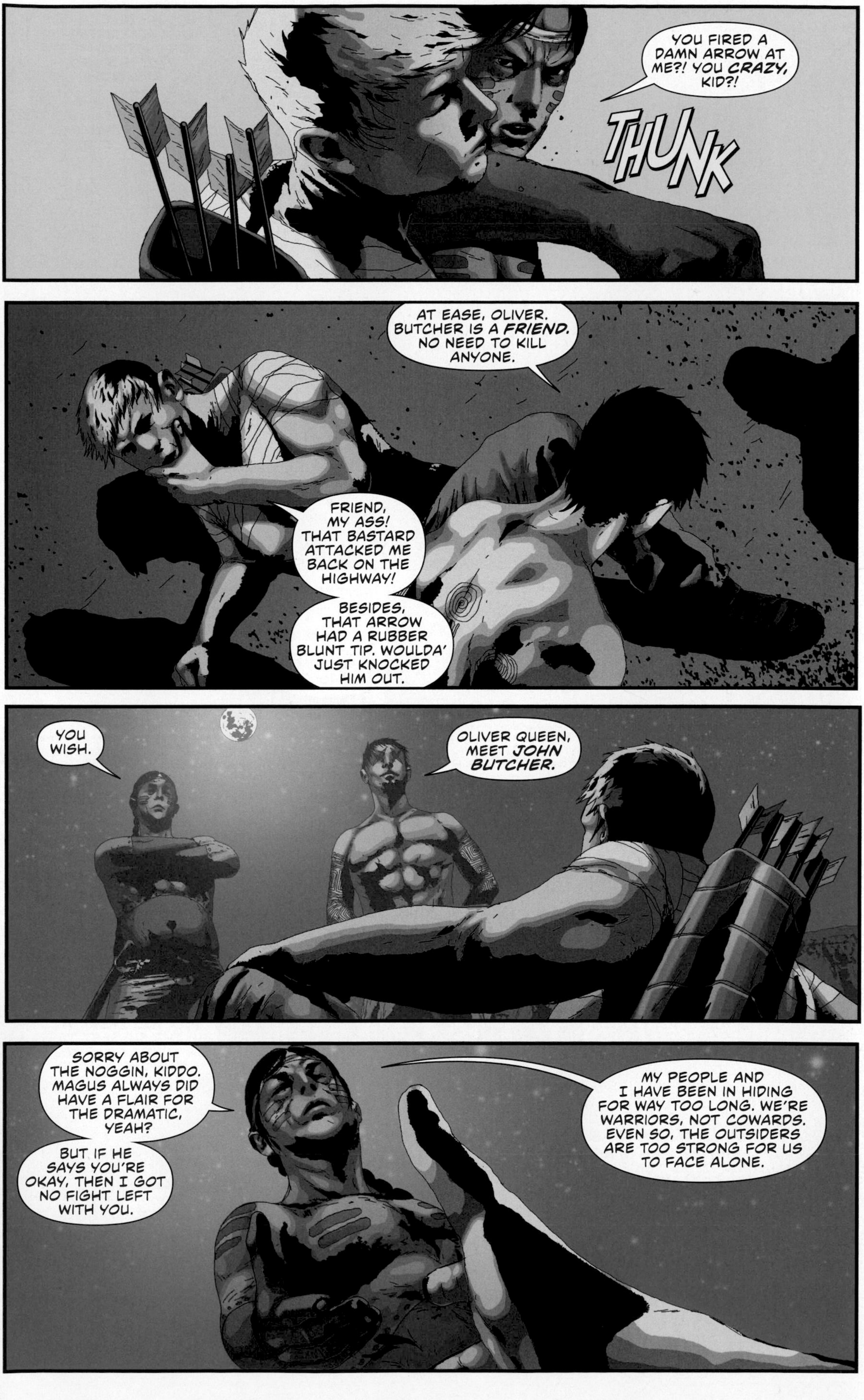

YOU FIRED A DAMN ARROW AT ME?! YOU CRAZY, KID?!
THUNK
AT EASE, OLIVER. BUTCHER IS A FRIEND. NO NEED TO KILL ANYONE.
FRIEND, MY ASS! THAT BASTARD ATTACKED ME BACK ON THE HIGHWAY!
BESIDES, THAT ARROW HAD A RUBBER BLUNT TIP. WOULDA' JUST KNOCKED HIM OUT.
YOU WISH.
OLIVER QUEEN, MEET JOHN BUTCHER.
SORRY ABOUT THE NOGGIN, KIDDO. MAGUS ALWAYS DID HAVE A FLAIR FOR THE DRAMATIC, YEAH?
BUT IF HE SAYS YOU'RE OKAY, THEN I GOT NO FIGHT LEFT WITH YOU.
MY PEOPLE AND I HAVE BEEN IN HIDING FOR WAY TOO LONG. WE'RE WARRIORS, NOT COWARDS. EVEN SO, THE OUTSIDERS ARE TOO STRONG FOR US TO FACE ALONE.

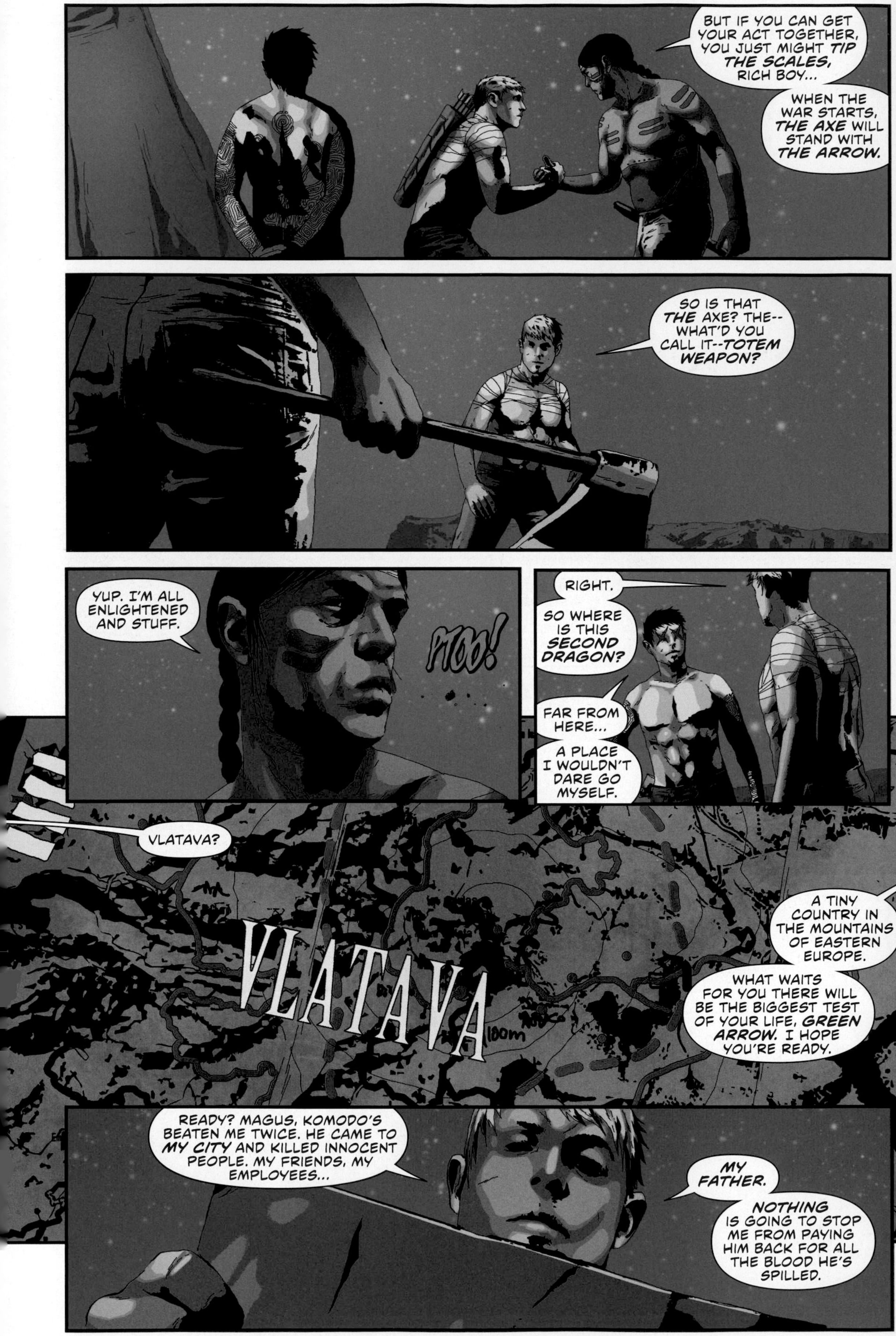
BUT IF YOU CAN GET YOUR ACT TOGETHER, YOU JUST MIGHT TIP THE SCALES, RICH BOY...
WHEN THE WAR STARTS, THE AXE WILL STAND WITH THE ARROW.
SO IS THAT THE AXE? THE--WHAT'D YOU CALL IT--TOTEM WEAPON?
YUP. I'M ALL ENLIGHTENED AND STUFF.
PTOO!
RIGHT.
SO WHERE IS THIS SECOND DRAGON?
FAR FROM HERE...
A PLACE I WOULDN'T DARE GO MYSELF.
VLATAVA?
VLATAVA
100m
A TINY COUNTRY IN THE MOUNTAINS OF EASTERN EUROPE.
WHAT WAITS FOR YOU THERE WILL BE THE BIGGEST TEST OF YOUR LIFE, GREEN ARROW. I HOPE YOU'RE READY.
READY? MAGUS, KOMODO'S BEATEN ME TWICE. HE CAME TO MY CITY AND KILLED INNOCENT PEOPLE. MY FRIENDS, MY EMPLOYEES...
MY FATHER.
NOTHING IS GOING TO STOP ME FROM PAYING HIM BACK FOR ALL THE BLOOD HE'S SPILLED.

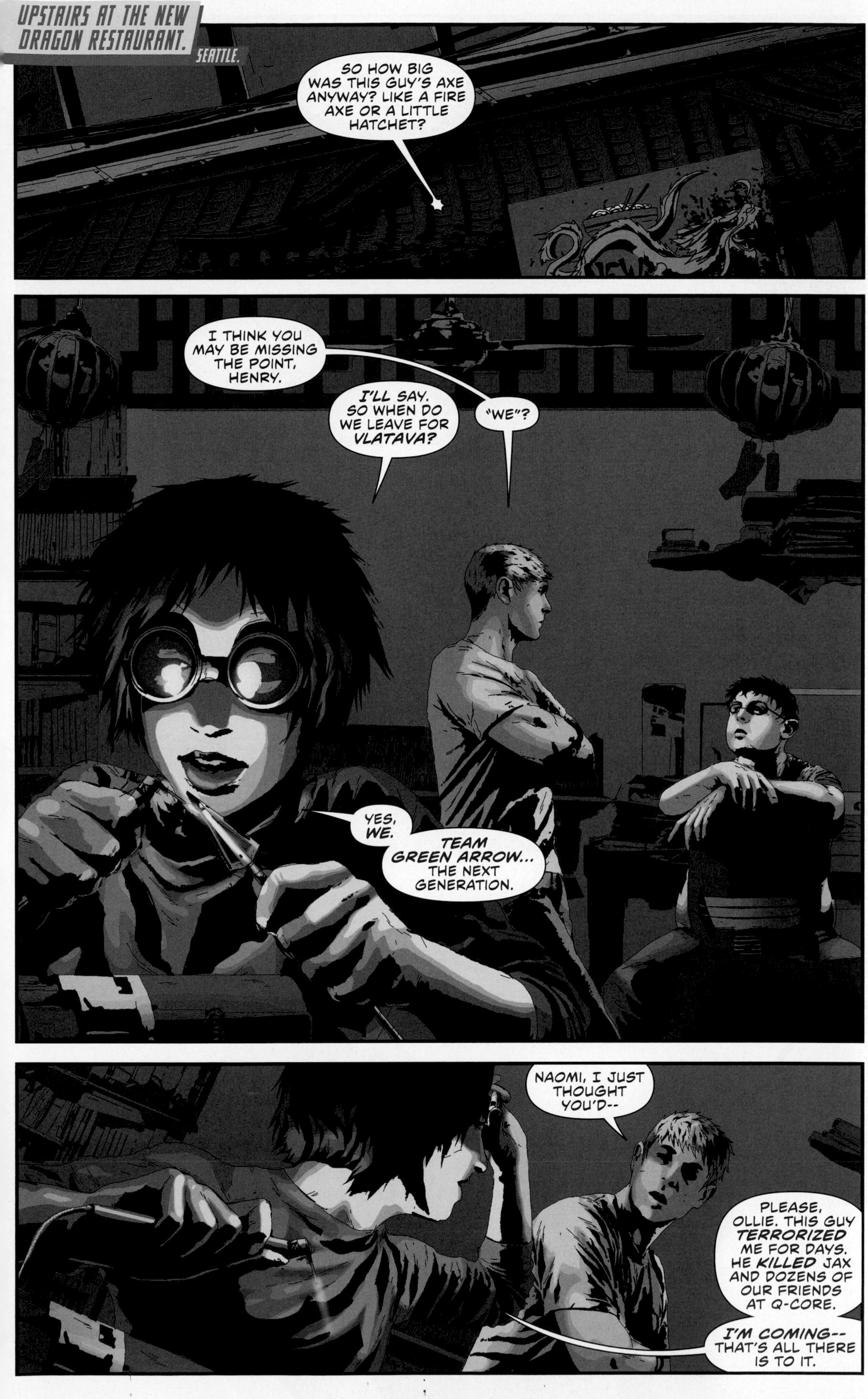
UPSTAIRS AT THE NEW DRAGON RESTAURANT.
SEATTLE.
SO HOW BIG WAS THIS GUY'S AXE ANYWAY? LIKE A FIRE AXE OR A LITTLE HATCHET?
I THINK YOU MAY BE MISSING THE POINT, HENRY.
I'LL SAY. SO WHEN DO WE LEAVE FOR VLATAVA?
"WE"?
YES, WE.
TEAM GREEN ARROW... THE NEXT GENERATION.
NAOMI, I JUST THOUGHT YOU'D--
PLEASE, OLLIE. THIS GUY TERRORIZED ME FOR DAYS. HE KILLED JAX AND DOZENS OF OUR FRIENDS AT Q-CORE.
I'M COMING-- THAT'S ALL THERE IS TO IT.

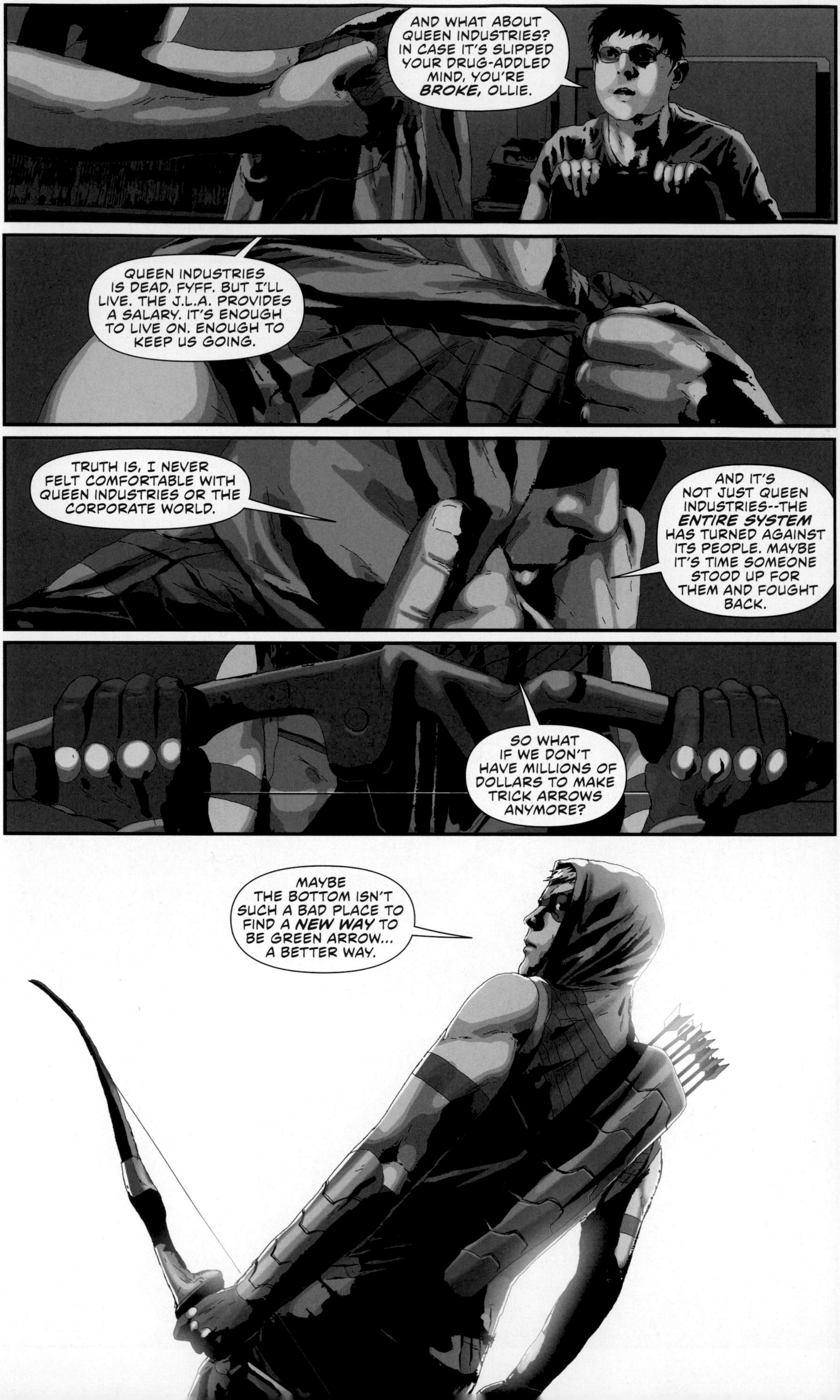
AND WHAT ABOUT QUEEN INDUSTRIES? IN CASE IT'S SLIPPED YOUR DRUG-ADDLED MIND, YOU'RE *BROKE,* OLLIE.
QUEEN INDUSTRIES IS DEAD, FYFF. BUT I'LL LIVE. THE J.L.A. PROVIDES A SALARY. IT'S ENOUGH TO LIVE ON. ENOUGH TO KEEP US GOING.
TRUTH IS, I NEVER FELT COMFORTABLE WITH QUEEN INDUSTRIES OR THE CORPORATE WORLD.
AND IT'S NOT JUST QUEEN INDUSTRIES--THE *ENTIRE SYSTEM* HAS TURNED AGAINST ITS PEOPLE. MAYBE IT'S TIME SOMEONE STOOD UP FOR THEM AND FOUGHT BACK.
SO WHAT IF WE DON'T HAVE MILLIONS OF DOLLARS TO MAKE TRICK ARROWS ANYMORE?
MAYBE THE BOTTOM ISN'T SUCH A BAD PLACE TO FIND A *NEW WAY* TO BE GREEN ARROW... A BETTER WAY.

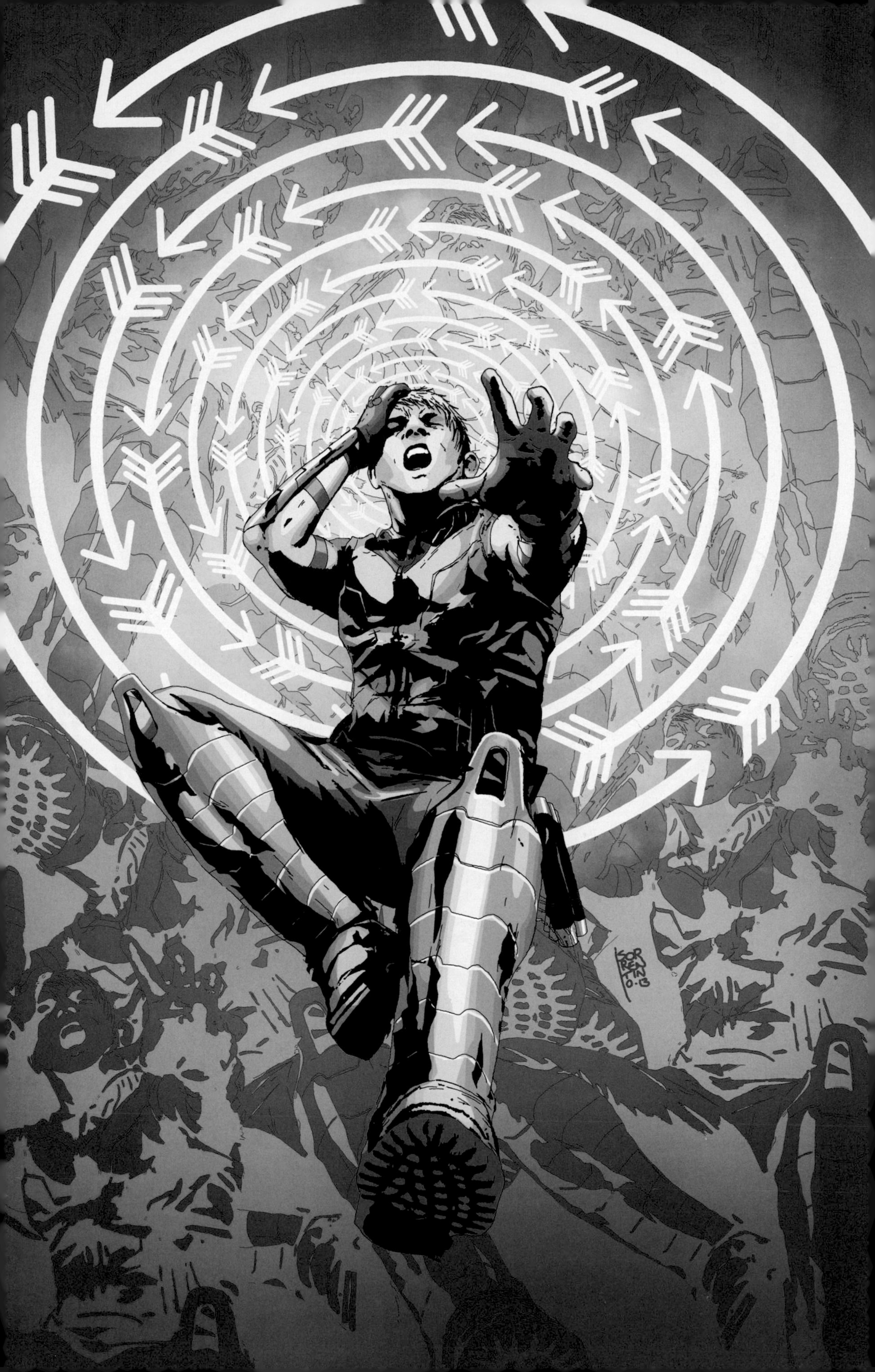

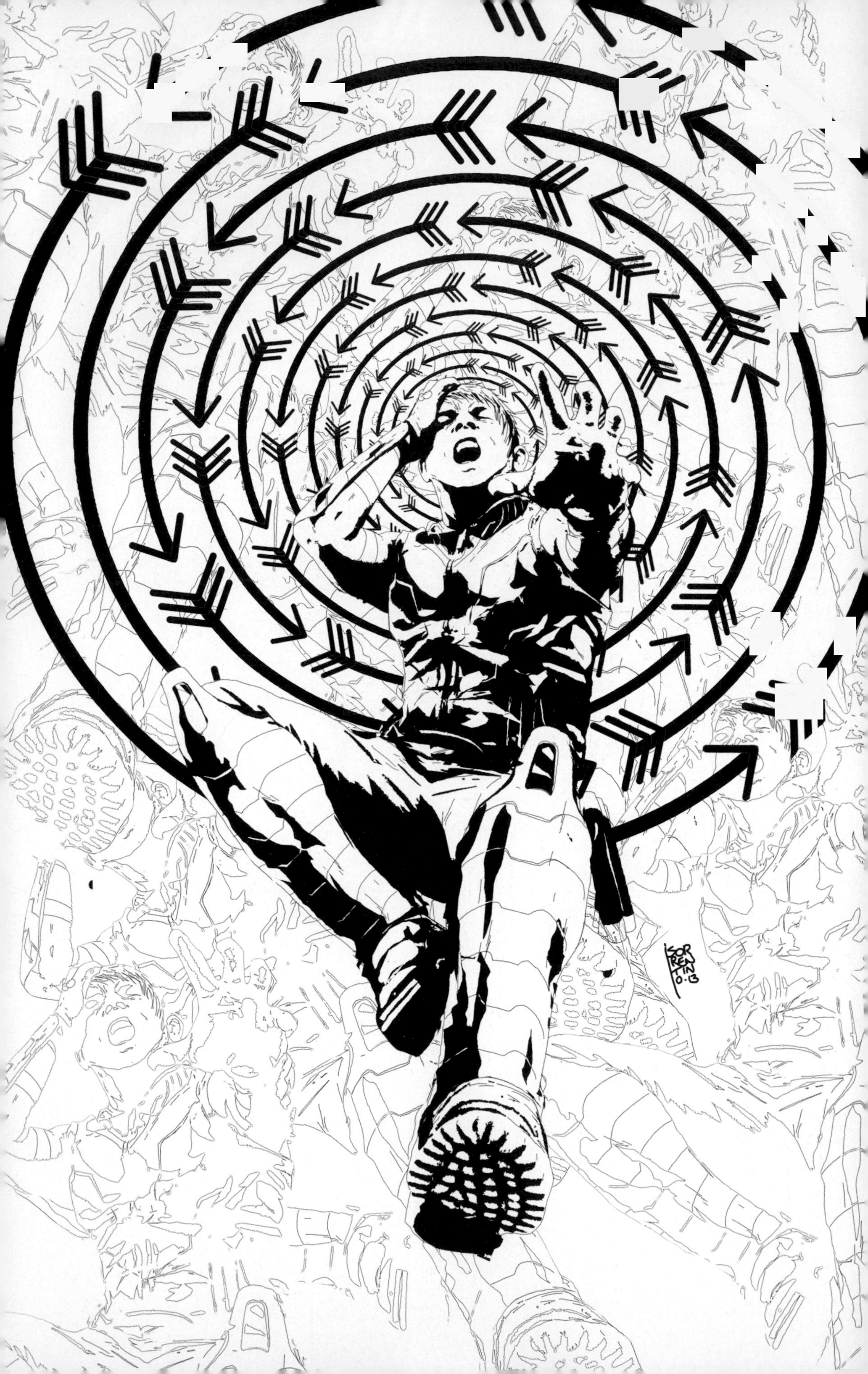

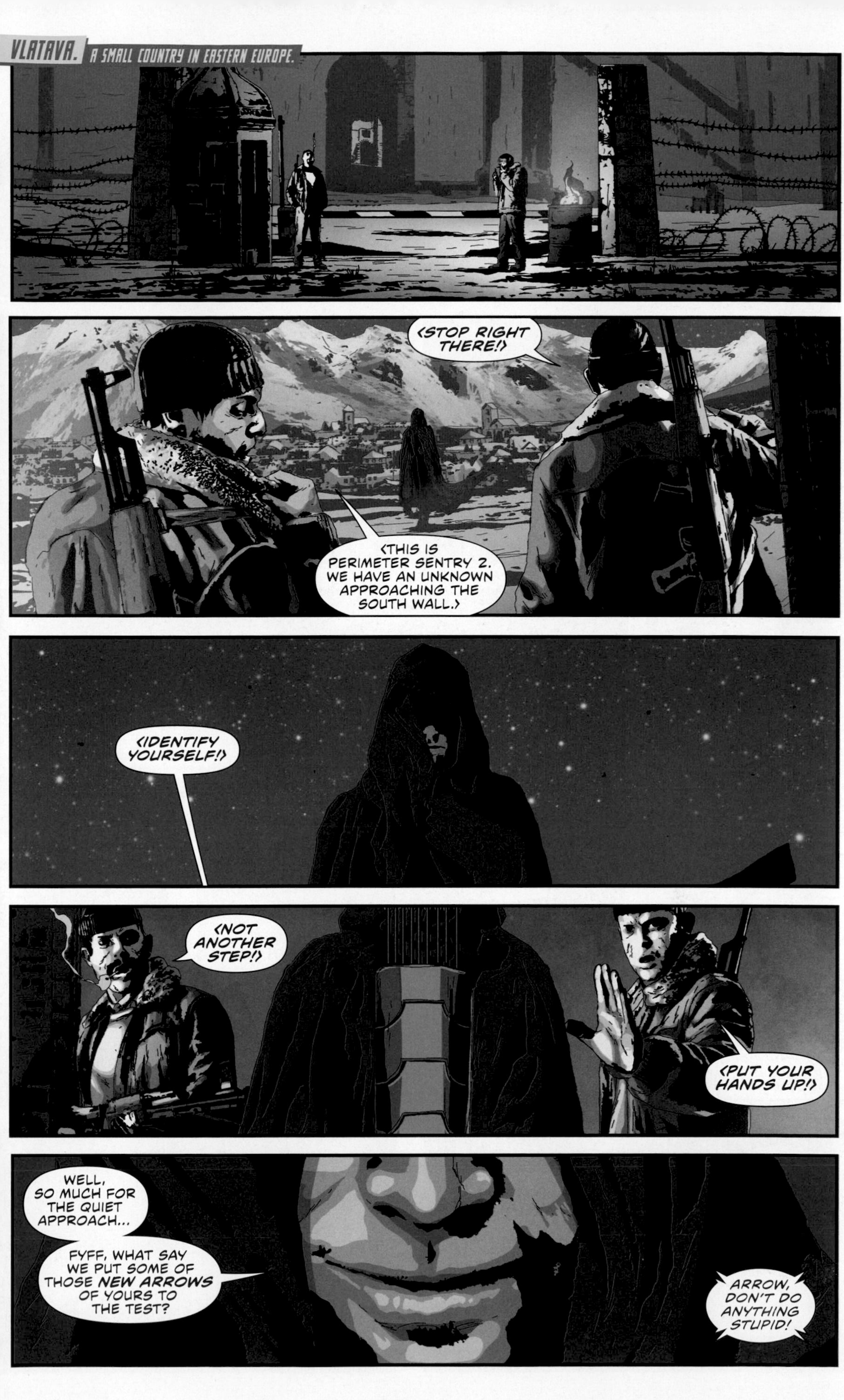
VLATAVA. A SMALL COUNTRY IN EASTERN EUROPE.
<STOP RIGHT THERE!>
<THIS IS PERIMETER SENTRY 2. WE HAVE AN UNKNOWN APPROACHING THE SOUTH WALL.>
<IDENTIFY YOURSELF!>
<NOT ANOTHER STEP!>
<PUT YOUR HANDS UP!>
WELL, SO MUCH FOR THE QUIET APPROACH...
FYFF, WHAT SAY WE PUT SOME OF THOSE NEW ARROWS OF YOURS TO THE TEST?
ARROW, DON'T DO ANYTHING STUPID!

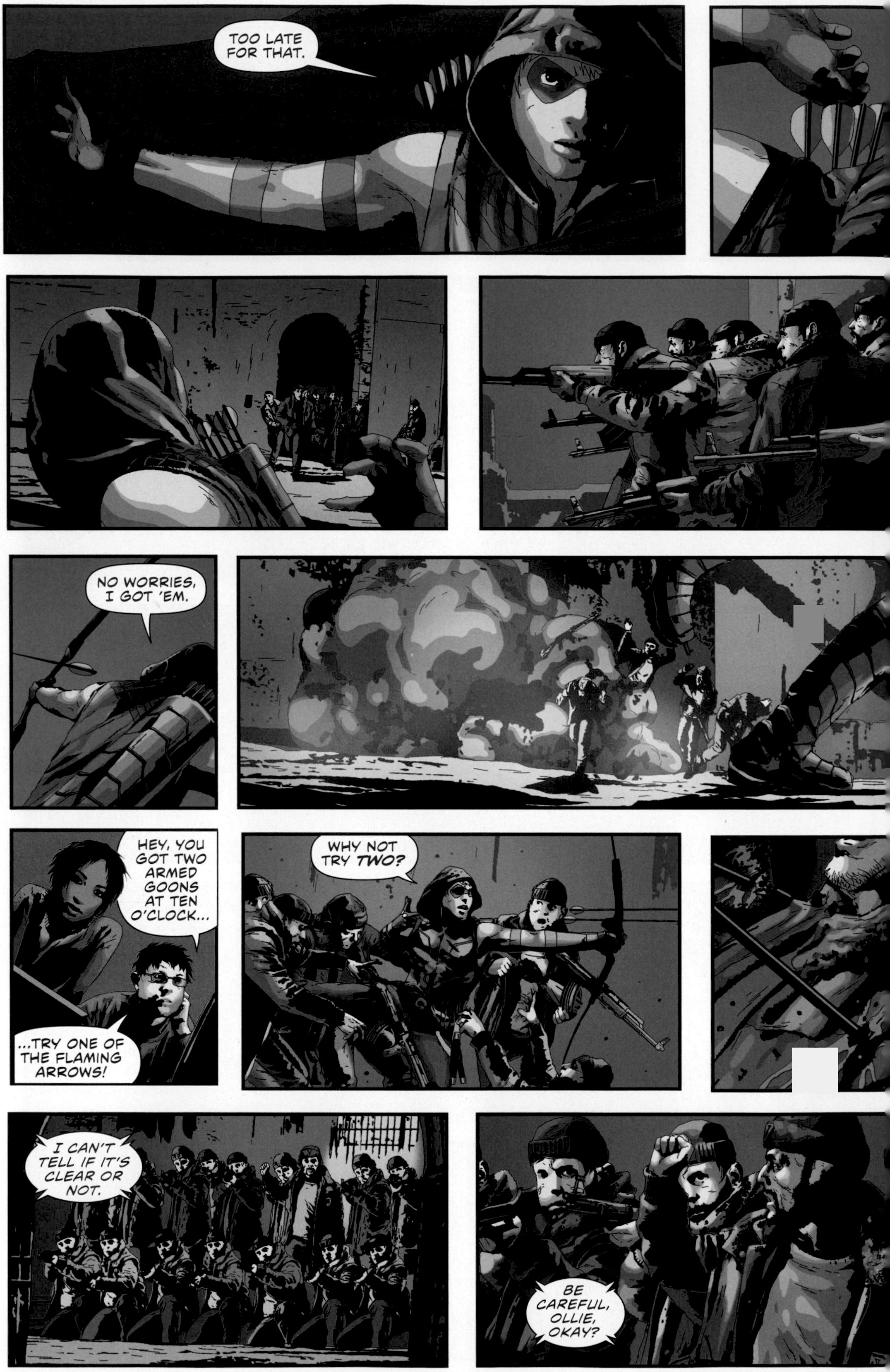
TOO LATE FOR THAT.
NO WORRIES, I GOT 'EM.
HEY, YOU GOT TWO ARMED GOONS AT TEN O'CLOCK...
...TRY ONE OF THE FLAMING ARROWS!
WHY NOT TRY *TWO*?
I CAN'T TELL IF IT'S CLEAR OR NOT.
BE CAREFUL, OLLIE, OKAY?

<AMERICAN!>

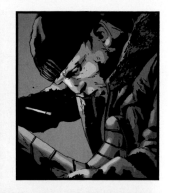

I HAVE FOUR MORE MERCS RUSHING FROM THE COMPOUND.

I'M IN... YOU GUYS STILL GOT ME ON SATELLITE?

YEAH-- THEY HAVE SOME KIND OF SCRAMBLER SET UP, BUT I HACKED THROUGH IT, NO PROBLEM.

FWOOSH
NICE! HOW DID YOU MAKE THE FLAMES GREEN?

A MAGICIAN NEVER REVEALS HIS SECRETS.

THE AREA AHEAD IS KINDA FUZZY ON THE SATELLITE...

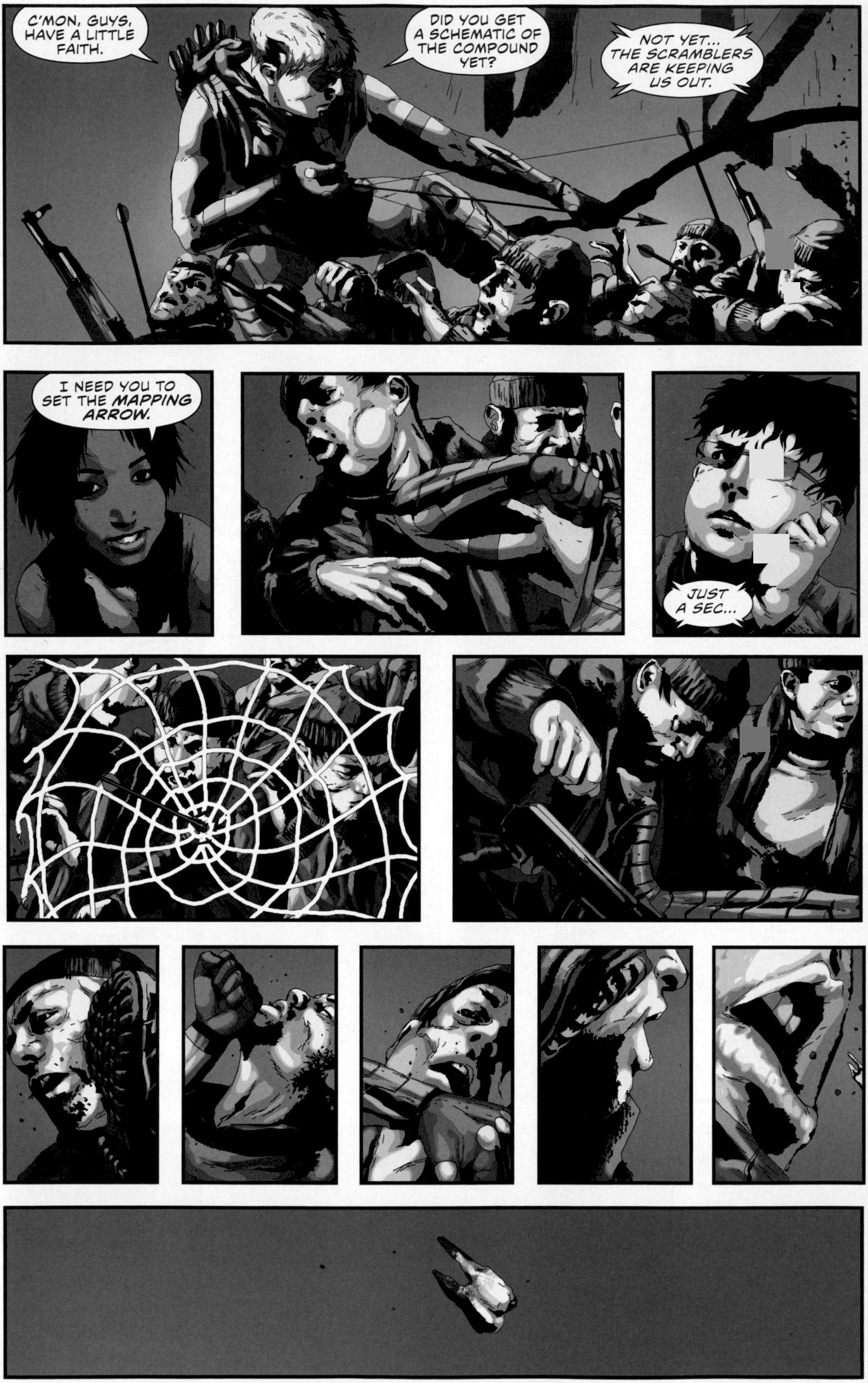
C'MON, GUYS, HAVE A LITTLE FAITH.
DID YOU GET A SCHEMATIC OF THE COMPOUND YET?
NOT YET... THE SCRAMBLERS ARE KEEPING US OUT.
I NEED YOU TO SET THE *MAPPING ARROW.*
JUST A SEC...

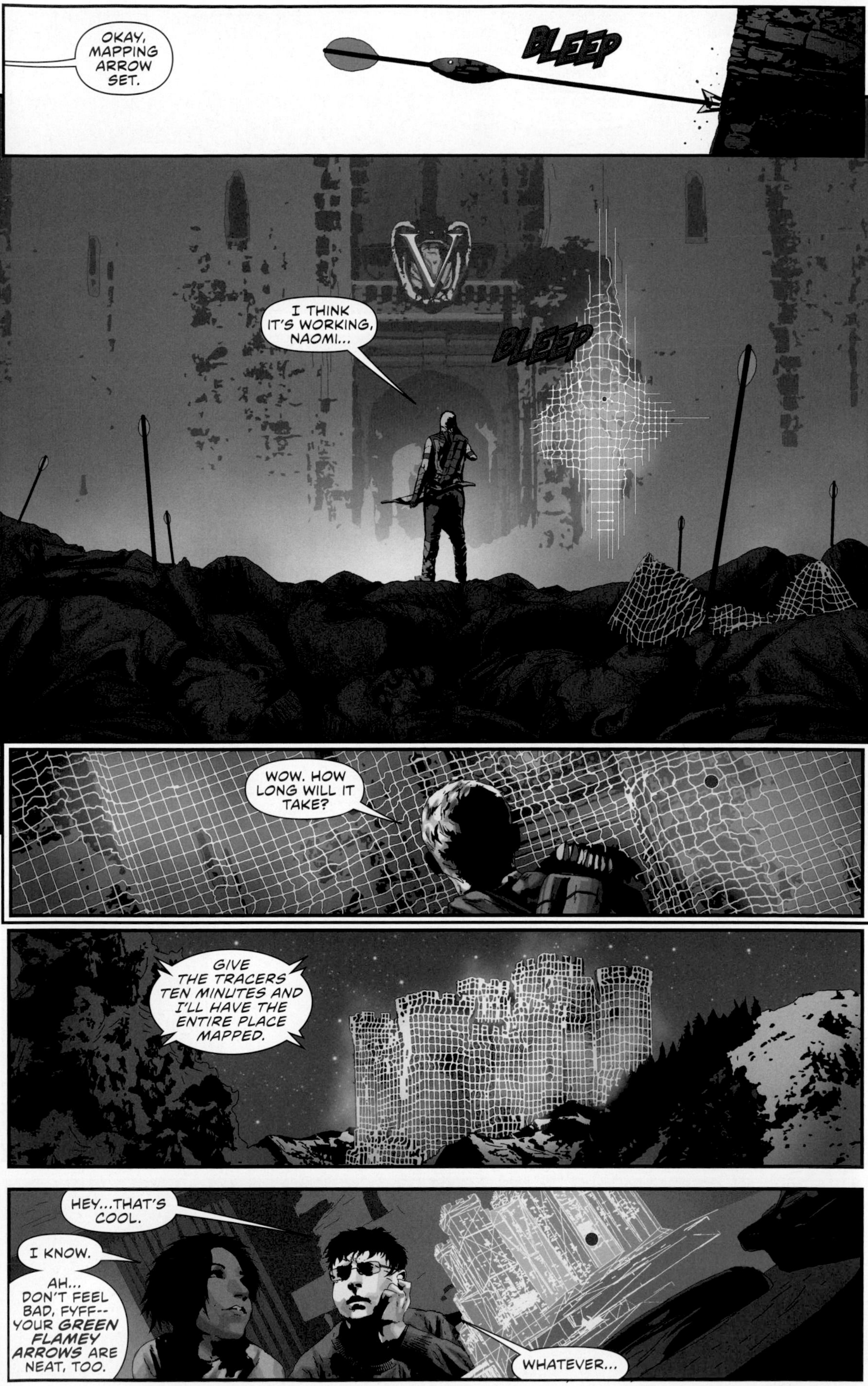

OKAY, MAPPING ARROW SET.
BLEEP
I THINK IT'S WORKING, NAOMI...
BLEEP
WOW. HOW LONG WILL IT TAKE?
GIVE THE TRACERS TEN MINUTES AND I'LL HAVE THE ENTIRE PLACE MAPPED.
HEY...THAT'S COOL.
I KNOW.
AH... DON'T FEEL BAD, FYFF-- YOUR GREEN FLAMEY ARROWS ARE NEAT, TOO.
WHATEVER...

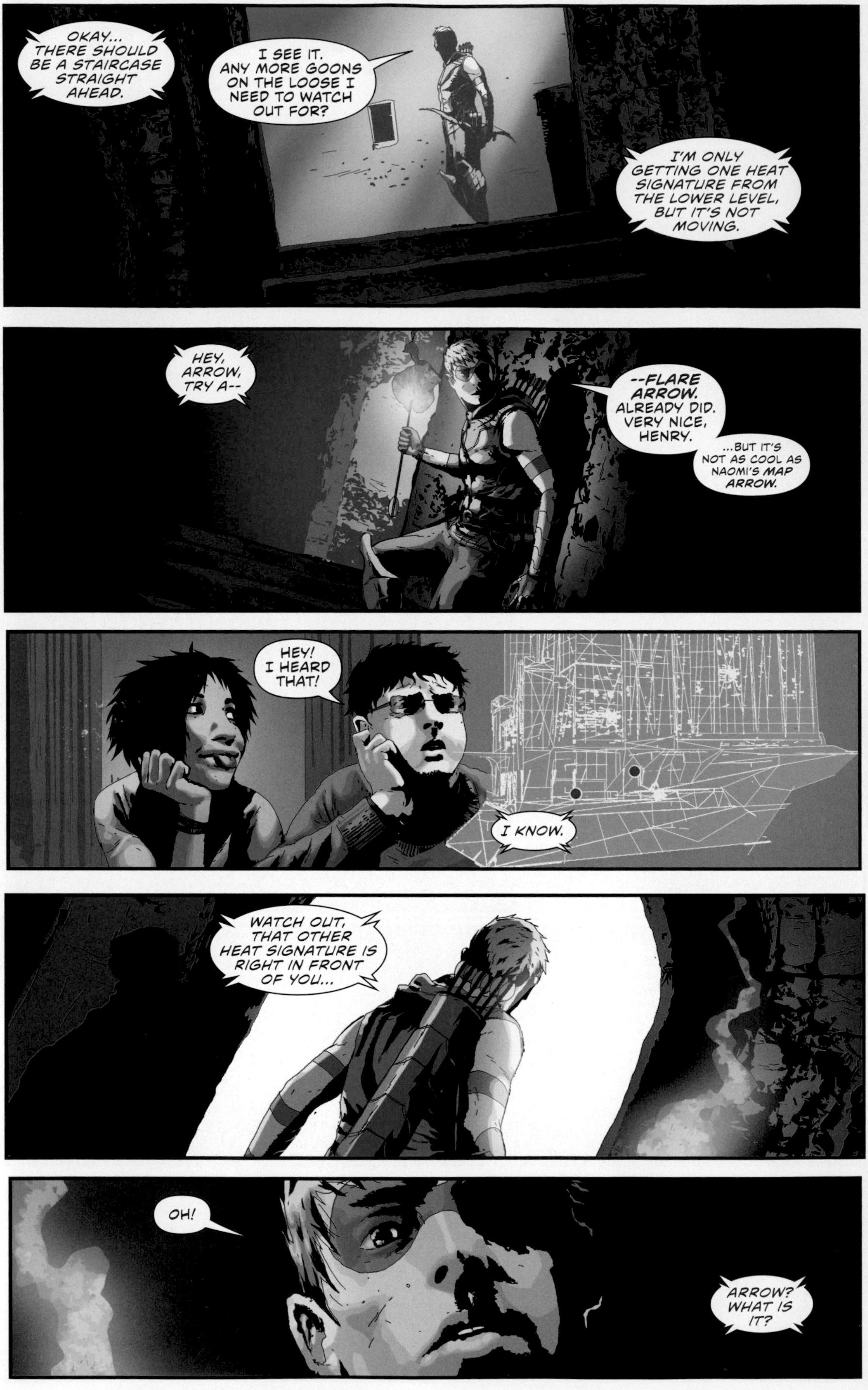
OKAY... THERE SHOULD BE A STAIRCASE STRAIGHT AHEAD.
I SEE IT. ANY MORE GOONS ON THE LOOSE I NEED TO WATCH OUT FOR?
I'M ONLY GETTING ONE HEAT SIGNATURE FROM THE LOWER LEVEL, BUT IT'S NOT MOVING.
HEY, ARROW, TRY A--
--FLARE ARROW. ALREADY DID. VERY NICE, HENRY.
...BUT IT'S NOT AS COOL AS NAOMI'S MAP ARROW.
HEY! I HEARD THAT!
I KNOW.
WATCH OUT, THAT OTHER HEAT SIGNATURE IS RIGHT IN FRONT OF YOU...
OH!
ARROW? WHAT IS IT?

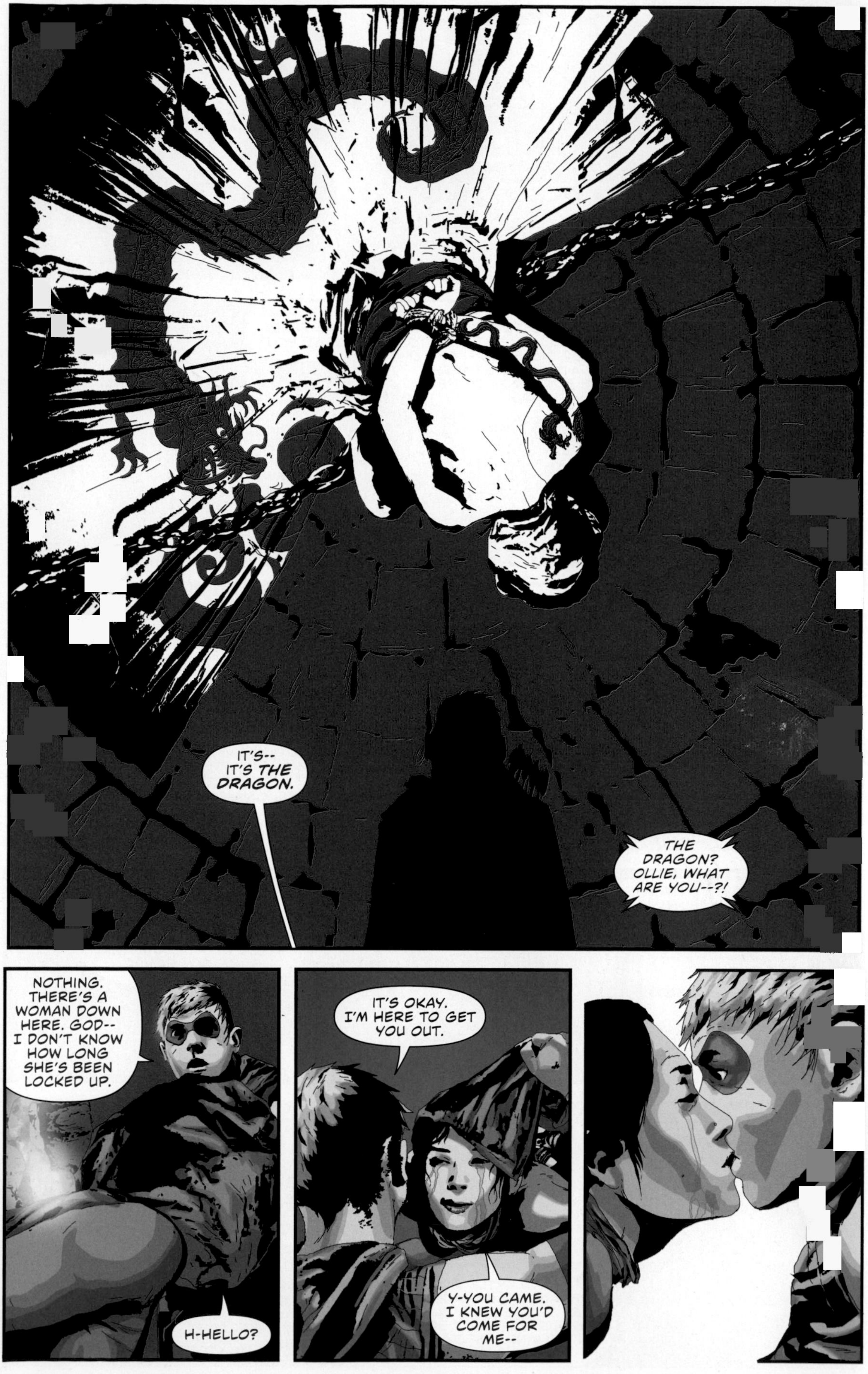
IT'S-- IT'S *THE DRAGON.*
THE DRAGON? OLLIE, WHAT ARE YOU--?!
NOTHING. THERE'S A WOMAN DOWN HERE. GOD-- I DON'T KNOW HOW LONG SHE'S BEEN LOCKED UP.
H-HELLO?
IT'S OKAY. I'M HERE TO GET YOU OUT.
Y-YOU CAME. I KNEW YOU'D COME FOR ME--

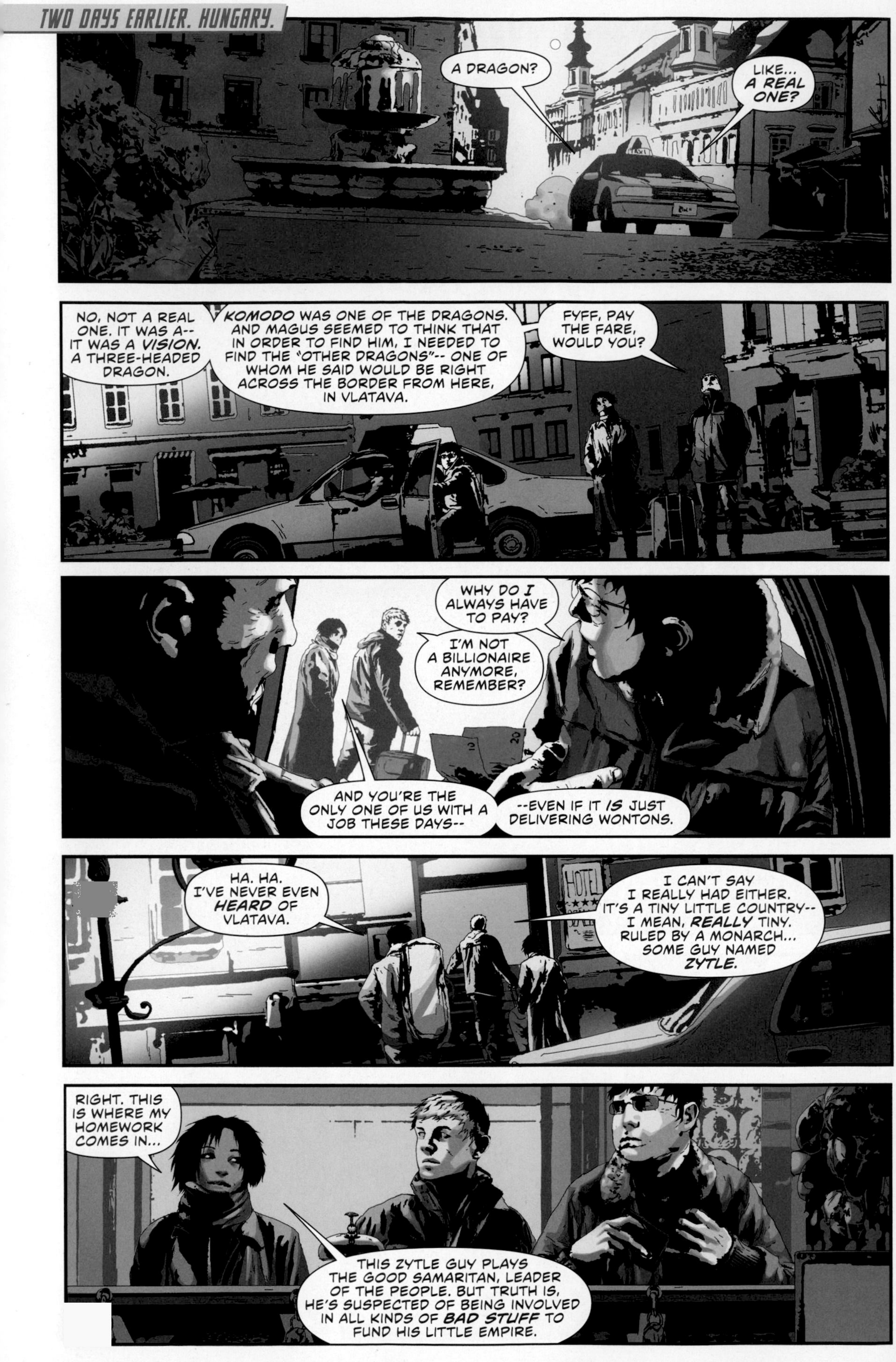
TWO DAYS EARLIER. HUNGARY.
A DRAGON?
LIKE... A REAL ONE?
NO, NOT A REAL ONE. IT WAS A-- IT WAS A VISION. A THREE-HEADED DRAGON.
KOMODO WAS ONE OF THE DRAGONS. AND MAGUS SEEMED TO THINK THAT IN ORDER TO FIND HIM, I NEEDED TO FIND THE "OTHER DRAGONS"-- ONE OF WHOM HE SAID WOULD BE RIGHT ACROSS THE BORDER FROM HERE, IN VLATAVA.
FYFF, PAY THE FARE, WOULD YOU?
WHY DO I ALWAYS HAVE TO PAY?
I'M NOT A BILLIONAIRE ANYMORE, REMEMBER?
AND YOU'RE THE ONLY ONE OF US WITH A JOB THESE DAYS--
--EVEN IF IT IS JUST DELIVERING WONTONS.
HA. HA. I'VE NEVER EVEN HEARD OF VLATAVA.
I CAN'T SAY I REALLY HAD EITHER. IT'S A TINY LITTLE COUNTRY-- I MEAN, REALLY TINY. RULED BY A MONARCH... SOME GUY NAMED ZYTLE.
RIGHT. THIS IS WHERE MY HOMEWORK COMES IN...
THIS ZYTLE GUY PLAYS THE GOOD SAMARITAN, LEADER OF THE PEOPLE. BUT TRUTH IS, HE'S SUSPECTED OF BEING INVOLVED IN ALL KINDS OF BAD STUFF TO FUND HIS LITTLE EMPIRE.

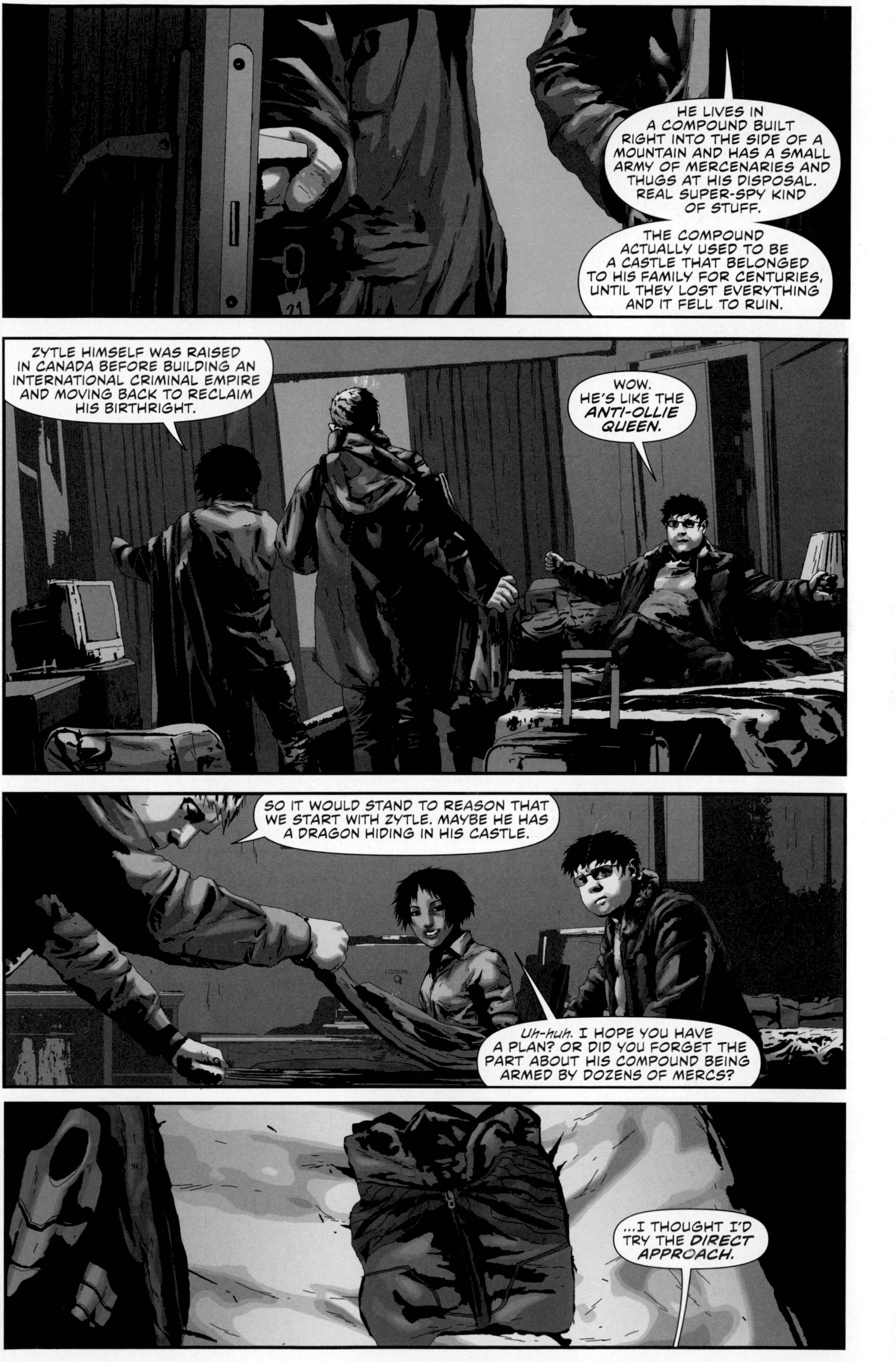
HE LIVES IN A COMPOUND BUILT RIGHT INTO THE SIDE OF A MOUNTAIN AND HAS A SMALL ARMY OF MERCENARIES AND THUGS AT HIS DISPOSAL. REAL SUPER-SPY KIND OF STUFF.
THE COMPOUND ACTUALLY USED TO BE A CASTLE THAT BELONGED TO HIS FAMILY FOR CENTURIES, UNTIL THEY LOST EVERYTHING AND IT FELL TO RUIN.
ZYTLE HIMSELF WAS RAISED IN CANADA BEFORE BUILDING AN INTERNATIONAL CRIMINAL EMPIRE AND MOVING BACK TO RECLAIM HIS BIRTHRIGHT.
WOW. HE'S LIKE THE *ANTI-OLLIE QUEEN.*
SO IT WOULD STAND TO REASON THAT WE START WITH ZYTLE. MAYBE HE HAS A DRAGON HIDING IN HIS CASTLE.
Uh-huh. I HOPE YOU HAVE A PLAN? OR DID YOU FORGET THE PART ABOUT HIS COMPOUND BEING ARMED BY DOZENS OF MERCS?
...I THOUGHT I'D TRY THE *DIRECT APPROACH.*

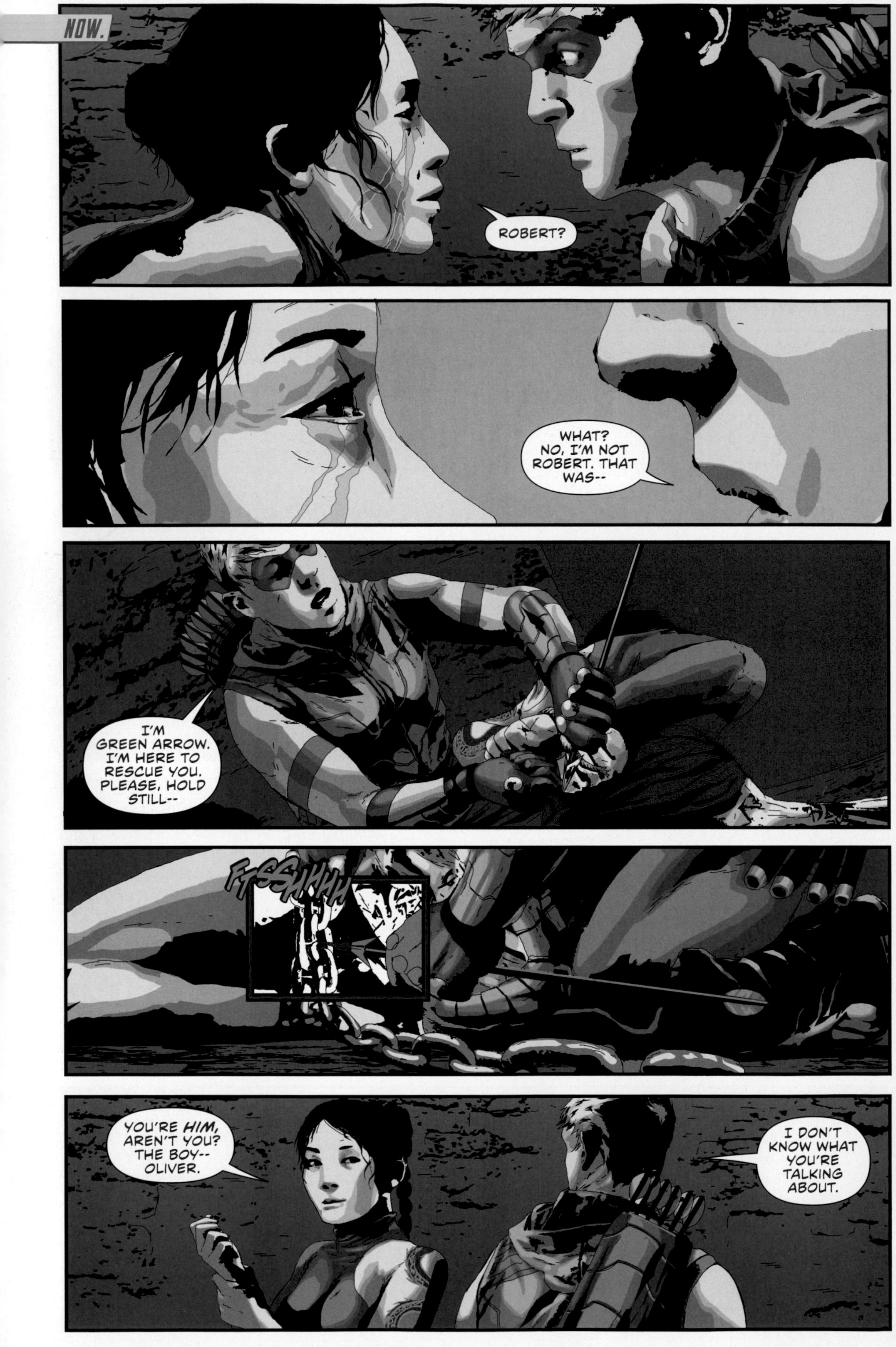
NOW.
ROBERT?
WHAT? NO, I'M NOT ROBERT. THAT WAS--
I'M GREEN ARROW. I'M HERE TO RESCUE YOU. PLEASE, HOLD STILL--
FTSSHHHH
YOU'RE *HIM*, AREN'T YOU? THE BOY-- OLIVER.
I DON'T KNOW WHAT YOU'RE TALKING ABOUT.

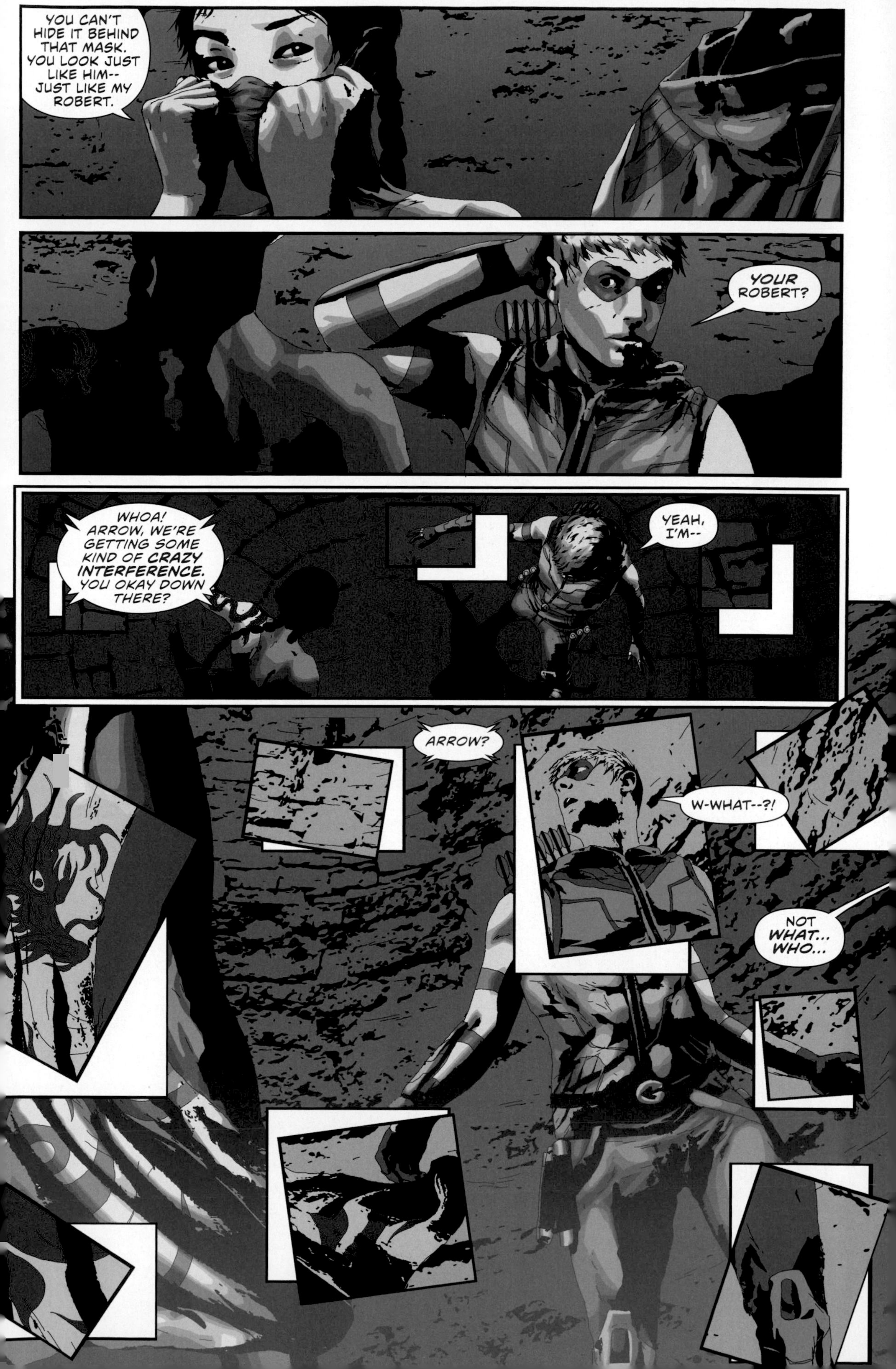
YOU CAN'T HIDE IT BEHIND THAT MASK. YOU LOOK JUST LIKE HIM-- JUST LIKE MY ROBERT.
YOUR ROBERT?
WHOA! ARROW, WE'RE GETTING SOME KIND OF CRAZY INTERFERENCE. YOU OKAY DOWN THERE?
YEAH, I'M--
ARROW?
W-WHAT--?!
NOT WHAT... WHO...

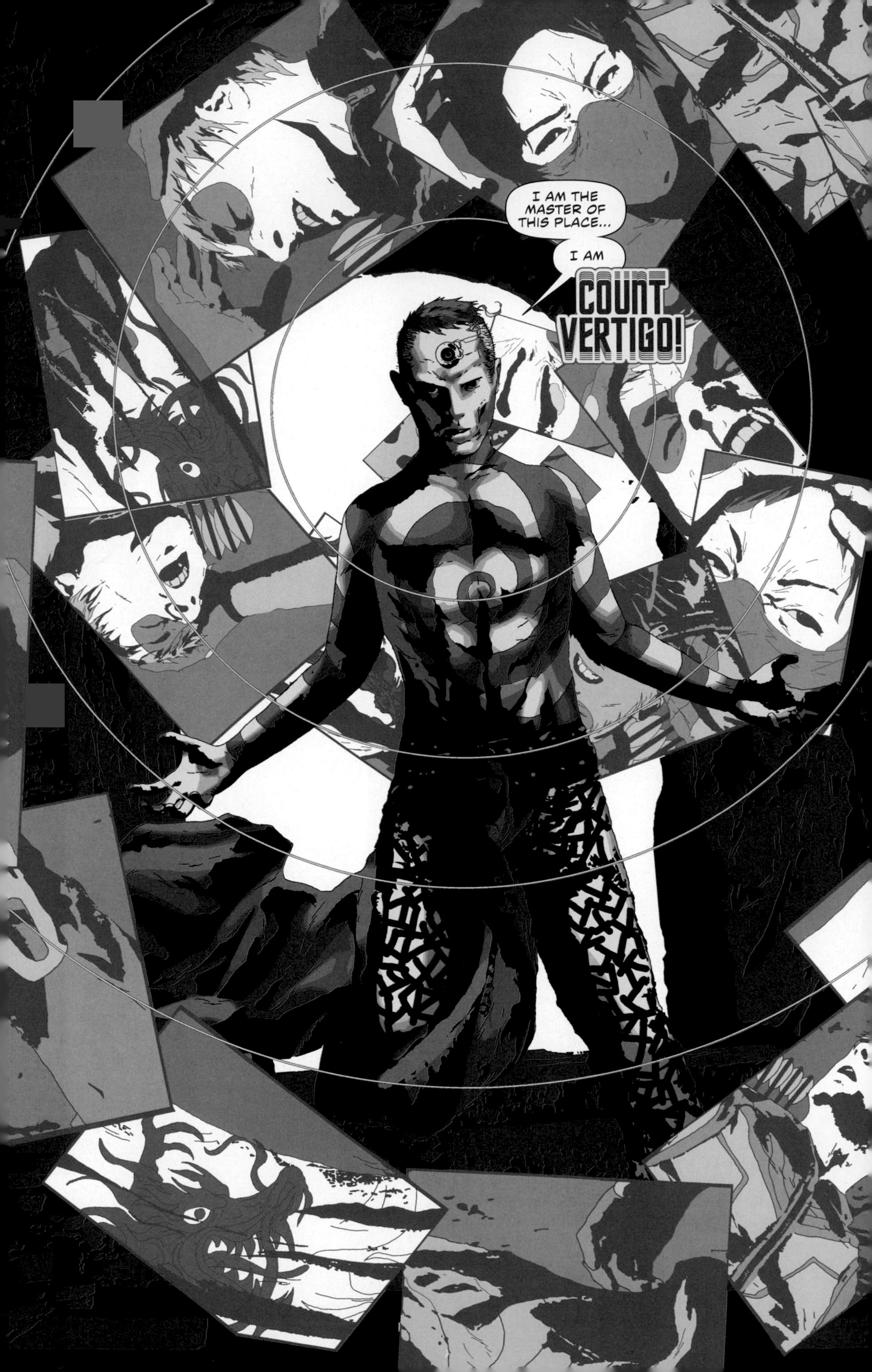
I AM THE MASTER OF THIS PLACE...
I AM
COUNT VERTIGO!

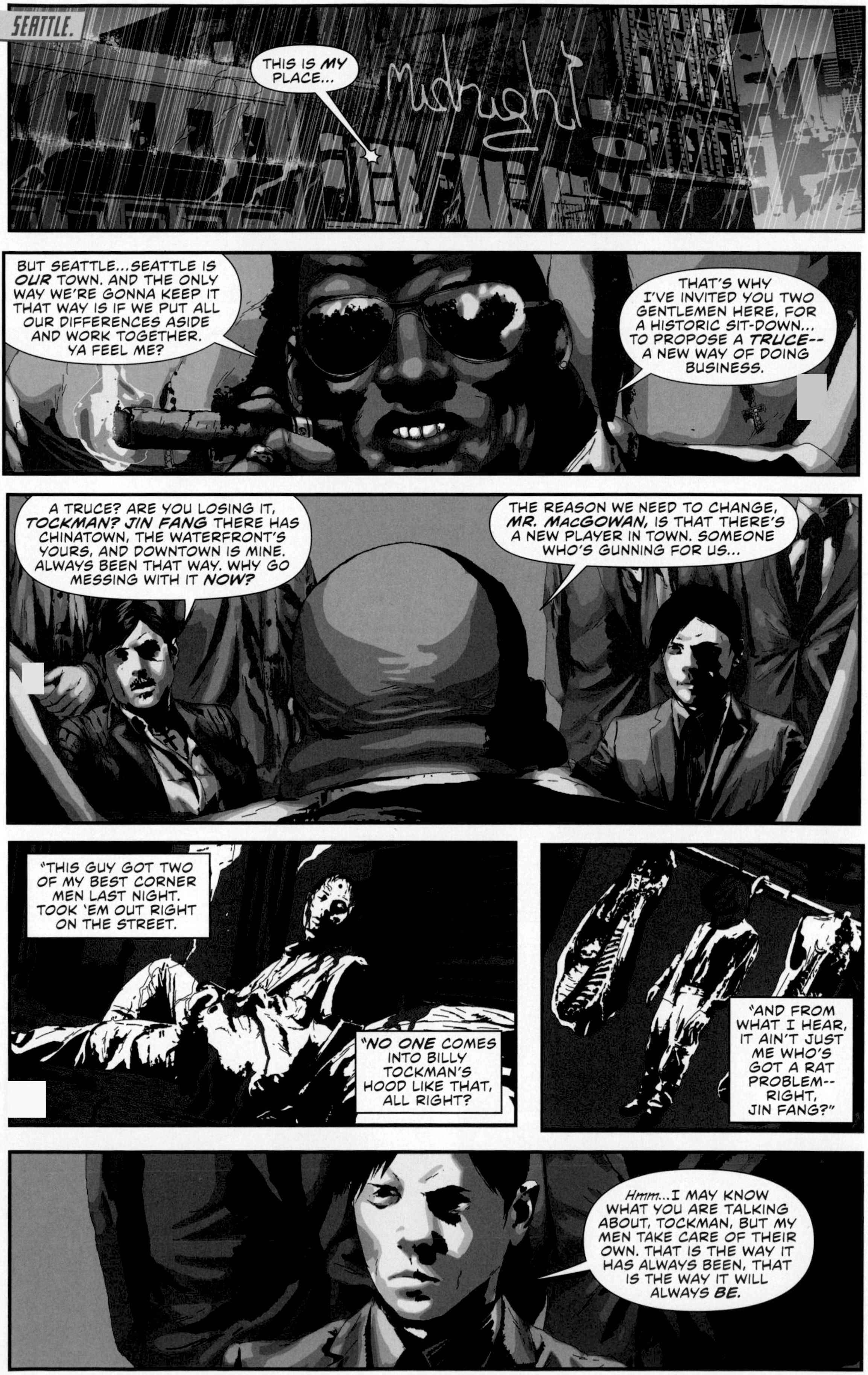
SEATTLE.
THIS IS MY PLACE...
midnight
BUT SEATTLE...SEATTLE IS OUR TOWN. AND THE ONLY WAY WE'RE GONNA KEEP IT THAT WAY IS IF WE PUT ALL OUR DIFFERENCES ASIDE AND WORK TOGETHER. YA FEEL ME?
THAT'S WHY I'VE INVITED YOU TWO GENTLEMEN HERE, FOR A HISTORIC SIT-DOWN... TO PROPOSE A TRUCE-- A NEW WAY OF DOING BUSINESS.
A TRUCE? ARE YOU LOSING IT, TOCKMAN? JIN FANG THERE HAS CHINATOWN, THE WATERFRONT'S YOURS, AND DOWNTOWN IS MINE. ALWAYS BEEN THAT WAY. WHY GO MESSING WITH IT NOW?
THE REASON WE NEED TO CHANGE, MR. MacGOWAN, IS THAT THERE'S A NEW PLAYER IN TOWN. SOMEONE WHO'S GUNNING FOR US...
"THIS GUY GOT TWO OF MY BEST CORNER MEN LAST NIGHT. TOOK 'EM OUT RIGHT ON THE STREET.
"NO ONE COMES INTO BILLY TOCKMAN'S HOOD LIKE THAT, ALL RIGHT?
"AND FROM WHAT I HEAR, IT AIN'T JUST ME WHO'S GOT A RAT PROBLEM-- RIGHT, JIN FANG?"
Hmm...I MAY KNOW WHAT YOU ARE TALKING ABOUT, TOCKMAN, BUT MY MEN TAKE CARE OF THEIR OWN. THAT IS THE WAY IT HAS ALWAYS BEEN, THAT IS THE WAY IT WILL ALWAYS BE.

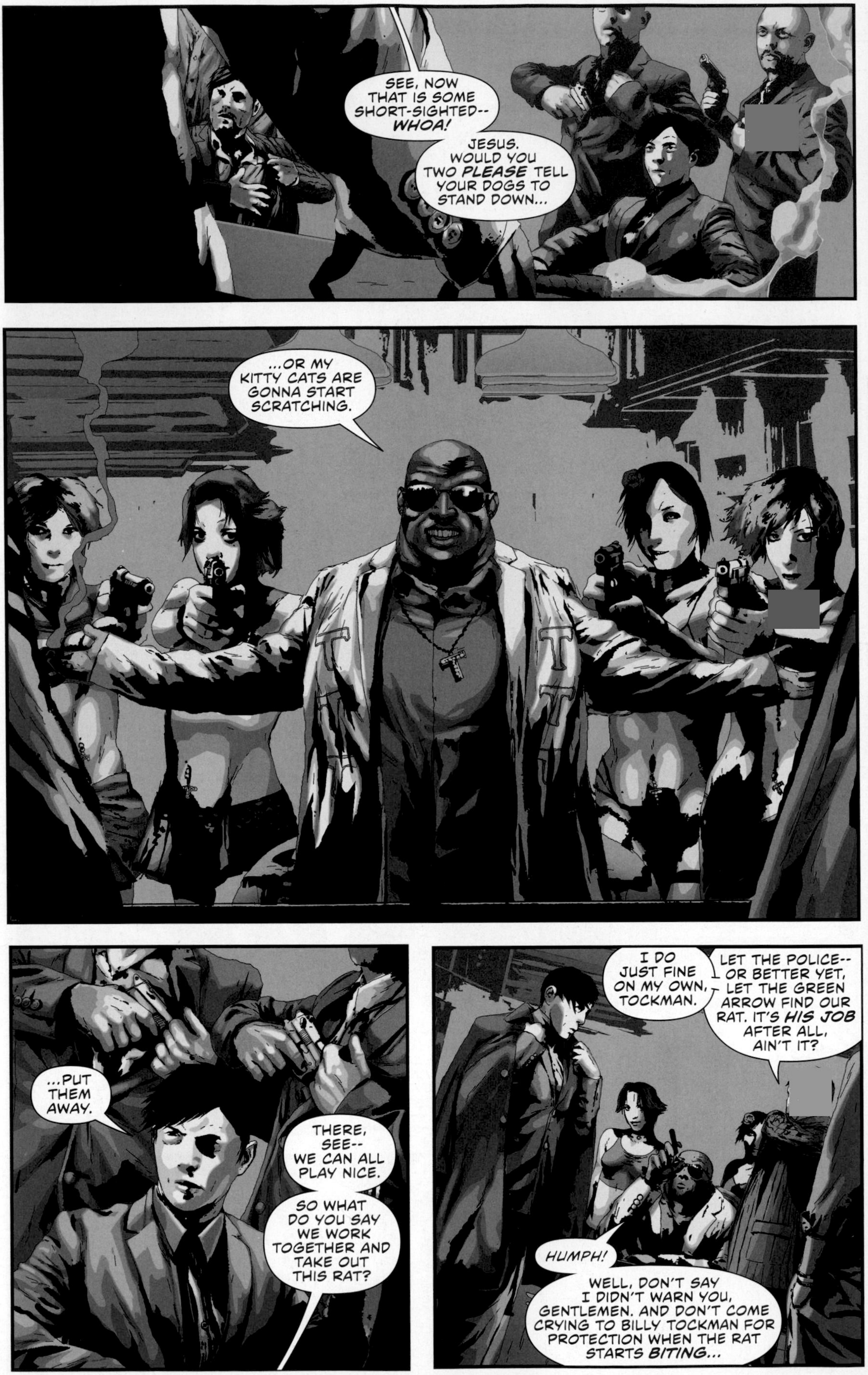
SEE, NOW THAT IS SOME SHORT-SIGHTED-- WHOA!
JESUS. WOULD YOU TWO PLEASE TELL YOUR DOGS TO STAND DOWN...
...OR MY KITTY CATS ARE GONNA START SCRATCHING.
...PUT THEM AWAY.
THERE, SEE-- WE CAN ALL PLAY NICE.
SO WHAT DO YOU SAY WE WORK TOGETHER AND TAKE OUT THIS RAT?
I DO JUST FINE ON MY OWN, TOCKMAN.
LET THE POLICE-- OR BETTER YET, LET THE GREEN ARROW FIND OUR RAT. IT'S HIS JOB AFTER ALL, AIN'T IT?
HUMPH!
WELL, DON'T SAY I DIDN'T WARN YOU, GENTLEMEN. AND DON'T COME CRYING TO BILLY TOCKMAN FOR PROTECTION WHEN THE RAT STARTS BITING...

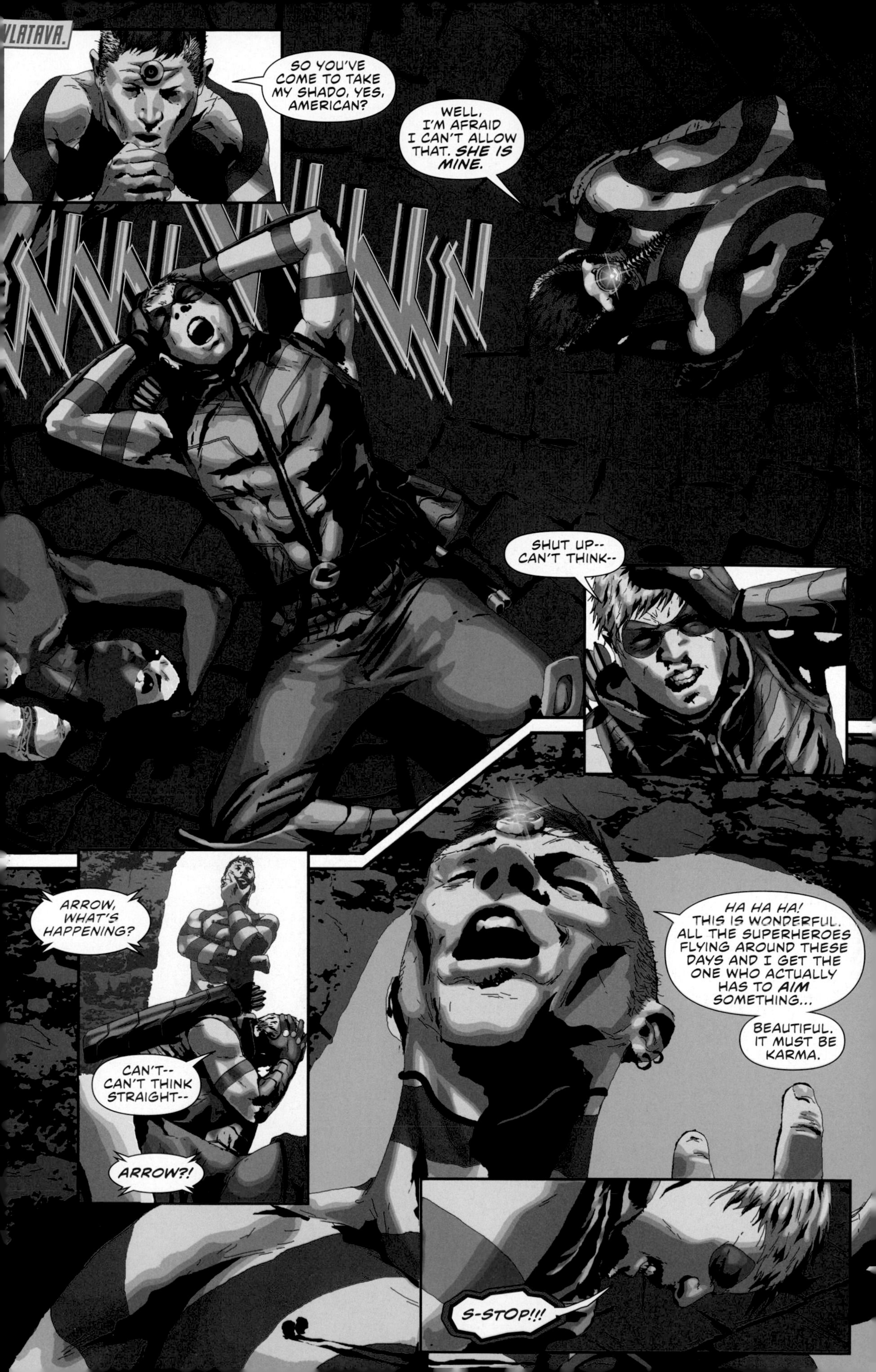
VLATAVA.
SO YOU'VE COME TO TAKE MY SHADO, YES, AMERICAN?
WELL, I'M AFRAID I CAN'T ALLOW THAT. SHE IS MINE.
SHUT UP-- CAN'T THINK--
ARROW, WHAT'S HAPPENING?
CAN'T-- CAN'T THINK STRAIGHT--
ARROW?!
HA HA HA! THIS IS WONDERFUL. ALL THE SUPERHEROES FLYING AROUND THESE DAYS AND I GET THE ONE WHO ACTUALLY HAS TO AIM SOMETHING...
BEAUTIFUL. IT MUST BE KARMA.
S-STOP!!!

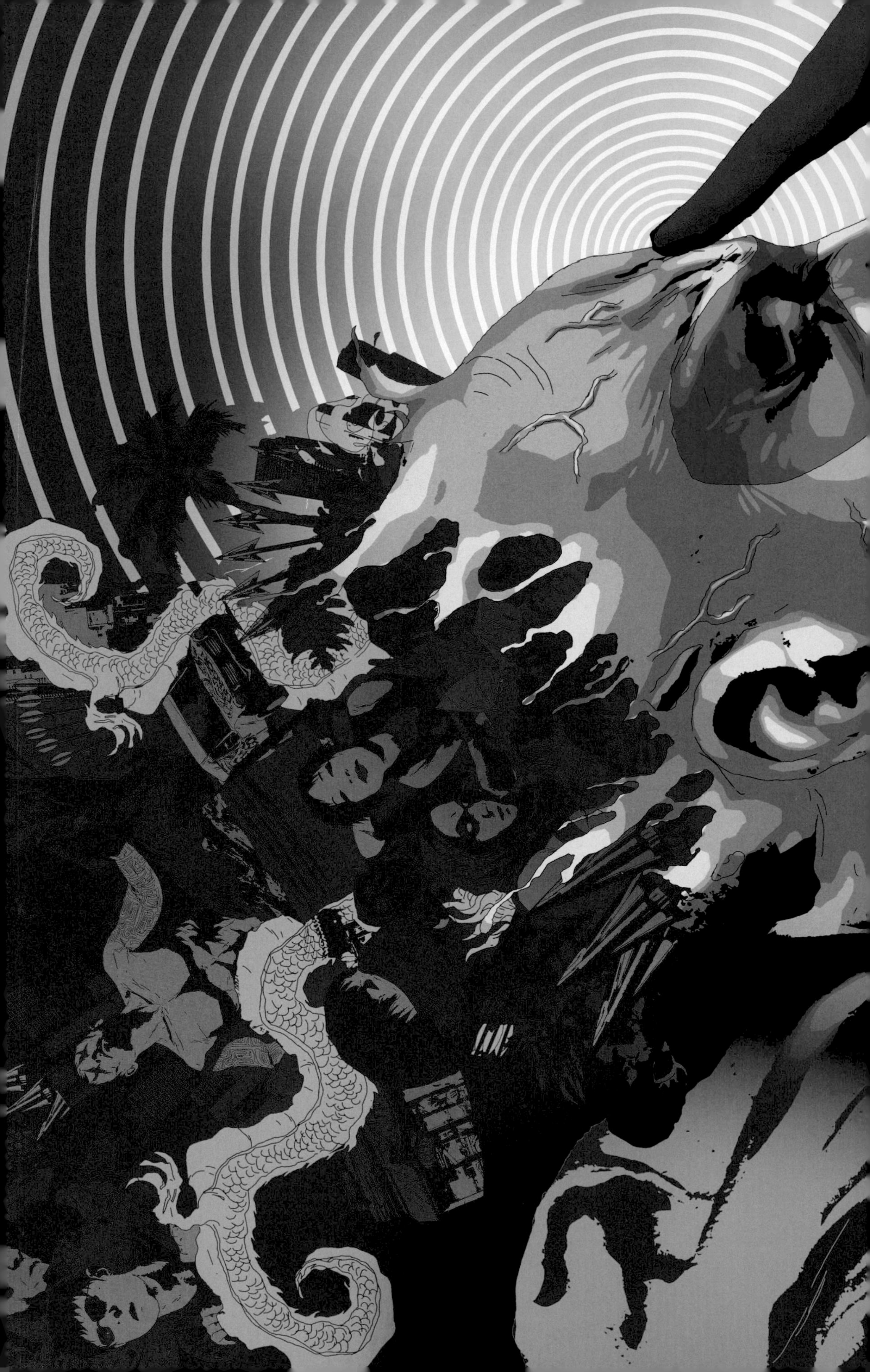

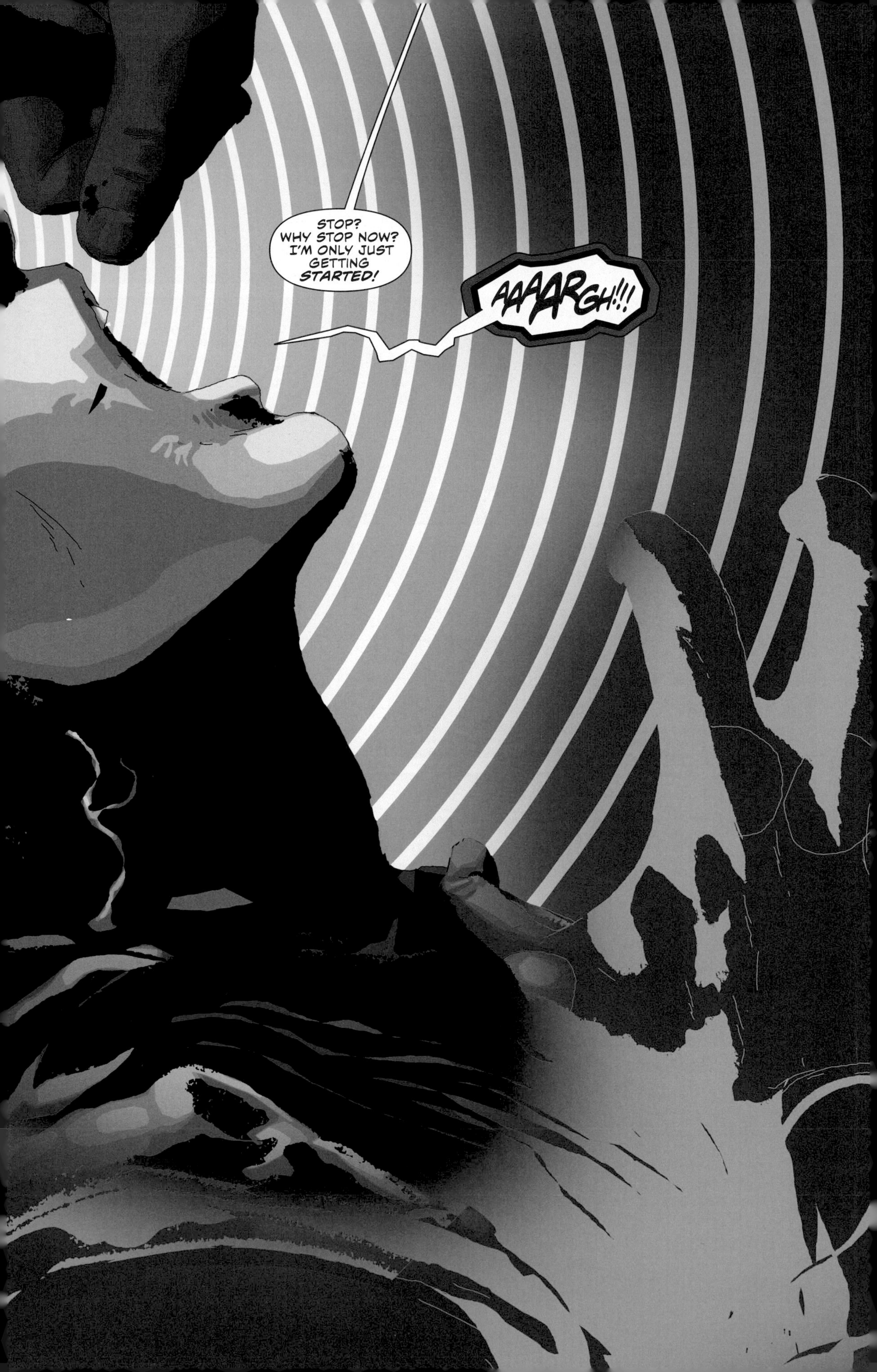
STOP? WHY STOP NOW? I'M ONLY JUST GETTING STARTED!
AAAAARGH!!!

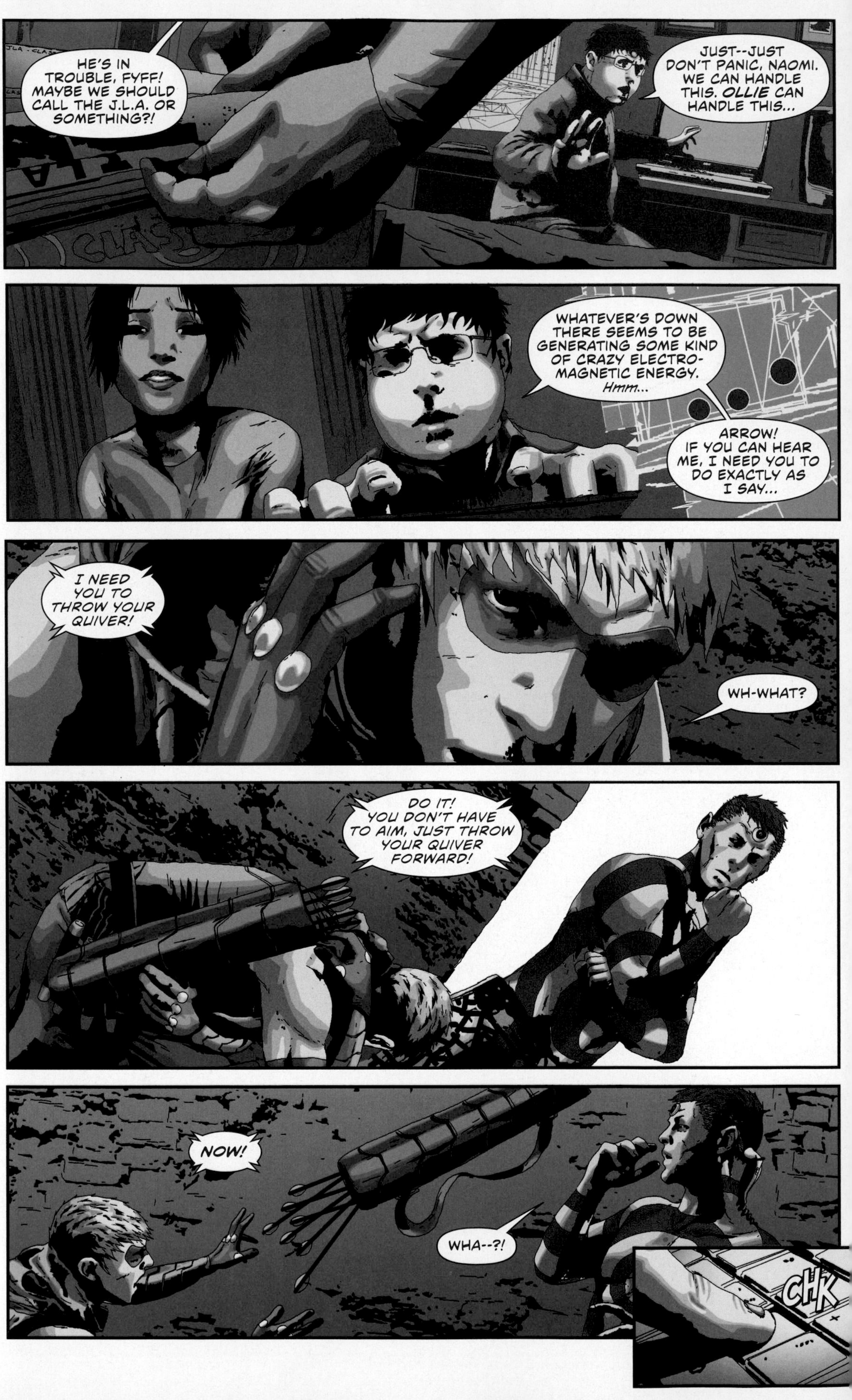
HE'S IN TROUBLE, FYFF! MAYBE WE SHOULD CALL THE J.L.A. OR SOMETHING?!
JUST--JUST DON'T PANIC, NAOMI. WE CAN HANDLE THIS. OLLIE CAN HANDLE THIS...
WHATEVER'S DOWN THERE SEEMS TO BE GENERATING SOME KIND OF CRAZY ELECTRO-MAGNETIC ENERGY. Hmm...
ARROW! IF YOU CAN HEAR ME, I NEED YOU TO DO EXACTLY AS I SAY...
I NEED YOU TO THROW YOUR QUIVER!
WH-WHAT?
DO IT! YOU DON'T HAVE TO AIM, JUST THROW YOUR QUIVER FORWARD!
NOW!
WHA--?!
CHK

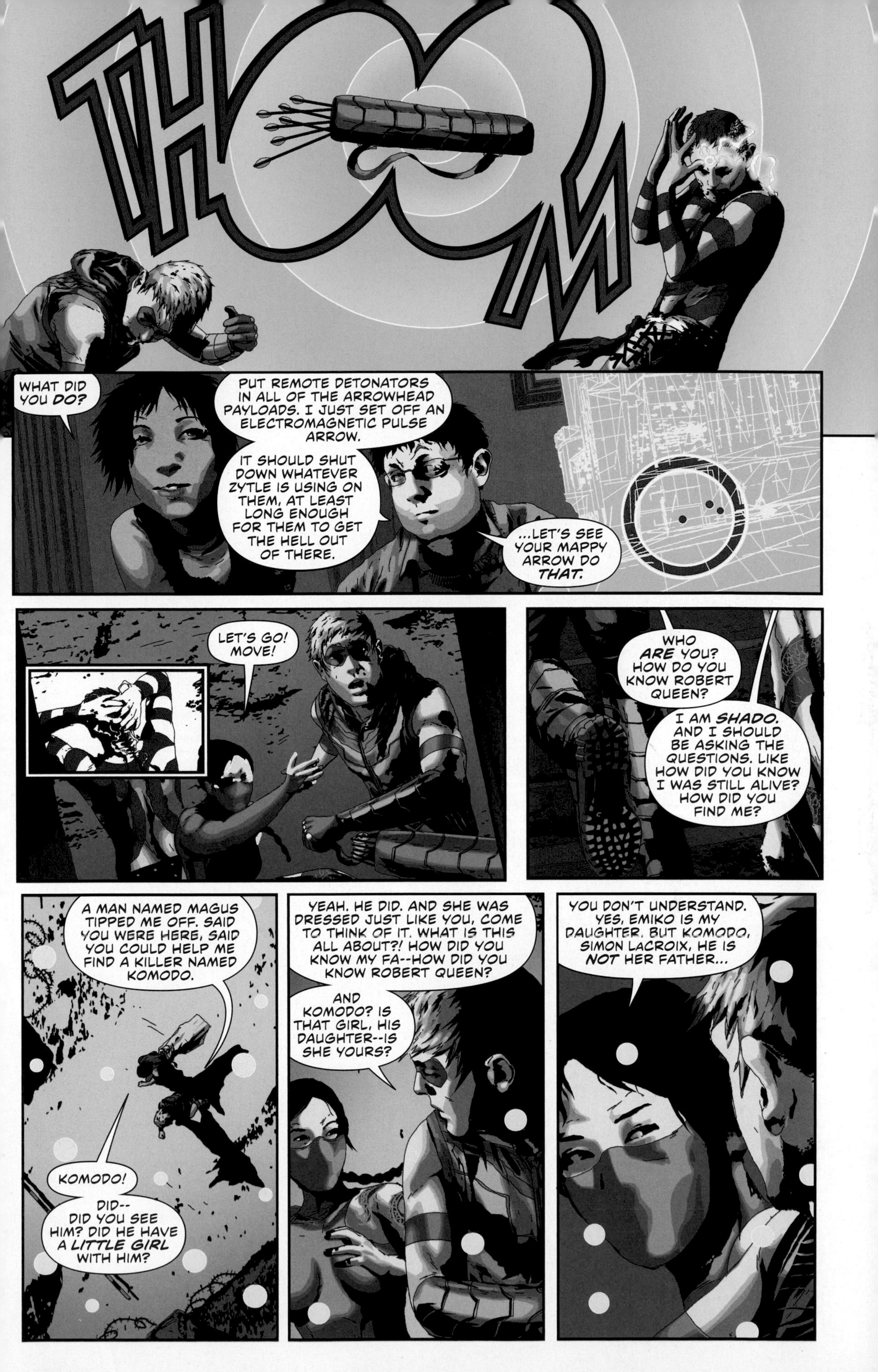
THOOM
WHAT DID YOU DO?
PUT REMOTE DETONATORS IN ALL OF THE ARROWHEAD PAYLOADS. I JUST SET OFF AN ELECTROMAGNETIC PULSE ARROW.
IT SHOULD SHUT DOWN WHATEVER ZYTLE IS USING ON THEM, AT LEAST LONG ENOUGH FOR THEM TO GET THE HELL OUT OF THERE.
...LET'S SEE YOUR MAPPY ARROW DO THAT.
LET'S GO! MOVE!
WHO ARE YOU? HOW DO YOU KNOW ROBERT QUEEN?
I AM SHADO. AND I SHOULD BE ASKING THE QUESTIONS. LIKE HOW DID YOU KNOW I WAS STILL ALIVE? HOW DID YOU FIND ME?
A MAN NAMED MAGUS TIPPED ME OFF. SAID YOU WERE HERE, SAID YOU COULD HELP ME FIND A KILLER NAMED KOMODO.
KOMODO!
DID-- DID YOU SEE HIM? DID HE HAVE A LITTLE GIRL WITH HIM?
YEAH. HE DID. AND SHE WAS DRESSED JUST LIKE YOU, COME TO THINK OF IT. WHAT IS THIS ALL ABOUT?! HOW DID YOU KNOW MY FA--HOW DID YOU KNOW ROBERT QUEEN?
AND KOMODO? IS THAT GIRL, HIS DAUGHTER--IS SHE YOURS?
YOU DON'T UNDERSTAND. YES, EMIKO IS MY DAUGHTER. BUT KOMODO, SIMON LACROIX, HE IS NOT HER FATHER...

ROBERT QUEEN IS EMIKO'S FATHER...
SHE IS YOUR SISTER.
SHADOS
PART 1 of 2

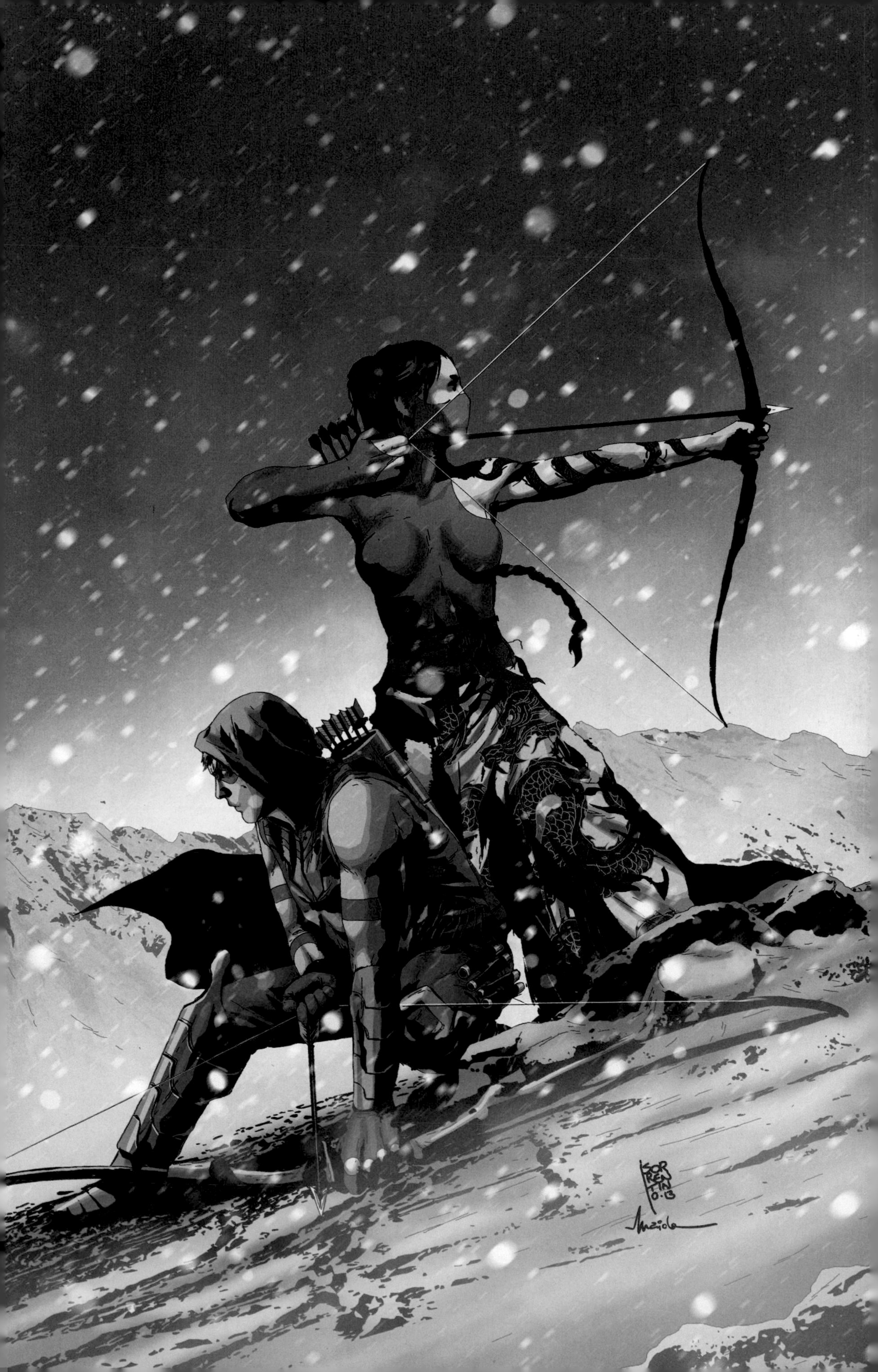

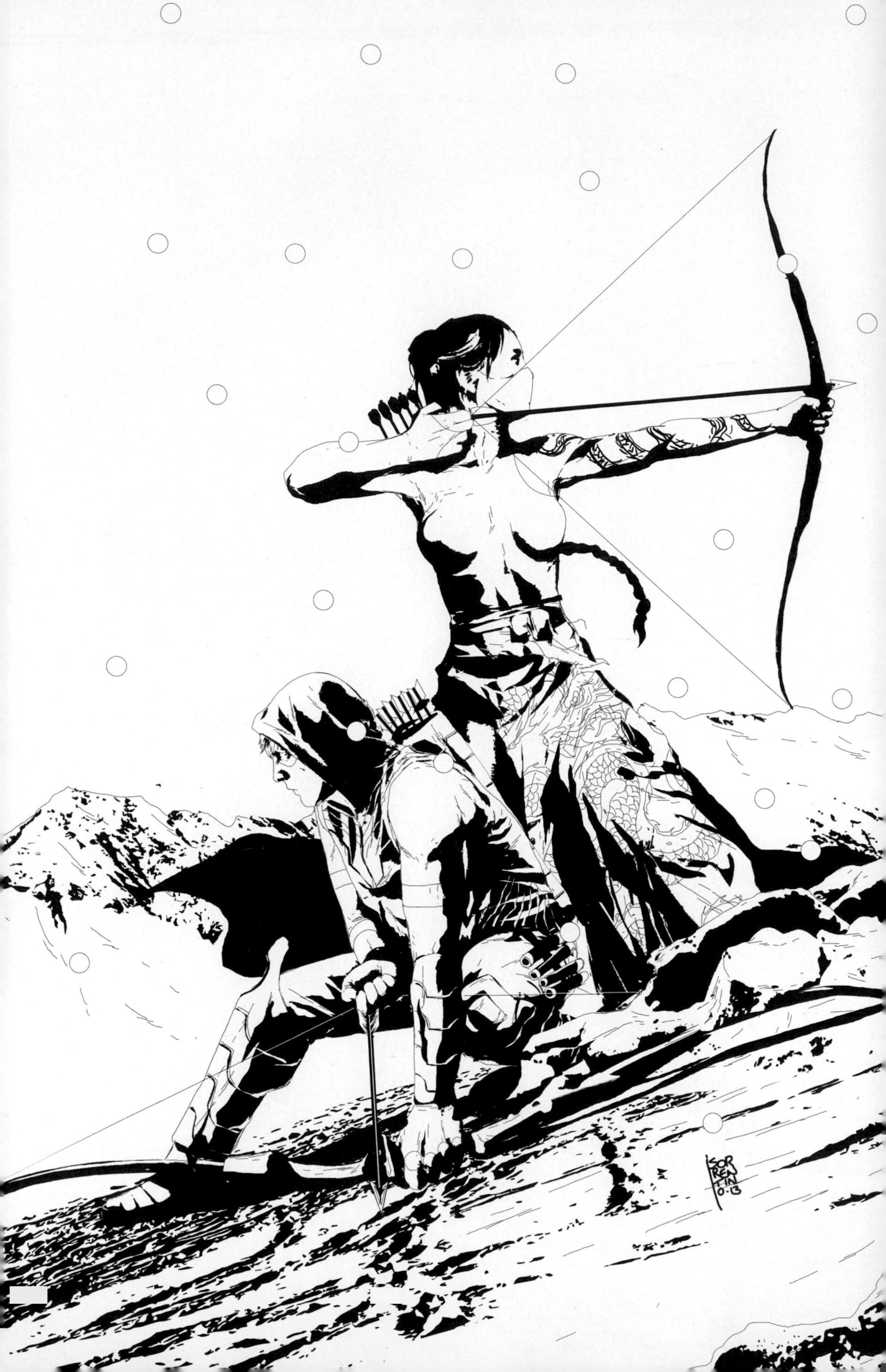

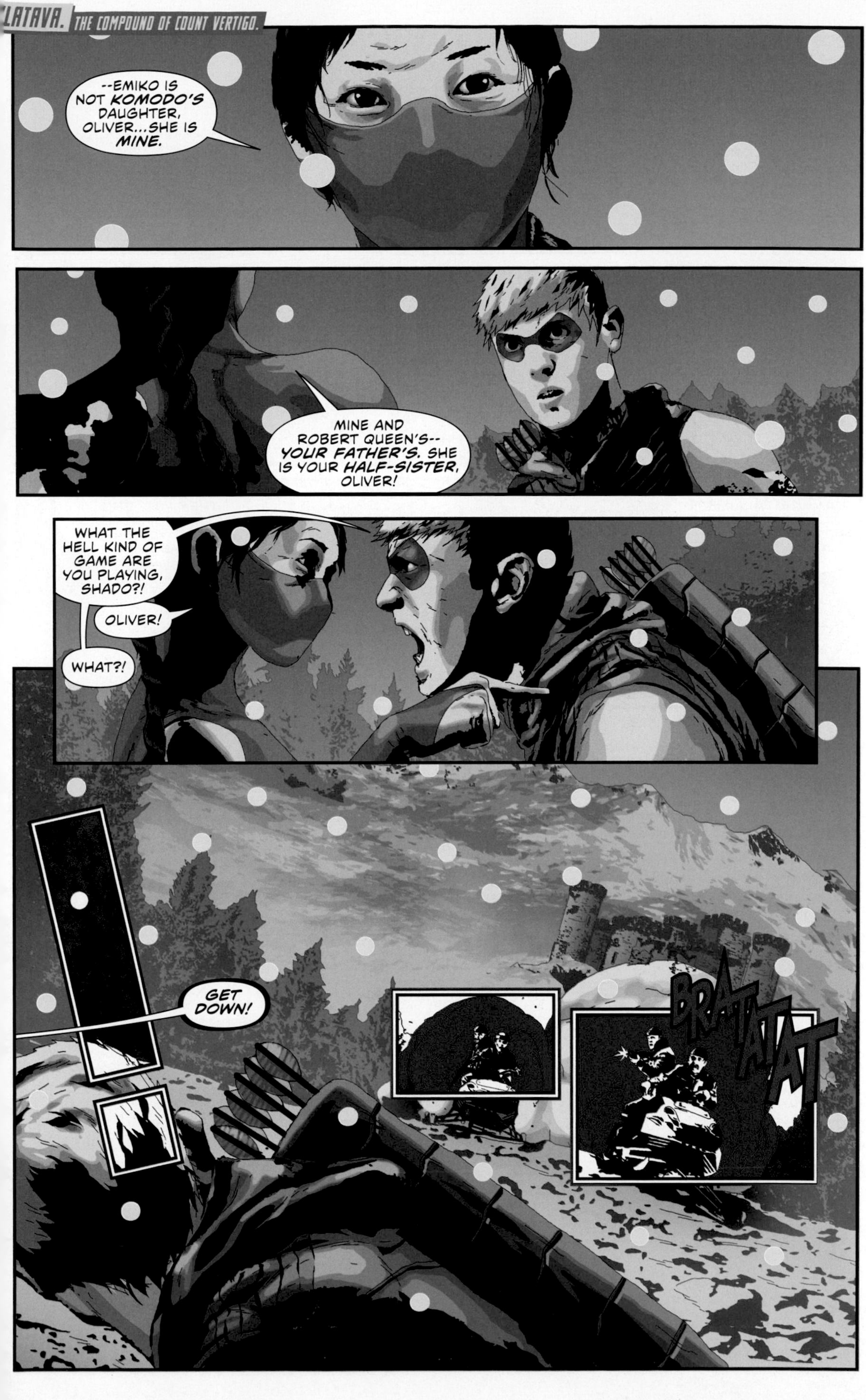
LATAVA. THE COMPOUND OF COUNT VERTIGO.
--EMIKO IS NOT KOMODO'S DAUGHTER, OLIVER...SHE IS MINE.
MINE AND ROBERT QUEEN'S-- YOUR FATHER'S. SHE IS YOUR HALF-SISTER, OLIVER!
WHAT THE HELL KIND OF GAME ARE YOU PLAYING, SHADO?!
OLIVER!
WHAT?!
GET DOWN!
BRATATAT

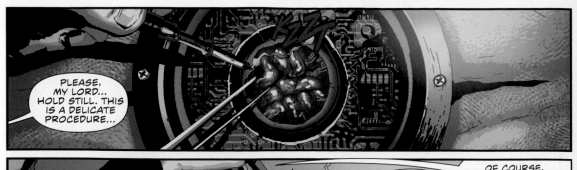

PLEASE, MY LORD... HOLD STILL. THIS IS A DELICATE PROCEDURE...

YES, I *KNOW* IT IS DELICATE... IT'S *MY DAMNED HEAD!* JUST HURRY UP.

OF COURSE, *COUNT VERTIGO.* BUT YOU SEE, THE INTRUDER'S ARROW EMITTED SOME SORT OF CONCENTRATED ELECTROMAGNETIC BURST.

IT HAS SEVERELY DAMAGED A NUMBER OF CIRCUITS IN YOUR IMPLANT. IT WILL TAKE A BIT OF TIME TO CORRECT.

HAVE MY MEN CAUGHT THEM YET? THIS AMERICAN SUPER-HERO... WHAT DID YOU SAY HIS NAME WAS?

I BELIEVE IT IS *GREEN ARROW,* MY LORD. AND I HAVE DISPATCHED THE REST OF YOUR SECURITY UNIT AS YOU ORDERED. I'M SURE IT'S ONLY A MATTER OF TIME UNTIL THEY ARE RECAPTURED.

NO! I'M GOING AFTER THEM MYSELF. *NO ONE* COMES TO *MY COUNTRY* AND STEALS FROM ME!

BUT, MY LORD, I STILL NEED TO CALIBRATE THE IMPLANT! AS IS, YOU WON'T BE ABLE TO PROPERLY CONTROL--

LATER! I CAN'T LET THEM GET OUT OF VLATAVA!

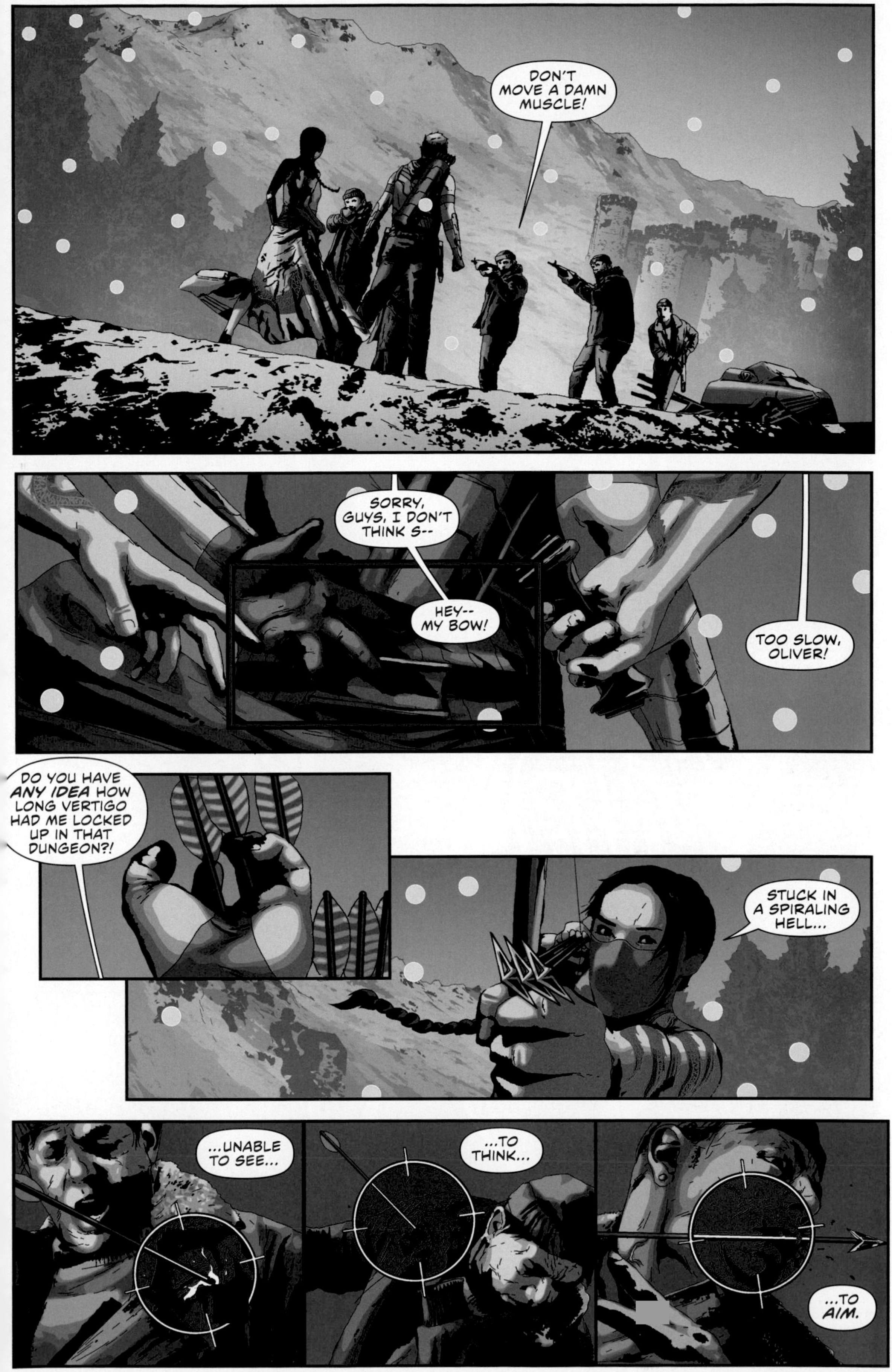
DON'T MOVE A DAMN MUSCLE!
SORRY, GUYS, I DON'T THINK S--
HEY-- MY BOW!
TOO SLOW, OLIVER!
DO YOU HAVE *ANY IDEA* HOW LONG VERTIGO HAD ME LOCKED UP IN THAT DUNGEON?!
STUCK IN A SPIRALING HELL...
...UNABLE TO SEE...
...TO THINK...
...TO *AIM.*

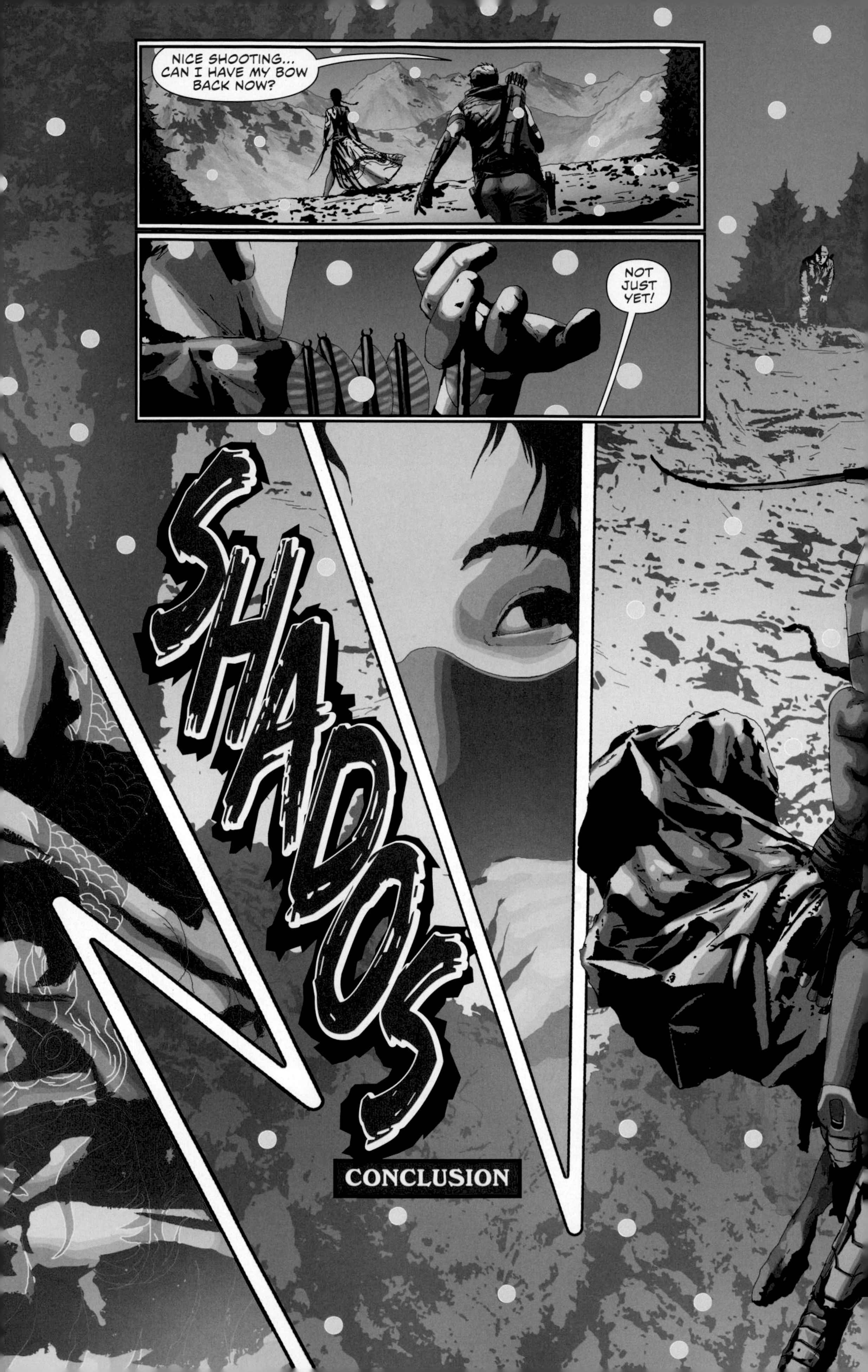
NICE SHOOTING... CAN I HAVE MY BOW BACK NOW?
NOT JUST YET!
SHADO'S
CONCLUSION

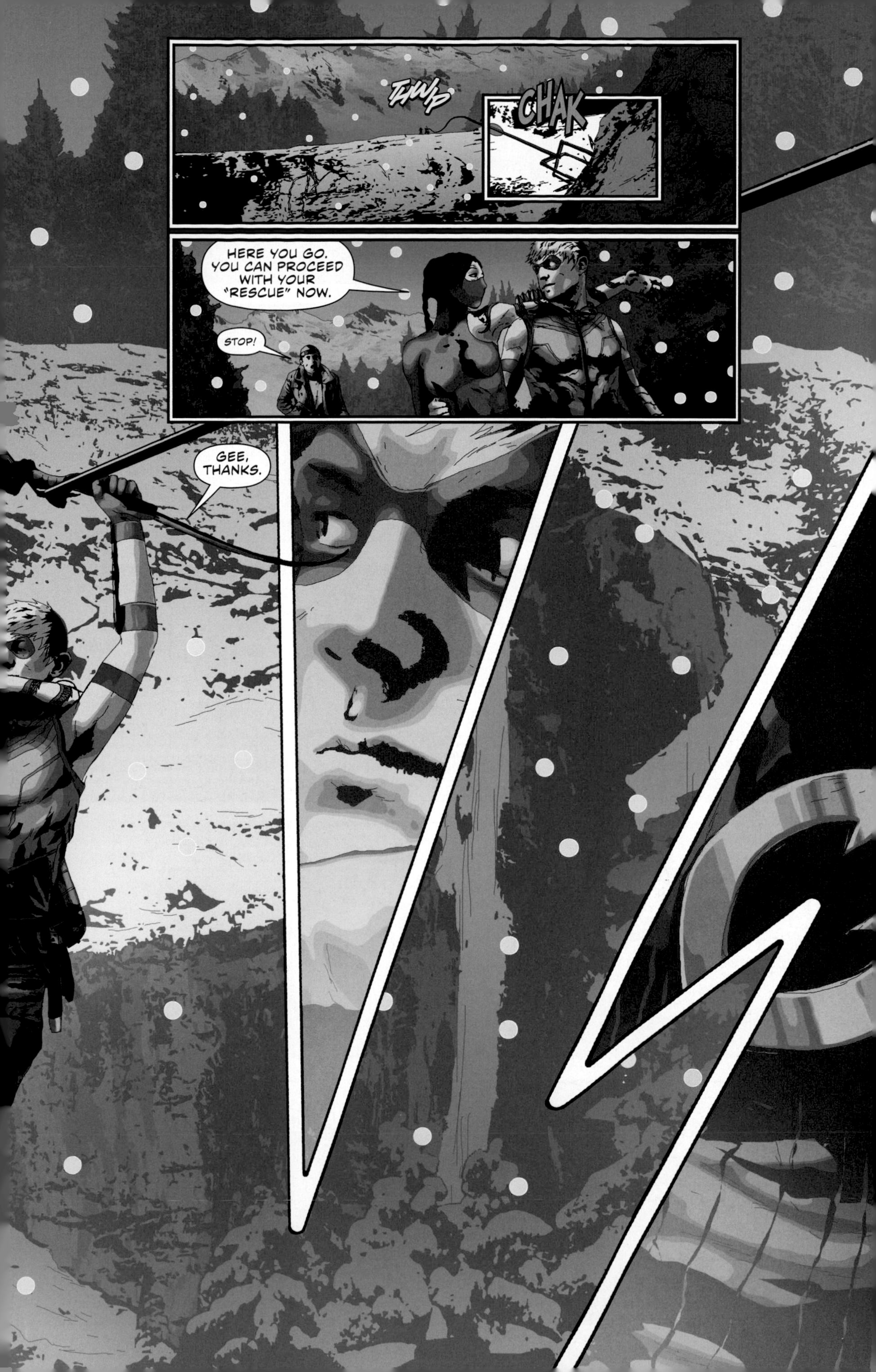
TWIP
CHAK
HERE YOU GO. YOU CAN PROCEED WITH YOUR "RESCUE" NOW.
STOP!
GEE, THANKS.

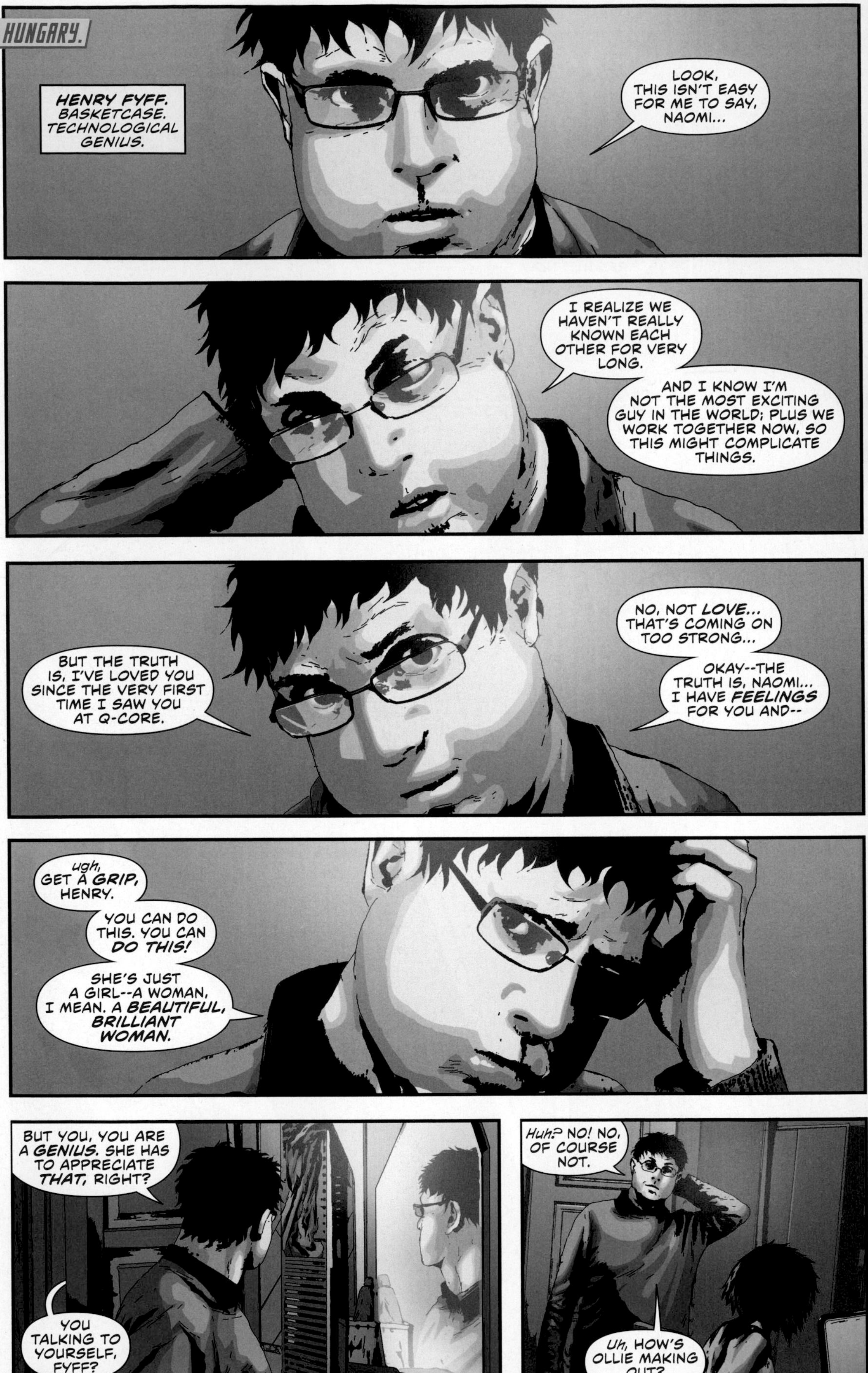
HUNGARY.
HENRY FYFF. BASKETCASE. TECHNOLOGICAL GENIUS.
LOOK, THIS ISN'T EASY FOR ME TO SAY, NAOMI...
I REALIZE WE HAVEN'T REALLY KNOWN EACH OTHER FOR VERY LONG.
AND I KNOW I'M NOT THE MOST EXCITING GUY IN THE WORLD; PLUS WE WORK TOGETHER NOW, SO THIS MIGHT COMPLICATE THINGS.
BUT THE TRUTH IS, I'VE LOVED YOU SINCE THE VERY FIRST TIME I SAW YOU AT Q-CORE.
NO, NOT LOVE... THAT'S COMING ON TOO STRONG...
OKAY--THE TRUTH IS, NAOMI... I HAVE FEELINGS FOR YOU AND--
ugh, GET A GRIP, HENRY.
YOU CAN DO THIS. YOU CAN DO THIS!
SHE'S JUST A GIRL--A WOMAN, I MEAN. A BEAUTIFUL, BRILLIANT WOMAN.
BUT YOU, YOU ARE A GENIUS. SHE HAS TO APPRECIATE THAT, RIGHT?
YOU TALKING TO YOURSELF, FYFF?
Huh? NO! NO, OF COURSE NOT.
Uh, HOW'S OLLIE MAKING OUT?

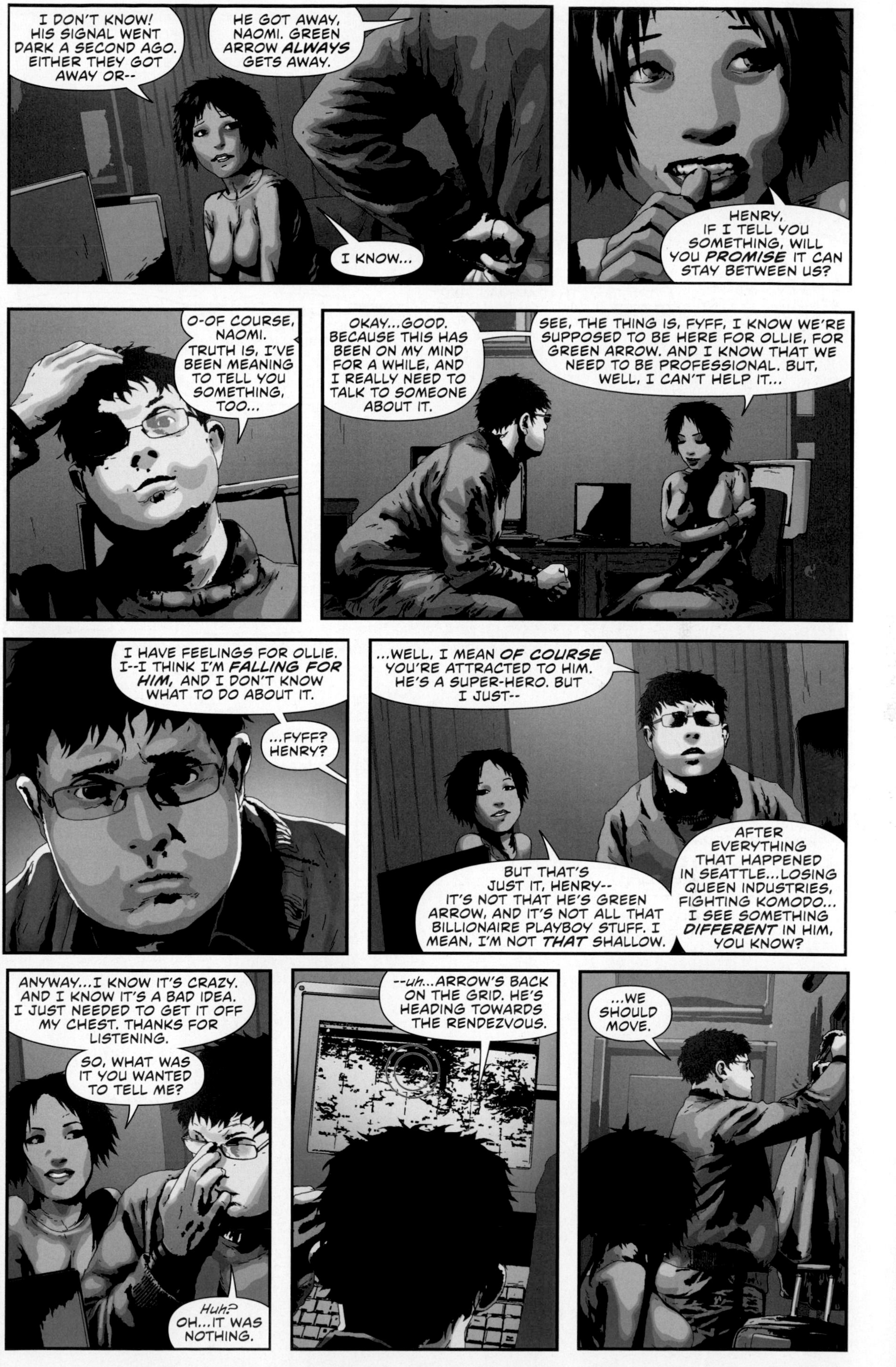
I DON'T KNOW! HIS SIGNAL WENT DARK A SECOND AGO. EITHER THEY GOT AWAY OR--
HE GOT AWAY, NAOMI. GREEN ARROW *ALWAYS* GETS AWAY.
I KNOW...
HENRY, IF I TELL YOU SOMETHING, WILL YOU *PROMISE* IT CAN STAY BETWEEN US?
O-OF COURSE, NAOMI. TRUTH IS, I'VE BEEN MEANING TO TELL YOU SOMETHING, TOO...
OKAY...GOOD. BECAUSE THIS HAS BEEN ON MY MIND FOR A WHILE, AND I REALLY NEED TO TALK TO SOMEONE ABOUT IT.
SEE, THE THING IS, FYFF, I KNOW WE'RE SUPPOSED TO BE HERE FOR OLLIE, FOR GREEN ARROW. AND I KNOW THAT WE NEED TO BE PROFESSIONAL. BUT, WELL, I CAN'T HELP IT...
I HAVE FEELINGS FOR OLLIE. I--I THINK I'M *FALLING FOR HIM,* AND I DON'T KNOW WHAT TO DO ABOUT IT.
...FYFF? HENRY?
...WELL, I MEAN *OF COURSE* YOU'RE ATTRACTED TO HIM. HE'S A SUPER-HERO. BUT I JUST--
BUT THAT'S JUST IT, HENRY-- IT'S NOT THAT HE'S GREEN ARROW, AND IT'S NOT ALL THAT BILLIONAIRE PLAYBOY STUFF. I MEAN, I'M NOT *THAT* SHALLOW.
AFTER EVERYTHING THAT HAPPENED IN SEATTLE...LOSING QUEEN INDUSTRIES, FIGHTING KOMODO... I SEE SOMETHING *DIFFERENT* IN HIM, YOU KNOW?
ANYWAY...I KNOW IT'S CRAZY. AND I KNOW IT'S A BAD IDEA. I JUST NEEDED TO GET IT OFF MY CHEST. THANKS FOR LISTENING.
SO, WHAT WAS IT YOU WANTED TO TELL ME?
Huh? OH...IT WAS NOTHING.
--*uh*...ARROW'S BACK ON THE GRID. HE'S HEADING TOWARDS THE RENDEZVOUS.
...WE SHOULD MOVE.

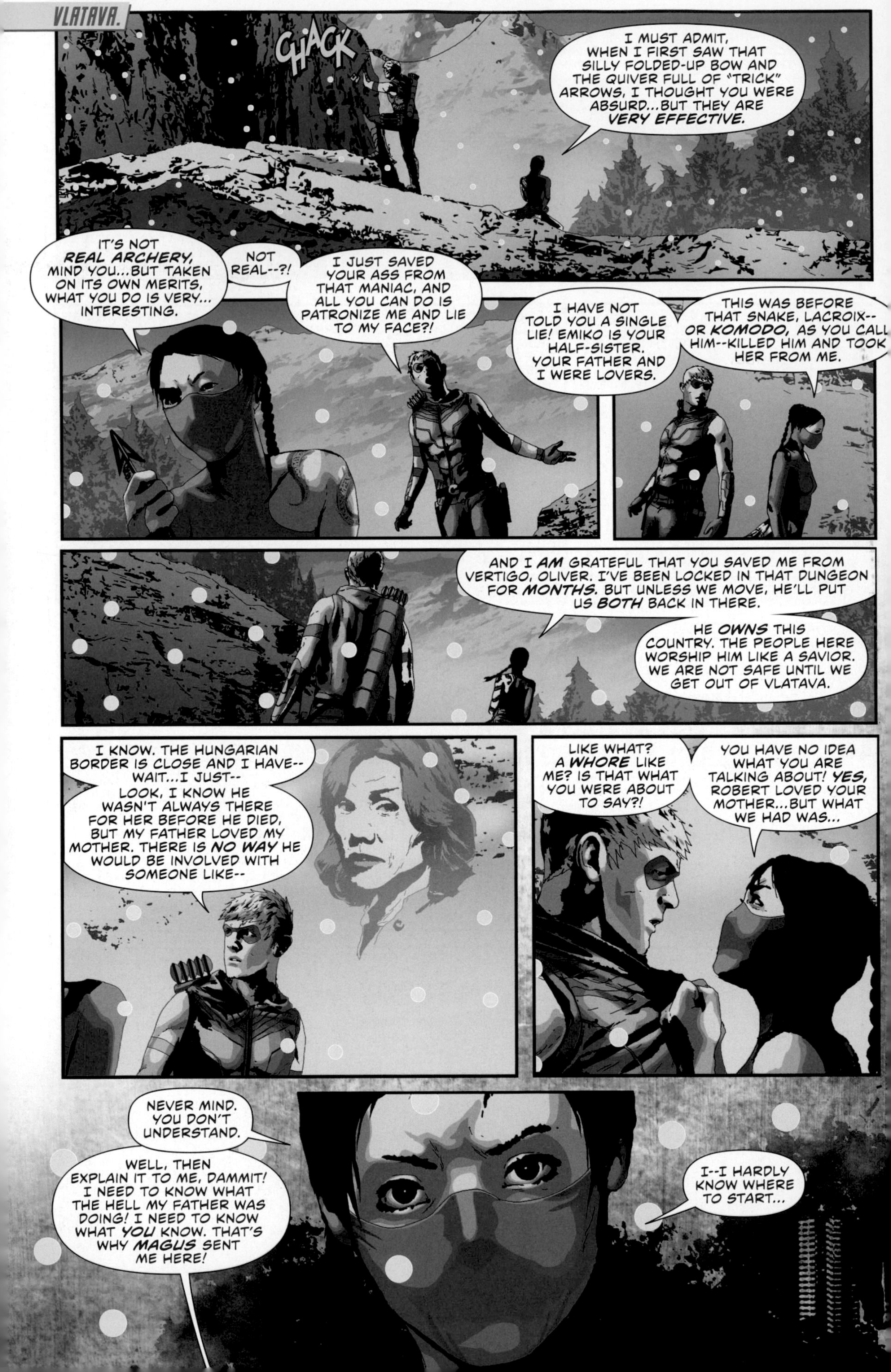
VLATAVA.
CHACK
I MUST ADMIT, WHEN I FIRST SAW THAT SILLY FOLDED-UP BOW AND THE QUIVER FULL OF "TRICK" ARROWS, I THOUGHT YOU WERE ABSURD...BUT THEY ARE VERY EFFECTIVE.
IT'S NOT REAL ARCHERY, MIND YOU...BUT TAKEN ON ITS OWN MERITS, WHAT YOU DO IS VERY... INTERESTING.
NOT REAL--?!
I JUST SAVED YOUR ASS FROM THAT MANIAC, AND ALL YOU CAN DO IS PATRONIZE ME AND LIE TO MY FACE?!
I HAVE NOT TOLD YOU A SINGLE LIE! EMIKO IS YOUR HALF-SISTER. YOUR FATHER AND I WERE LOVERS.
THIS WAS BEFORE THAT SNAKE, LACROIX--OR KOMODO, AS YOU CALL HIM--KILLED HIM AND TOOK HER FROM ME.
AND I AM GRATEFUL THAT YOU SAVED ME FROM VERTIGO, OLIVER. I'VE BEEN LOCKED IN THAT DUNGEON FOR MONTHS. BUT UNLESS WE MOVE, HE'LL PUT US BOTH BACK IN THERE.
HE OWNS THIS COUNTRY. THE PEOPLE HERE WORSHIP HIM LIKE A SAVIOR. WE ARE NOT SAFE UNTIL WE GET OUT OF VLATAVA.
I KNOW. THE HUNGARIAN BORDER IS CLOSE AND I HAVE-- WAIT...I JUST--
LOOK, I KNOW HE WASN'T ALWAYS THERE FOR HER BEFORE HE DIED, BUT MY FATHER LOVED MY MOTHER. THERE IS NO WAY HE WOULD BE INVOLVED WITH SOMEONE LIKE--
LIKE WHAT? A WHORE LIKE ME? IS THAT WHAT YOU WERE ABOUT TO SAY?!
YOU HAVE NO IDEA WHAT YOU ARE TALKING ABOUT! YES, ROBERT LOVED YOUR MOTHER...BUT WHAT WE HAD WAS...
NEVER MIND. YOU DON'T UNDERSTAND.
WELL, THEN EXPLAIN IT TO ME, DAMMIT! I NEED TO KNOW WHAT THE HELL MY FATHER WAS DOING! I NEED TO KNOW WHAT YOU KNOW. THAT'S WHY MAGUS SENT ME HERE!
I--I HARDLY KNOW WHERE TO START...

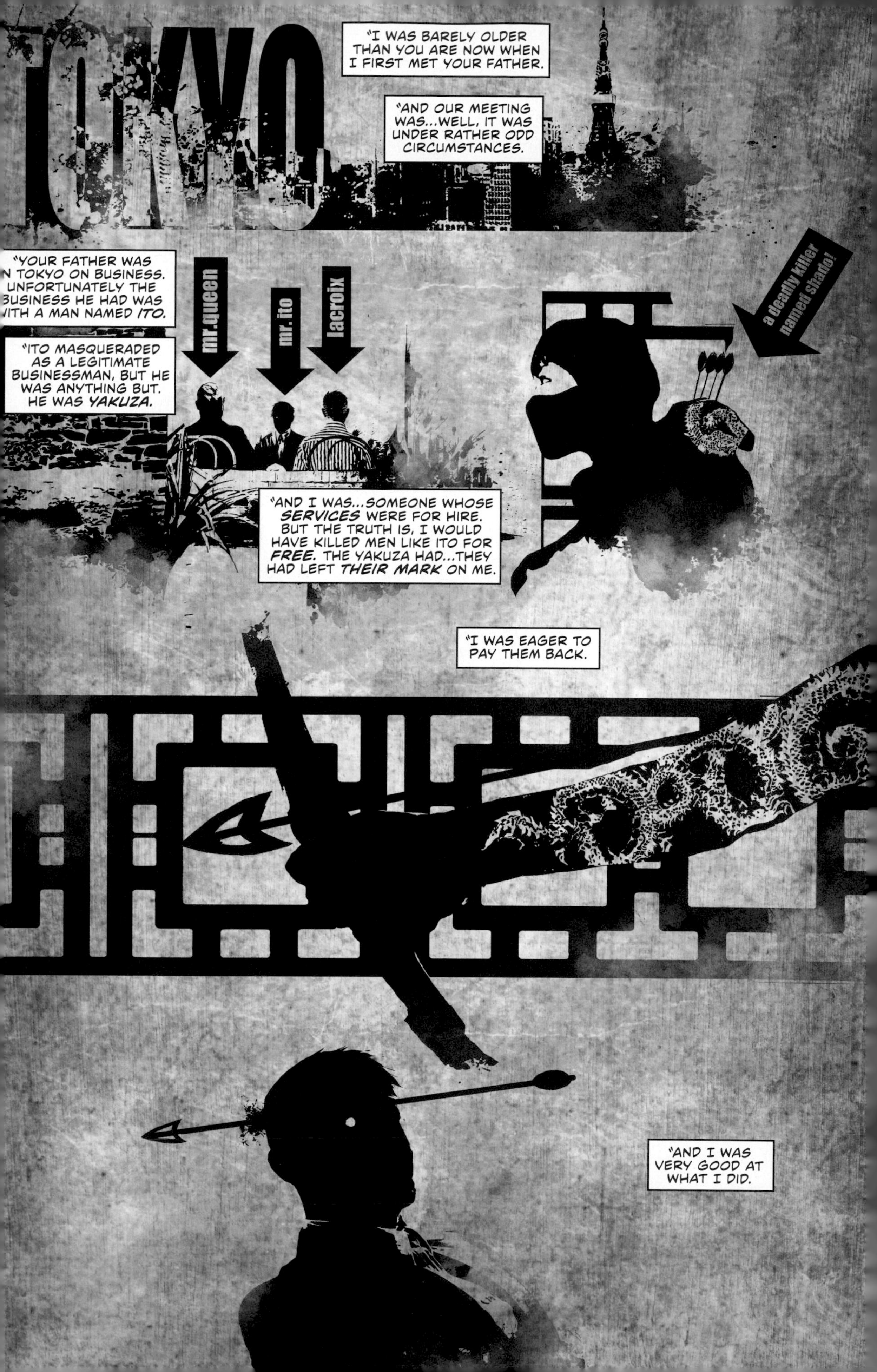
TOKYO
"I WAS BARELY OLDER THAN YOU ARE NOW WHEN I FIRST MET YOUR FATHER.
"AND OUR MEETING WAS...WELL, IT WAS UNDER RATHER ODD CIRCUMSTANCES.
"YOUR FATHER WAS IN TOKYO ON BUSINESS. UNFORTUNATELY THE BUSINESS HE HAD WAS WITH A MAN NAMED ITO.
mr.queen
mr.ito
lacroix
a deadly killer named shado!
"ITO MASQUERADED AS A LEGITIMATE BUSINESSMAN, BUT HE WAS ANYTHING BUT. HE WAS YAKUZA.
"AND I WAS...SOMEONE WHOSE SERVICES WERE FOR HIRE. BUT THE TRUTH IS, I WOULD HAVE KILLED MEN LIKE ITO FOR FREE. THE YAKUZA HAD...THEY HAD LEFT THEIR MARK ON ME.
"I WAS EAGER TO PAY THEM BACK.
"AND I WAS VERY GOOD AT WHAT I DID.

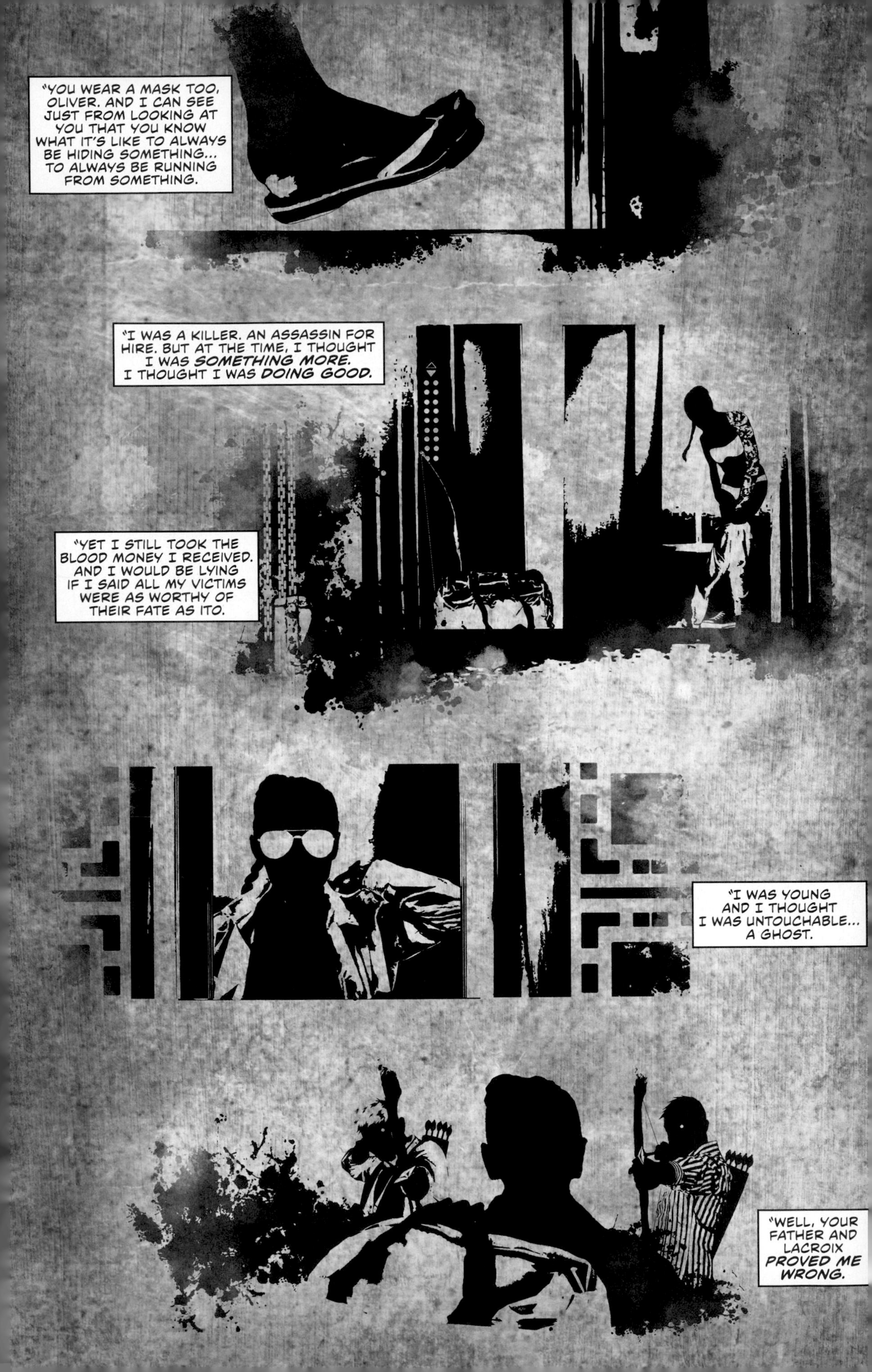
"YOU WEAR A MASK TOO, OLIVER. AND I CAN SEE JUST FROM LOOKING AT YOU THAT YOU KNOW WHAT IT'S LIKE TO ALWAYS BE HIDING SOMETHING... TO ALWAYS BE RUNNING FROM SOMETHING.
"I WAS A KILLER. AN ASSASSIN FOR HIRE. BUT AT THE TIME, I THOUGHT I WAS SOMETHING MORE. I THOUGHT I WAS DOING GOOD.
"YET I STILL TOOK THE BLOOD MONEY I RECEIVED. AND I WOULD BE LYING IF I SAID ALL MY VICTIMS WERE AS WORTHY OF THEIR FATE AS ITO.
"I WAS YOUNG AND I THOUGHT I WAS UNTOUCHABLE... A GHOST.
"WELL, YOUR FATHER AND LACROIX PROVED ME WRONG.

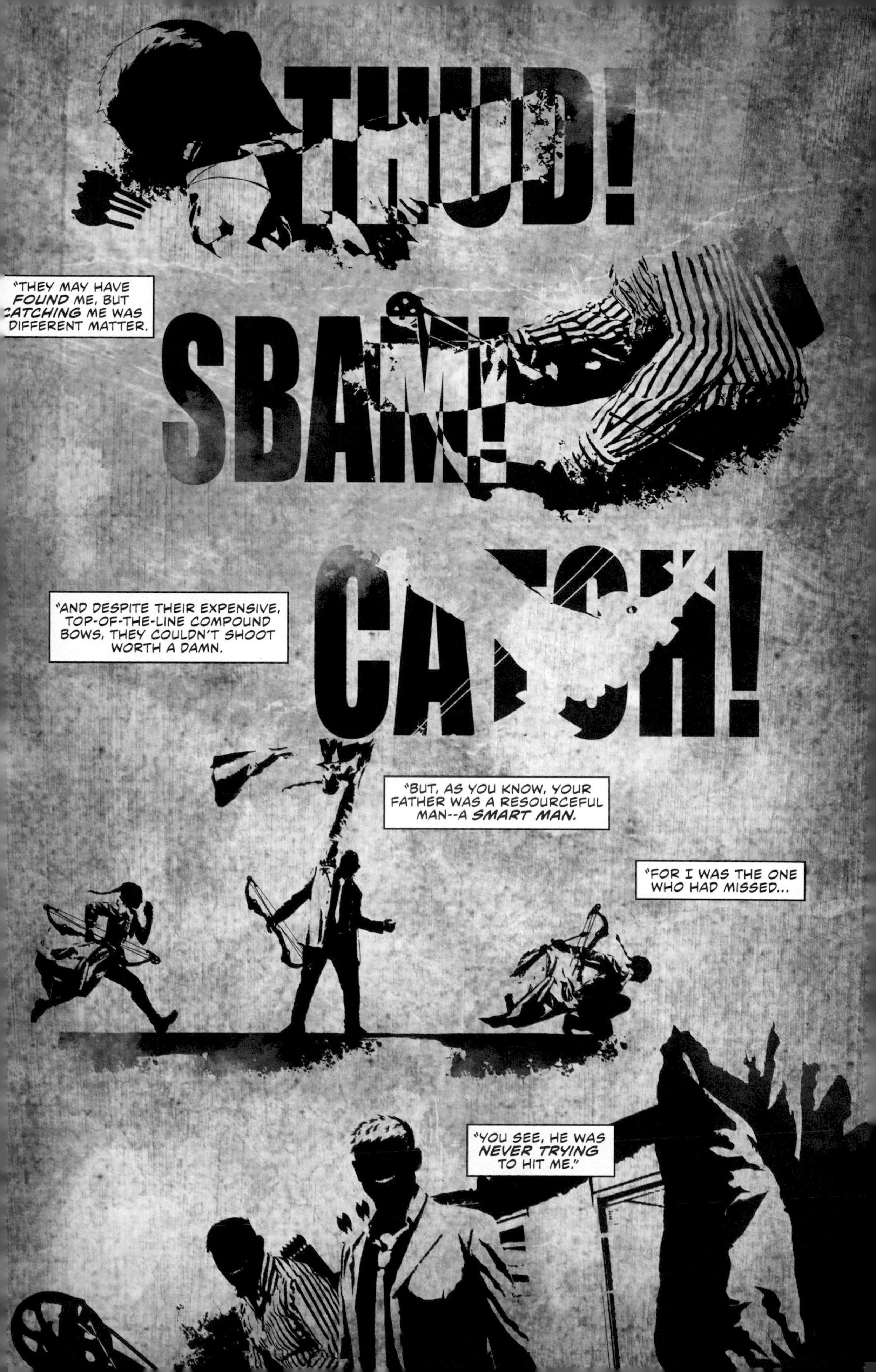
THUD!
SBAM!
"THEY MAY HAVE FOUND ME, BUT CATCHING ME WAS DIFFERENT MATTER.
"AND DESPITE THEIR EXPENSIVE, TOP-OF-THE-LINE COMPOUND BOWS, THEY COULDN'T SHOOT WORTH A DAMN.
"BUT, AS YOU KNOW, YOUR FATHER WAS A RESOURCEFUL MAN--A SMART MAN.
"FOR I WAS THE ONE WHO HAD MISSED...
"YOU SEE, HE WAS NEVER TRYING TO HIT ME."

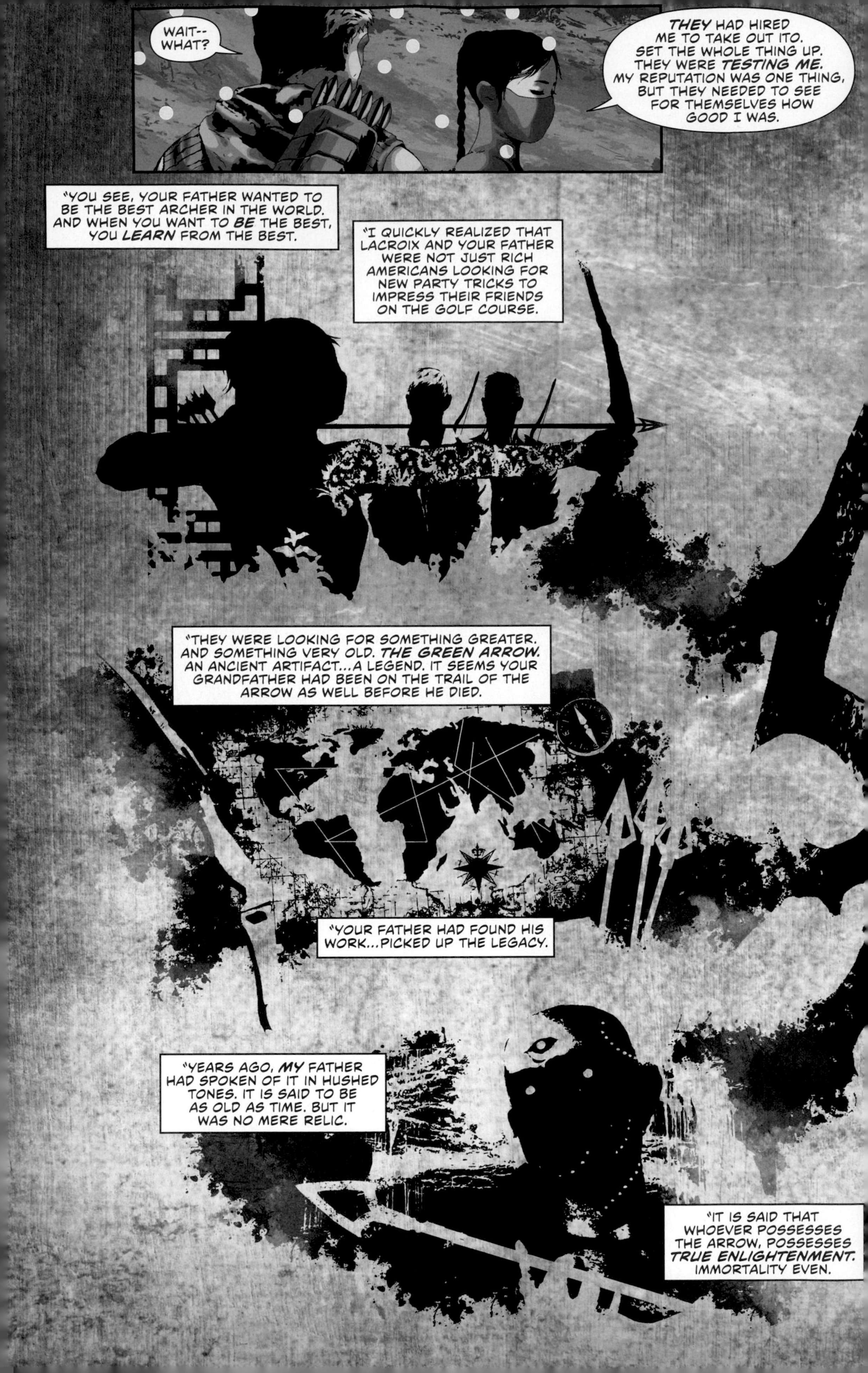
WAIT-- WHAT?
THEY HAD HIRED ME TO TAKE OUT ITO. SET THE WHOLE THING UP. THEY WERE TESTING ME. MY REPUTATION WAS ONE THING, BUT THEY NEEDED TO SEE FOR THEMSELVES HOW GOOD I WAS.
"YOU SEE, YOUR FATHER WANTED TO BE THE BEST ARCHER IN THE WORLD. AND WHEN YOU WANT TO BE THE BEST, YOU LEARN FROM THE BEST.
"I QUICKLY REALIZED THAT LACROIX AND YOUR FATHER WERE NOT JUST RICH AMERICANS LOOKING FOR NEW PARTY TRICKS TO IMPRESS THEIR FRIENDS ON THE GOLF COURSE.
"THEY WERE LOOKING FOR SOMETHING GREATER. AND SOMETHING VERY OLD. THE GREEN ARROW. AN ANCIENT ARTIFACT...A LEGEND. IT SEEMS YOUR GRANDFATHER HAD BEEN ON THE TRAIL OF THE ARROW AS WELL BEFORE HE DIED.
"YOUR FATHER HAD FOUND HIS WORK...PICKED UP THE LEGACY.
"YEARS AGO, MY FATHER HAD SPOKEN OF IT IN HUSHED TONES. IT IS SAID TO BE AS OLD AS TIME. BUT IT WAS NO MERE RELIC.
"IT IS SAID THAT WHOEVER POSSESSES THE ARROW, POSSESSES TRUE ENLIGHTENMENT. IMMORTALITY EVEN.

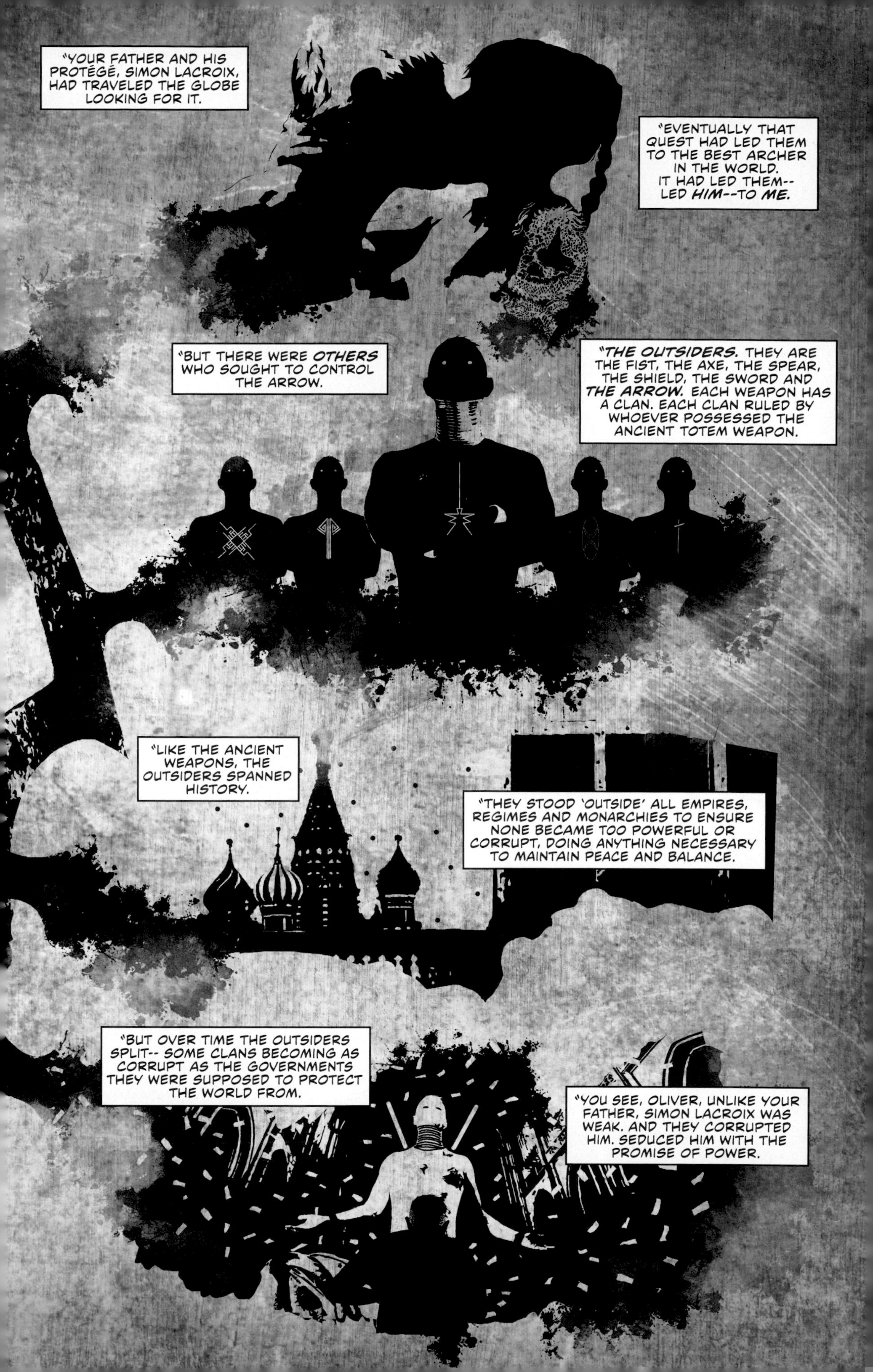
"YOUR FATHER AND HIS PROTÉGÉ, SIMON LACROIX, HAD TRAVELED THE GLOBE LOOKING FOR IT.
"EVENTUALLY THAT QUEST HAD LED THEM TO THE BEST ARCHER IN THE WORLD. IT HAD LED THEM-- LED *HIM*--TO *ME.*
"BUT THERE WERE *OTHERS* WHO SOUGHT TO CONTROL THE ARROW.
"*THE OUTSIDERS.* THEY ARE THE FIST, THE AXE, THE SPEAR, THE SHIELD, THE SWORD AND *THE ARROW.* EACH WEAPON HAS A CLAN. EACH CLAN RULED BY WHOEVER POSSESSED THE ANCIENT TOTEM WEAPON.
"LIKE THE ANCIENT WEAPONS, THE OUTSIDERS SPANNED HISTORY.
"THEY STOOD 'OUTSIDE' ALL EMPIRES, REGIMES AND MONARCHIES TO ENSURE NONE BECAME TOO POWERFUL OR CORRUPT, DOING ANYTHING NECESSARY TO MAINTAIN PEACE AND BALANCE.
"BUT OVER TIME THE OUTSIDERS SPLIT-- SOME CLANS BECOMING AS CORRUPT AS THE GOVERNMENTS THEY WERE SUPPOSED TO PROTECT THE WORLD FROM.
"YOU SEE, OLIVER, UNLIKE YOUR FATHER, SIMON LACROIX WAS WEAK. AND THEY CORRUPTED HIM. SEDUCED HIM WITH THE PROMISE OF POWER.

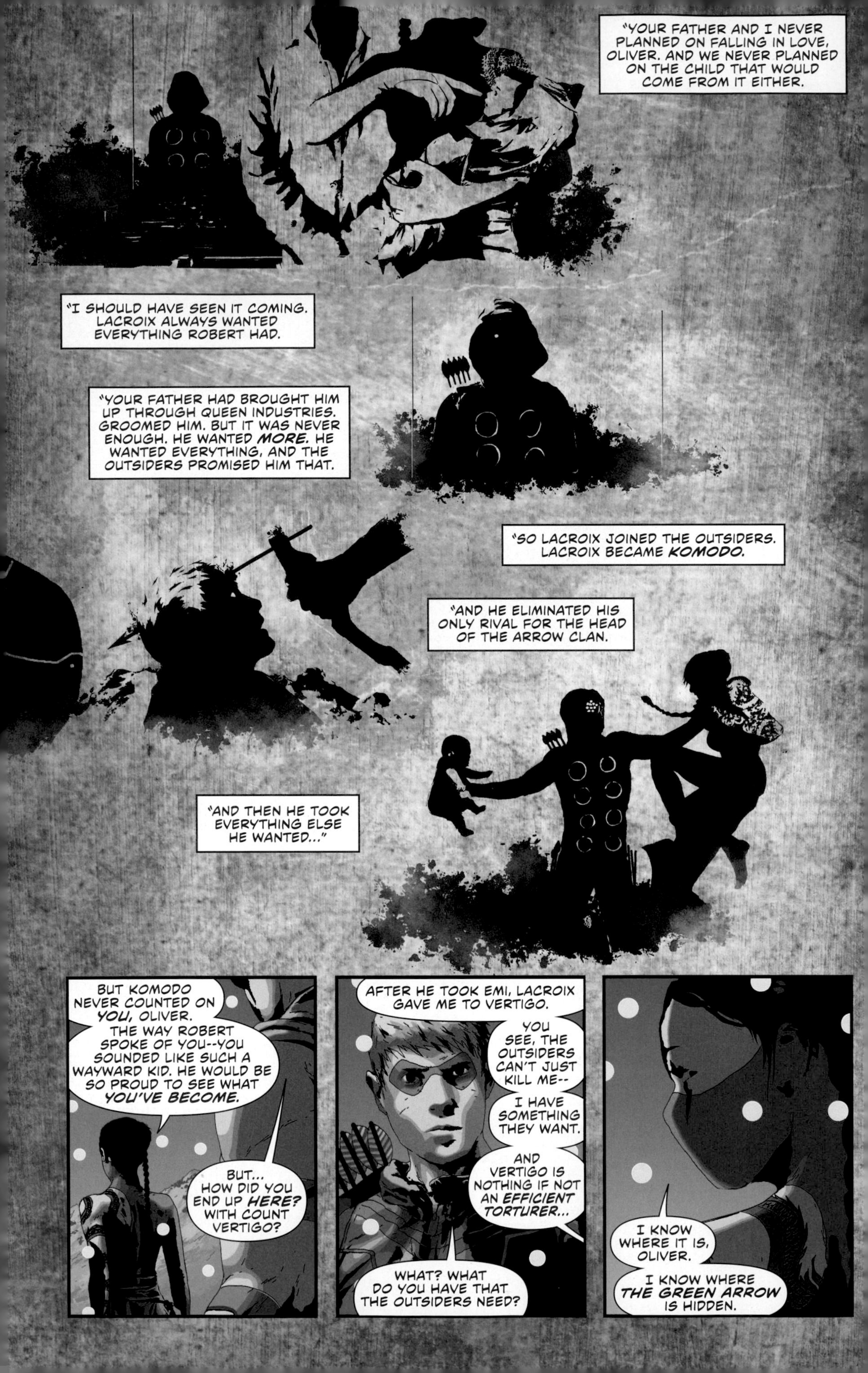
"YOUR FATHER AND I NEVER PLANNED ON FALLING IN LOVE, OLIVER. AND WE NEVER PLANNED ON THE CHILD THAT WOULD COME FROM IT EITHER.
"I SHOULD HAVE SEEN IT COMING. LACROIX ALWAYS WANTED EVERYTHING ROBERT HAD.
"YOUR FATHER HAD BROUGHT HIM UP THROUGH QUEEN INDUSTRIES. GROOMED HIM. BUT IT WAS NEVER ENOUGH. HE WANTED *MORE.* HE WANTED EVERYTHING, AND THE OUTSIDERS PROMISED HIM THAT.
"SO LACROIX JOINED THE OUTSIDERS. LACROIX BECAME *KOMODO.*
"AND HE ELIMINATED HIS ONLY RIVAL FOR THE HEAD OF THE ARROW CLAN.
"AND THEN HE TOOK EVERYTHING ELSE HE WANTED..."
BUT KOMODO NEVER COUNTED ON *YOU,* OLIVER.
THE WAY ROBERT SPOKE OF YOU--YOU SOUNDED LIKE SUCH A WAYWARD KID. HE WOULD BE SO PROUD TO SEE WHAT *YOU'VE BECOME.*
BUT... HOW DID YOU END UP *HERE?* WITH COUNT VERTIGO?
AFTER HE TOOK EMI, LACROIX GAVE ME TO VERTIGO.
YOU SEE, THE OUTSIDERS CAN'T JUST KILL ME--
I HAVE SOMETHING THEY WANT.
AND VERTIGO IS NOTHING IF NOT AN *EFFICIENT TORTURER...*
WHAT? WHAT DO YOU HAVE THAT THE OUTSIDERS NEED?
I KNOW WHERE IT IS, OLIVER.
I KNOW WHERE *THE GREEN ARROW* IS HIDDEN.

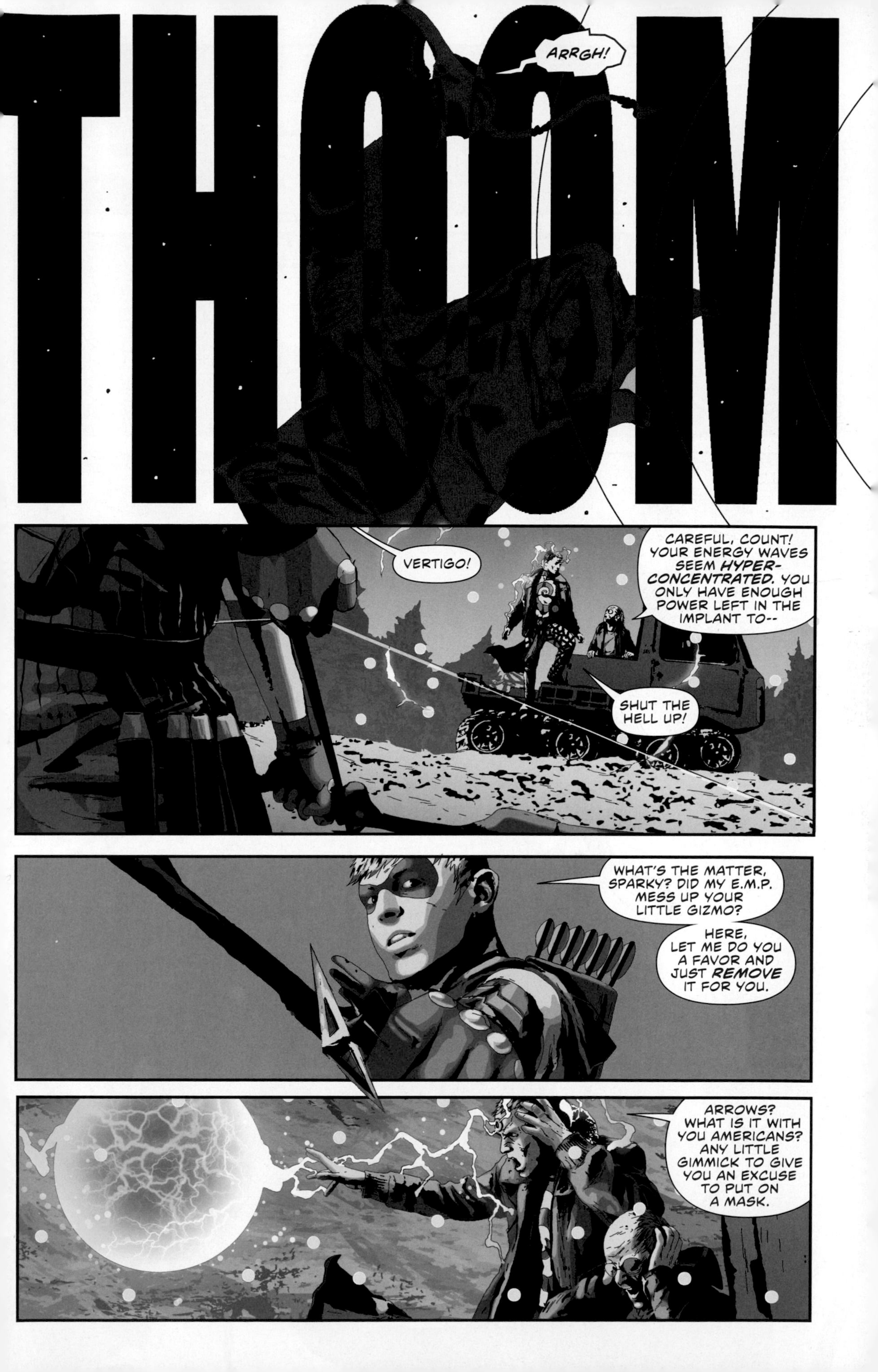
THOOM
ARRGH!
VERTIGO!
CAREFUL, COUNT! YOUR ENERGY WAVES SEEM HYPER-CONCENTRATED. YOU ONLY HAVE ENOUGH POWER LEFT IN THE IMPLANT TO--
SHUT THE HELL UP!
WHAT'S THE MATTER, SPARKY? DID MY E.M.P. MESS UP YOUR LITTLE GIZMO?
HERE, LET ME DO YOU A FAVOR AND JUST REMOVE IT FOR YOU.
ARROWS? WHAT IS IT WITH YOU AMERICANS? ANY LITTLE GIMMICK TO GIVE YOU AN EXCUSE TO PUT ON A MASK.

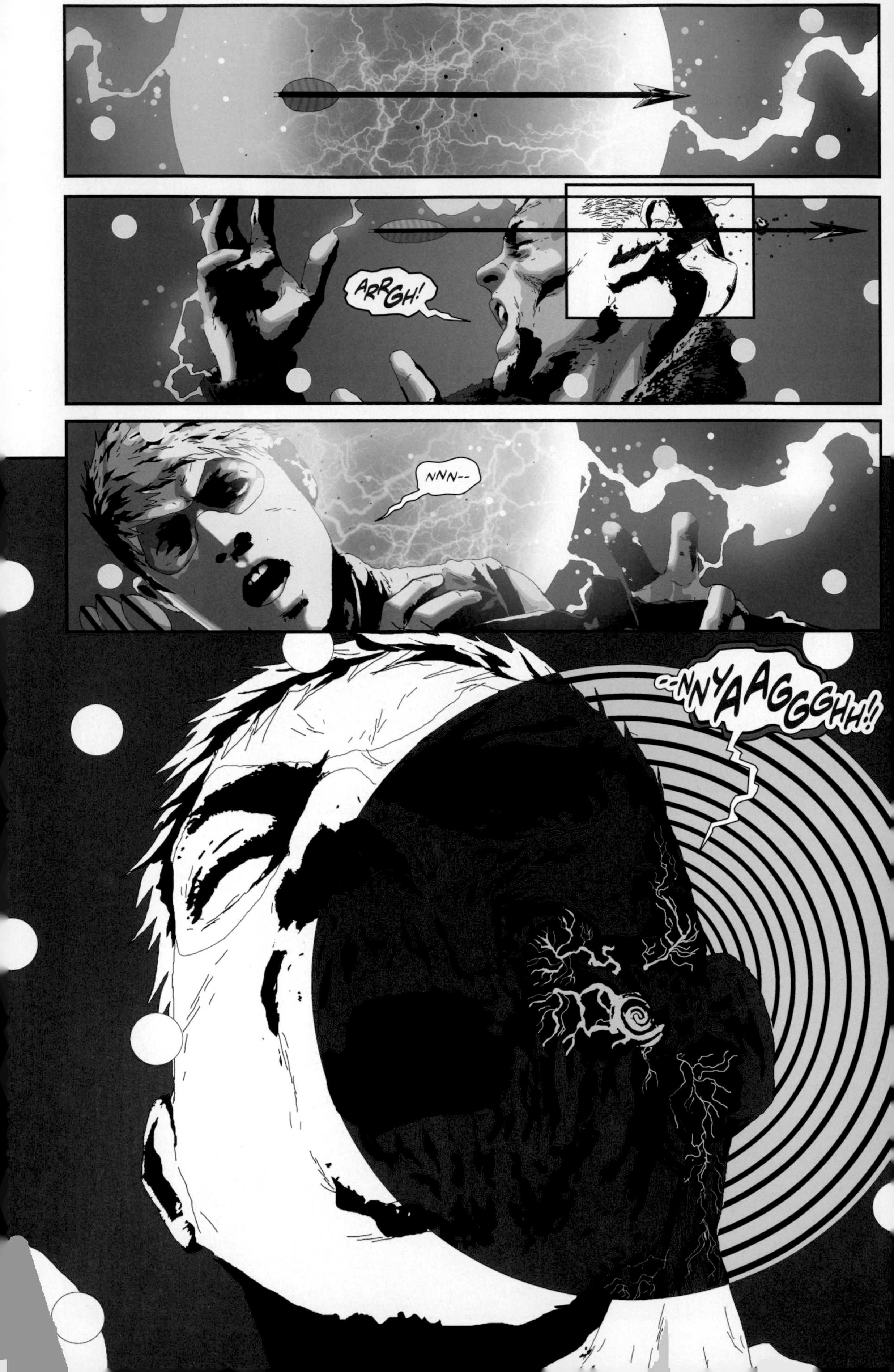
ARRGH!
NNN--
--NNYAAGGGHH!

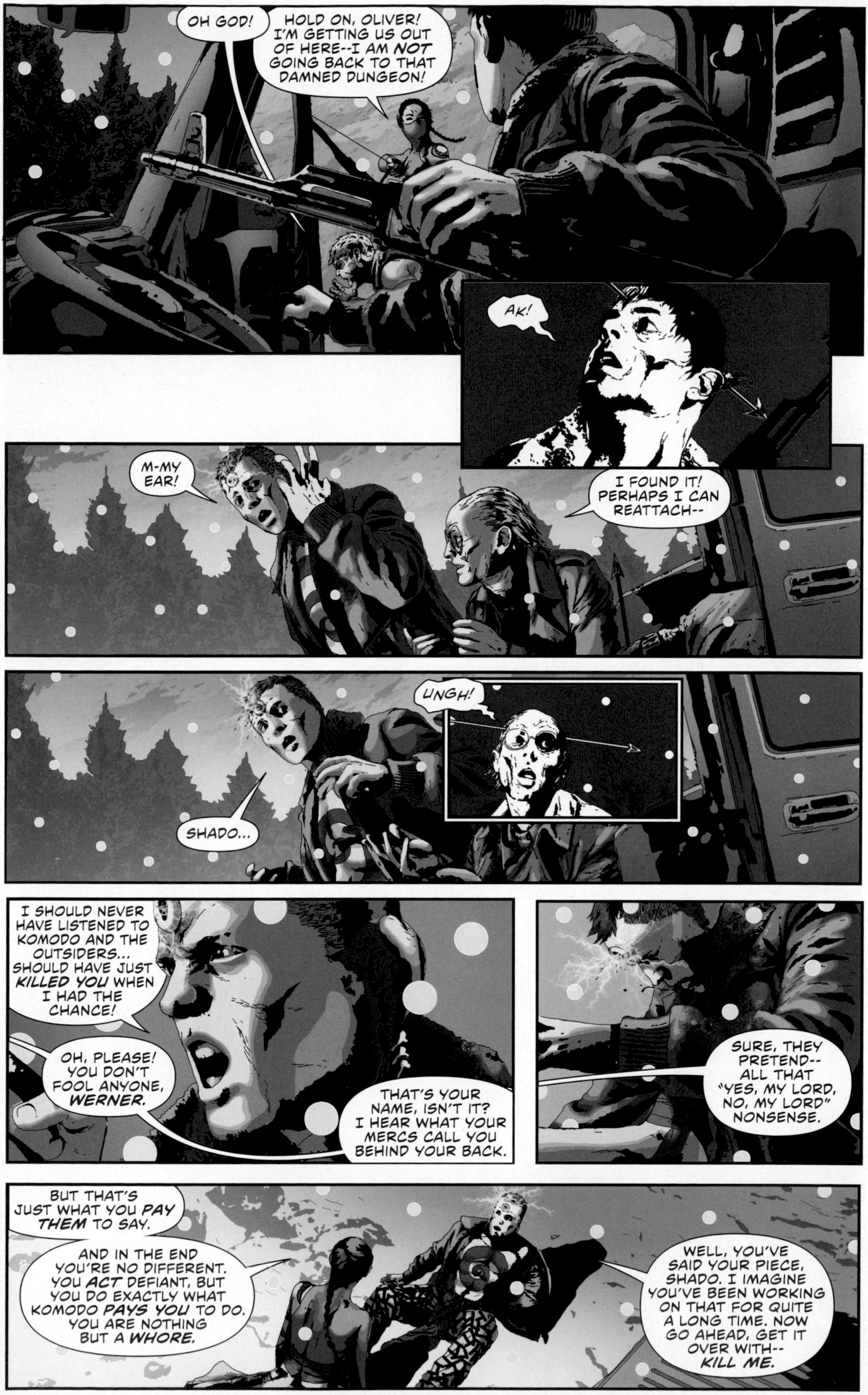
OH GOD!
HOLD ON, OLIVER! I'M GETTING US OUT OF HERE--I AM NOT GOING BACK TO THAT DAMNED DUNGEON!
AK!
M-MY EAR!
I FOUND IT! PERHAPS I CAN REATTACH--
UNGH!
SHADO...
I SHOULD NEVER HAVE LISTENED TO KOMODO AND THE OUTSIDERS... SHOULD HAVE JUST KILLED YOU WHEN I HAD THE CHANCE!
OH, PLEASE! YOU DON'T FOOL ANYONE, WERNER.
THAT'S YOUR NAME, ISN'T IT? I HEAR WHAT YOUR MERCS CALL YOU BEHIND YOUR BACK.
SURE, THEY PRETEND-- ALL THAT "YES, MY LORD, NO, MY LORD" NONSENSE.
BUT THAT'S JUST WHAT YOU PAY THEM TO SAY.
AND IN THE END YOU'RE NO DIFFERENT. YOU ACT DEFIANT, BUT YOU DO EXACTLY WHAT KOMODO PAYS YOU TO DO. YOU ARE NOTHING BUT A WHORE.
WELL, YOU'VE SAID YOUR PIECE, SHADO. I IMAGINE YOU'VE BEEN WORKING ON THAT FOR QUITE A LONG TIME. NOW GO AHEAD, GET IT OVER WITH-- KILL ME.

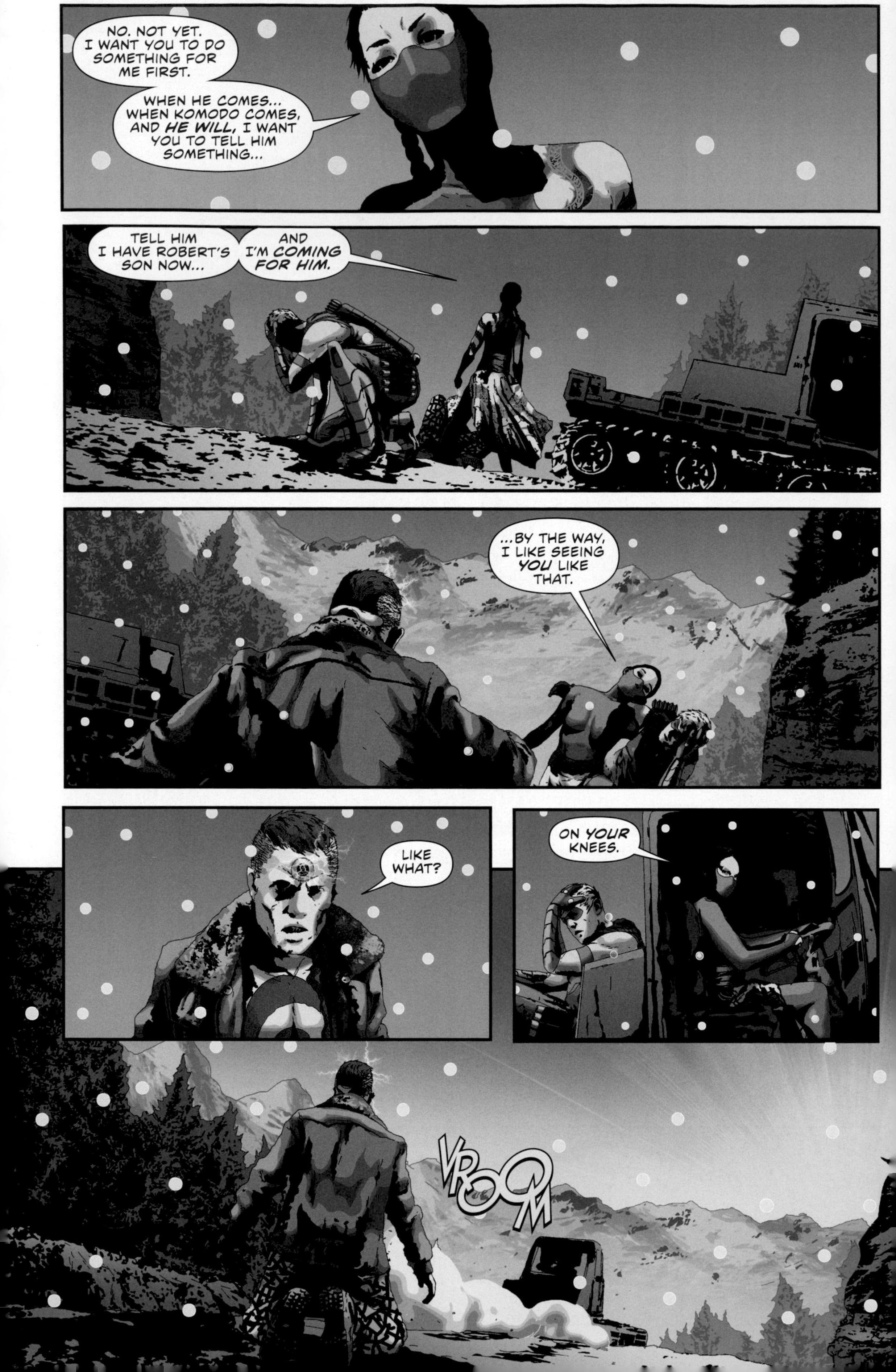
NO. NOT YET. I WANT YOU TO DO SOMETHING FOR ME FIRST.
WHEN HE COMES... WHEN KOMODO COMES, AND HE WILL, I WANT YOU TO TELL HIM SOMETHING...
TELL HIM I HAVE ROBERT'S SON NOW...
AND I'M COMING FOR HIM.
...BY THE WAY, I LIKE SEEING YOU LIKE THAT.
LIKE WHAT?
ON YOUR KNEES.
VROOM

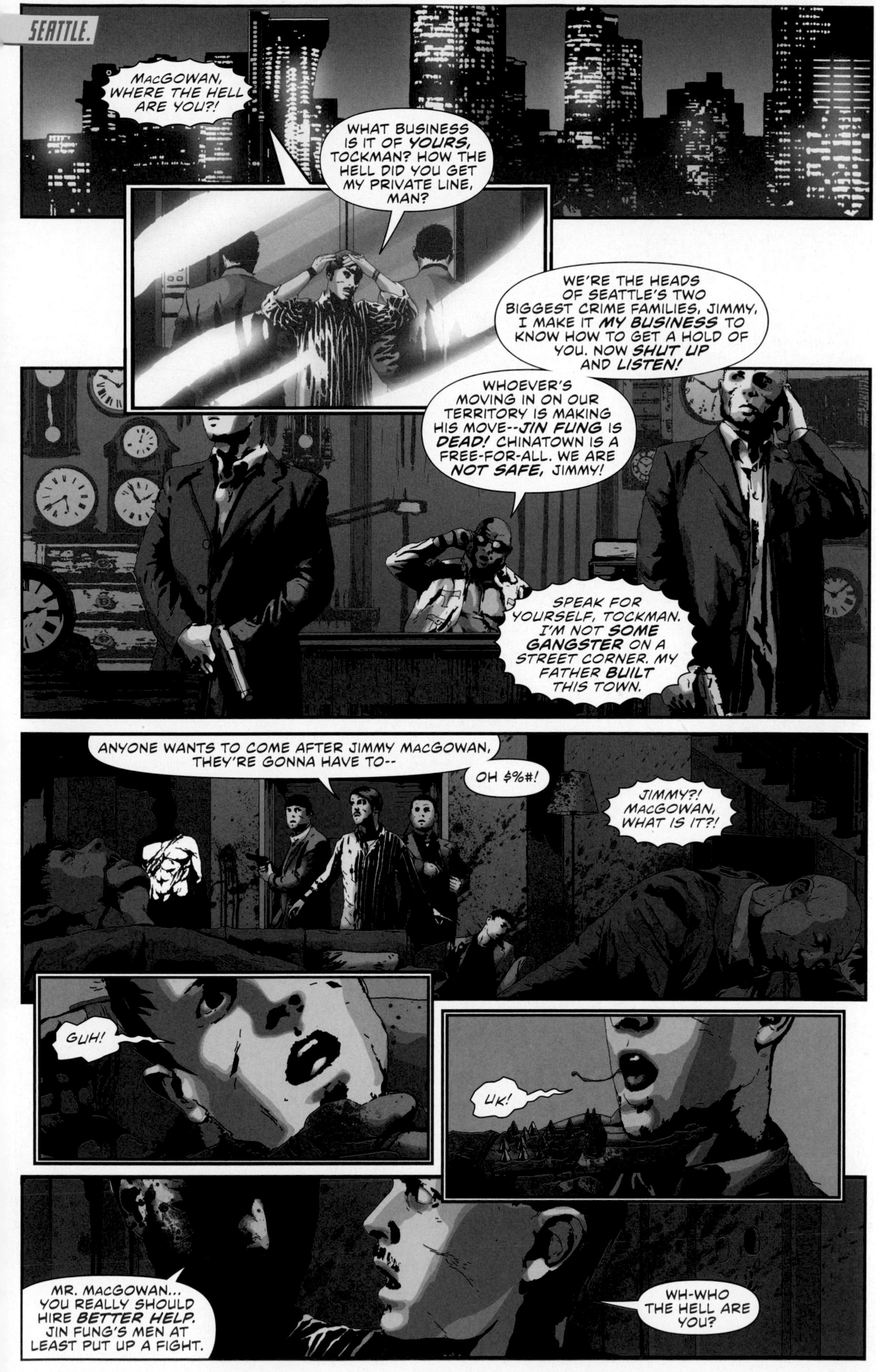
SEATTLE.
MacGOWAN, WHERE THE HELL ARE YOU?!
WHAT BUSINESS IS IT OF YOURS, TOCKMAN? HOW THE HELL DID YOU GET MY PRIVATE LINE, MAN?
WE'RE THE HEADS OF SEATTLE'S TWO BIGGEST CRIME FAMILIES, JIMMY, I MAKE IT MY BUSINESS TO KNOW HOW TO GET A HOLD OF YOU. NOW SHUT UP AND LISTEN!
WHOEVER'S MOVING IN ON OUR TERRITORY IS MAKING HIS MOVE--JIN FUNG IS DEAD! CHINATOWN IS A FREE-FOR-ALL. WE ARE NOT SAFE, JIMMY!
SPEAK FOR YOURSELF, TOCKMAN. I'M NOT SOME GANGSTER ON A STREET CORNER. MY FATHER BUILT THIS TOWN.
ANYONE WANTS TO COME AFTER JIMMY MACGOWAN, THEY'RE GONNA HAVE TO--
OH $%#!
JIMMY?! MACGOWAN, WHAT IS IT?!
GUH!
UK!
MR. MACGOWAN... YOU REALLY SHOULD HIRE BETTER HELP. JIN FUNG'S MEN AT LEAST PUT UP A FIGHT.
WH-WHO THE HELL ARE YOU?

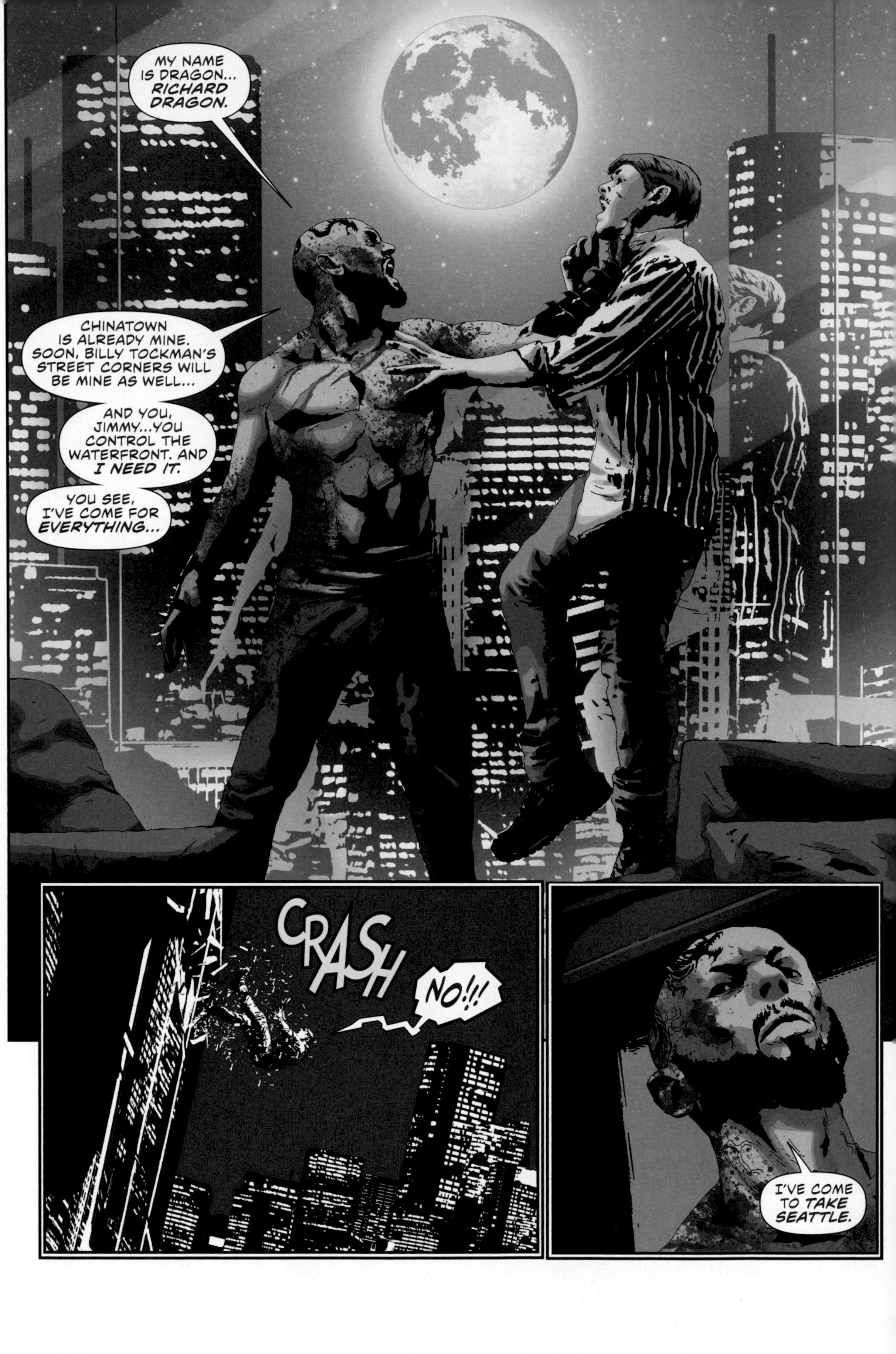
MY NAME IS DRAGON... RICHARD DRAGON.
CHINATOWN IS ALREADY MINE. SOON, BILLY TOCKMAN'S STREET CORNERS WILL BE MINE AS WELL...
AND YOU, JIMMY...YOU CONTROL THE WATERFRONT. AND I NEED IT.
YOU SEE, I'VE COME FOR EVERYTHING...
CRASH
NO!!!
I'VE COME TO TAKE SEATTLE.

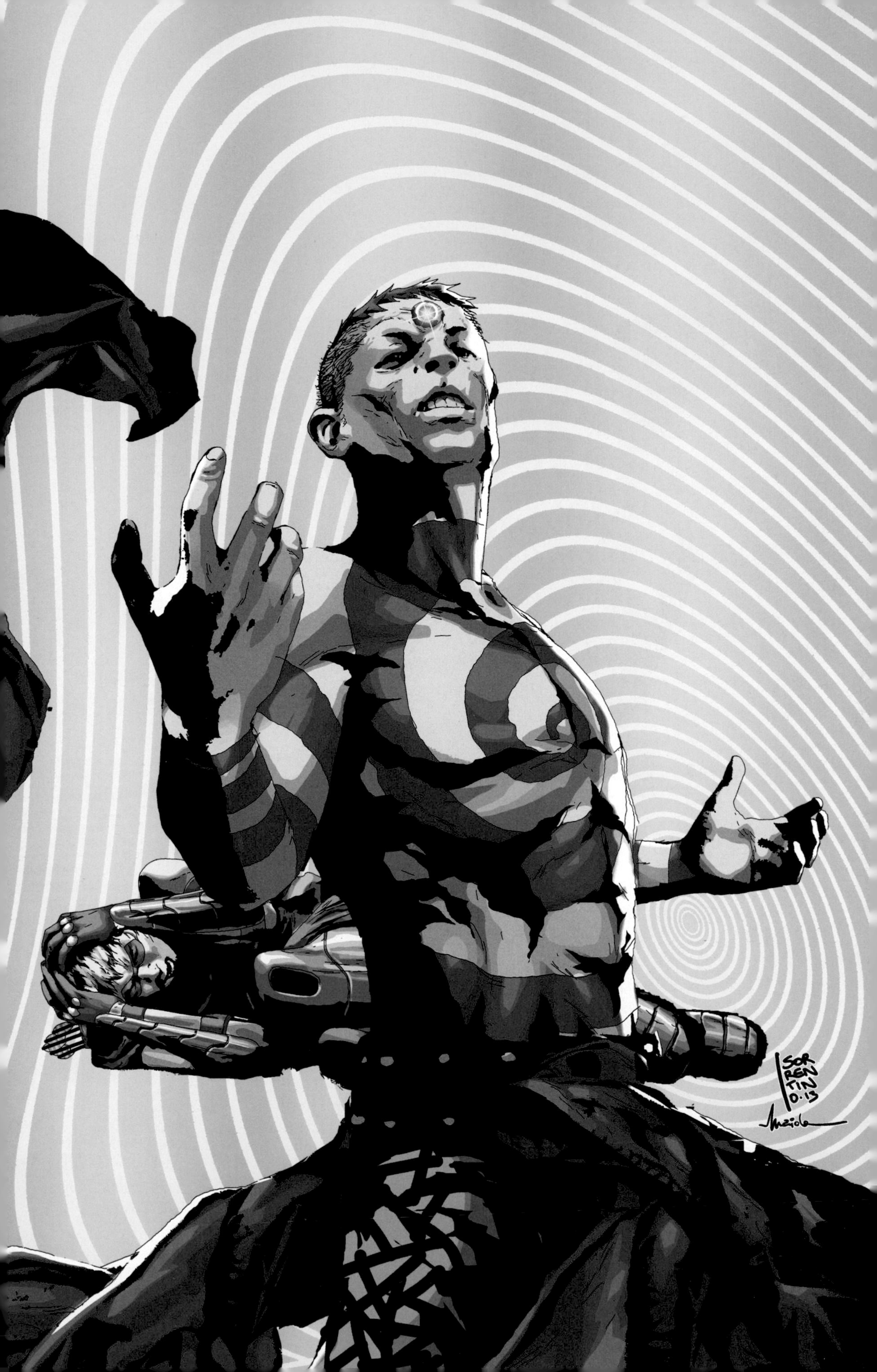
SOR
REN
TIN
O·13

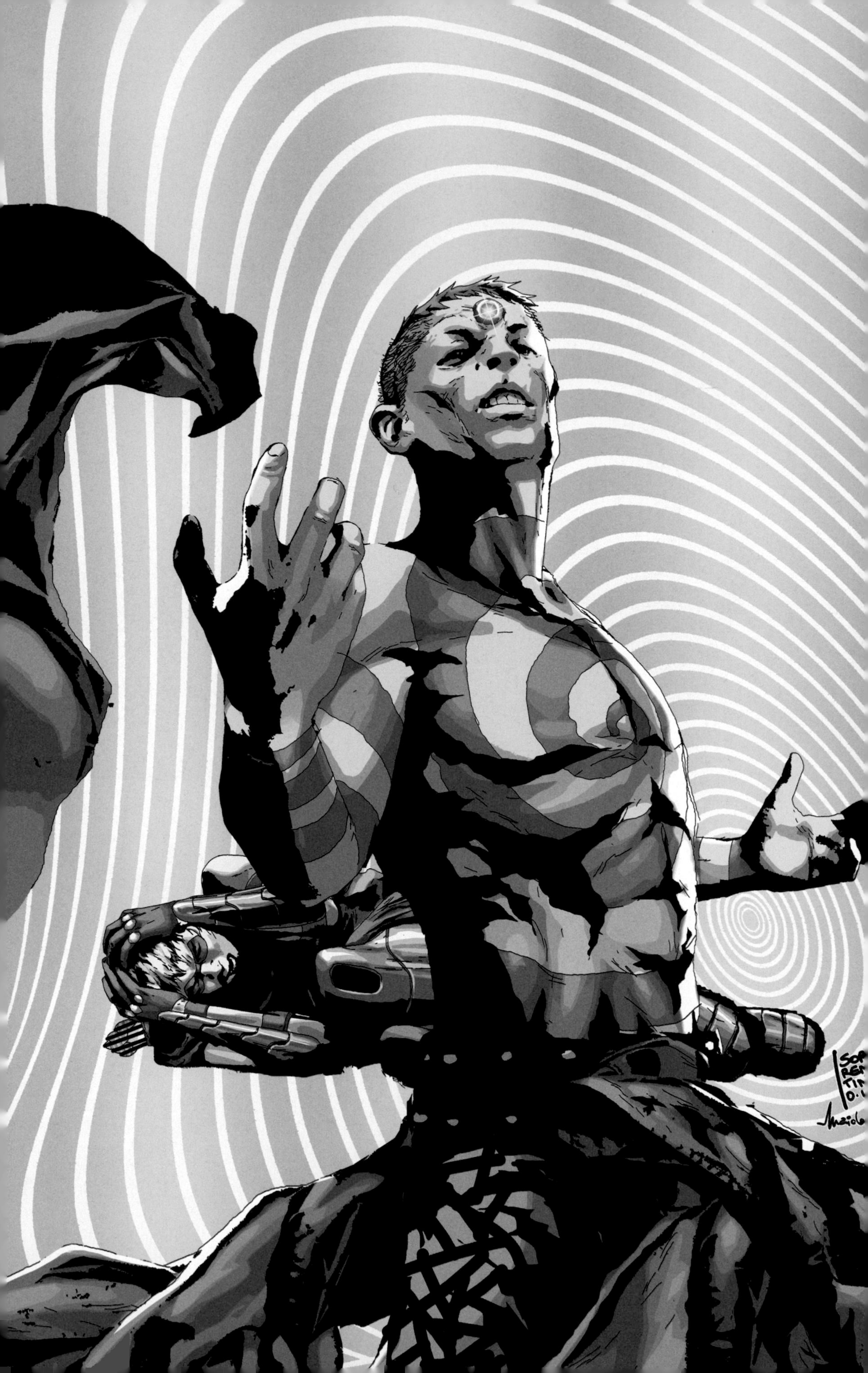

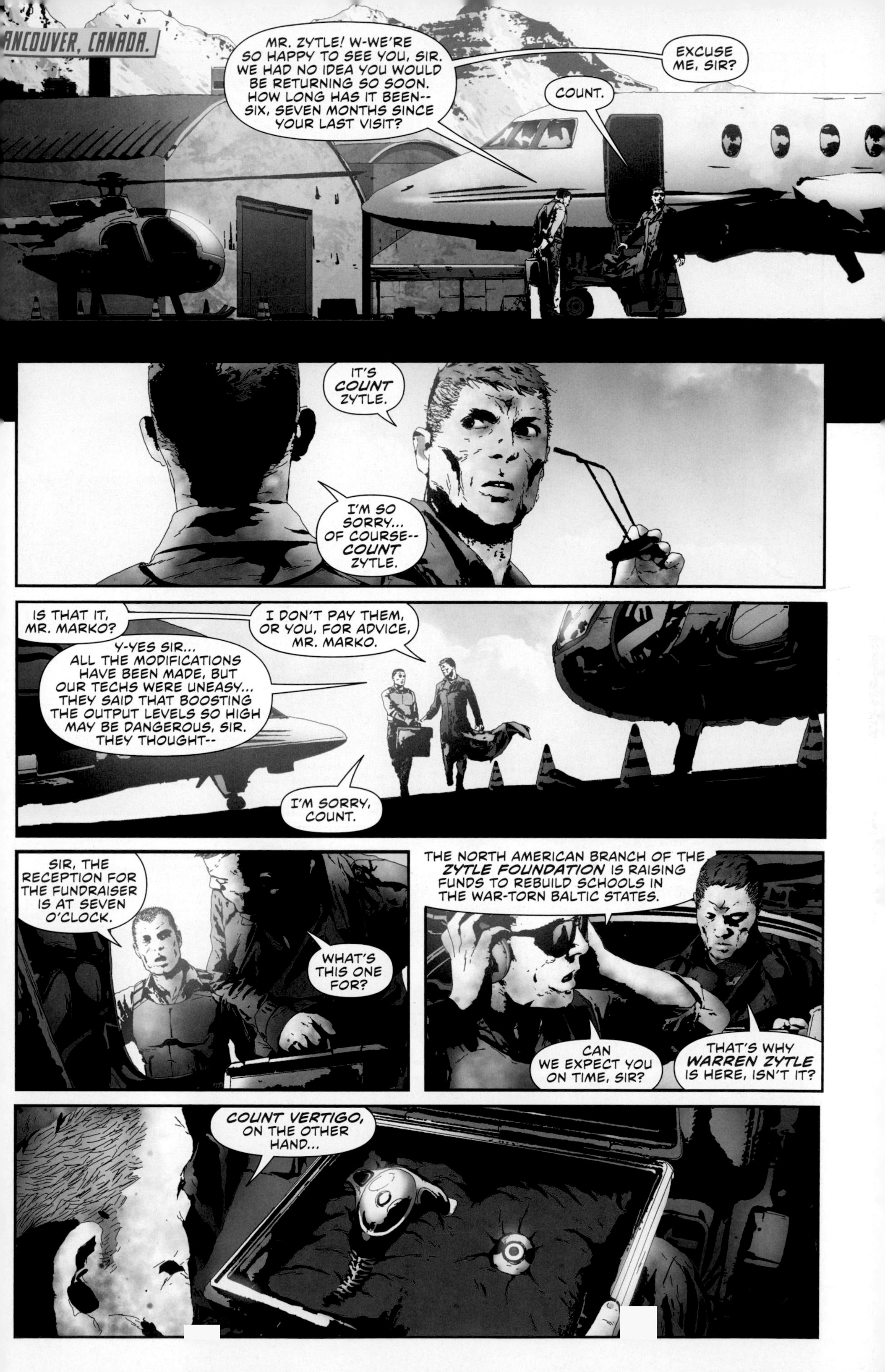
ANCOUVER, CANADA.
MR. ZYTLE! W-WE'RE SO HAPPY TO SEE YOU, SIR. WE HAD NO IDEA YOU WOULD BE RETURNING SO SOON. HOW LONG HAS IT BEEN-- SIX, SEVEN MONTHS SINCE YOUR LAST VISIT?
EXCUSE ME, SIR?
COUNT.
IT'S COUNT ZYTLE.
I'M SO SORRY... OF COURSE-- COUNT ZYTLE.
IS THAT IT, MR. MARKO?
Y-YES SIR... ALL THE MODIFICATIONS HAVE BEEN MADE, BUT OUR TECHS WERE UNEASY... THEY SAID THAT BOOSTING THE OUTPUT LEVELS SO HIGH MAY BE DANGEROUS, SIR. THEY THOUGHT--
I DON'T PAY THEM, OR YOU, FOR ADVICE, MR. MARKO.
I'M SORRY, COUNT.
SIR, THE RECEPTION FOR THE FUNDRAISER IS AT SEVEN O'CLOCK.
WHAT'S THIS ONE FOR?
THE NORTH AMERICAN BRANCH OF THE ZYTLE FOUNDATION IS RAISING FUNDS TO REBUILD SCHOOLS IN THE WAR-TORN BALTIC STATES.
CAN WE EXPECT YOU ON TIME, SIR?
THAT'S WHY WARREN ZYTLE IS HERE, ISN'T IT?
COUNT VERTIGO, ON THE OTHER HAND...

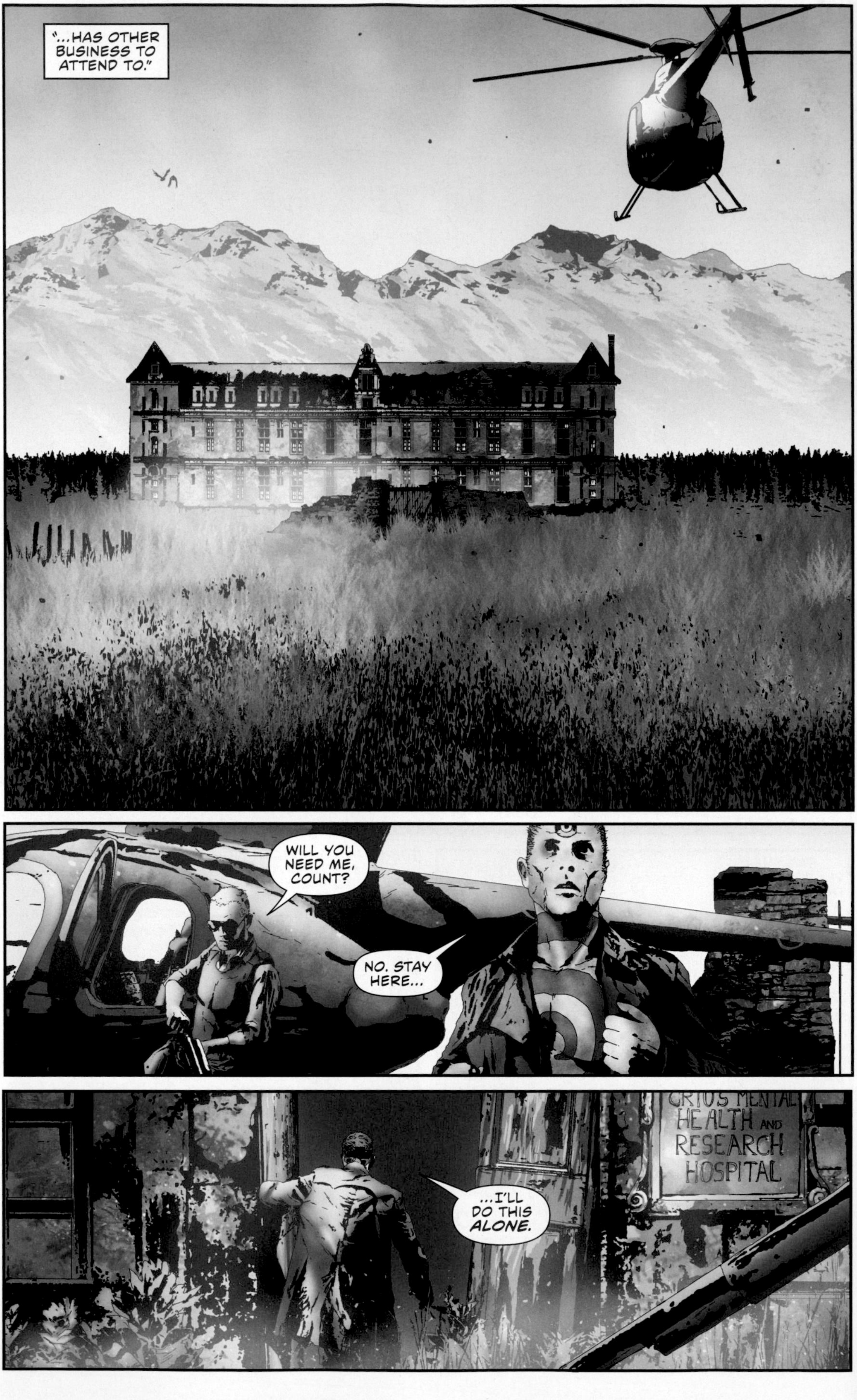
"...HAS OTHER BUSINESS TO ATTEND TO."
WILL YOU NEED ME, COUNT?
NO. STAY HERE...
HEALTH AND RESEARCH HOSPITAL
...I'LL DO THIS *ALONE*.

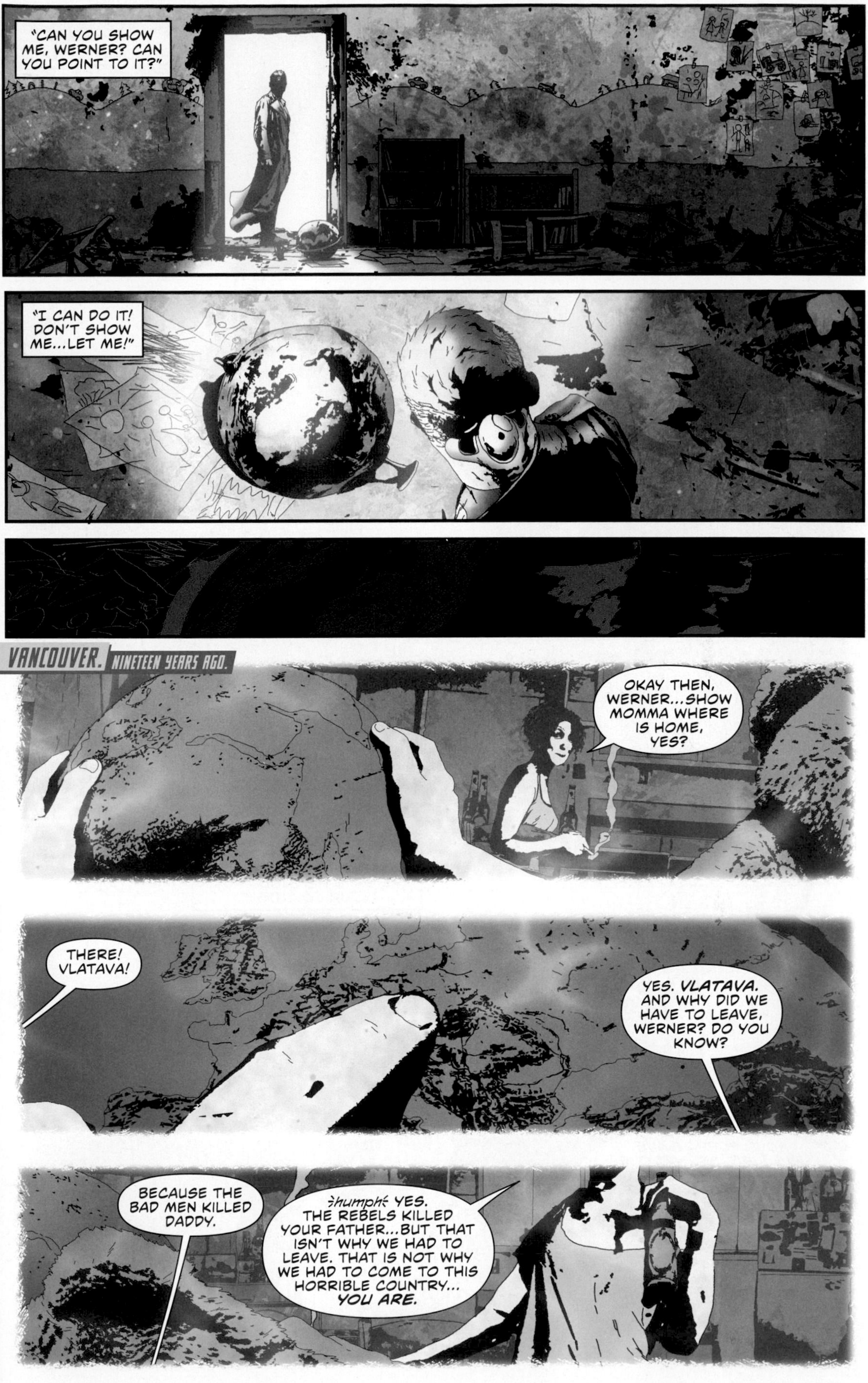
"CAN YOU SHOW ME, WERNER? CAN YOU POINT TO IT?"
"I CAN DO IT! DON'T SHOW ME...LET ME!"
VANCOUVER. NINETEEN YEARS AGO.
OKAY THEN, WERNER...SHOW MOMMA WHERE IS HOME, YES?
THERE! VLATAVA!
YES. VLATAVA. AND WHY DID WE HAVE TO LEAVE, WERNER? DO YOU KNOW?
BECAUSE THE BAD MEN KILLED DADDY.
humph YES. THE REBELS KILLED YOUR FATHER...BUT THAT ISN'T WHY WE HAD TO LEAVE. THAT IS NOT WHY WE HAD TO COME TO THIS HORRIBLE COUNTRY... YOU ARE.

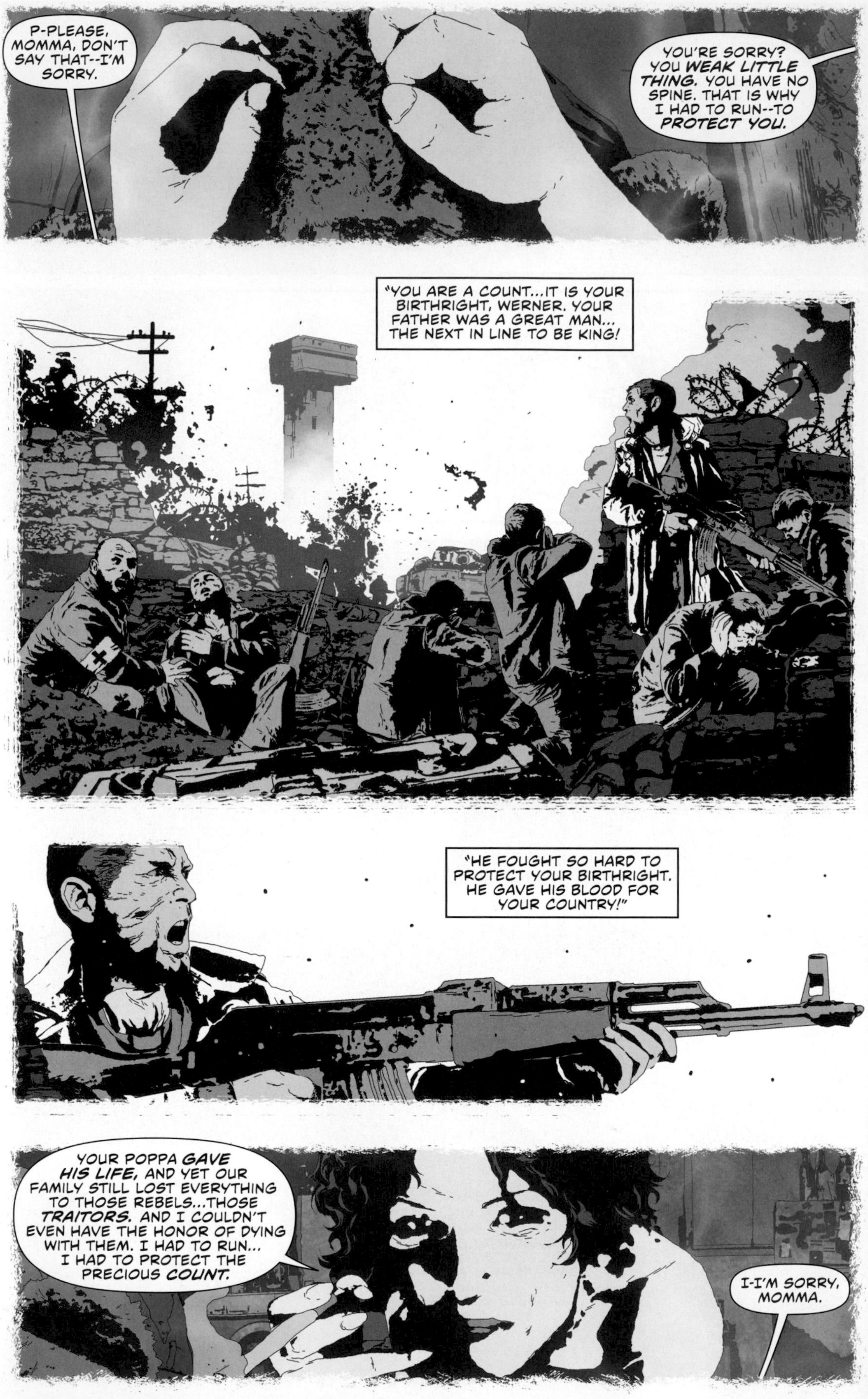
P-PLEASE, MOMMA, DON'T SAY THAT--I'M SORRY.
YOU'RE SORRY? YOU WEAK LITTLE THING. YOU HAVE NO SPINE. THAT IS WHY I HAD TO RUN--TO PROTECT YOU.
"YOU ARE A COUNT...IT IS YOUR BIRTHRIGHT, WERNER. YOUR FATHER WAS A GREAT MAN... THE NEXT IN LINE TO BE KING!
"HE FOUGHT SO HARD TO PROTECT YOUR BIRTHRIGHT. HE GAVE HIS BLOOD FOR YOUR COUNTRY!"
YOUR POPPA GAVE HIS LIFE, AND YET OUR FAMILY STILL LOST EVERYTHING TO THOSE REBELS...THOSE TRAITORS. AND I COULDN'T EVEN HAVE THE HONOR OF DYING WITH THEM. I HAD TO RUN... I HAD TO PROTECT THE PRECIOUS COUNT.
I-I'M SORRY, MOMMA.

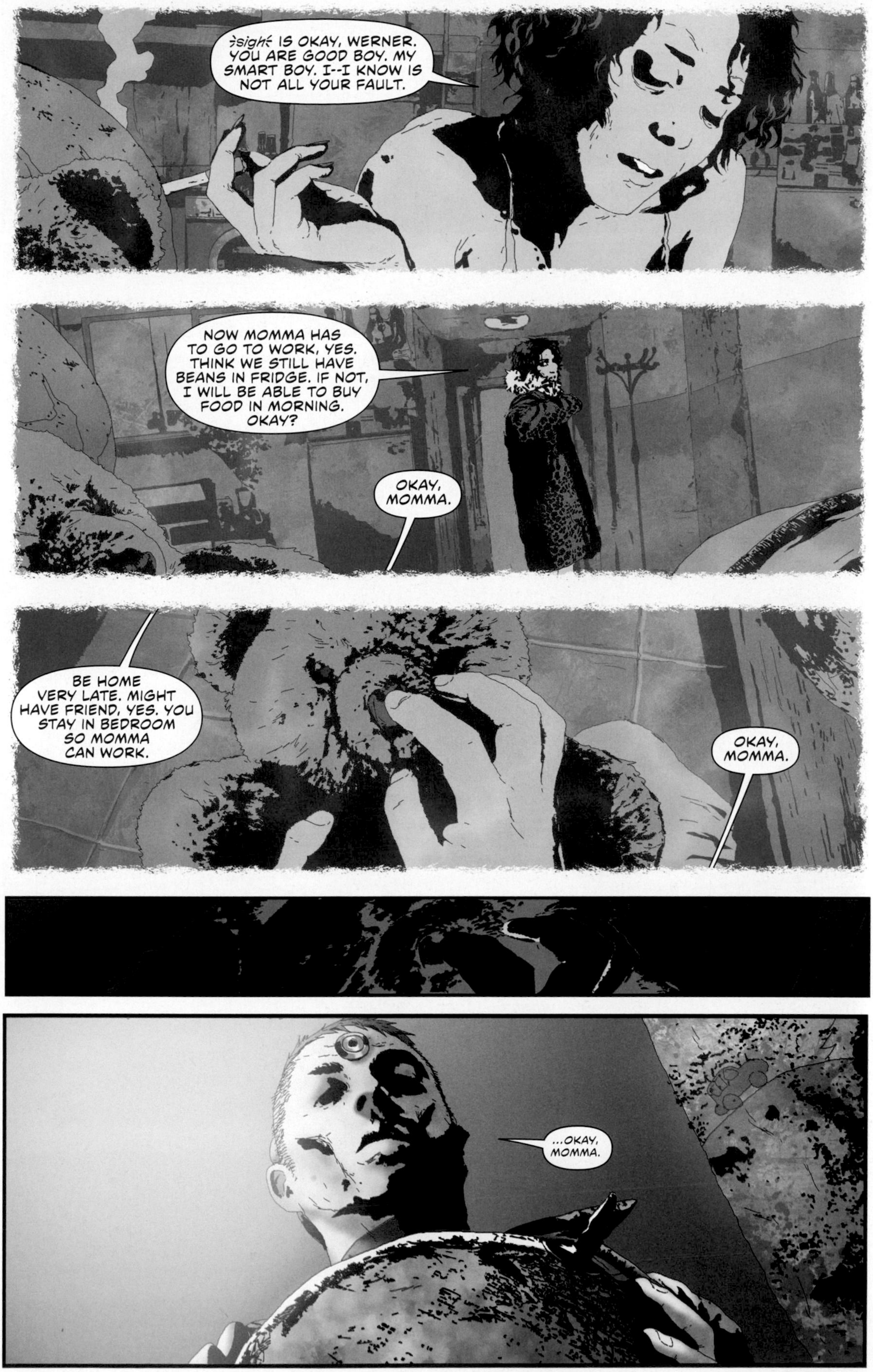

sigh IS OKAY, WERNER. YOU ARE GOOD BOY. MY SMART BOY. I--I KNOW IS NOT ALL YOUR FAULT.
NOW MOMMA HAS TO GO TO WORK, YES. THINK WE STILL HAVE BEANS IN FRIDGE. IF NOT, I WILL BE ABLE TO BUY FOOD IN MORNING. OKAY?
OKAY, MOMMA.
BE HOME VERY LATE. MIGHT HAVE FRIEND, YES. YOU STAY IN BEDROOM SO MOMMA CAN WORK.
OKAY, MOMMA.
...OKAY, MOMMA.

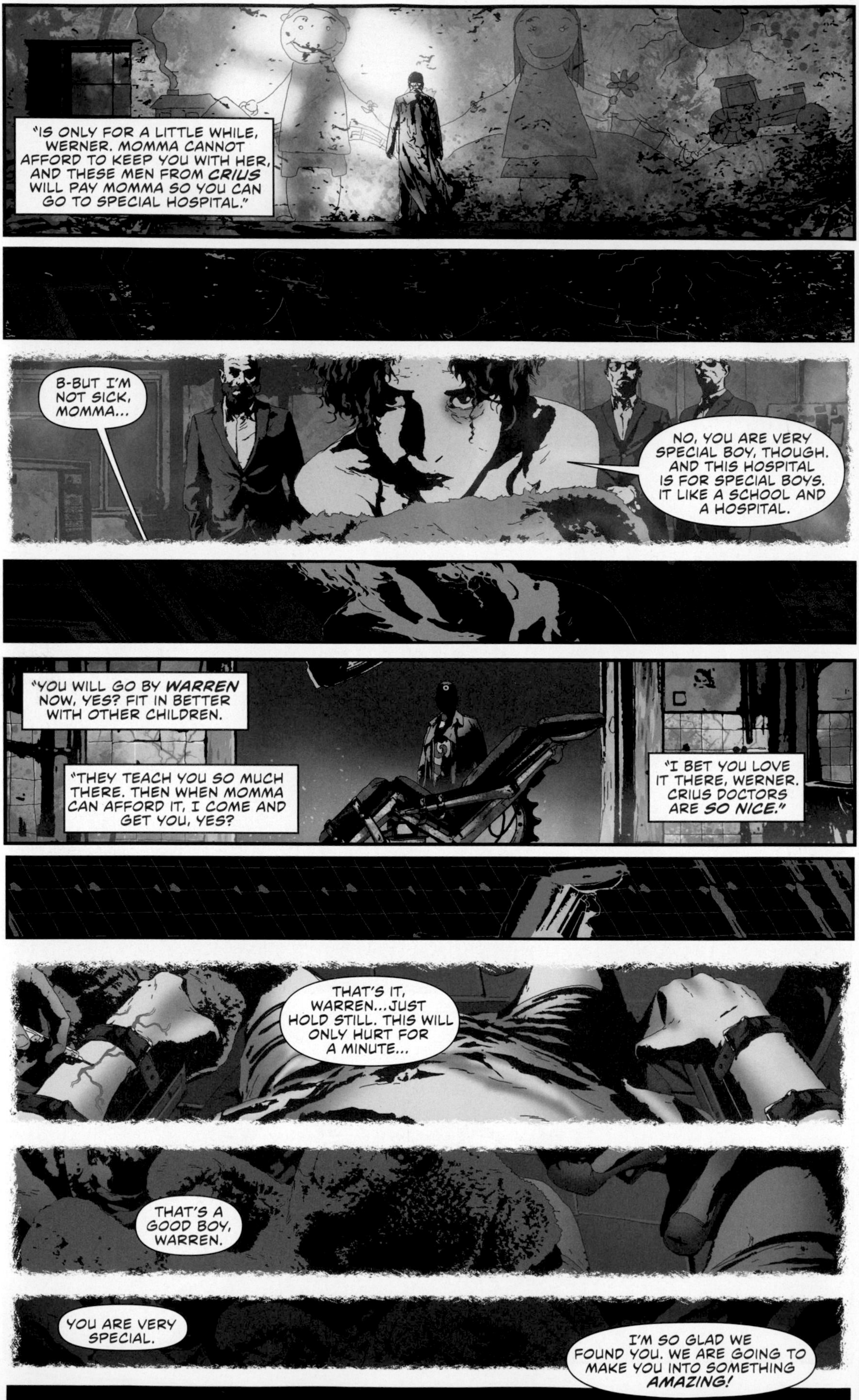
"IS ONLY FOR A LITTLE WHILE, WERNER. MOMMA CANNOT AFFORD TO KEEP YOU WITH HER, AND THESE MEN FROM CRIUS WILL PAY MOMMA SO YOU CAN GO TO SPECIAL HOSPITAL."
B-BUT I'M NOT SICK, MOMMA...
NO, YOU ARE VERY SPECIAL BOY, THOUGH. AND THIS HOSPITAL IS FOR SPECIAL BOYS. IT LIKE A SCHOOL AND A HOSPITAL.
"YOU WILL GO BY WARREN NOW, YES? FIT IN BETTER WITH OTHER CHILDREN.
"THEY TEACH YOU SO MUCH THERE. THEN WHEN MOMMA CAN AFFORD IT, I COME AND GET YOU, YES?
"I BET YOU LOVE IT THERE, WERNER. CRIUS DOCTORS ARE SO NICE."
THAT'S IT, WARREN...JUST HOLD STILL. THIS WILL ONLY HURT FOR A MINUTE...
THAT'S A GOOD BOY, WARREN.
YOU ARE VERY SPECIAL.
I'M SO GLAD WE FOUND YOU. WE ARE GOING TO MAKE YOU INTO SOMETHING AMAZING!

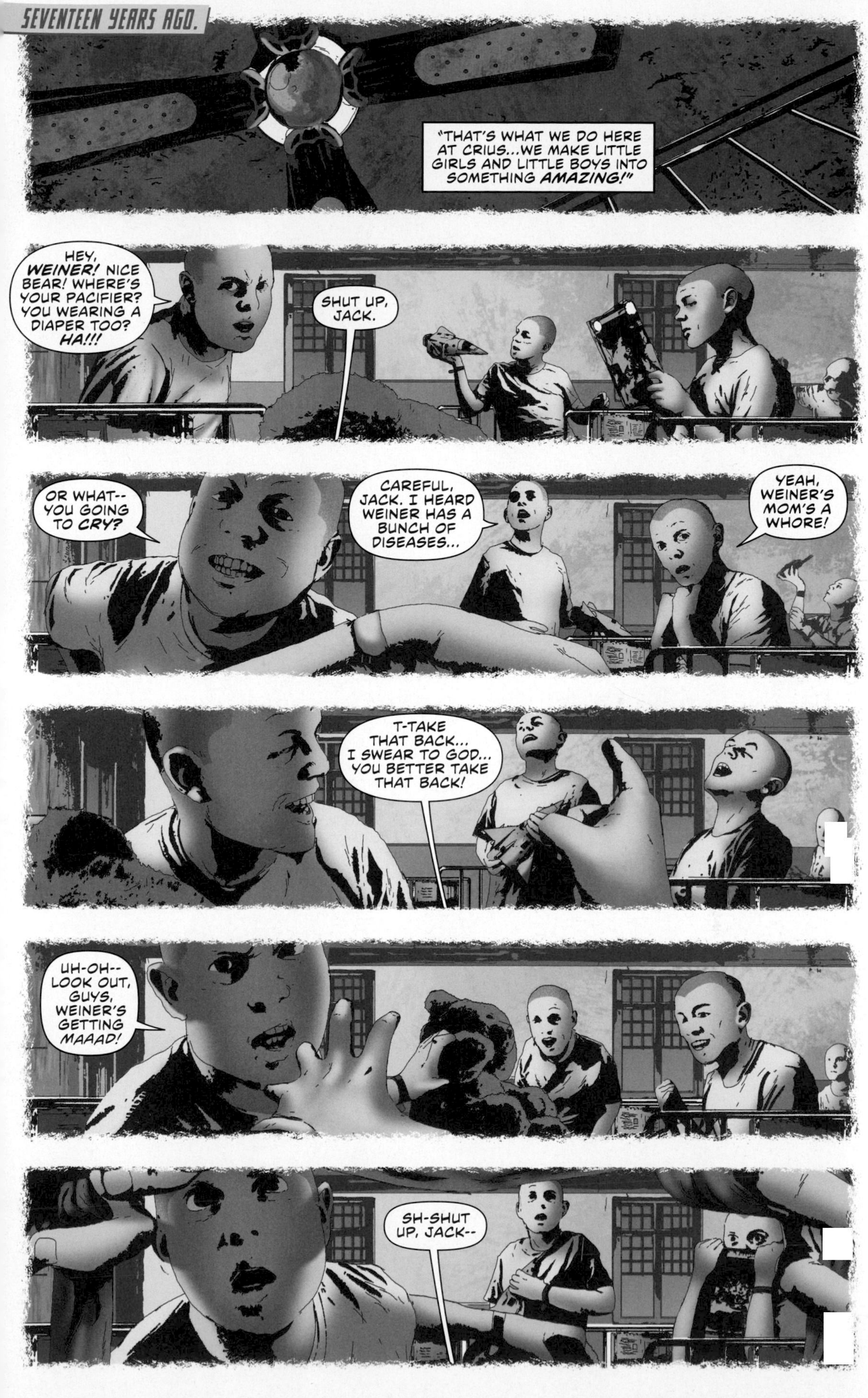
SEVENTEEN YEARS AGO.
"THAT'S WHAT WE DO HERE AT CRIUS...WE MAKE LITTLE GIRLS AND LITTLE BOYS INTO SOMETHING AMAZING!"
HEY, WEINER! NICE BEAR! WHERE'S YOUR PACIFIER? YOU WEARING A DIAPER TOO? HA!!!
SHUT UP, JACK.
OR WHAT--YOU GOING TO CRY?
CAREFUL, JACK. I HEARD WEINER HAS A BUNCH OF DISEASES...
YEAH, WEINER'S MOM'S A WHORE!
T-TAKE THAT BACK... I SWEAR TO GOD... YOU BETTER TAKE THAT BACK!
UH-OH--LOOK OUT, GUYS, WEINER'S GETTING MAAAD!
SH-SHUT UP, JACK--

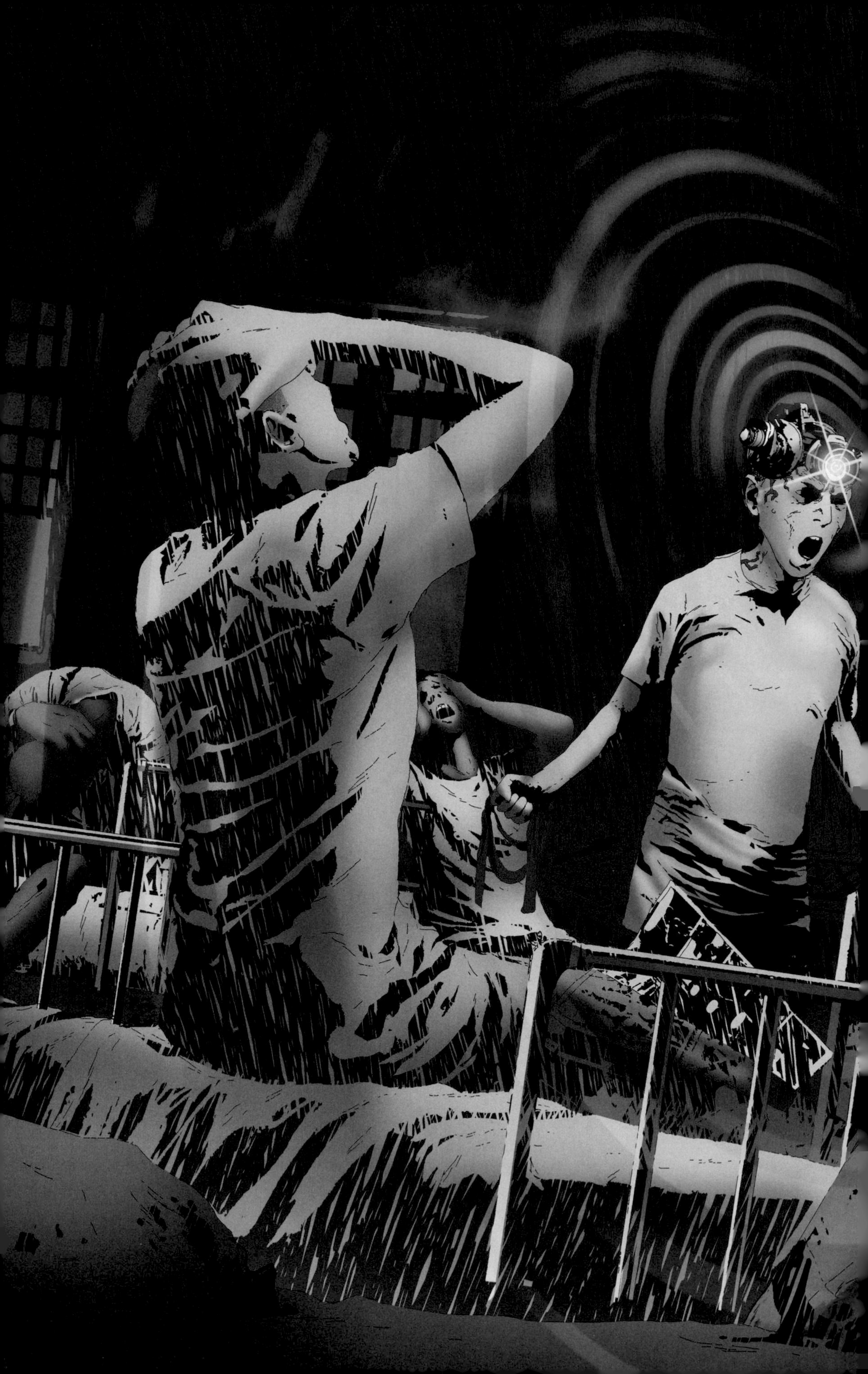

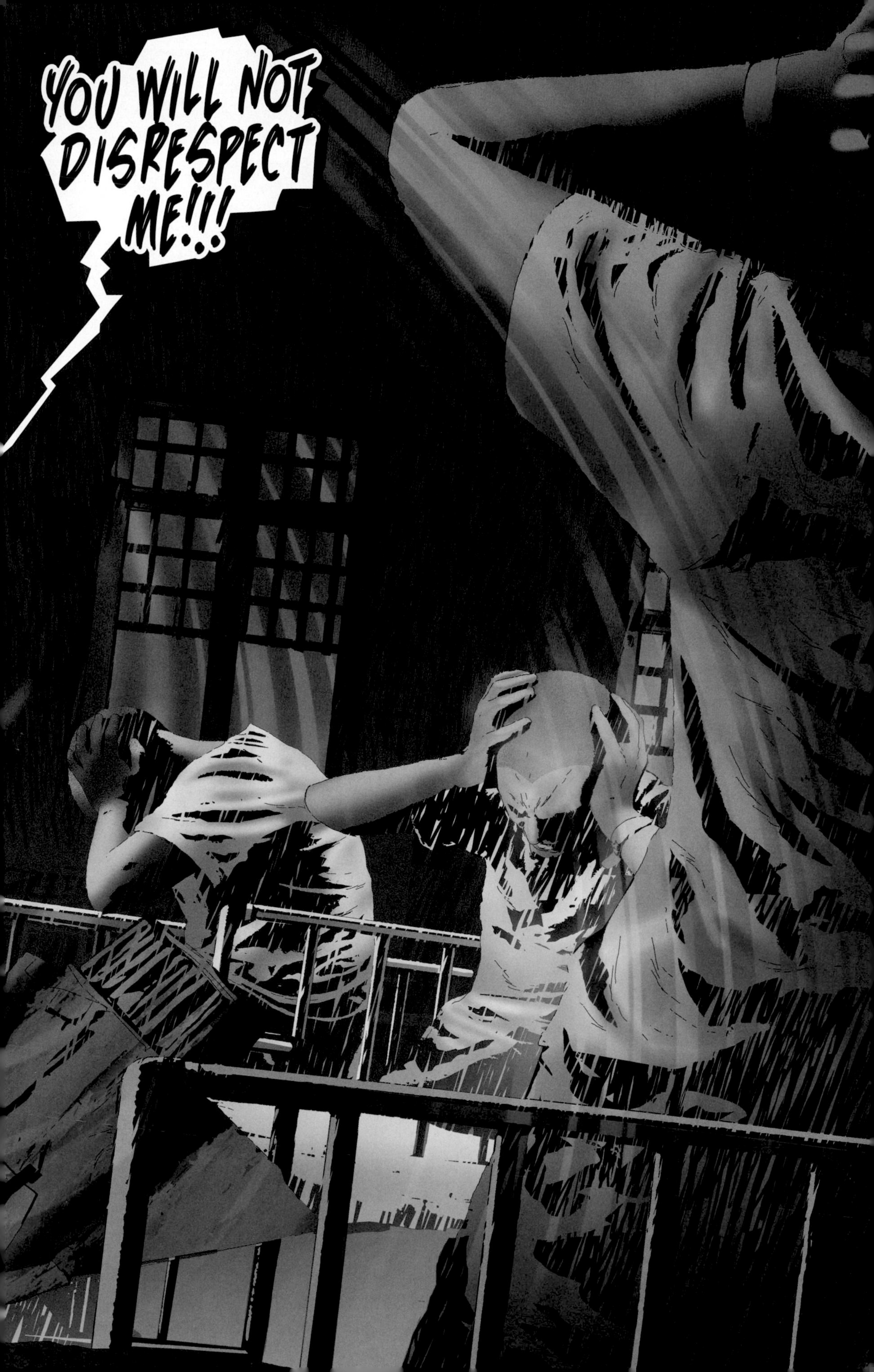
YOU WILL NOT DISRESPECT ME!!!

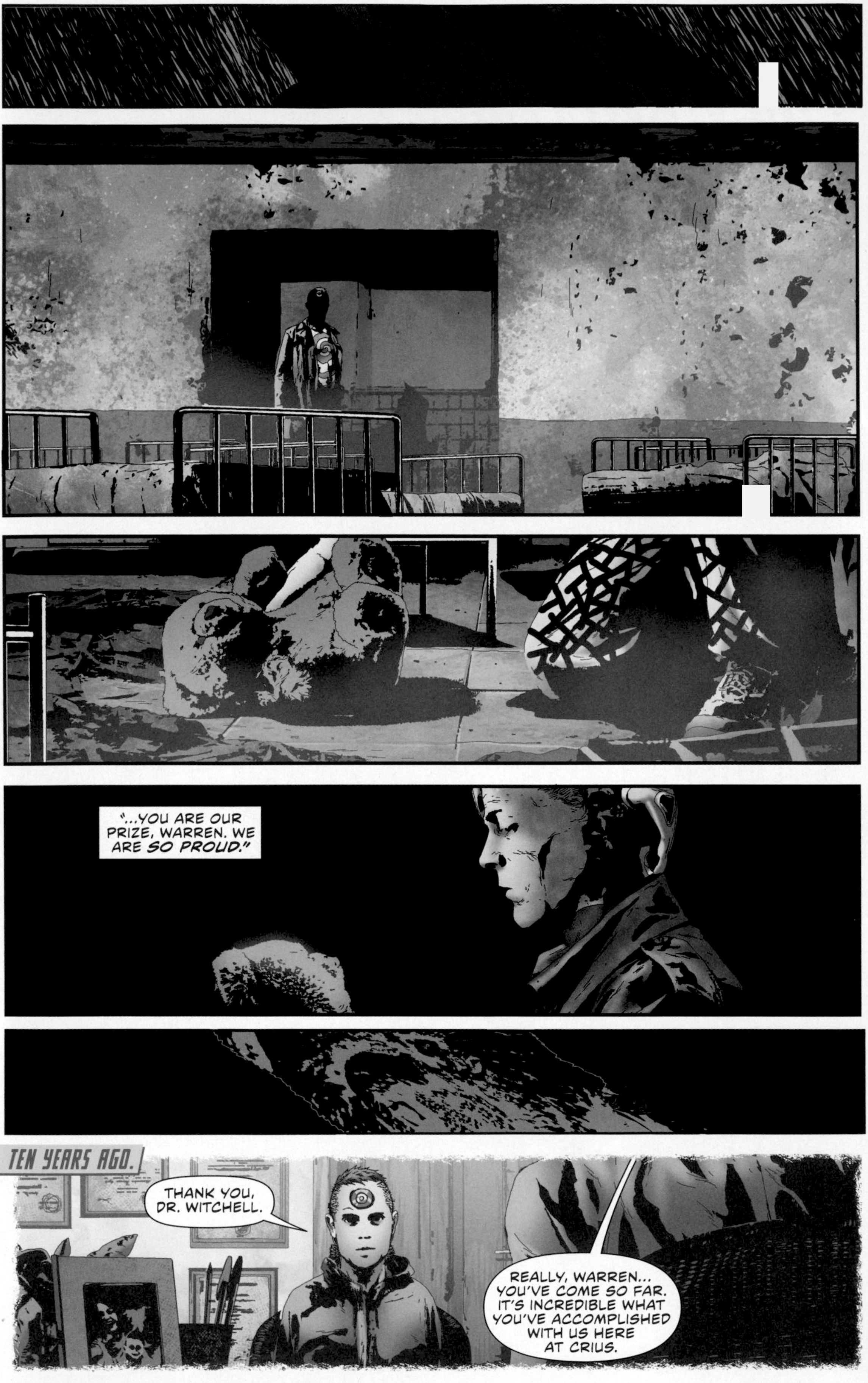
"...YOU ARE OUR PRIZE, WARREN. WE ARE *SO PROUD.*"
TEN YEARS AGO.
THANK YOU, DR. WITCHELL.
REALLY, WARREN... YOU'VE COME SO FAR. IT'S INCREDIBLE WHAT YOU'VE ACCOMPLISHED WITH US HERE AT CRIUS.

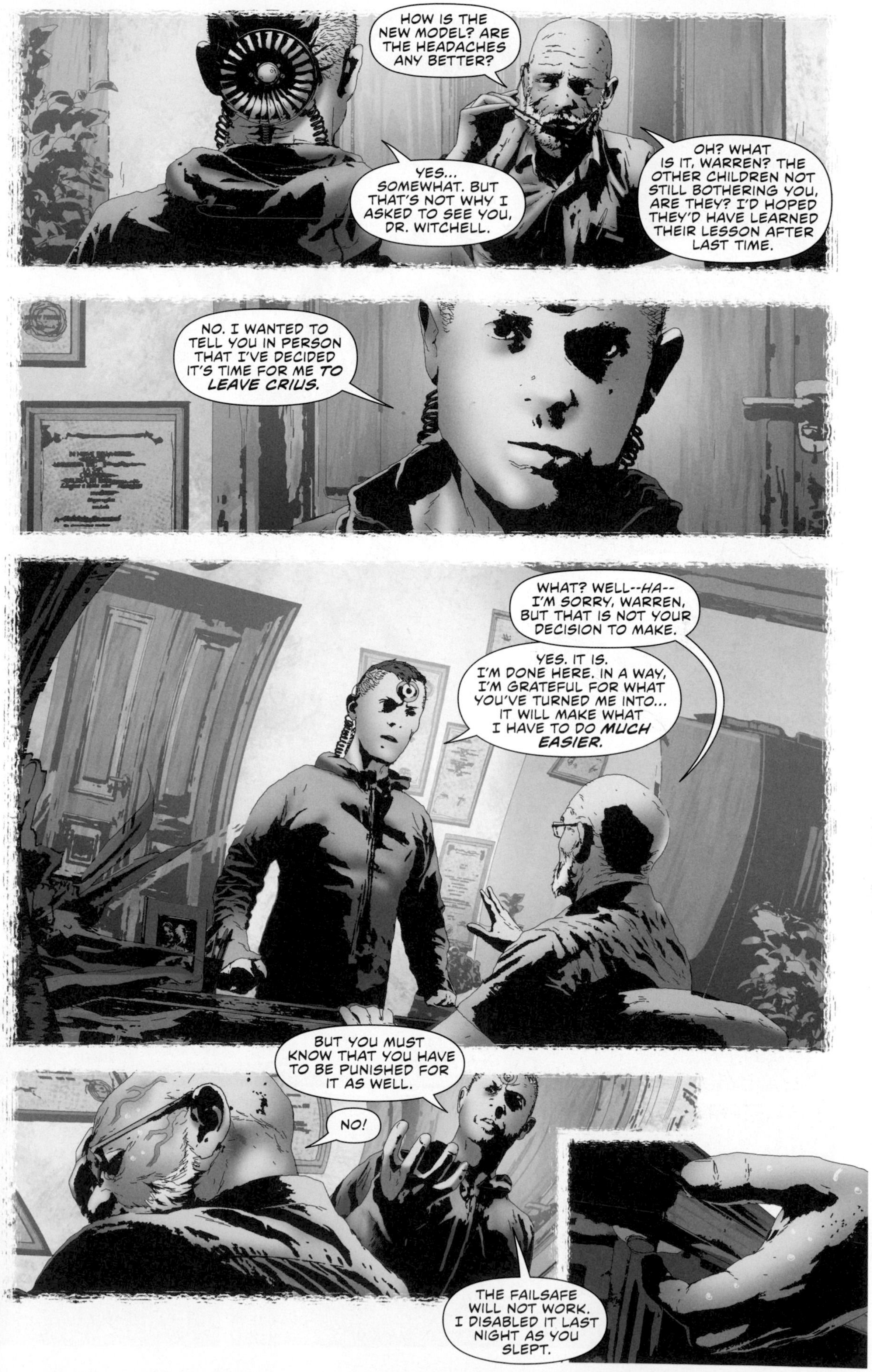
HOW IS THE NEW MODEL? ARE THE HEADACHES ANY BETTER?
YES... SOMEWHAT. BUT THAT'S NOT WHY I ASKED TO SEE YOU, DR. WITCHELL.
OH? WHAT IS IT, WARREN? THE OTHER CHILDREN NOT STILL BOTHERING YOU, ARE THEY? I'D HOPED THEY'D HAVE LEARNED THEIR LESSON AFTER LAST TIME.
NO. I WANTED TO TELL YOU IN PERSON THAT I'VE DECIDED IT'S TIME FOR ME TO LEAVE CRIUS.
WHAT? WELL--HA-- I'M SORRY, WARREN, BUT THAT IS NOT YOUR DECISION TO MAKE.
YES. IT IS. I'M DONE HERE. IN A WAY, I'M GRATEFUL FOR WHAT YOU'VE TURNED ME INTO... IT WILL MAKE WHAT I HAVE TO DO MUCH EASIER.
BUT YOU MUST KNOW THAT YOU HAVE TO BE PUNISHED FOR IT AS WELL.
NO!
THE FAILSAFE WILL NOT WORK. I DISABLED IT LAST NIGHT AS YOU SLEPT.

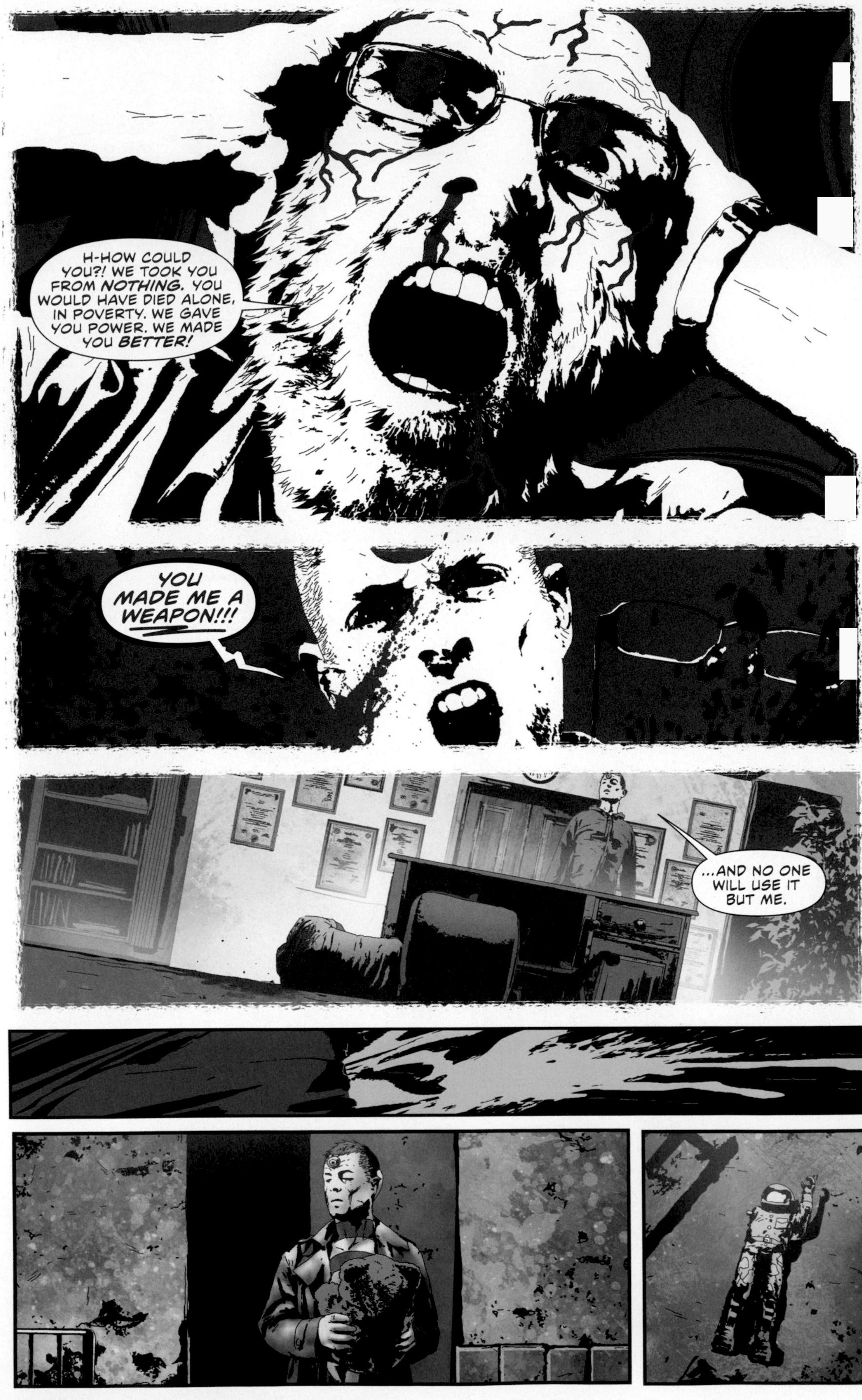
H-HOW COULD YOU?! WE TOOK YOU FROM NOTHING. YOU WOULD HAVE DIED ALONE, IN POVERTY. WE GAVE YOU POWER. WE MADE YOU BETTER!
YOU MADE ME A WEAPON!!!
...AND NO ONE WILL USE IT BUT ME.

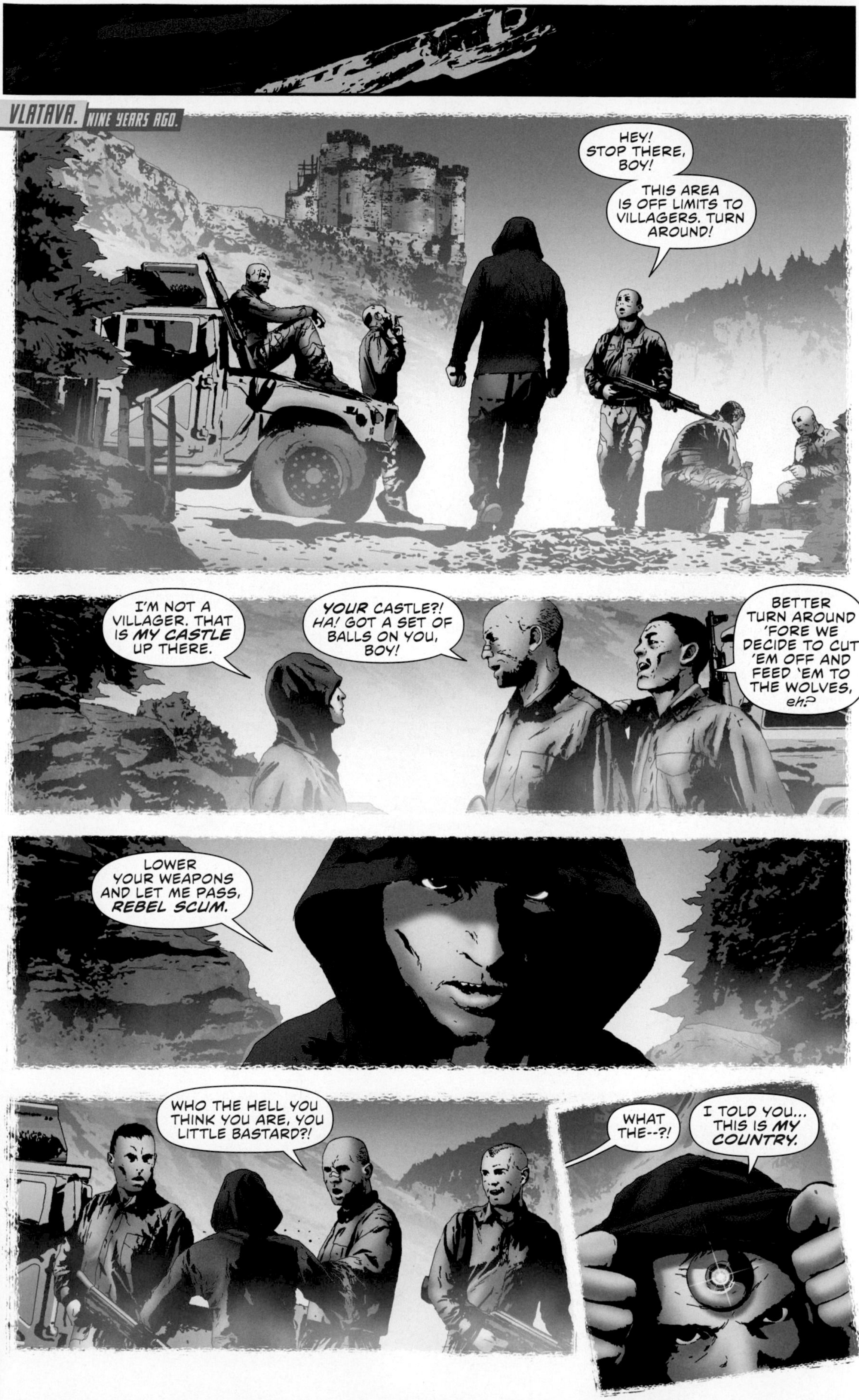
VLATAVA. NINE YEARS AGO.
HEY! STOP THERE, BOY!
THIS AREA IS OFF LIMITS TO VILLAGERS. TURN AROUND!
I'M NOT A VILLAGER. THAT IS MY CASTLE UP THERE.
YOUR CASTLE?! HA! GOT A SET OF BALLS ON YOU, BOY!
BETTER TURN AROUND 'FORE WE DECIDE TO CUT 'EM OFF AND FEED 'EM TO THE WOLVES, eh?
LOWER YOUR WEAPONS AND LET ME PASS, REBEL SCUM.
WHO THE HELL YOU THINK YOU ARE, YOU LITTLE BASTARD?!
WHAT THE--?!
I TOLD YOU... THIS IS MY COUNTRY.

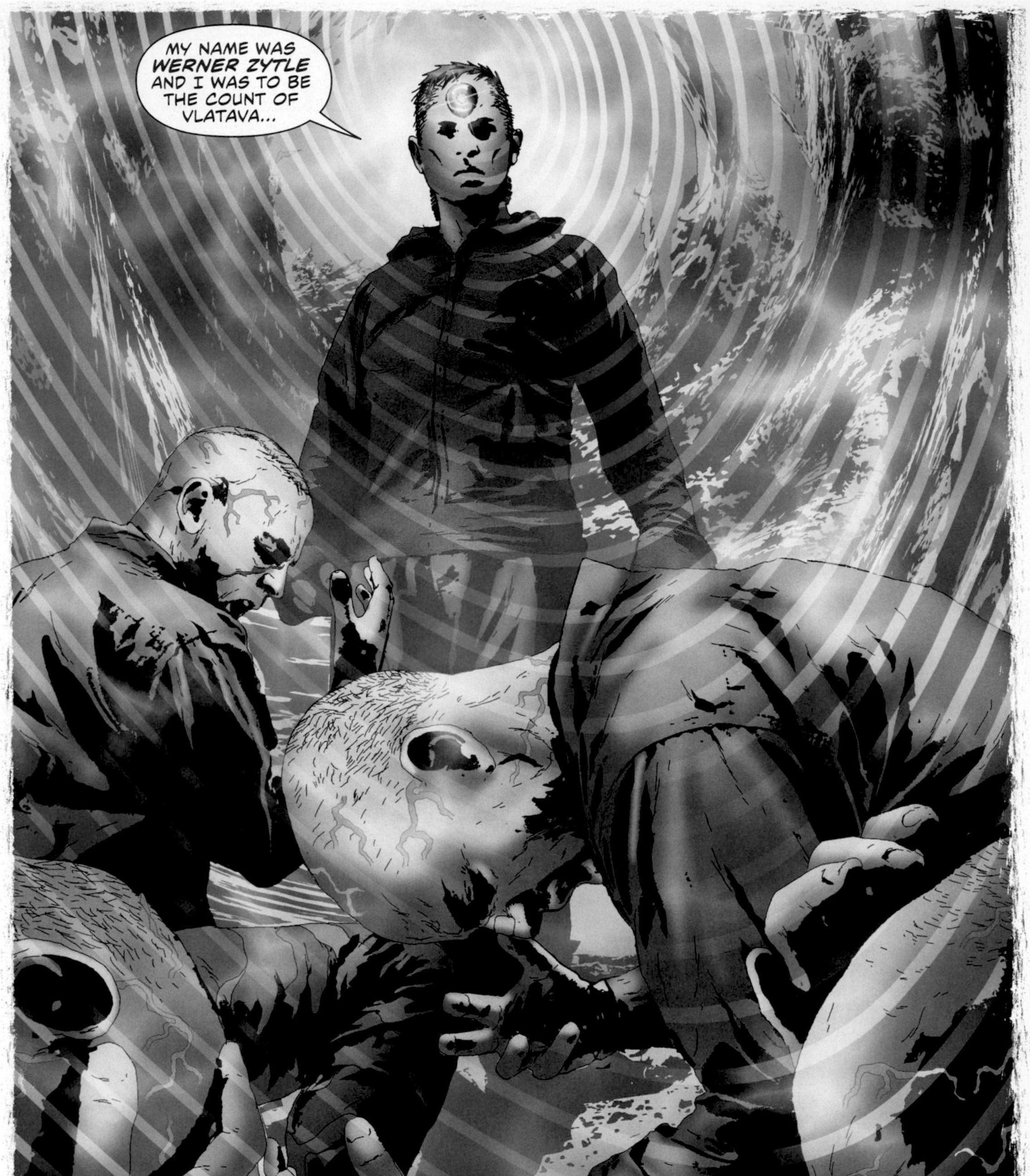
MY NAME WAS WERNER ZYTLE AND I WAS TO BE THE COUNT OF VLATAVA...

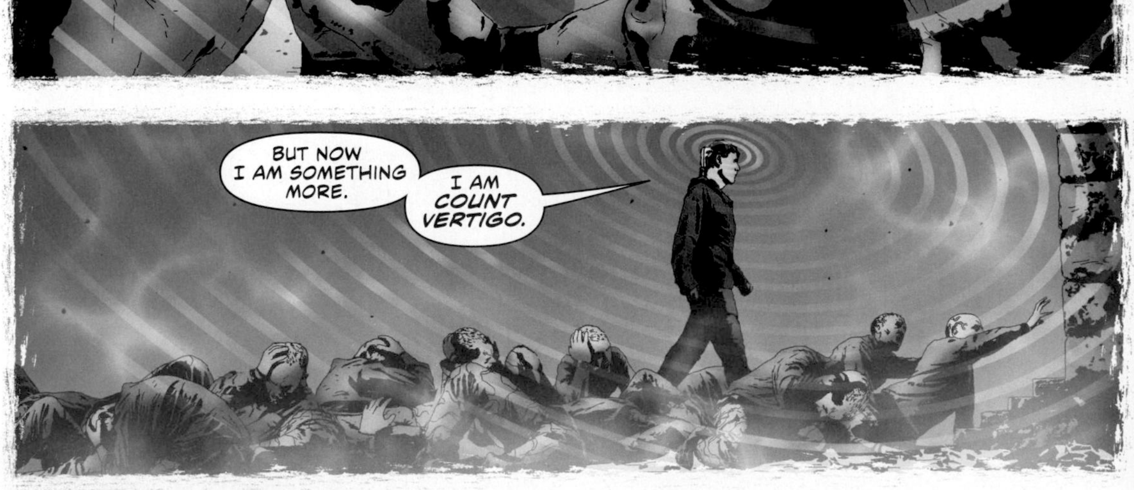
BUT NOW I AM SOMETHING MORE.
I AM COUNT VERTIGO.

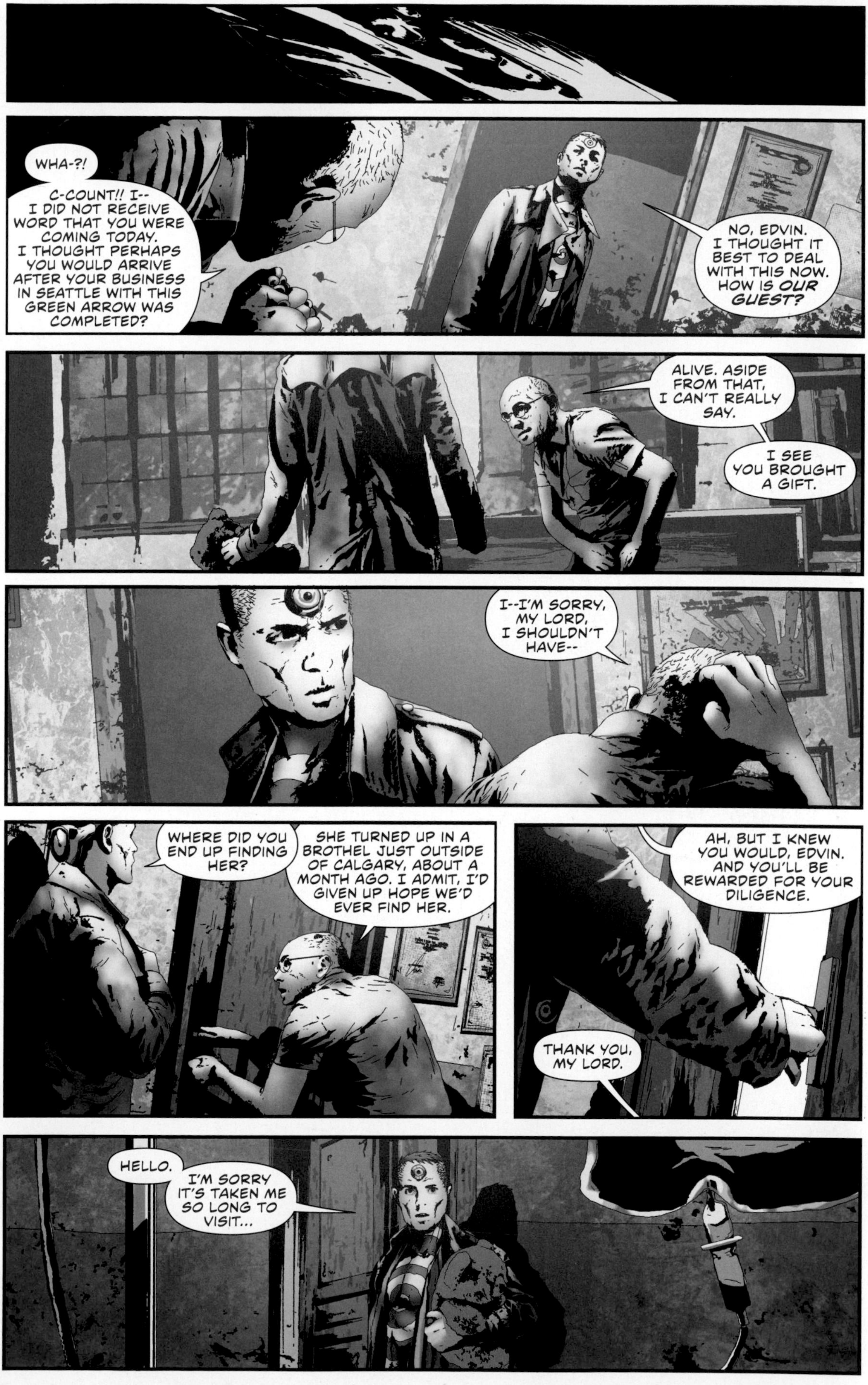
WHA-?!
C-COUNT!! I--
I DID NOT RECEIVE WORD THAT YOU WERE COMING TODAY. I THOUGHT PERHAPS YOU WOULD ARRIVE AFTER YOUR BUSINESS IN SEATTLE WITH THIS GREEN ARROW WAS COMPLETED?
NO, EDVIN. I THOUGHT IT BEST TO DEAL WITH THIS NOW. HOW IS OUR GUEST?
ALIVE. ASIDE FROM THAT, I CAN'T REALLY SAY.
I SEE YOU BROUGHT A GIFT.
I--I'M SORRY, MY LORD, I SHOULDN'T HAVE--
WHERE DID YOU END UP FINDING HER?
SHE TURNED UP IN A BROTHEL JUST OUTSIDE OF CALGARY, ABOUT A MONTH AGO. I ADMIT, I'D GIVEN UP HOPE WE'D EVER FIND HER.
AH, BUT I KNEW YOU WOULD, EDVIN. AND YOU'LL BE REWARDED FOR YOUR DILIGENCE.
THANK YOU, MY LORD.
HELLO.
I'M SORRY IT'S TAKEN ME SO LONG TO VISIT...

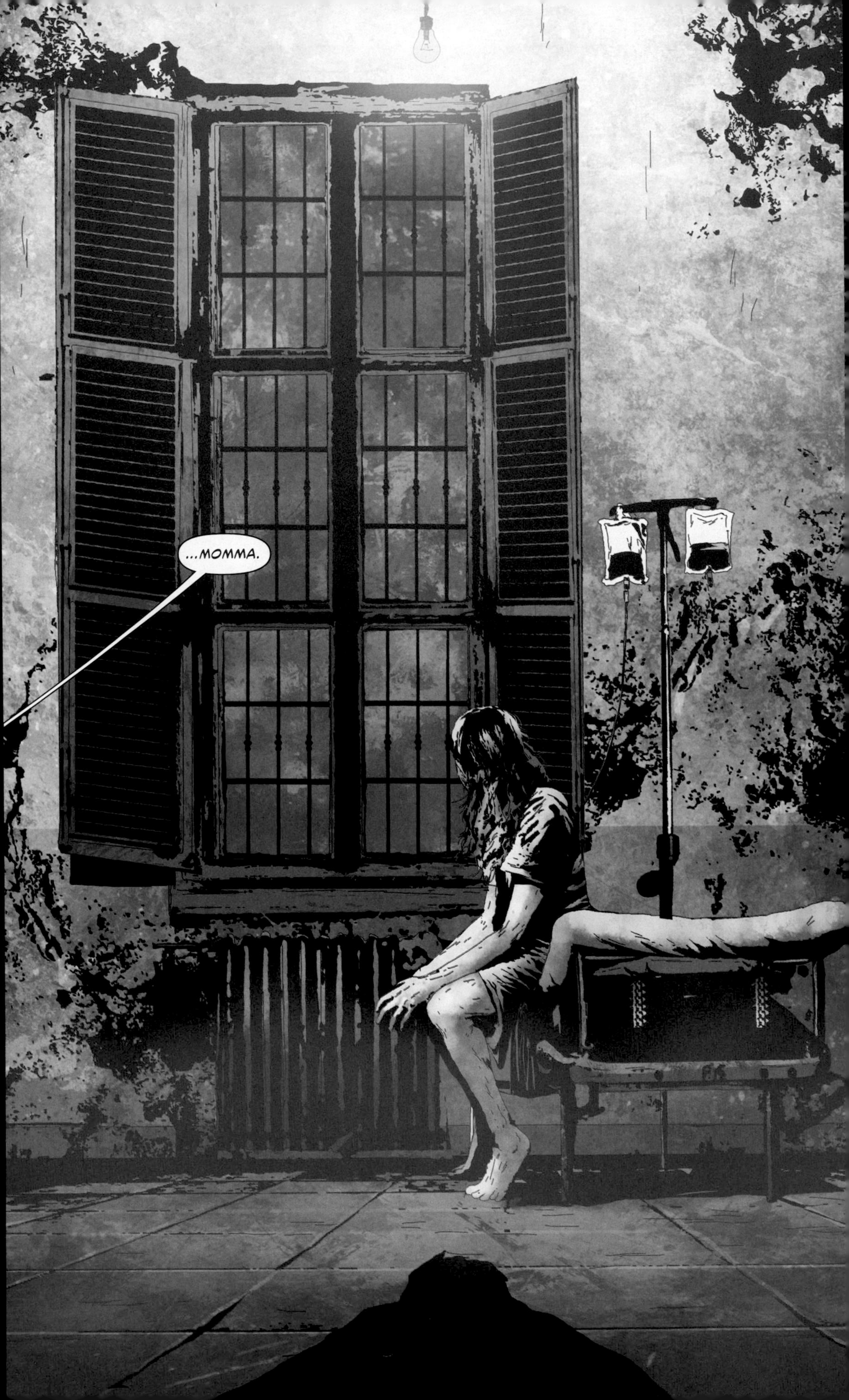
...MOMMA.

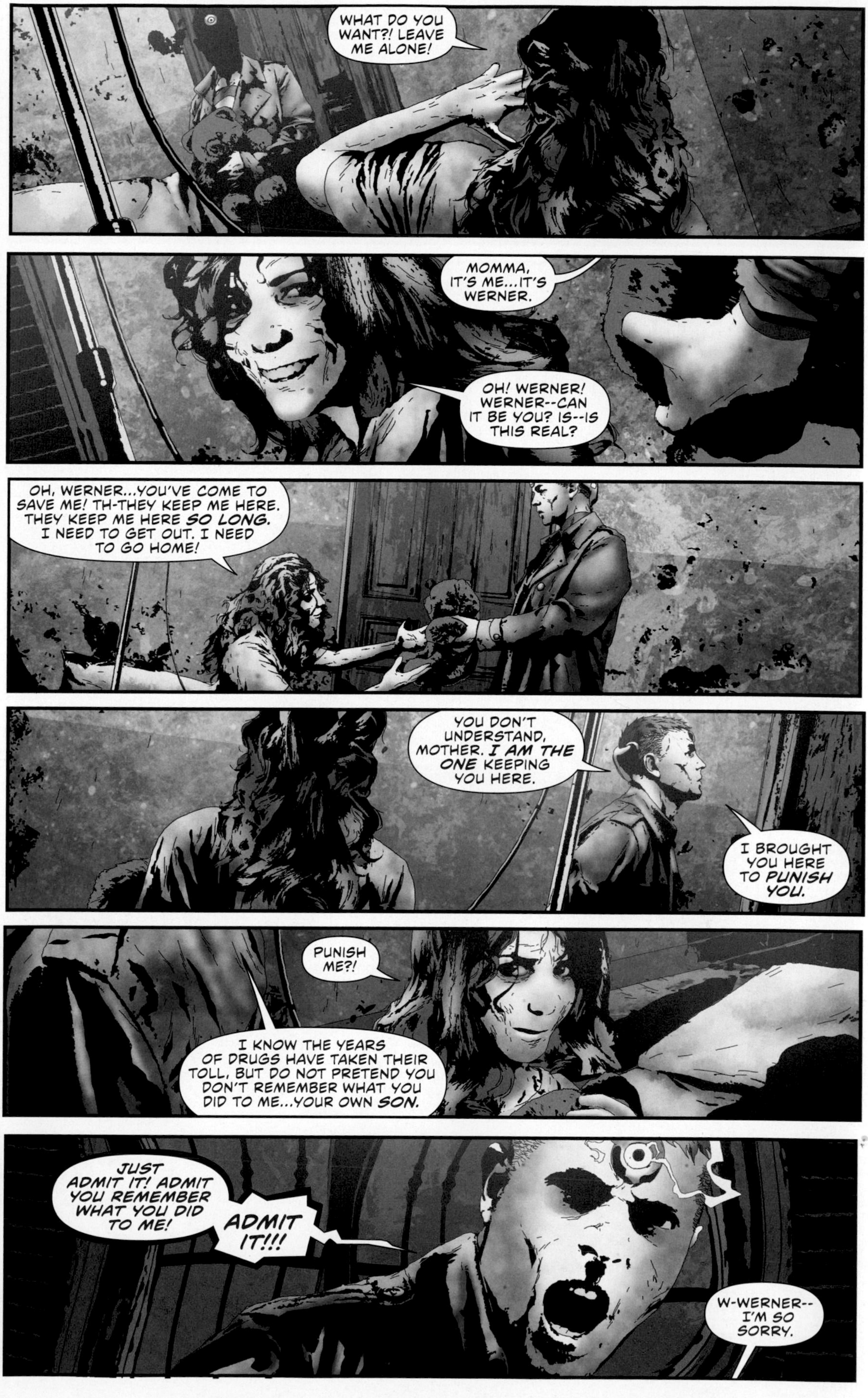
WHAT DO YOU WANT?! LEAVE ME ALONE!
MOMMA, IT'S ME...IT'S WERNER.
OH! WERNER! WERNER--CAN IT BE YOU? IS--IS THIS REAL?
OH, WERNER...YOU'VE COME TO SAVE ME! TH-THEY KEEP ME HERE. THEY KEEP ME HERE SO LONG. I NEED TO GET OUT. I NEED TO GO HOME!
YOU DON'T UNDERSTAND, MOTHER. I AM THE ONE KEEPING YOU HERE.
I BROUGHT YOU HERE TO PUNISH YOU.
PUNISH ME?!
I KNOW THE YEARS OF DRUGS HAVE TAKEN THEIR TOLL, BUT DO NOT PRETEND YOU DON'T REMEMBER WHAT YOU DID TO ME...YOUR OWN SON.
JUST ADMIT IT! ADMIT YOU REMEMBER WHAT YOU DID TO ME!
ADMIT IT!!!
W-WERNER-- I'M SO SORRY.

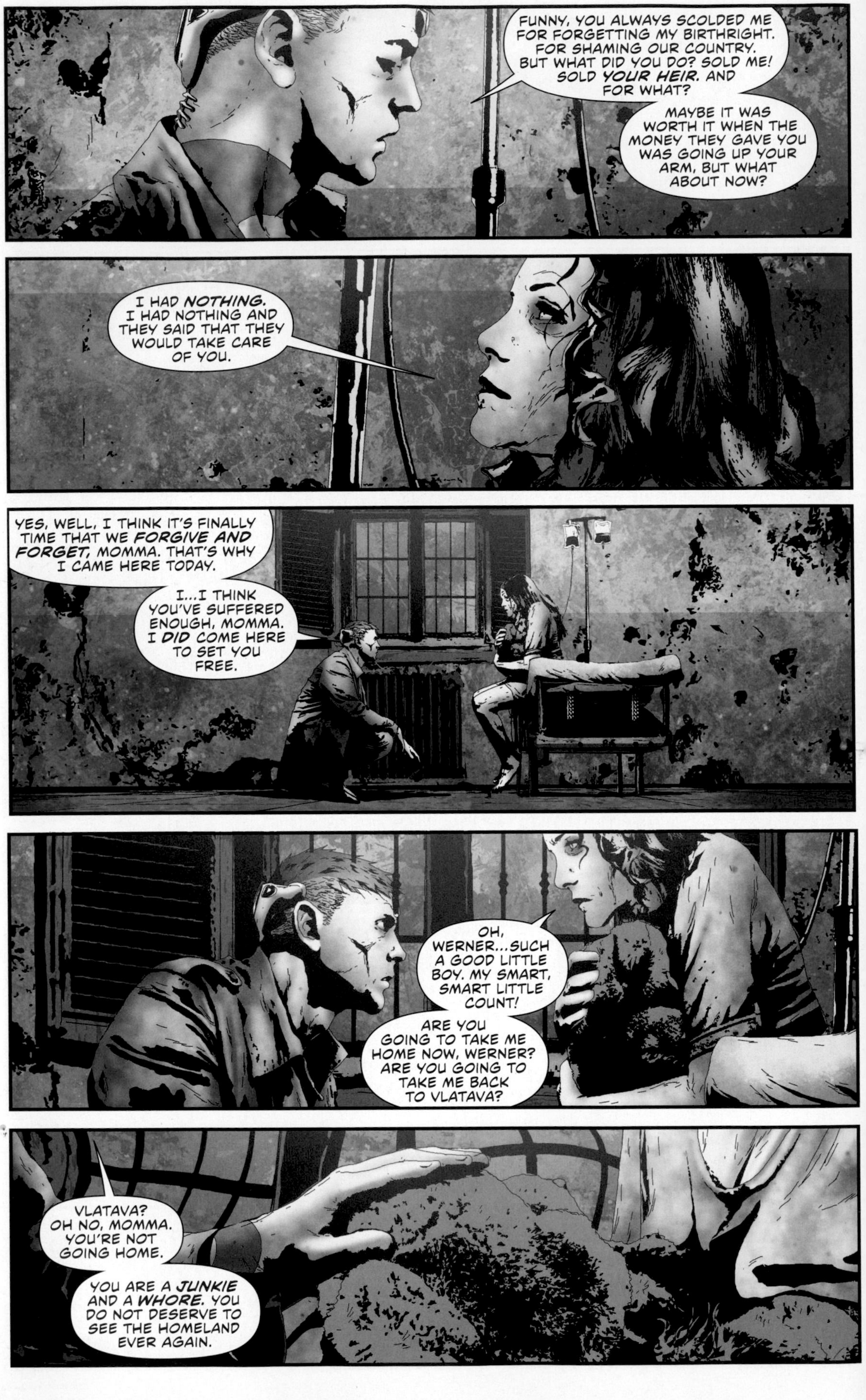
FUNNY, YOU ALWAYS SCOLDED ME FOR FORGETTING MY BIRTHRIGHT. FOR SHAMING OUR COUNTRY. BUT WHAT DID YOU DO? SOLD ME! SOLD *YOUR HEIR.* AND FOR WHAT?
MAYBE IT WAS WORTH IT WHEN THE MONEY THEY GAVE YOU WAS GOING UP YOUR ARM, BUT WHAT ABOUT NOW?
I HAD *NOTHING.* I HAD NOTHING AND THEY SAID THAT THEY WOULD TAKE CARE OF YOU.
YES, WELL, I THINK IT'S FINALLY TIME THAT WE *FORGIVE AND FORGET,* MOMMA. THAT'S WHY I CAME HERE TODAY.
I...I THINK YOU'VE SUFFERED ENOUGH, MOMMA. I *DID* COME HERE TO SET YOU FREE.
OH, WERNER...SUCH A GOOD LITTLE BOY. MY SMART, SMART LITTLE COUNT!
ARE YOU GOING TO TAKE ME HOME NOW, WERNER? ARE YOU GOING TO TAKE ME BACK TO VLATAVA?
VLATAVA? OH NO, MOMMA. YOU'RE NOT GOING HOME.
YOU ARE A *JUNKIE* AND A *WHORE.* YOU DO NOT DESERVE TO SEE THE HOMELAND EVER AGAIN.

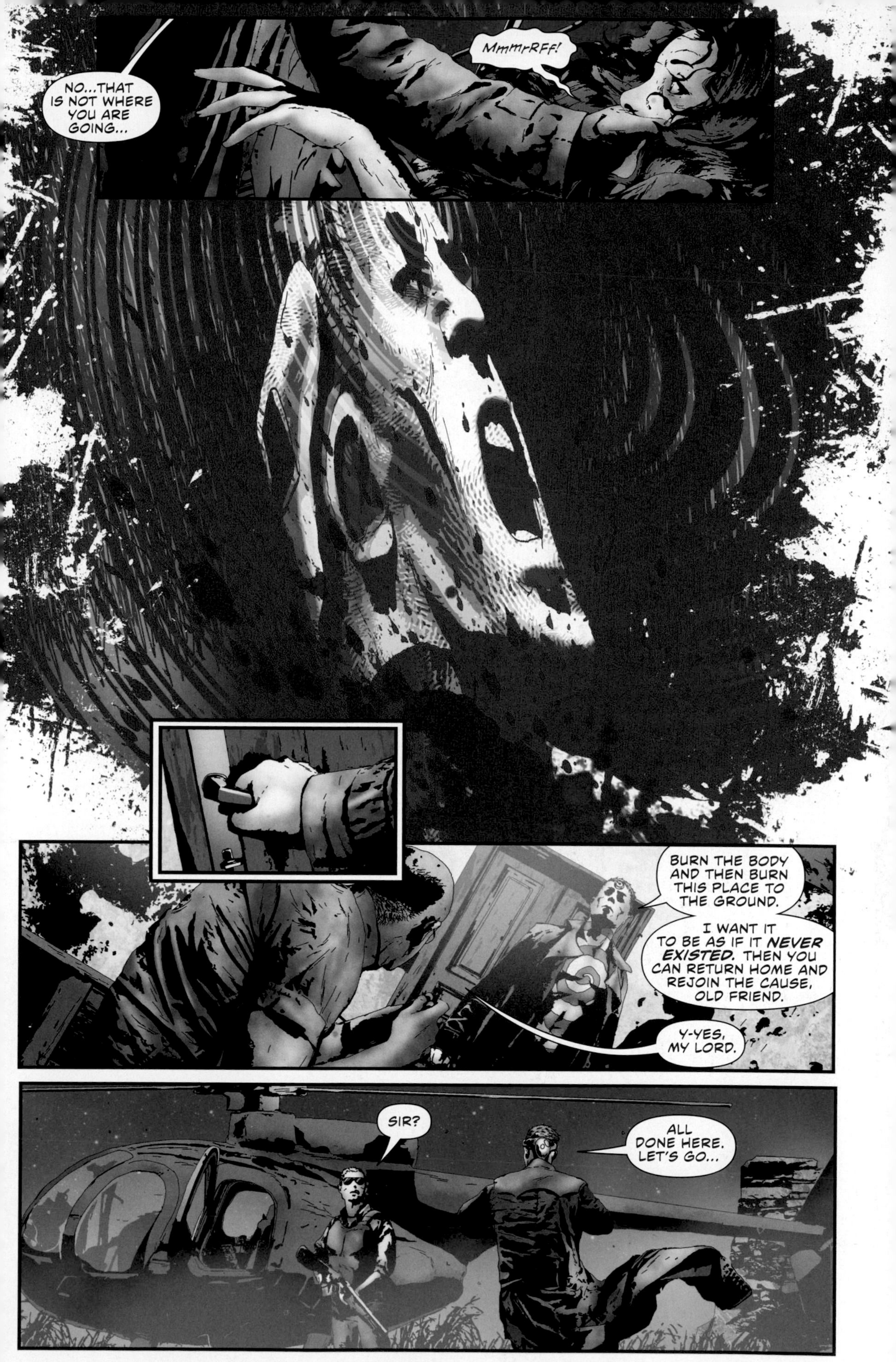
MmmrRFF!
NO...THAT IS NOT WHERE YOU ARE GOING...
BURN THE BODY AND THEN BURN THIS PLACE TO THE GROUND.
I WANT IT TO BE AS IF IT NEVER EXISTED. THEN YOU CAN RETURN HOME AND REJOIN THE CAUSE, OLD FRIEND.
Y-YES, MY LORD.
SIR?
ALL DONE HERE. LET'S GO...

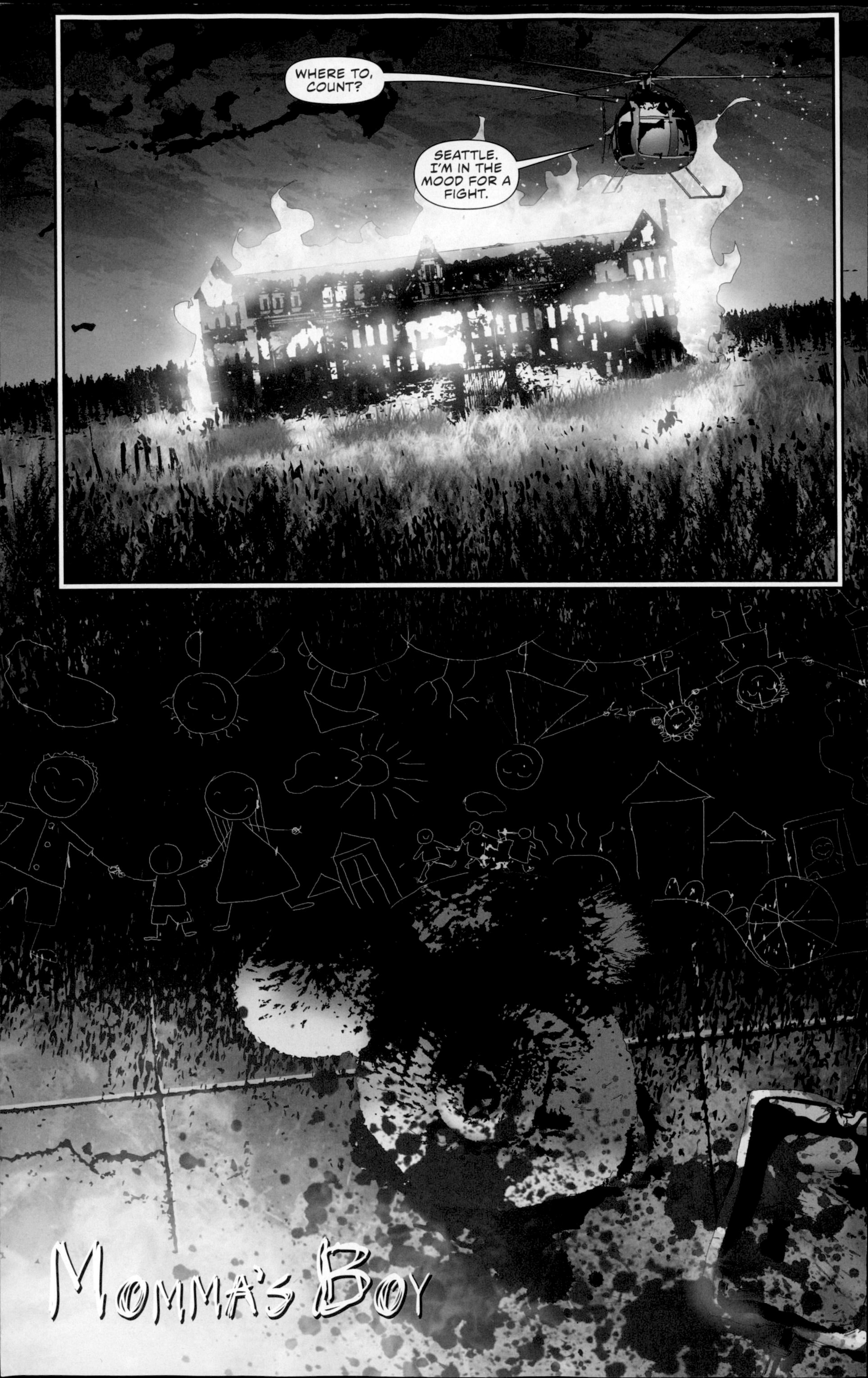
WHERE TO, COUNT?
SEATTLE. I'M IN THE MOOD FOR A FIGHT.
MOMMA'S BOY

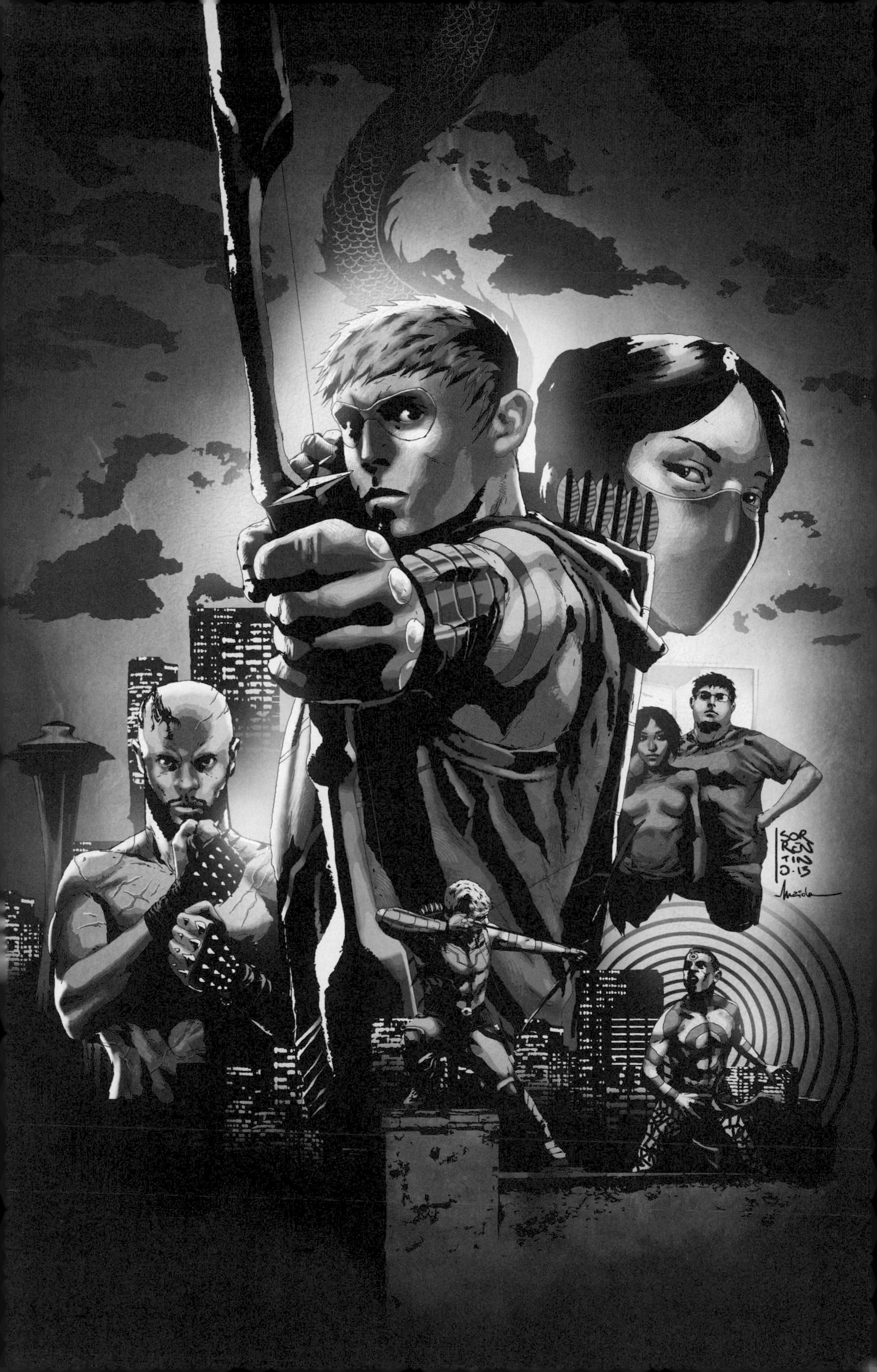

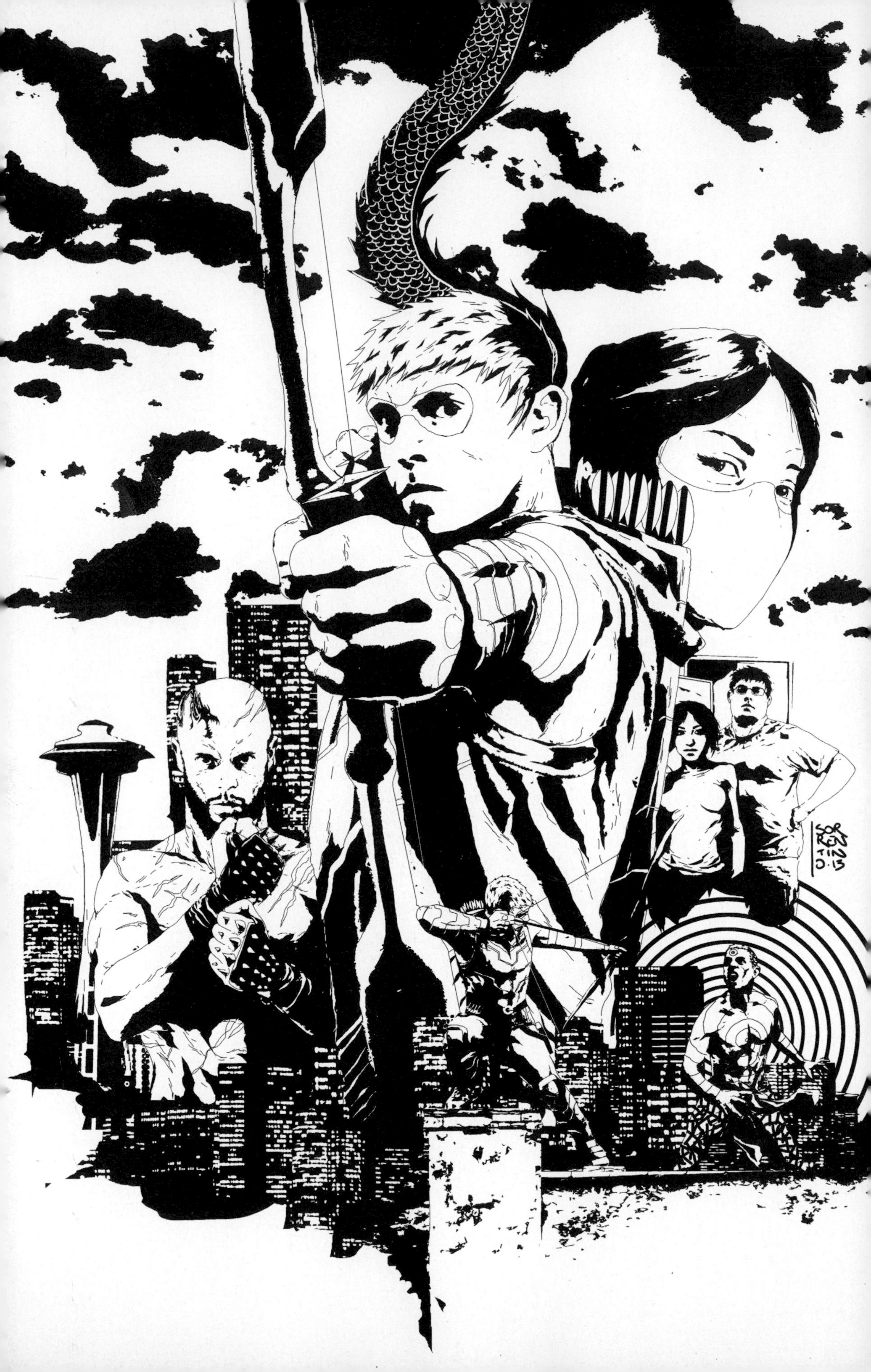

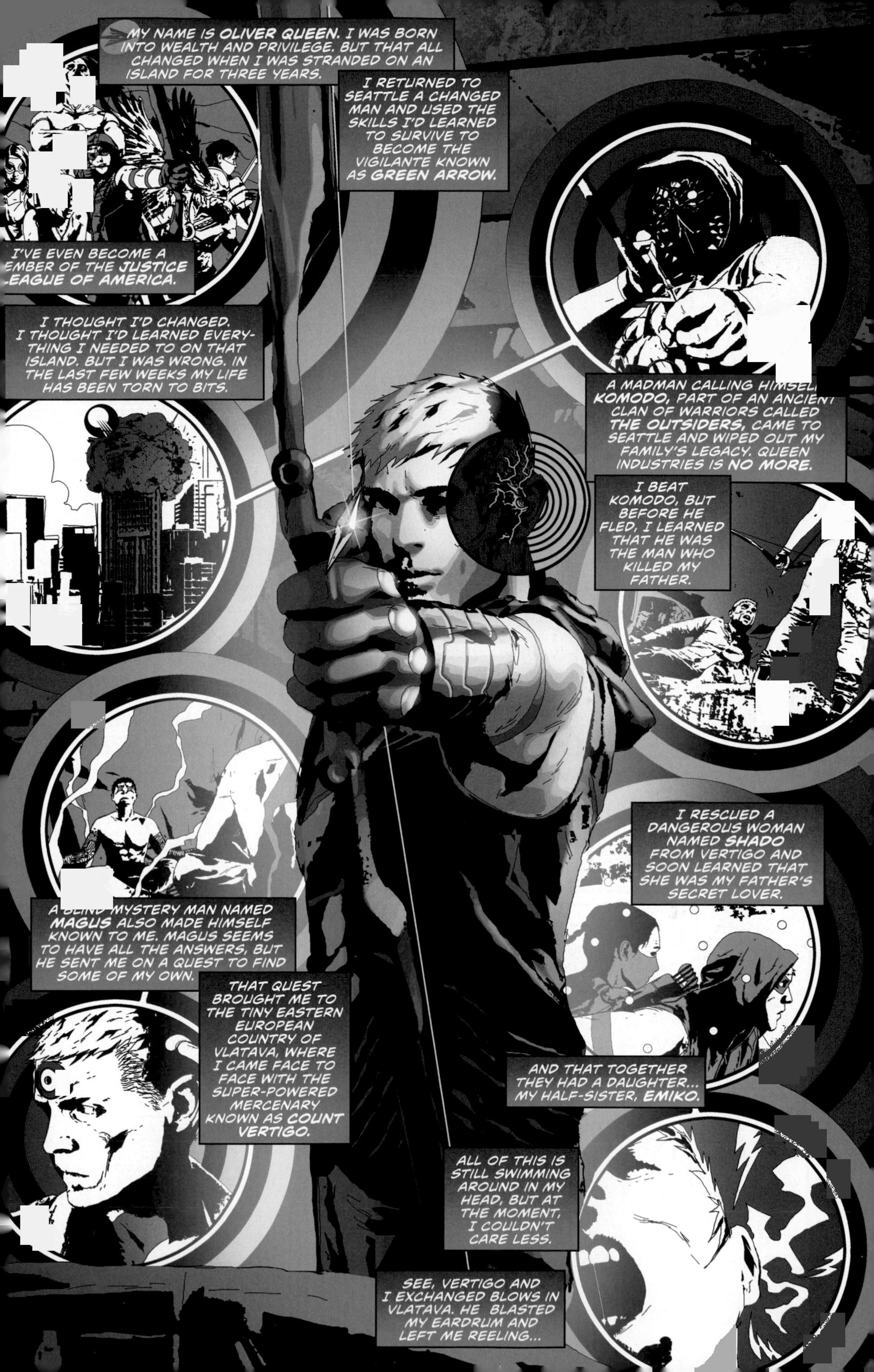

MY NAME IS OLIVER QUEEN. I WAS BORN INTO WEALTH AND PRIVILEGE. BUT THAT ALL CHANGED WHEN I WAS STRANDED ON AN ISLAND FOR THREE YEARS.
I RETURNED TO SEATTLE A CHANGED MAN AND USED THE SKILLS I'D LEARNED TO SURVIVE TO BECOME THE VIGILANTE KNOWN AS GREEN ARROW.
I'VE EVEN BECOME A EMBER OF THE JUSTICE EAGUE OF AMERICA.
I THOUGHT I'D CHANGED. I THOUGHT I'D LEARNED EVERYTHING I NEEDED TO ON THAT ISLAND. BUT I WAS WRONG. IN THE LAST FEW WEEKS MY LIFE HAS BEEN TORN TO BITS.
A MADMAN CALLING HIMSEL KOMODO, PART OF AN ANCIEN CLAN OF WARRIORS CALLED THE OUTSIDERS, CAME TO SEATTLE AND WIPED OUT MY FAMILY'S LEGACY. QUEEN INDUSTRIES IS NO MORE.
I BEAT KOMODO, BUT BEFORE HE FLED, I LEARNED THAT HE WAS THE MAN WHO KILLED MY FATHER.
A BLIND MYSTERY MAN NAMED MAGUS ALSO MADE HIMSELF KNOWN TO ME. MAGUS SEEMS TO HAVE ALL THE ANSWERS, BUT HE SENT ME ON A QUEST TO FIND SOME OF MY OWN.
THAT QUEST BROUGHT ME TO THE TINY EASTERN EUROPEAN COUNTRY OF VLATAVA, WHERE I CAME FACE TO FACE WITH THE SUPER-POWERED MERCENARY KNOWN AS COUNT VERTIGO.
I RESCUED A DANGEROUS WOMAN NAMED SHADO FROM VERTIGO AND SOON LEARNED THAT SHE WAS MY FATHER'S SECRET LOVER.
AND THAT TOGETHER THEY HAD A DAUGHTER... MY HALF-SISTER, EMIKO.
ALL OF THIS IS STILL SWIMMING AROUND IN MY HEAD, BUT AT THE MOMENT, I COULDN'T CARE LESS.
SEE, VERTIGO AND I EXCHANGED BLOWS IN VLATAVA. HE BLASTED MY EARDRUM AND LEFT ME REELING...

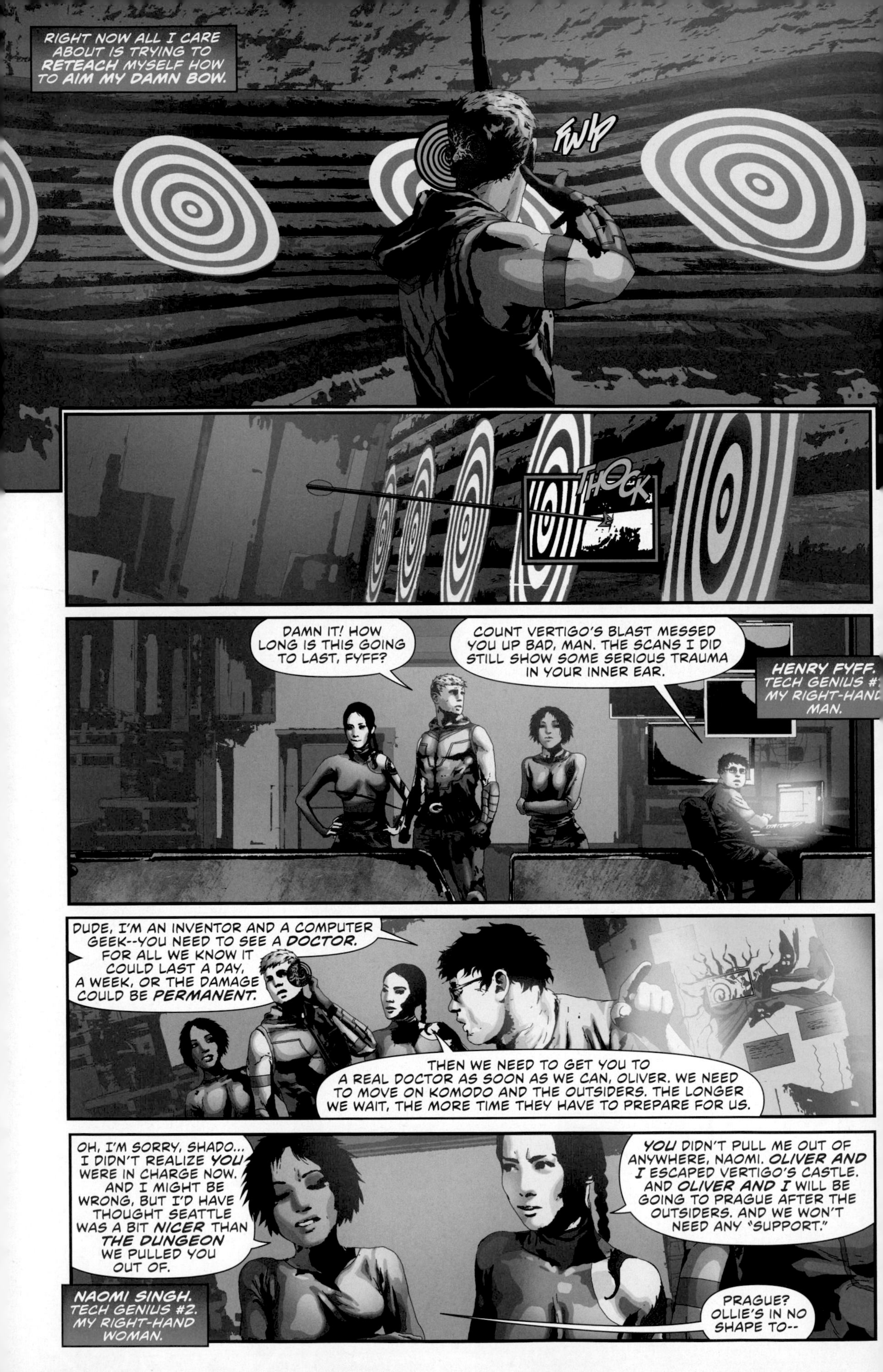
RIGHT NOW ALL I CARE ABOUT IS TRYING TO RETEACH MYSELF HOW TO AIM MY DAMN BOW.
FWIP
THOCK
DAMN IT! HOW LONG IS THIS GOING TO LAST, FYFF?
COUNT VERTIGO'S BLAST MESSED YOU UP BAD, MAN. THE SCANS I DID STILL SHOW SOME SERIOUS TRAUMA IN YOUR INNER EAR.
HENRY FYFF. TECH GENIUS #1. MY RIGHT-HAND MAN.
DUDE, I'M AN INVENTOR AND A COMPUTER GEEK--YOU NEED TO SEE A DOCTOR. FOR ALL WE KNOW IT COULD LAST A DAY, A WEEK, OR THE DAMAGE COULD BE PERMANENT.
THEN WE NEED TO GET YOU TO A REAL DOCTOR AS SOON AS WE CAN, OLIVER. WE NEED TO MOVE ON KOMODO AND THE OUTSIDERS. THE LONGER WE WAIT, THE MORE TIME THEY HAVE TO PREPARE FOR US.
OH, I'M SORRY, SHADO... I DIDN'T REALIZE YOU WERE IN CHARGE NOW. AND I MIGHT BE WRONG, BUT I'D HAVE THOUGHT SEATTLE WAS A BIT NICER THAN THE DUNGEON WE PULLED YOU OUT OF.
NAOMI SINGH. TECH GENIUS #2. MY RIGHT-HAND WOMAN.
YOU DIDN'T PULL ME OUT OF ANYWHERE, NAOMI. OLIVER AND I ESCAPED VERTIGO'S CASTLE. AND OLIVER AND I WILL BE GOING TO PRAGUE AFTER THE OUTSIDERS. AND WE WON'T NEED ANY "SUPPORT."
PRAGUE? OLLIE'S IN NO SHAPE TO--

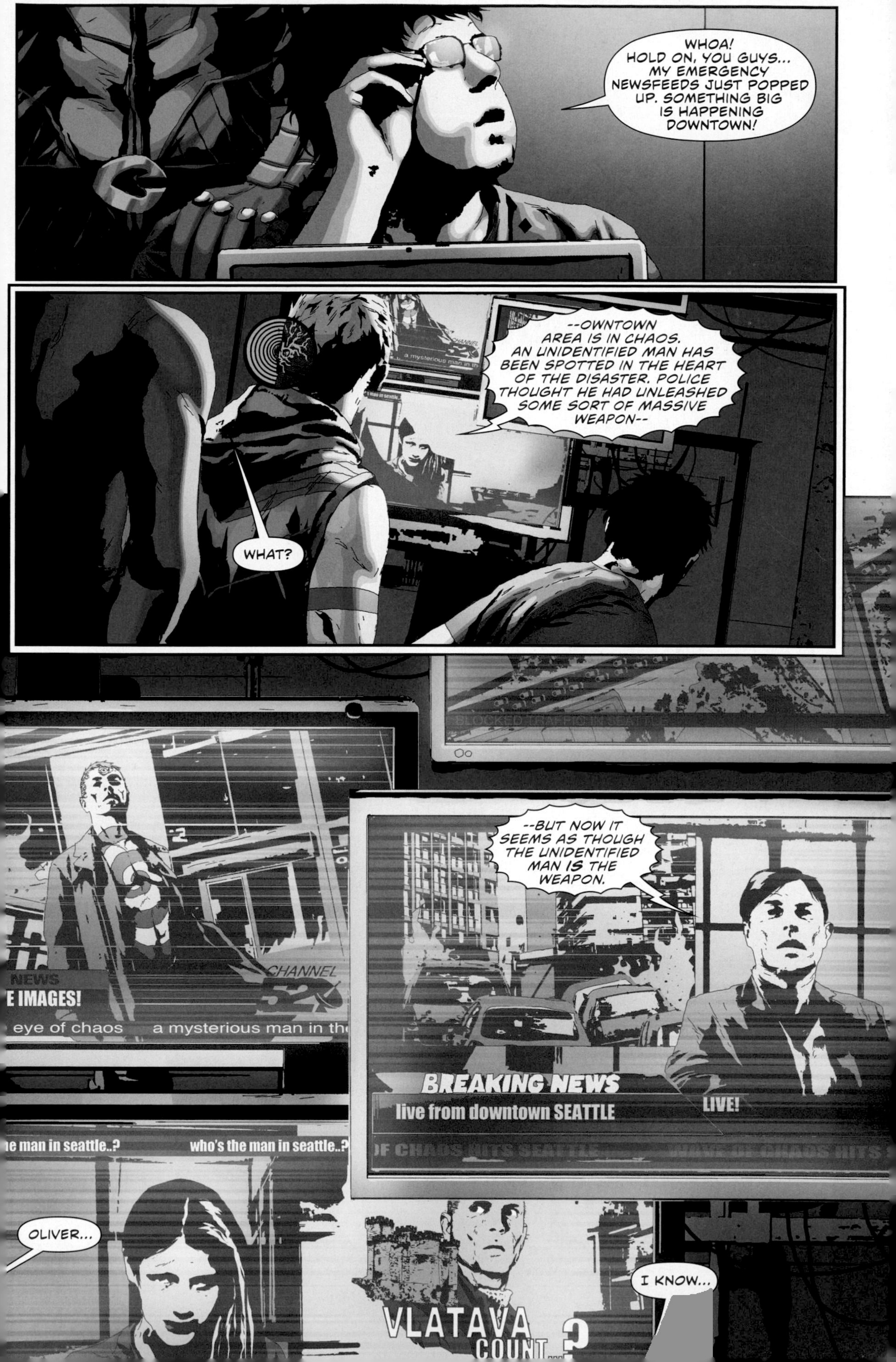
WHOA! HOLD ON, YOU GUYS... MY EMERGENCY NEWSFEEDS JUST POPPED UP. SOMETHING BIG IS HAPPENING DOWNTOWN!
--OWNTOWN AREA IS IN CHAOS. AN UNIDENTIFIED MAN HAS BEEN SPOTTED IN THE HEART OF THE DISASTER. POLICE THOUGHT HE HAD UNLEASHED SOME SORT OF MASSIVE WEAPON--
WHAT?
BLOCKED TRAFFIC IN SEATTLE
NEWS
E IMAGES!
CHANNEL
eye of chaos a mysterious man in the
--BUT NOW IT SEEMS AS THOUGH THE UNIDENTIFIED MAN IS THE WEAPON.
BREAKING NEWS
live from downtown SEATTLE
LIVE!
e man in seattle..? who's the man in seattle..?
OLIVER...
I KNOW...
VLATAVA
COUNT...?

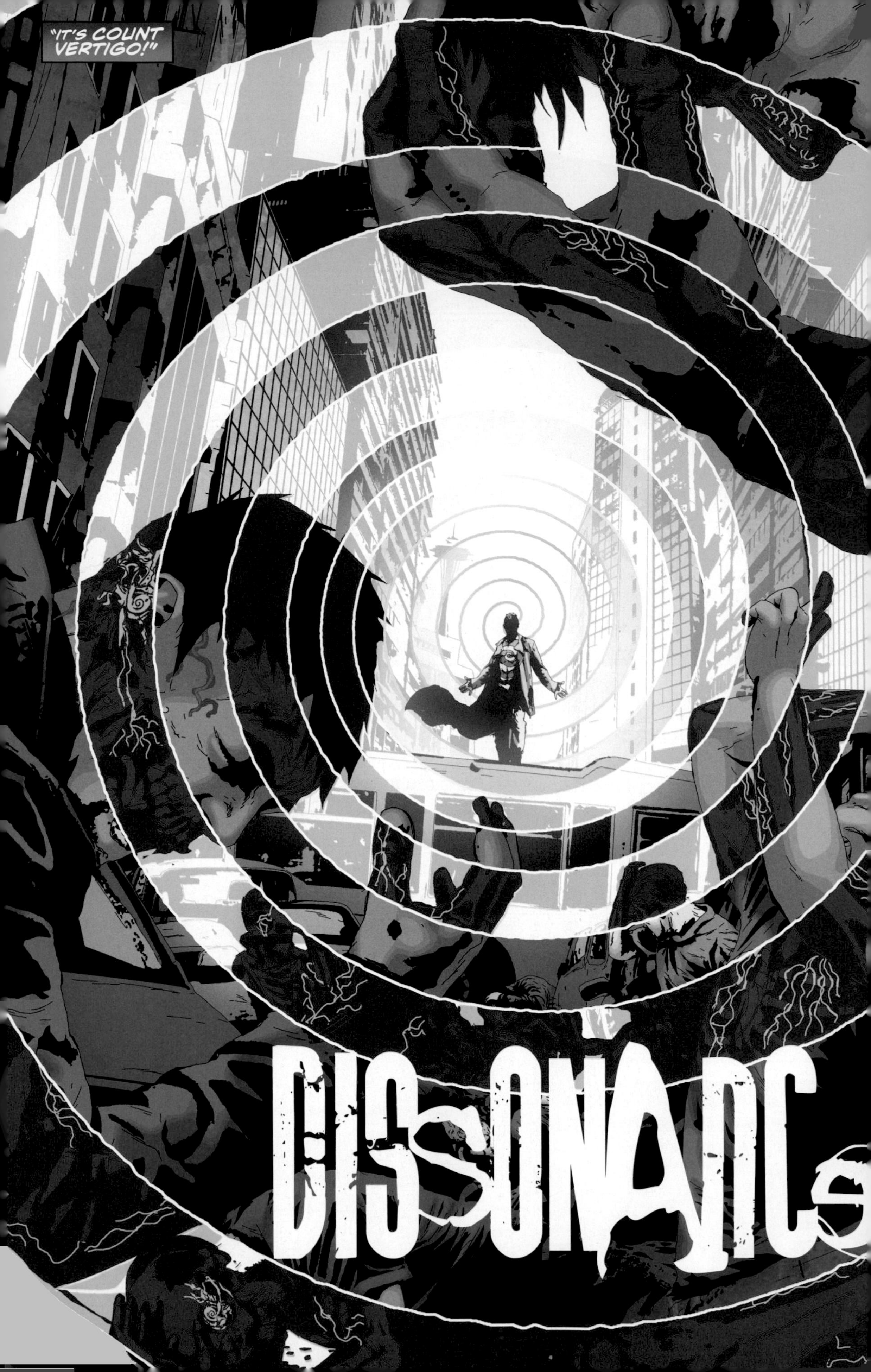
"IT'S COUNT VERTIGO!"
DISSONANCE

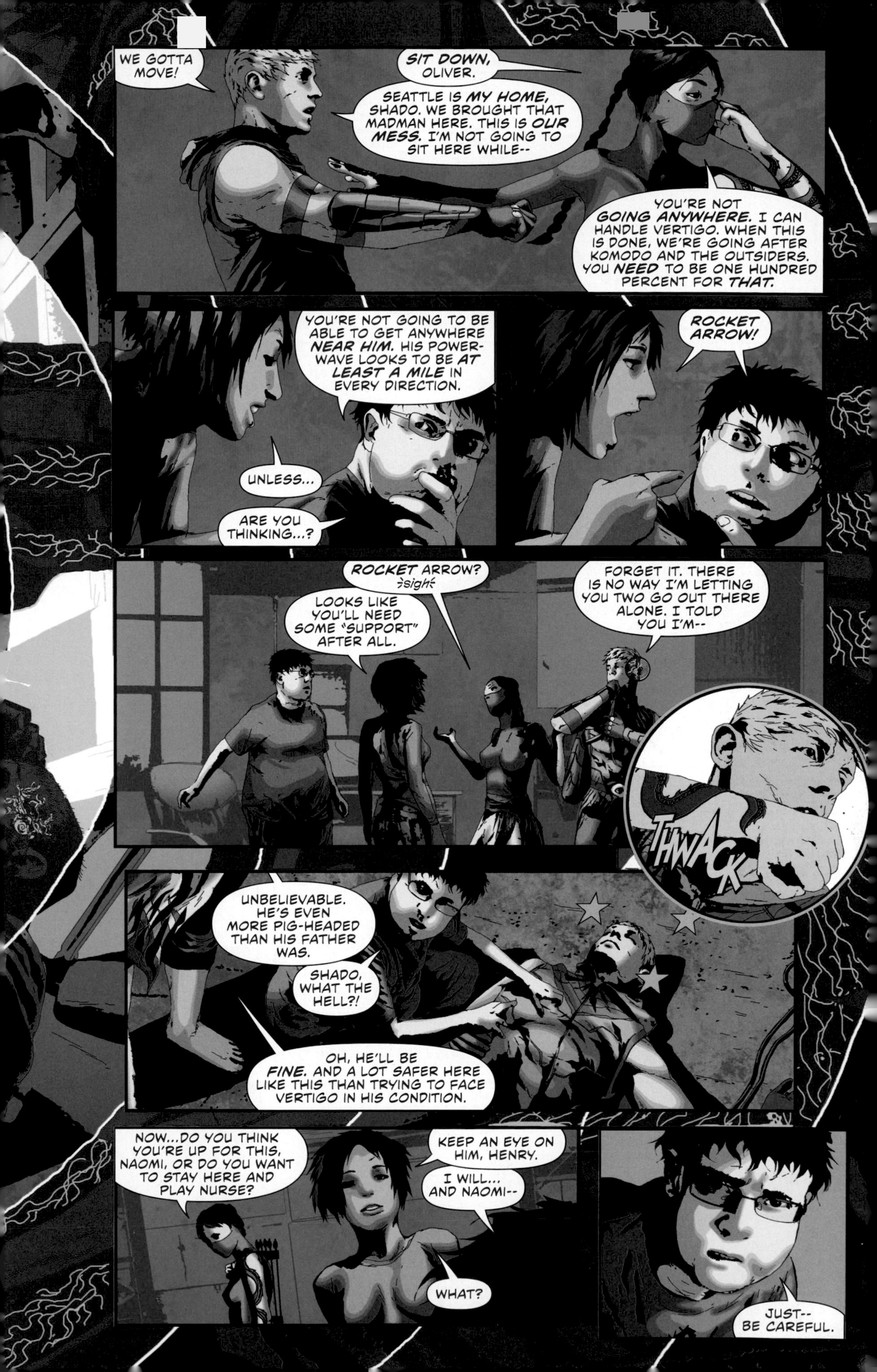
WE GOTTA MOVE!
SIT DOWN, OLIVER.
SEATTLE IS MY HOME, SHADO. WE BROUGHT THAT MADMAN HERE. THIS IS OUR MESS. I'M NOT GOING TO SIT HERE WHILE--
YOU'RE NOT GOING ANYWHERE. I CAN HANDLE VERTIGO. WHEN THIS IS DONE, WE'RE GOING AFTER KOMODO AND THE OUTSIDERS. YOU NEED TO BE ONE HUNDRED PERCENT FOR THAT.
YOU'RE NOT GOING TO BE ABLE TO GET ANYWHERE NEAR HIM. HIS POWER-WAVE LOOKS TO BE AT LEAST A MILE IN EVERY DIRECTION.
UNLESS...
ARE YOU THINKING...?
ROCKET ARROW!
ROCKET ARROW? sigh
LOOKS LIKE YOU'LL NEED SOME "SUPPORT" AFTER ALL.
FORGET IT. THERE IS NO WAY I'M LETTING YOU TWO GO OUT THERE ALONE. I TOLD YOU I'M--
THWACK
UNBELIEVABLE. HE'S EVEN MORE PIG-HEADED THAN HIS FATHER WAS.
SHADO, WHAT THE HELL?!
OH, HE'LL BE FINE. AND A LOT SAFER HERE LIKE THIS THAN TRYING TO FACE VERTIGO IN HIS CONDITION.
NOW...DO YOU THINK YOU'RE UP FOR THIS, NAOMI, OR DO YOU WANT TO STAY HERE AND PLAY NURSE?
KEEP AN EYE ON HIM, HENRY.
I WILL... AND NAOMI--
WHAT?
JUST-- BE CAREFUL.

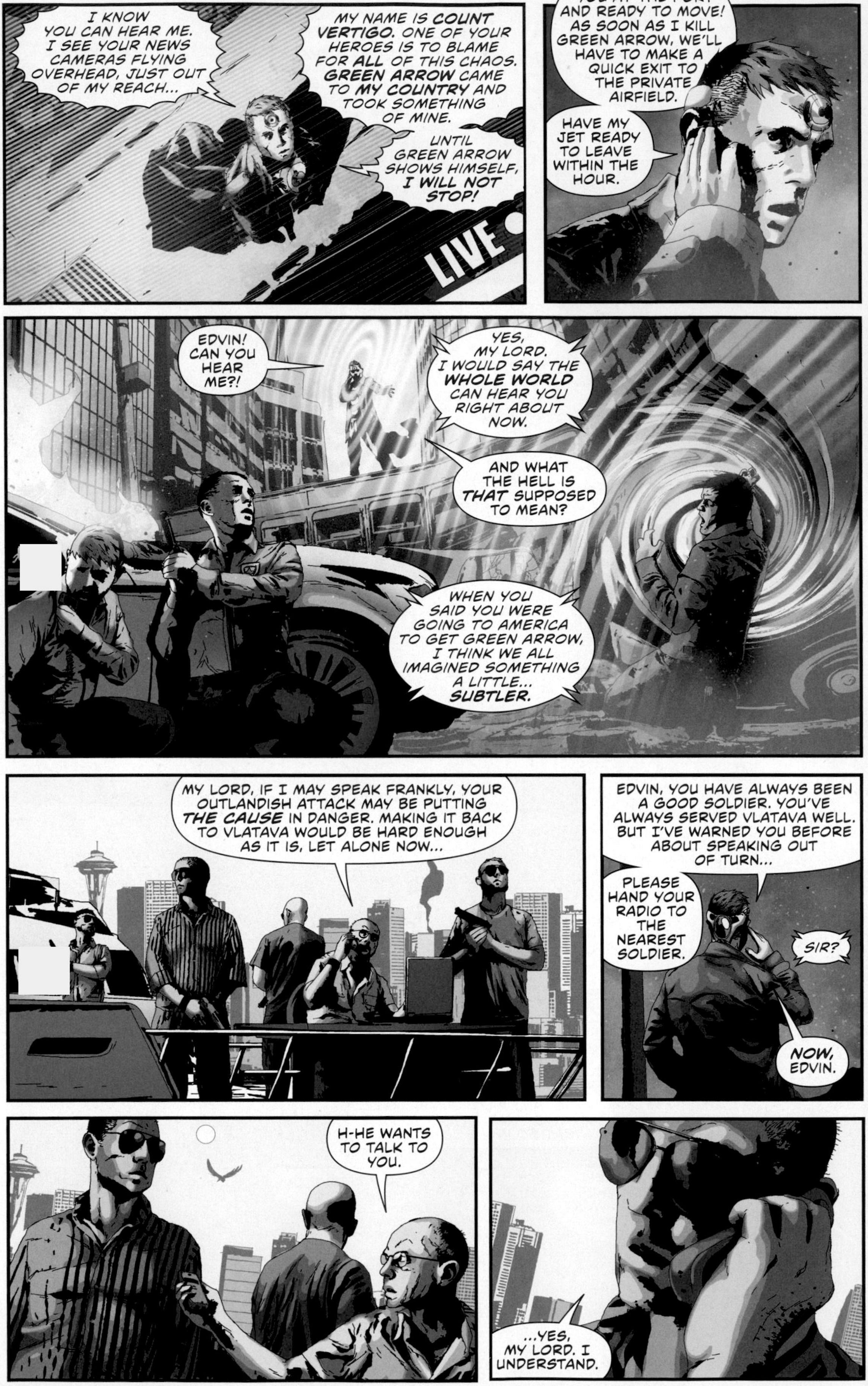
I KNOW YOU CAN HEAR ME. I SEE YOUR NEWS CAMERAS FLYING OVERHEAD, JUST OUT OF MY REACH...
MY NAME IS COUNT VERTIGO. ONE OF YOUR HEROES IS TO BLAME FOR ALL OF THIS CHAOS. GREEN ARROW CAME TO MY COUNTRY AND TOOK SOMETHING OF MINE.
UNTIL GREEN ARROW SHOWS HIMSELF, I WILL NOT STOP!
LIVE
EDVIN, I WANT YOU AT THE PORT AND READY TO MOVE! AS SOON AS I KILL GREEN ARROW, WE'LL HAVE TO MAKE A QUICK EXIT TO THE PRIVATE AIRFIELD.
HAVE MY JET READY TO LEAVE WITHIN THE HOUR.
EDVIN! CAN YOU HEAR ME?!
YES, MY LORD. I WOULD SAY THE WHOLE WORLD CAN HEAR YOU RIGHT ABOUT NOW.
AND WHAT THE HELL IS THAT SUPPOSED TO MEAN?
WHEN YOU SAID YOU WERE GOING TO AMERICA TO GET GREEN ARROW, I THINK WE ALL IMAGINED SOMETHING A LITTLE... SUBTLER.
MY LORD, IF I MAY SPEAK FRANKLY, YOUR OUTLANDISH ATTACK MAY BE PUTTING THE CAUSE IN DANGER. MAKING IT BACK TO VLATAVA WOULD BE HARD ENOUGH AS IT IS, LET ALONE NOW...
EDVIN, YOU HAVE ALWAYS BEEN A GOOD SOLDIER. YOU'VE ALWAYS SERVED VLATAVA WELL. BUT I'VE WARNED YOU BEFORE ABOUT SPEAKING OUT OF TURN...
PLEASE HAND YOUR RADIO TO THE NEAREST SOLDIER.
SIR?
NOW, EDVIN.
H-HE WANTS TO TALK TO YOU.
...YES, MY LORD. I UNDERSTAND.

IT IS DONE, MY LORD.

GOOD. AND I TRUST I CAN RELY ON YOU TO HAVE THE BOAT READY TO GET US OUT OF HERE WHEN IT'S DONE? FOR YOUR COUNT? FOR VLATAVA?

YES, MY LORD...

...FOR VLATAVA.

--SO FAR NO POLICE OR RESCUE CREWS HAVE BEEN ABLE TO GET ANYWHERE NEAR THE BLAST-WAVE AS PANIC GRIPS THE CITY.

--LIVE FOOTAGE AS THE INTERNATIONAL TERRORIST KNOWN AS COUNT VERTIGO CALLS OUT SEATTLE'S OWN GREEN ARROW.

WHAT THE HELL HIT ME?

THAT WOULD BE THE LOVELY SHADO. SHE'S A PIECE OF WORK, OLLIE. MAYBE YOU SHOULD HAVE LEFT HER IN EUROPE...

HAVING SAID THAT, I STILL THINK IT'S BEST YOU STAY PUT. YOU'RE IN NO SHAPE TO DEAL WITH VERTIGO.

HE'S CALLING ME OUT, FYFF! I WON'T LET ANYONE ELSE GET HURT IN THIS CITY BECAUSE OF ME. NOT AFTER KOMODO...

I UNDERSTAND WHAT YOU'RE FEELING, OLLIE, BUT YOU KNOW YOU CAN'T EVEN AIM YOUR DAMNED BOW. YOU NEED TO STEP BACK...

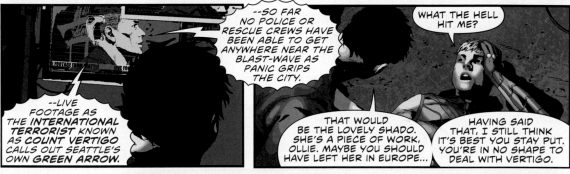

"SHADO HAS THIS UNDER CONTROL..."

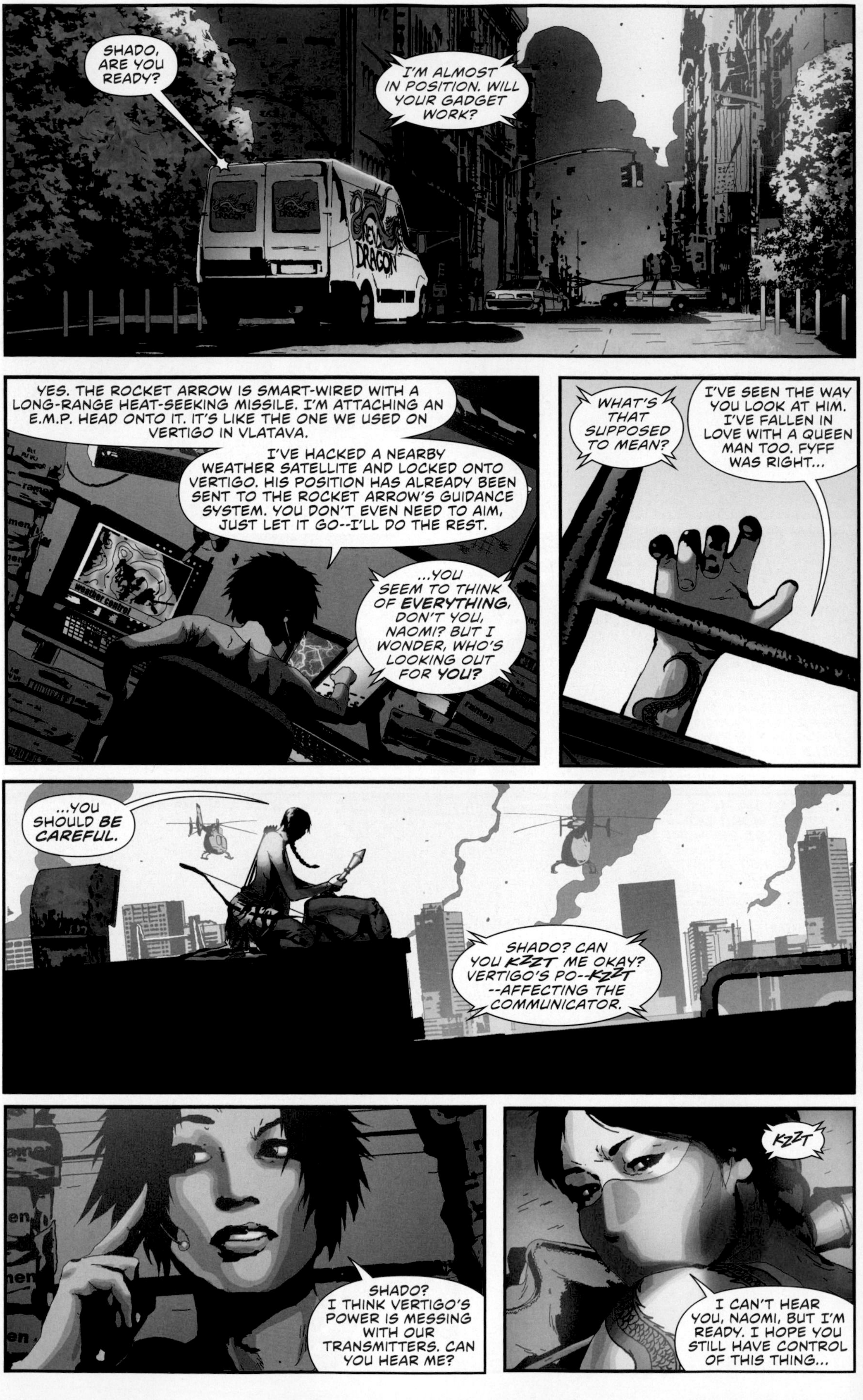
SHADO, ARE YOU READY?
I'M ALMOST IN POSITION. WILL YOUR GADGET WORK?
NEW DRAGON
YES. THE ROCKET ARROW IS SMART-WIRED WITH A LONG-RANGE HEAT-SEEKING MISSILE. I'M ATTACHING AN E.M.P. HEAD ONTO IT. IT'S LIKE THE ONE WE USED ON VERTIGO IN VLATAVA.
I'VE HACKED A NEARBY WEATHER SATELLITE AND LOCKED ONTO VERTIGO. HIS POSITION HAS ALREADY BEEN SENT TO THE ROCKET ARROW'S GUIDANCE SYSTEM. YOU DON'T EVEN NEED TO AIM, JUST LET IT GO--I'LL DO THE REST.
...YOU SEEM TO THINK OF EVERYTHING, DON'T YOU, NAOMI? BUT I WONDER, WHO'S LOOKING OUT FOR YOU?
weather control
WHAT'S THAT SUPPOSED TO MEAN?
I'VE SEEN THE WAY YOU LOOK AT HIM. I'VE FALLEN IN LOVE WITH A QUEEN MAN TOO. FYFF WAS RIGHT...
...YOU SHOULD BE CAREFUL.
SHADO? CAN YOU KZZT ME OKAY? VERTIGO'S PO--KZZT --AFFECTING THE COMMUNICATOR.
SHADO? I THINK VERTIGO'S POWER IS MESSING WITH OUR TRANSMITTERS. CAN YOU HEAR ME?
KZZT
I CAN'T HEAR YOU, NAOMI, BUT I'M READY. I HOPE YOU STILL HAVE CONTROL OF THIS THING...

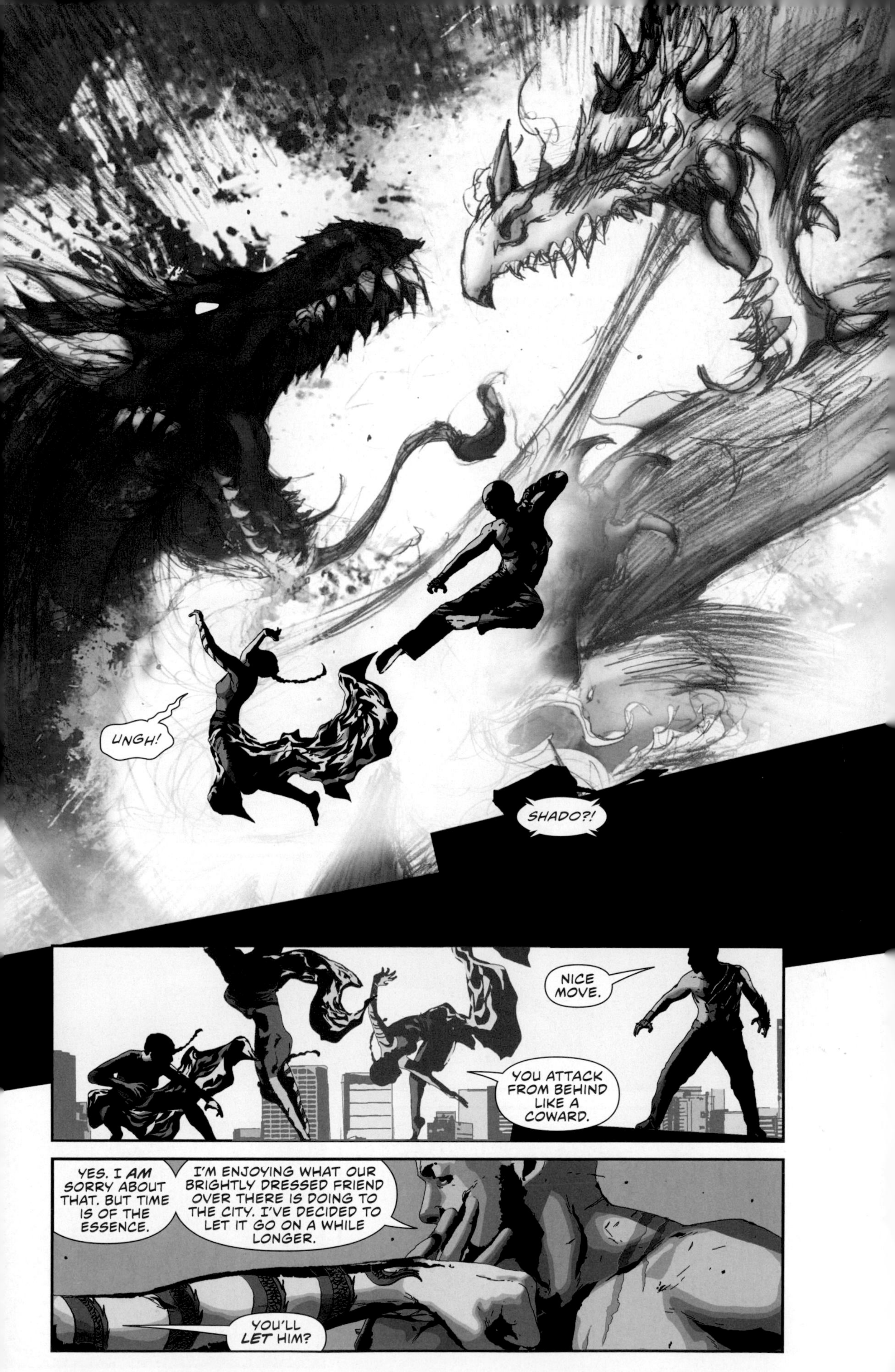
UNGH!
SHADO?!
NICE MOVE.
YOU ATTACK FROM BEHIND LIKE A COWARD.
YES. I *AM* SORRY ABOUT THAT. BUT TIME IS OF THE ESSENCE.
I'M ENJOYING WHAT OUR BRIGHTLY DRESSED FRIEND OVER THERE IS DOING TO THE CITY. I'VE DECIDED TO LET IT GO ON A WHILE LONGER.
YOU'LL *LET* HIM?

YES, LET HIM.
AND I MAY BE WRONG, BUT YOUR CHOICE OF WEAPON LEADS ME TO BELIEVE YOU MAY KNOW THE GREEN ARROW?
UNGH!
WELL, I WANT YOU TO DELIVER A MESSAGE TO HIM FOR ME, WILL YOU?
FROM NOW ON, NOTHING HAPPENS IN THIS CITY ANYMORE UNLESS I WANT IT TO. SO HE CAN EITHER FOLLOW THE NEW RULES, OR I'M AFRAID THERE WON'T BE ROOM FOR HIM HERE ANYMORE.
WHO THE HELL DO YOU THINK YOU ARE TO BE MAKING SUCH DEMANDS?!
exposed temple: lethal damage
thin fingers: easy to break
right shoulder: key point for her offensive capability
cape: can be used to incapacitate
breastbone: incapacitate
spleen: death by blood loss
estimated weight: 121 lb.
estimated height: 5 ft. 3 in.
weight now unbalanced– all on the left leg
key point to hit!
SOMEONE WHO SEES EVERYTHING.
THOK
WHAM
ANGH!
KZZT SHADO? SHADO, CAN YOU HEAR ME?!

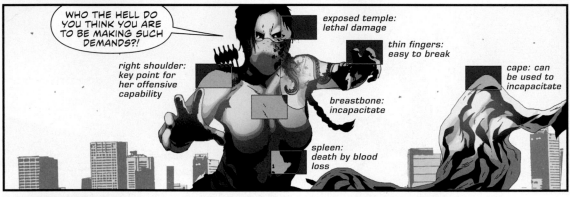

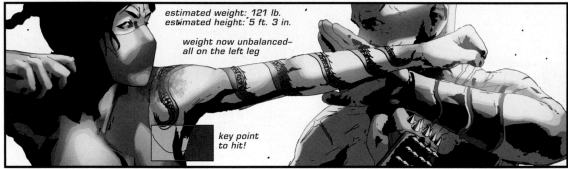

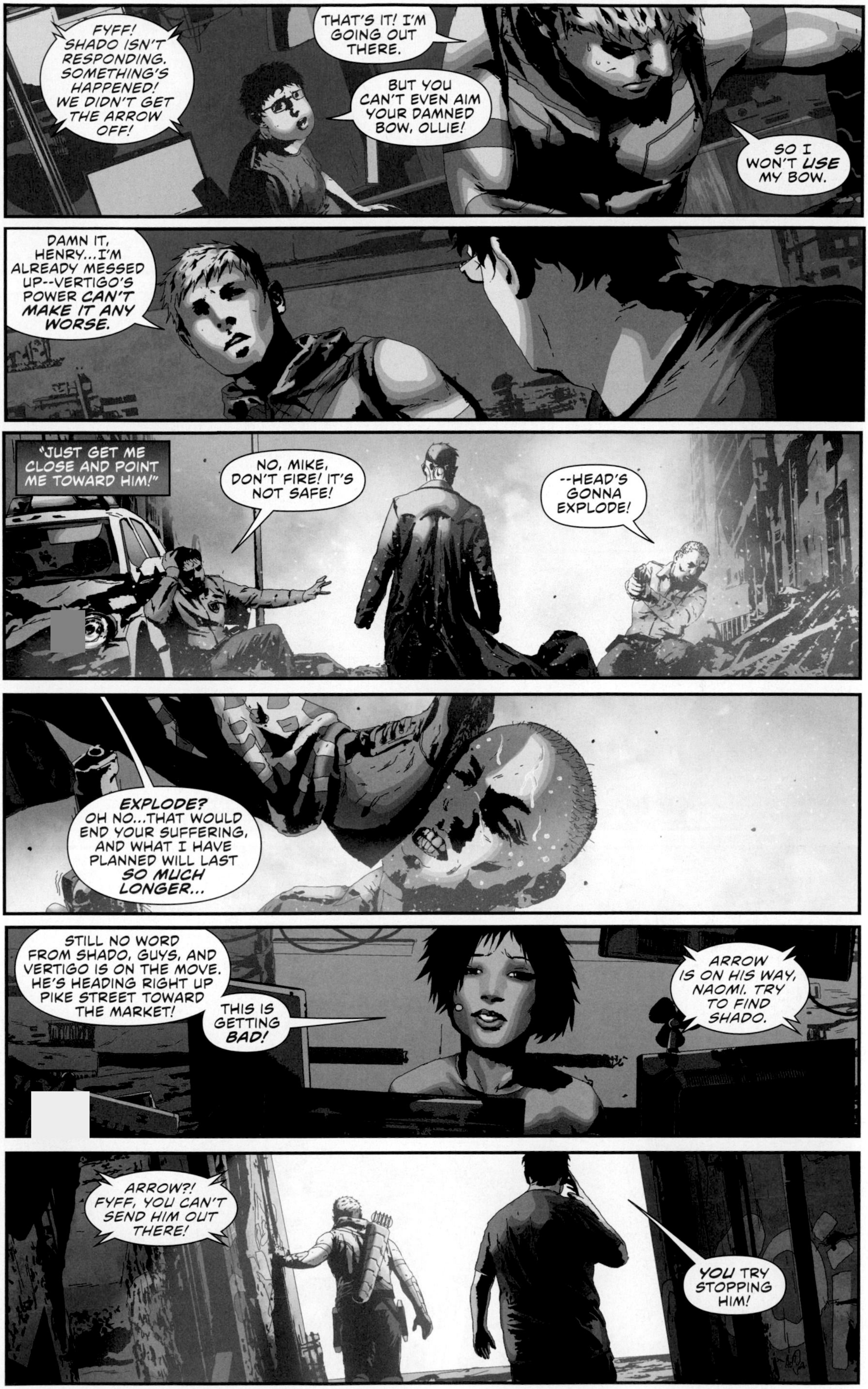
FYFF! SHADO ISN'T RESPONDING. SOMETHING'S HAPPENED! WE DIDN'T GET THE ARROW OFF!
THAT'S IT! I'M GOING OUT THERE.
BUT YOU CAN'T EVEN AIM YOUR DAMNED BOW, OLLIE!
SO I WON'T USE MY BOW.
DAMN IT, HENRY...I'M ALREADY MESSED UP--VERTIGO'S POWER CAN'T MAKE IT ANY WORSE.
"JUST GET ME CLOSE AND POINT ME TOWARD HIM!"
NO, MIKE, DON'T FIRE! IT'S NOT SAFE!
--HEAD'S GONNA EXPLODE!
EXPLODE? OH NO...THAT WOULD END YOUR SUFFERING, AND WHAT I HAVE PLANNED WILL LAST SO MUCH LONGER...
STILL NO WORD FROM SHADO, GUYS, AND VERTIGO IS ON THE MOVE. HE'S HEADING RIGHT UP PIKE STREET TOWARD THE MARKET!
THIS IS GETTING BAD!
ARROW IS ON HIS WAY, NAOMI. TRY TO FIND SHADO.
ARROW?! FYFF, YOU CAN'T SEND HIM OUT THERE!
YOU TRY STOPPING HIM!

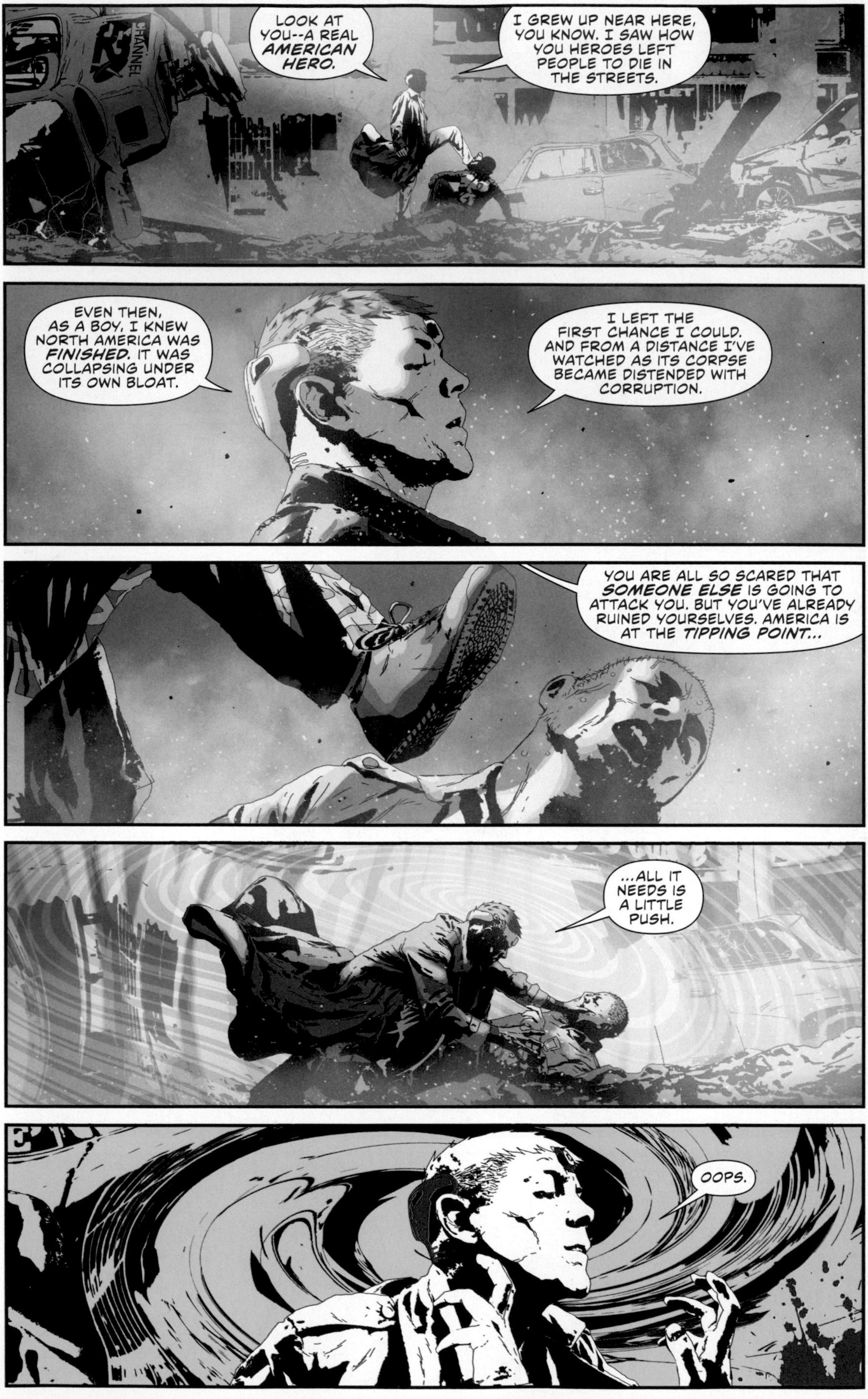
LOOK AT YOU--A REAL AMERICAN HERO.
I GREW UP NEAR HERE, YOU KNOW. I SAW HOW YOU HEROES LEFT PEOPLE TO DIE IN THE STREETS.
CHANNEL
EVEN THEN, AS A BOY, I KNEW NORTH AMERICA WAS FINISHED. IT WAS COLLAPSING UNDER ITS OWN BLOAT.
I LEFT THE FIRST CHANCE I COULD. AND FROM A DISTANCE I'VE WATCHED AS ITS CORPSE BECAME DISTENDED WITH CORRUPTION.
YOU ARE ALL SO SCARED THAT SOMEONE ELSE IS GOING TO ATTACK YOU. BUT YOU'VE ALREADY RUINED YOURSELVES. AMERICA IS AT THE TIPPING POINT...
...ALL IT NEEDS IS A LITTLE PUSH.
OOPS.

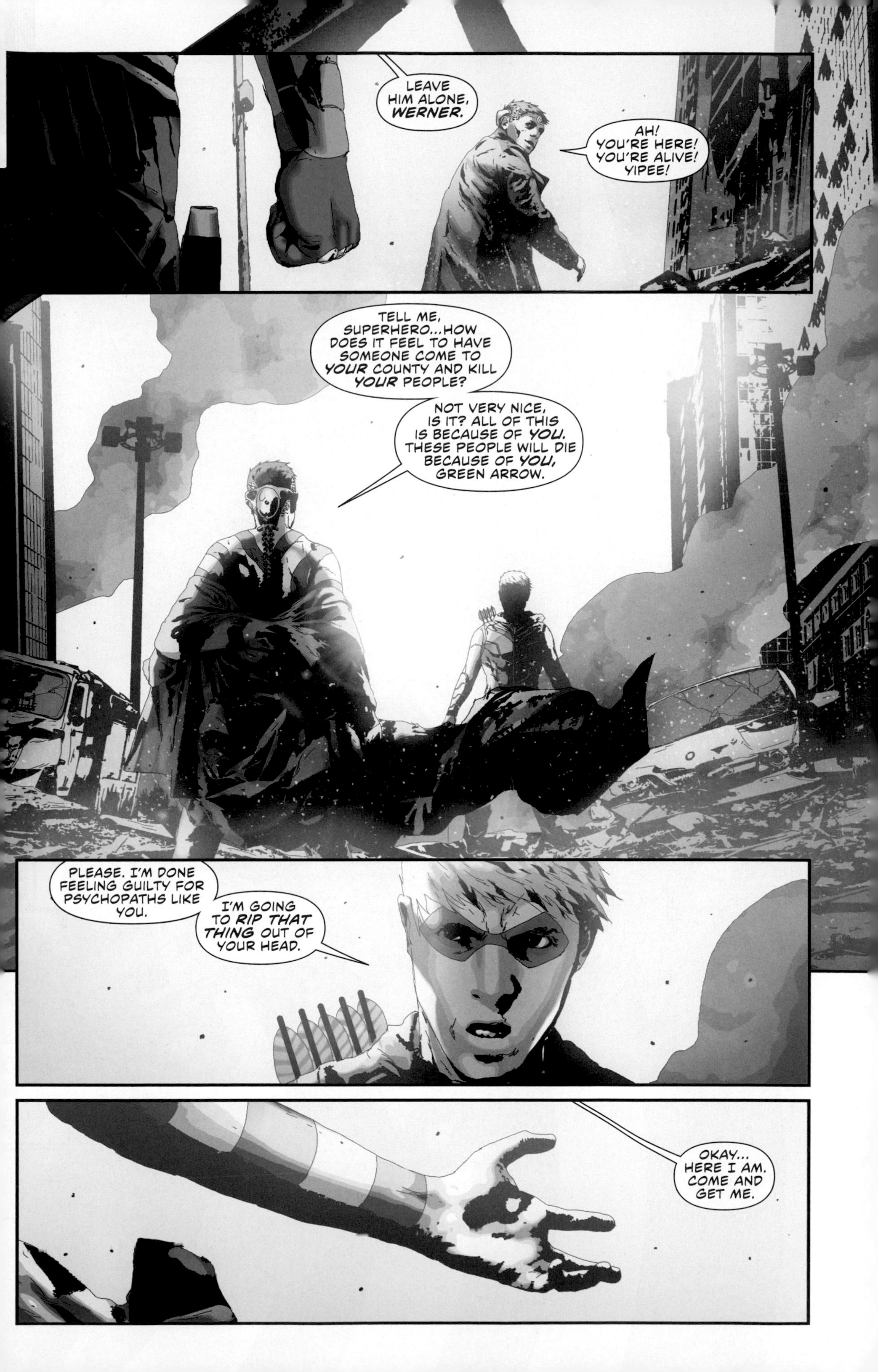
LEAVE HIM ALONE, WERNER.
AH! YOU'RE HERE! YOU'RE ALIVE! YIPEE!
TELL ME, SUPERHERO...HOW DOES IT FEEL TO HAVE SOMEONE COME TO YOUR COUNTY AND KILL YOUR PEOPLE?
NOT VERY NICE, IS IT? ALL OF THIS IS BECAUSE OF YOU. THESE PEOPLE WILL DIE BECAUSE OF YOU, GREEN ARROW.
PLEASE. I'M DONE FEELING GUILTY FOR PSYCHOPATHS LIKE YOU.
I'M GOING TO RIP THAT THING OUT OF YOUR HEAD.
OKAY... HERE I AM. COME AND GET ME.

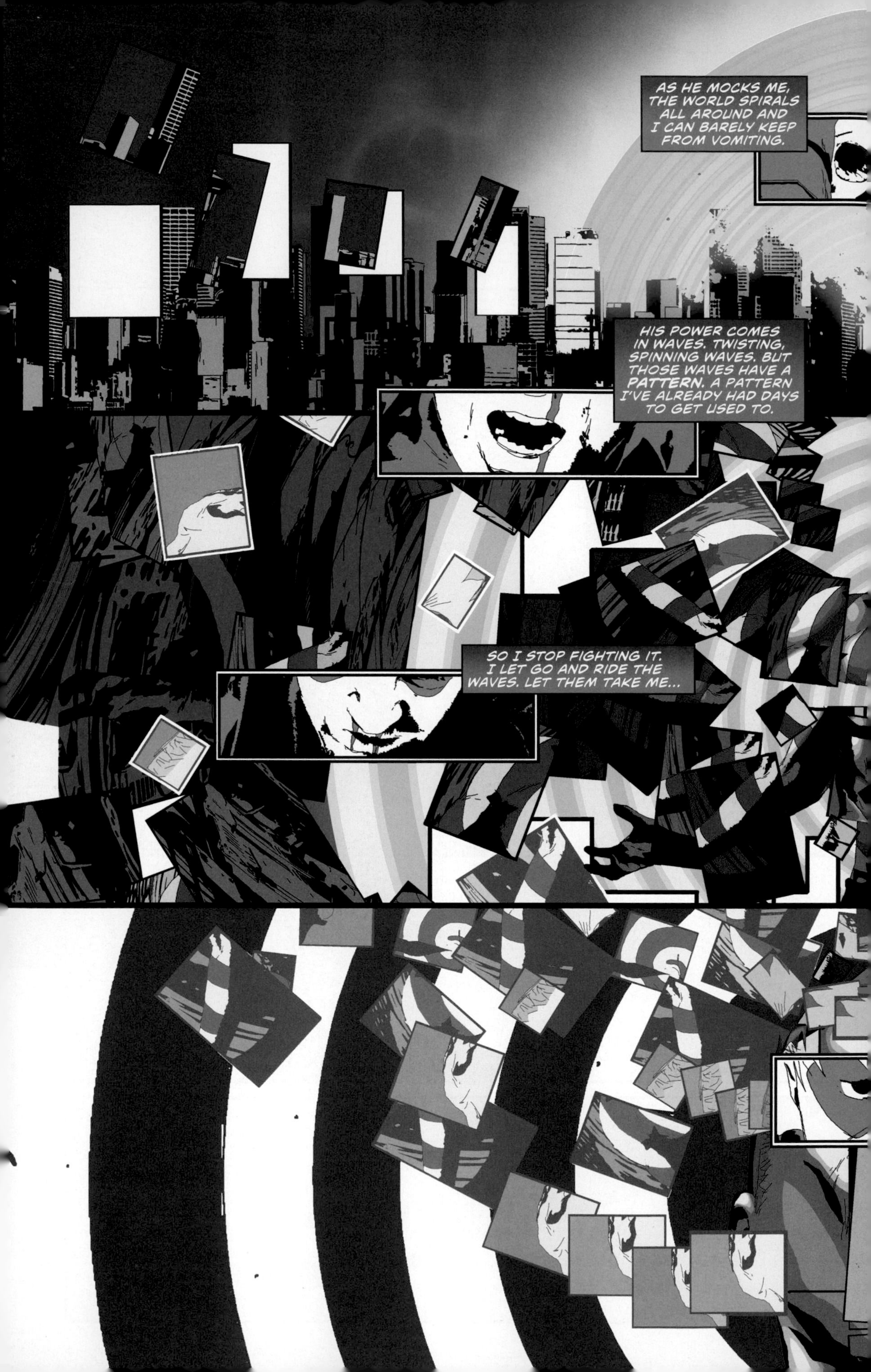
AS HE MOCKS ME, THE WORLD SPIRALS ALL AROUND AND I CAN BARELY KEEP FROM VOMITING.
HIS POWER COMES IN WAVES. TWISTING, SPINNING WAVES. BUT THOSE WAVES HAVE A PATTERN. A PATTERN I'VE ALREADY HAD DAYS TO GET USED TO.
SO I STOP FIGHTING IT. I LET GO AND RIDE THE WAVES. LET THEM TAKE ME...

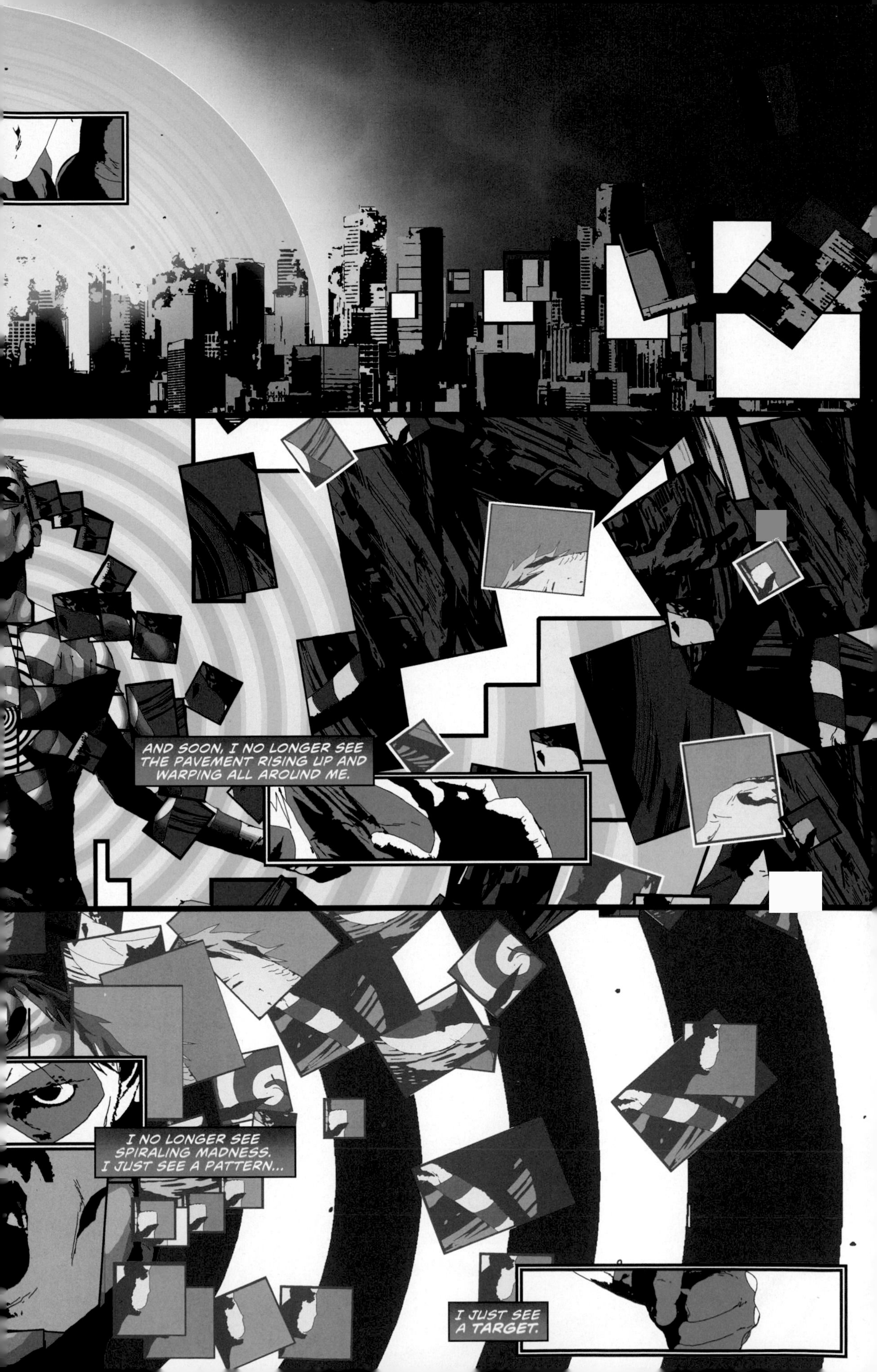
AND SOON, I NO LONGER SEE THE PAVEMENT RISING UP AND WARPING ALL AROUND ME.
I NO LONGER SEE SPIRALING MADNESS. I JUST SEE A PATTERN...
I JUST SEE A TARGET.

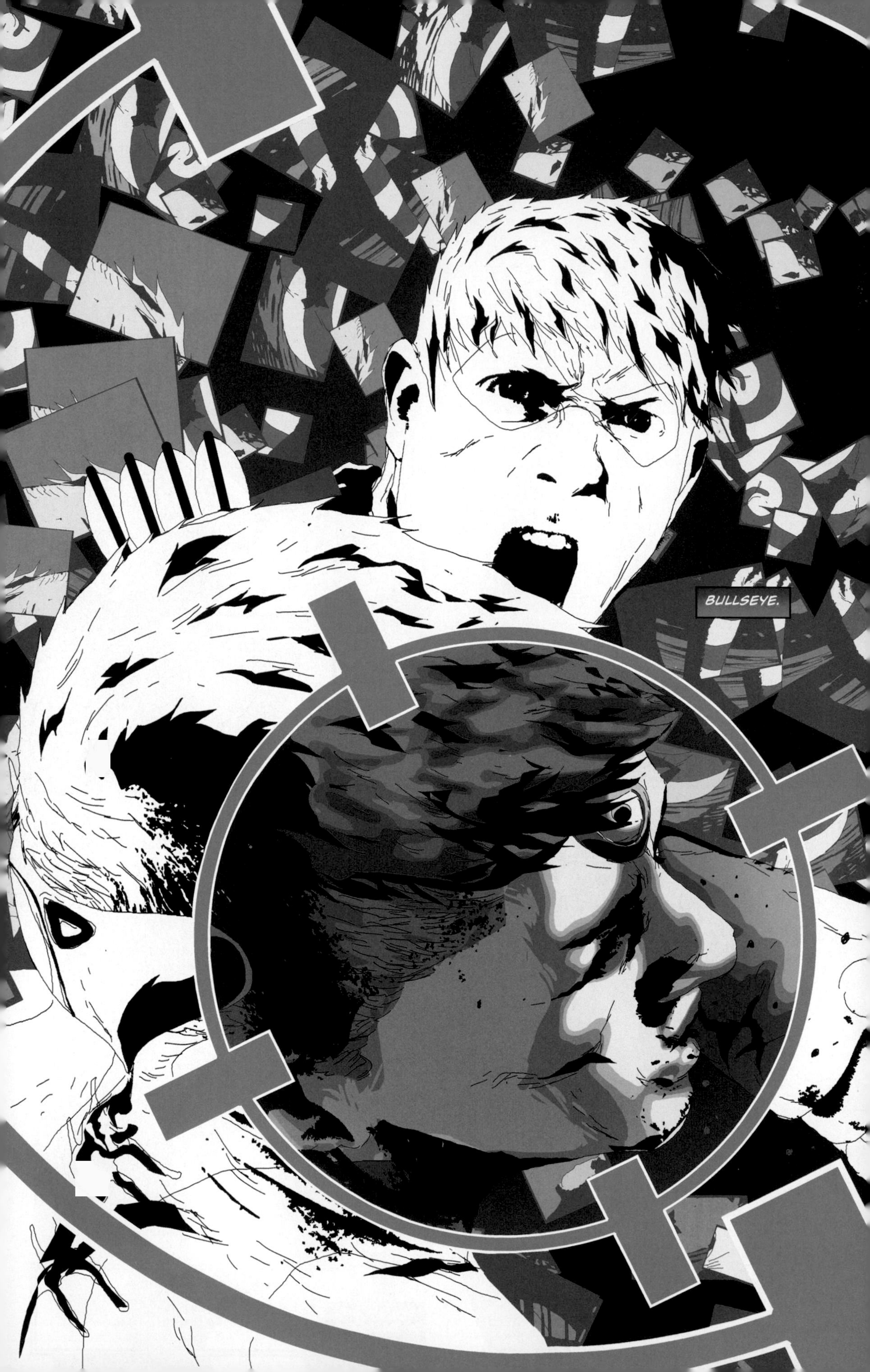
BULLSEYE.

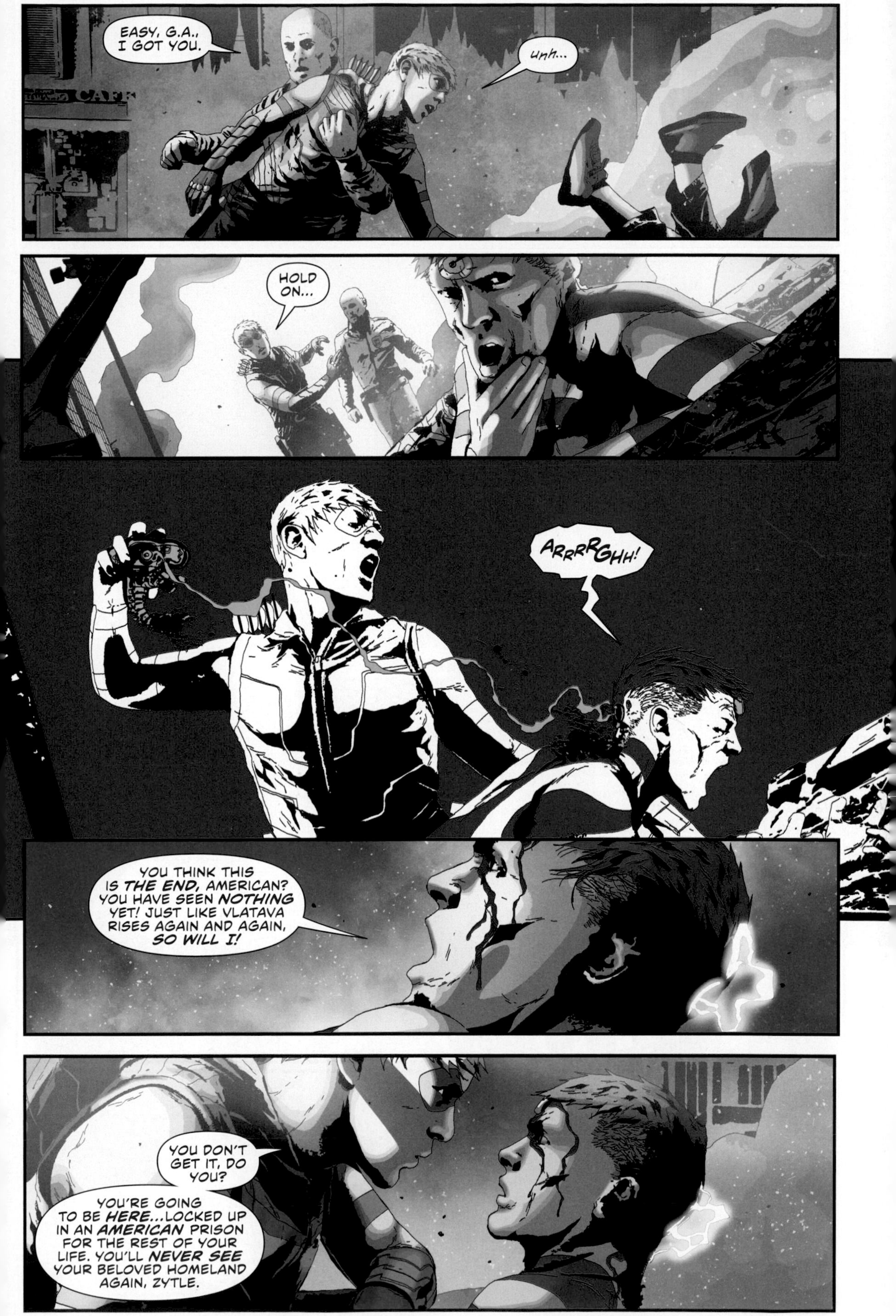
EASY, G.A., I GOT YOU.
unh...
HOLD ON...
ARRRRGHH!
YOU THINK THIS IS THE END, AMERICAN? YOU HAVE SEEN NOTHING YET! JUST LIKE VLATAVA RISES AGAIN AND AGAIN, SO WILL I!
YOU DON'T GET IT, DO YOU?
YOU'RE GOING TO BE HERE...LOCKED UP IN AN AMERICAN PRISON FOR THE REST OF YOUR LIFE. YOU'LL NEVER SEE YOUR BELOVED HOMELAND AGAIN, ZYTLE.
CAFE

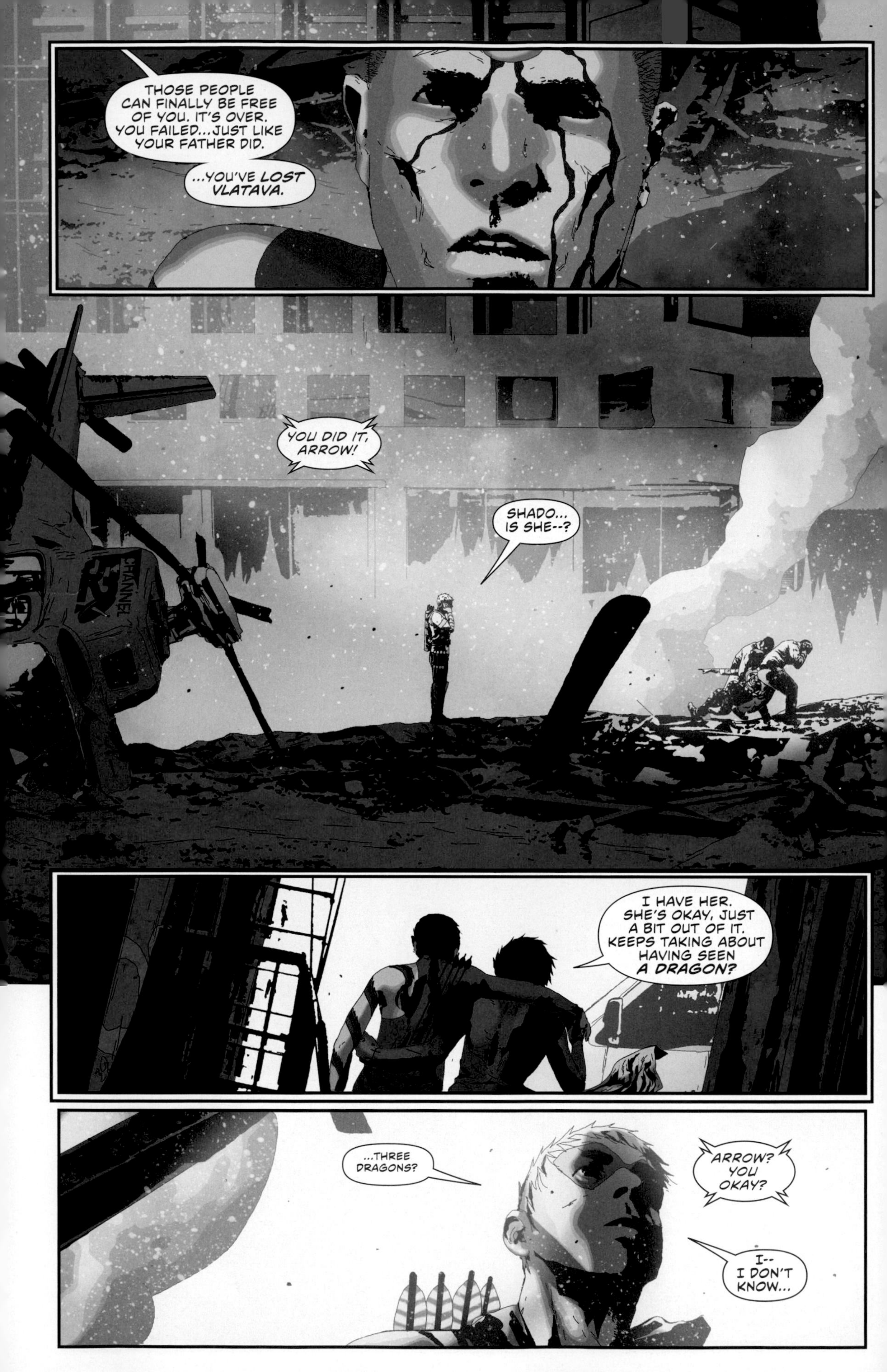
THOSE PEOPLE CAN FINALLY BE FREE OF YOU. IT'S OVER. YOU FAILED...JUST LIKE YOUR FATHER DID.
...YOU'VE *LOST* VLATAVA.
YOU DID IT, ARROW!
SHADO... IS SHE--?
I HAVE HER. SHE'S OKAY, JUST A BIT OUT OF IT. KEEPS TAKING ABOUT HAVING SEEN ***A DRAGON?***
...THREE DRAGONS?
ARROW? YOU OKAY?
I-- I DON'T KNOW...

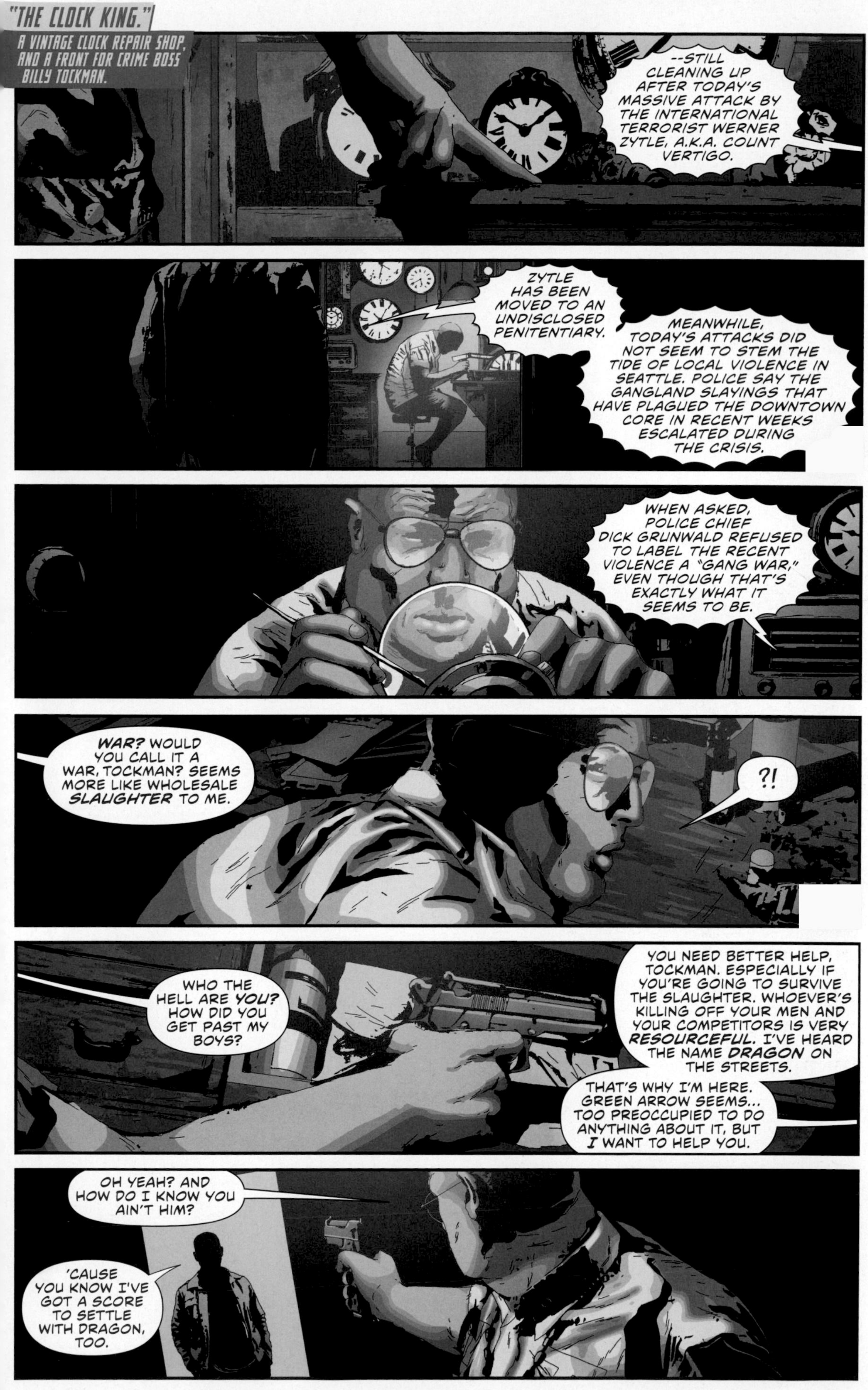
"THE CLOCK KING."
A VINTAGE CLOCK REPAIR SHOP, AND A FRONT FOR CRIME BOSS BILLY TOCKMAN.
--STILL CLEANING UP AFTER TODAY'S MASSIVE ATTACK BY THE INTERNATIONAL TERRORIST WERNER ZYTLE, A.K.A. COUNT VERTIGO.
ZYTLE HAS BEEN MOVED TO AN UNDISCLOSED PENITENTIARY.
MEANWHILE, TODAY'S ATTACKS DID NOT SEEM TO STEM THE TIDE OF LOCAL VIOLENCE IN SEATTLE. POLICE SAY THE GANGLAND SLAYINGS THAT HAVE PLAGUED THE DOWNTOWN CORE IN RECENT WEEKS ESCALATED DURING THE CRISIS.
WHEN ASKED, POLICE CHIEF DICK GRUNWALD REFUSED TO LABEL THE RECENT VIOLENCE A "GANG WAR," EVEN THOUGH THAT'S EXACTLY WHAT IT SEEMS TO BE.
WAR? WOULD YOU CALL IT A WAR, TOCKMAN? SEEMS MORE LIKE WHOLESALE SLAUGHTER TO ME.
?!
WHO THE HELL ARE YOU? HOW DID YOU GET PAST MY BOYS?
YOU NEED BETTER HELP, TOCKMAN. ESPECIALLY IF YOU'RE GOING TO SURVIVE THE SLAUGHTER. WHOEVER'S KILLING OFF YOUR MEN AND YOUR COMPETITORS IS VERY RESOURCEFUL. I'VE HEARD THE NAME DRAGON ON THE STREETS.
THAT'S WHY I'M HERE. GREEN ARROW SEEMS... TOO PREOCCUPIED TO DO ANYTHING ABOUT IT, BUT I WANT TO HELP YOU.
OH YEAH? AND HOW DO I KNOW YOU AIN'T HIM?
'CAUSE YOU KNOW I'VE GOT A SCORE TO SETTLE WITH DRAGON, TOO.

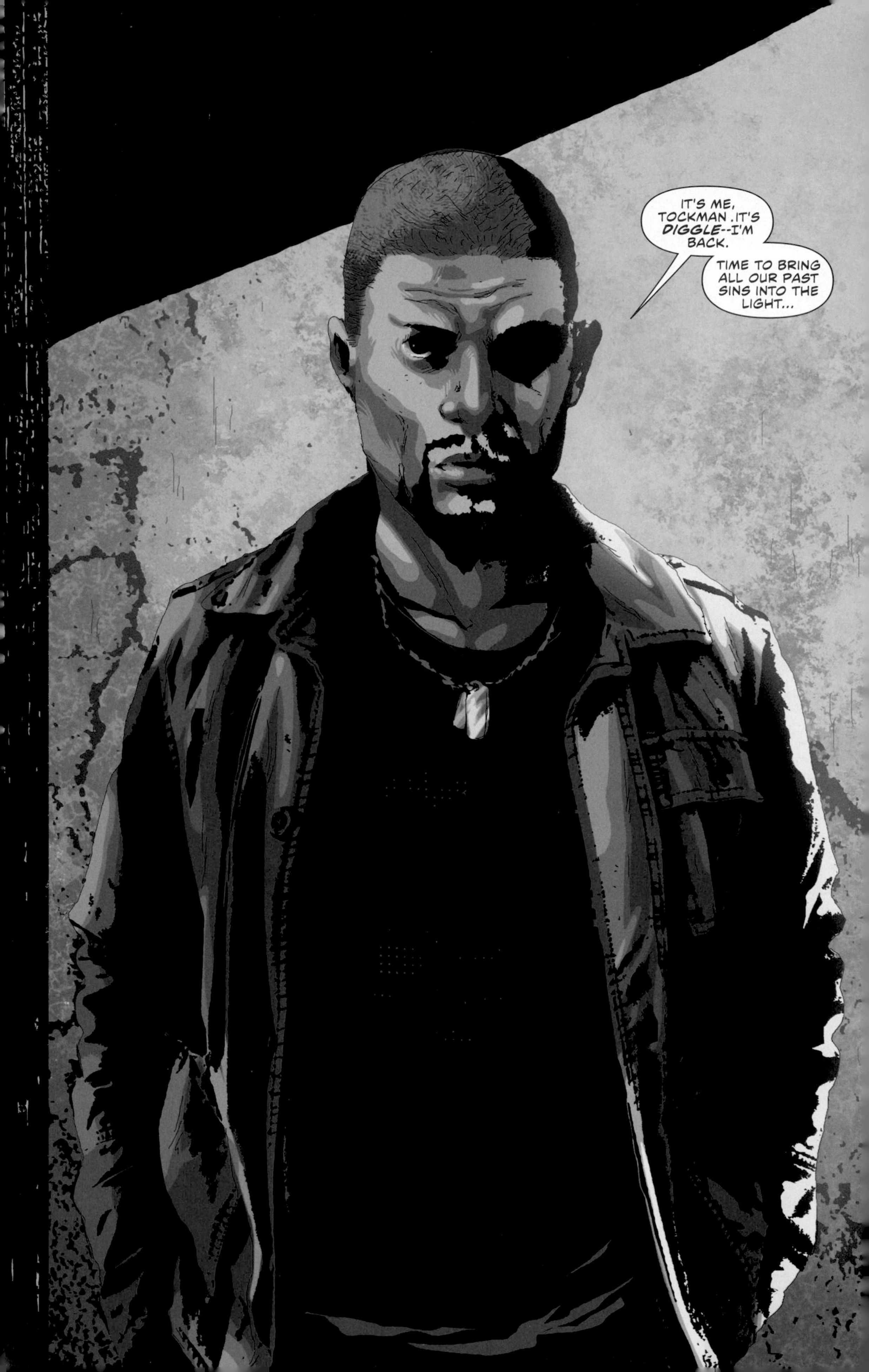
IT'S ME, TOCKMAN .IT'S DIGGLE--I'M BACK.
TIME TO BRING ALL OUR PAST SINS INTO THE LIGHT...

GREEN ARROW
CHARACTER DESIGNS BY ANDREA SORRENTINO

Komodo

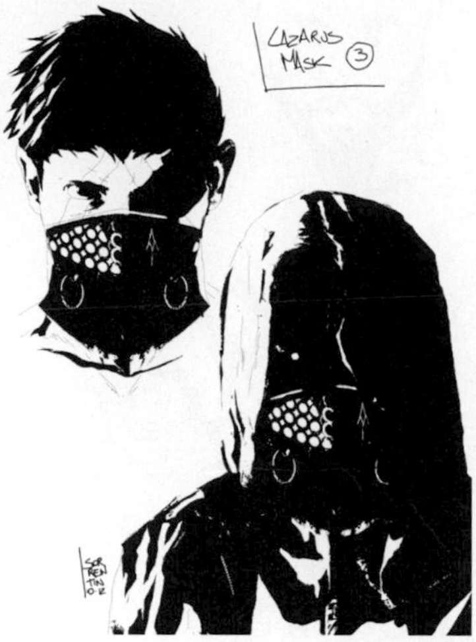
LAZARUS MASK 3

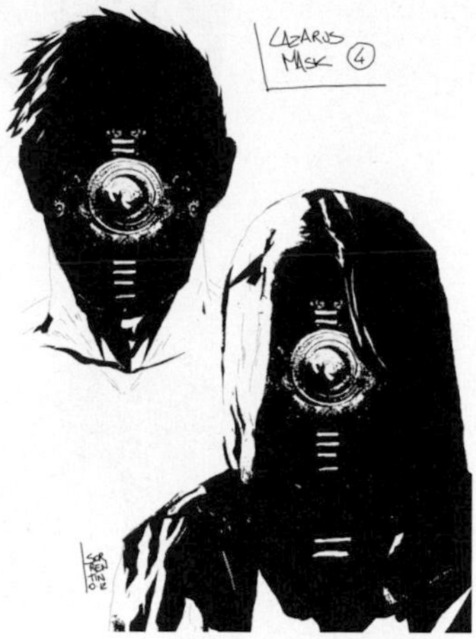
LAZARUS MASK 4

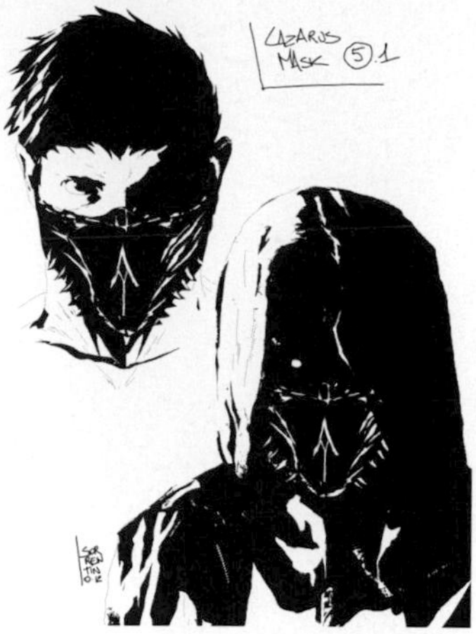
LAZARUS MASK 5.1

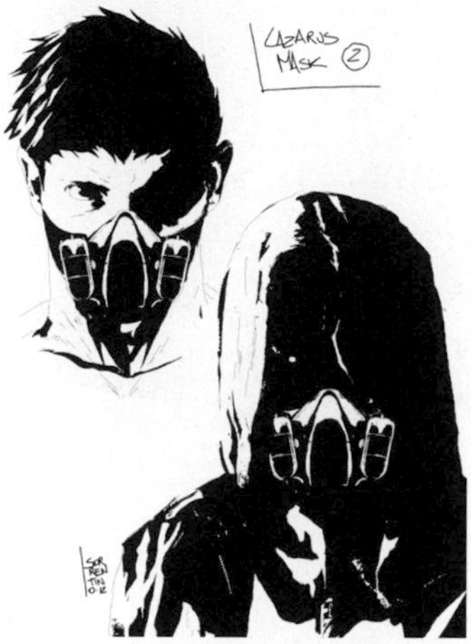
LAZARUS MASK 2

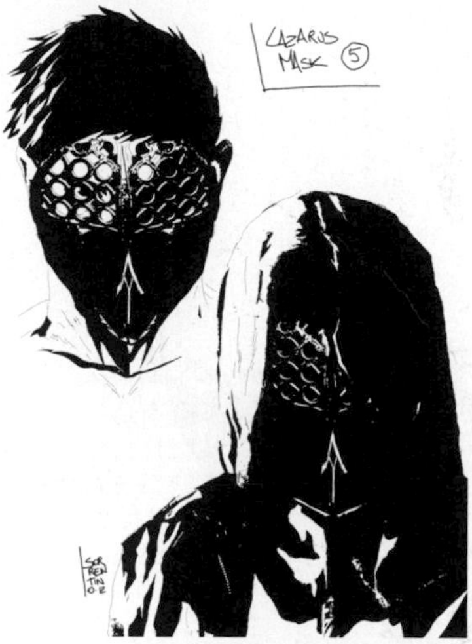
LAZARUS MASK 5

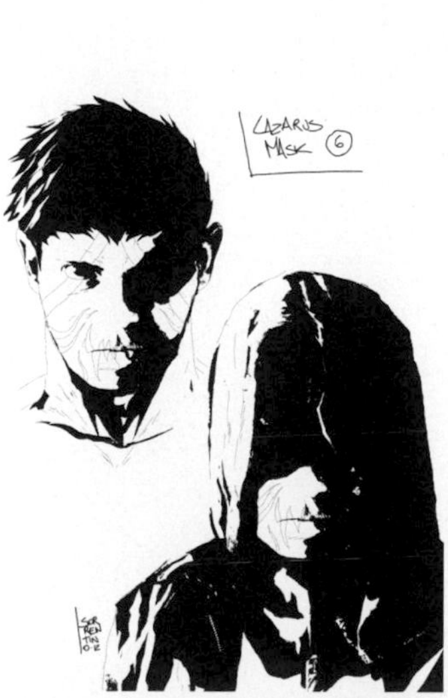
LAZARUS MASK 6

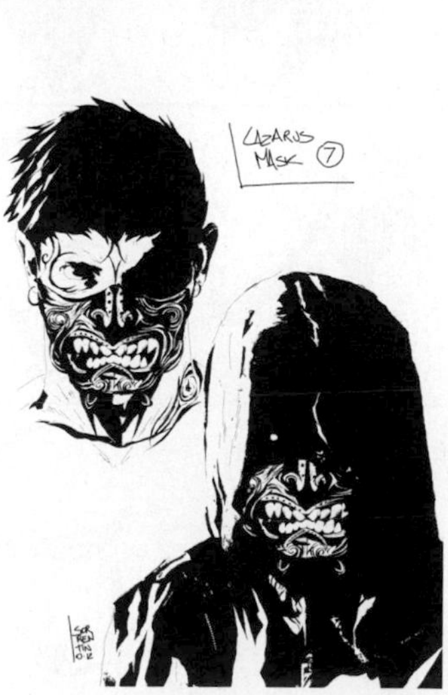
LAZARUS MASK 7

RICHARD
DRAGON

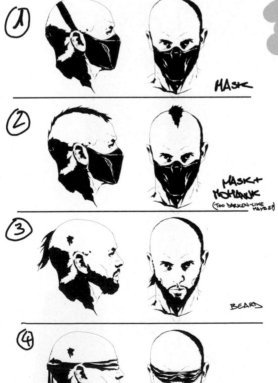

① MASK

② MASK +
MOHAWK
(TOO DARKON-LIKE MAYBE?)

③ BEARD

④ BLIND-FIGHT
MODE

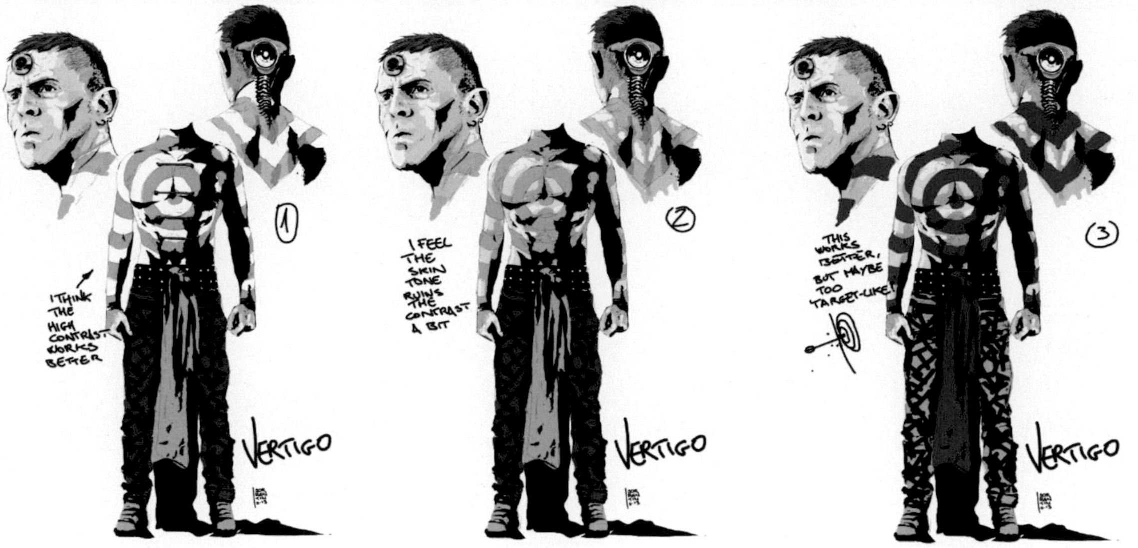
1
I THINK THE HIGH CONTRAST WORKS BETTER
VERTIGO
2
I FEEL THE SKIN TONE RUINS THE CONTRAST A BIT
VERTIGO
3
THIS WORKS BETTER, BUT MAYBE TOO TARGET-LIKE!
VERTIGO

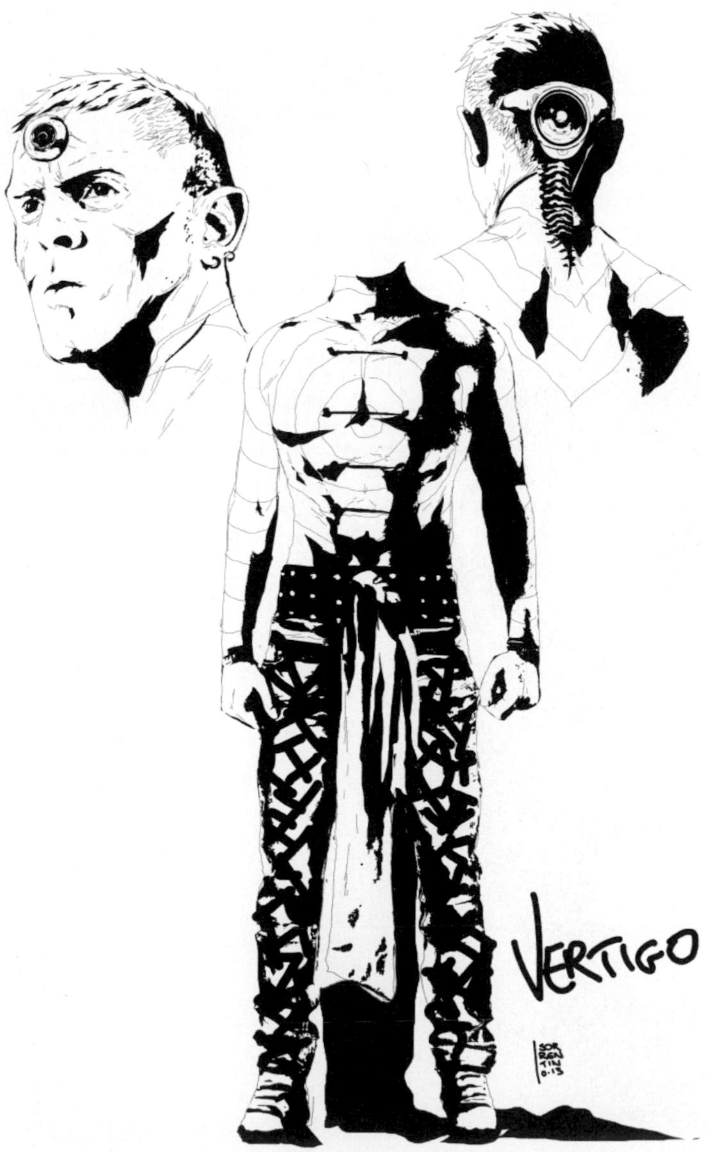
VERTIGO
SOR REN TIN 0.13

GREEN ARROW

VARIANT COVER FOR ISSUE #19 BY JOHN CALDWELL

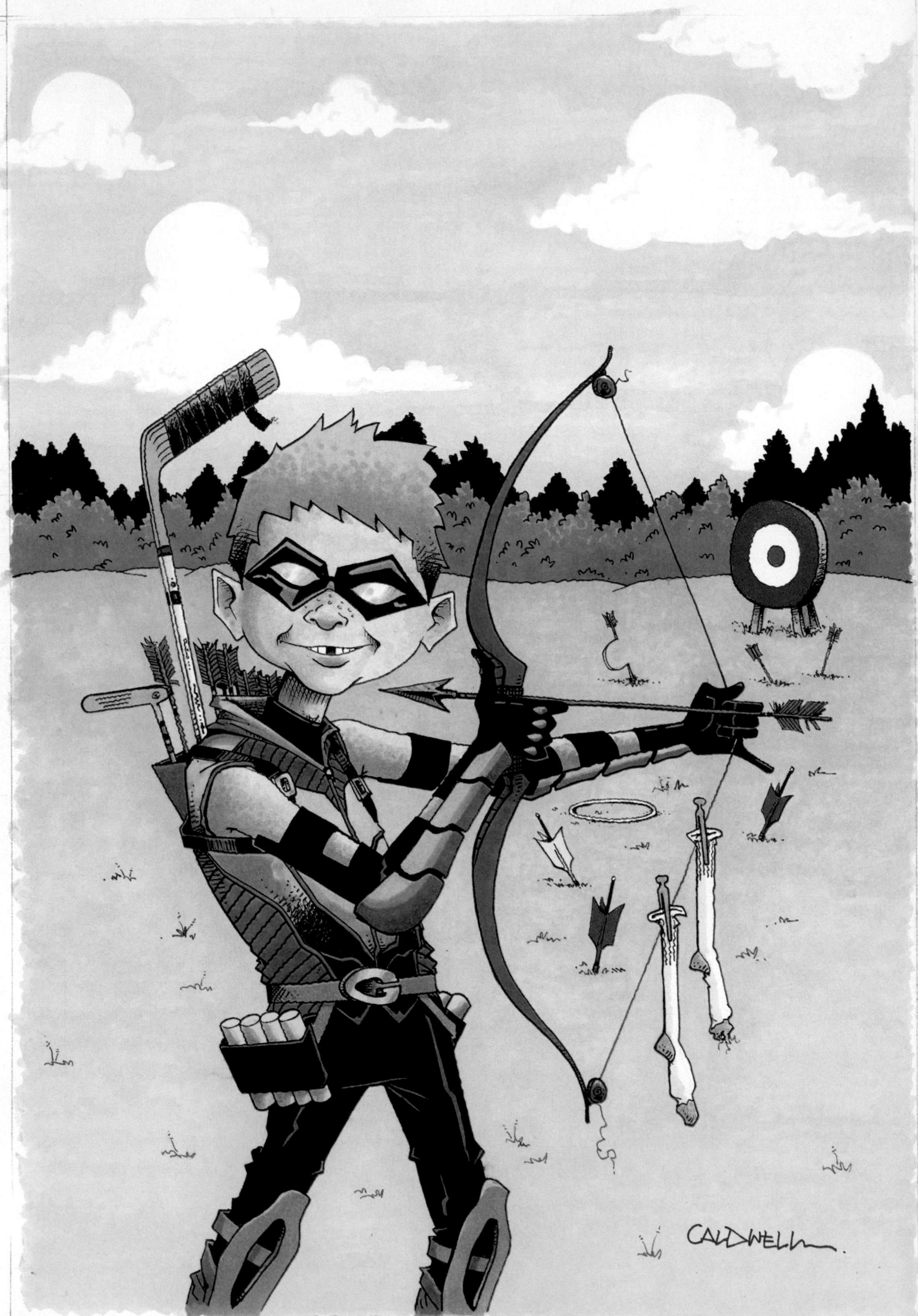
CALDWELL

GREEN ARROW

FULL COVER SPREAD SKETCH FOR ISSUE #19 BY ANDREA SORRENTINO

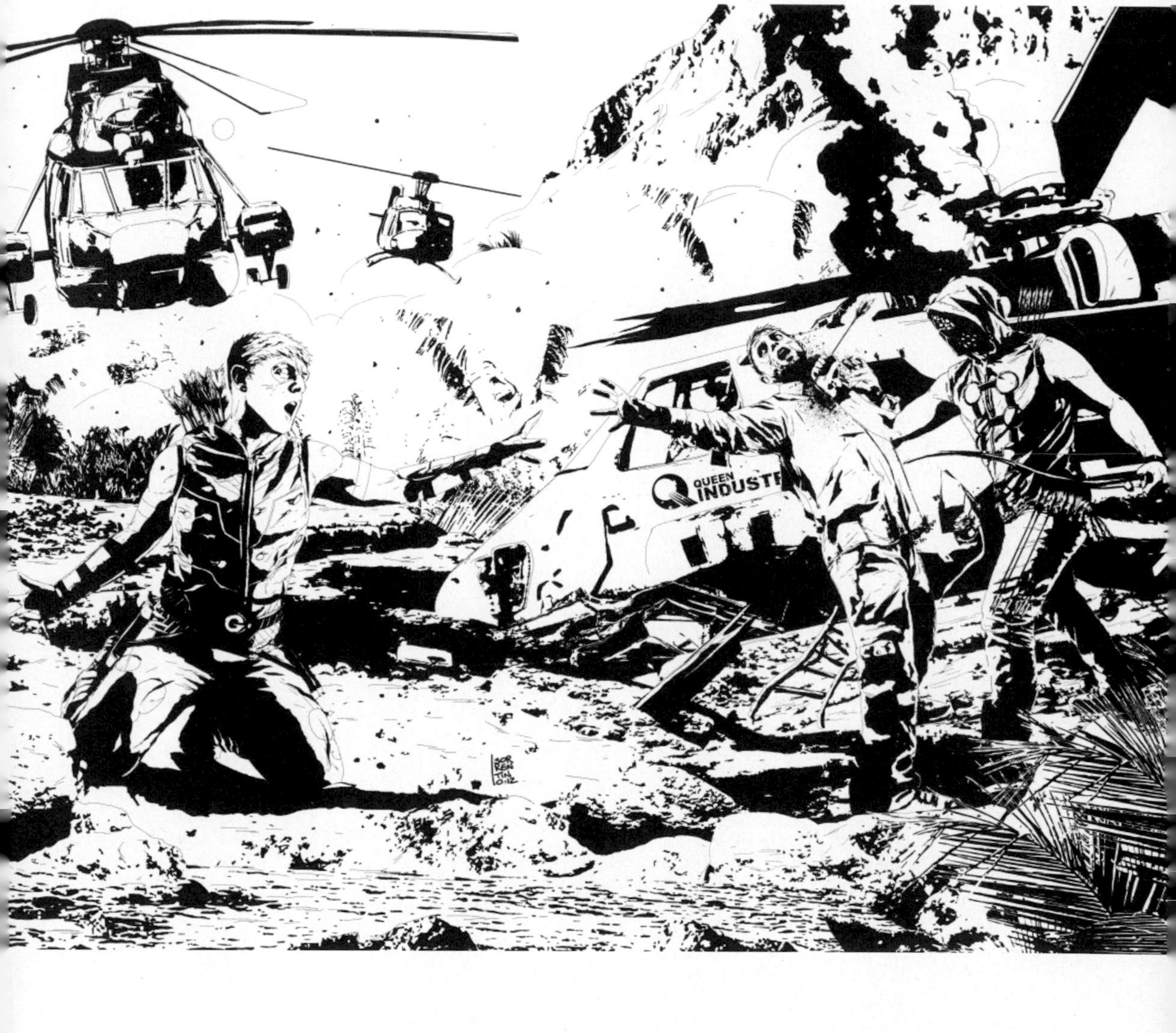
QUEEN
INDUSTR

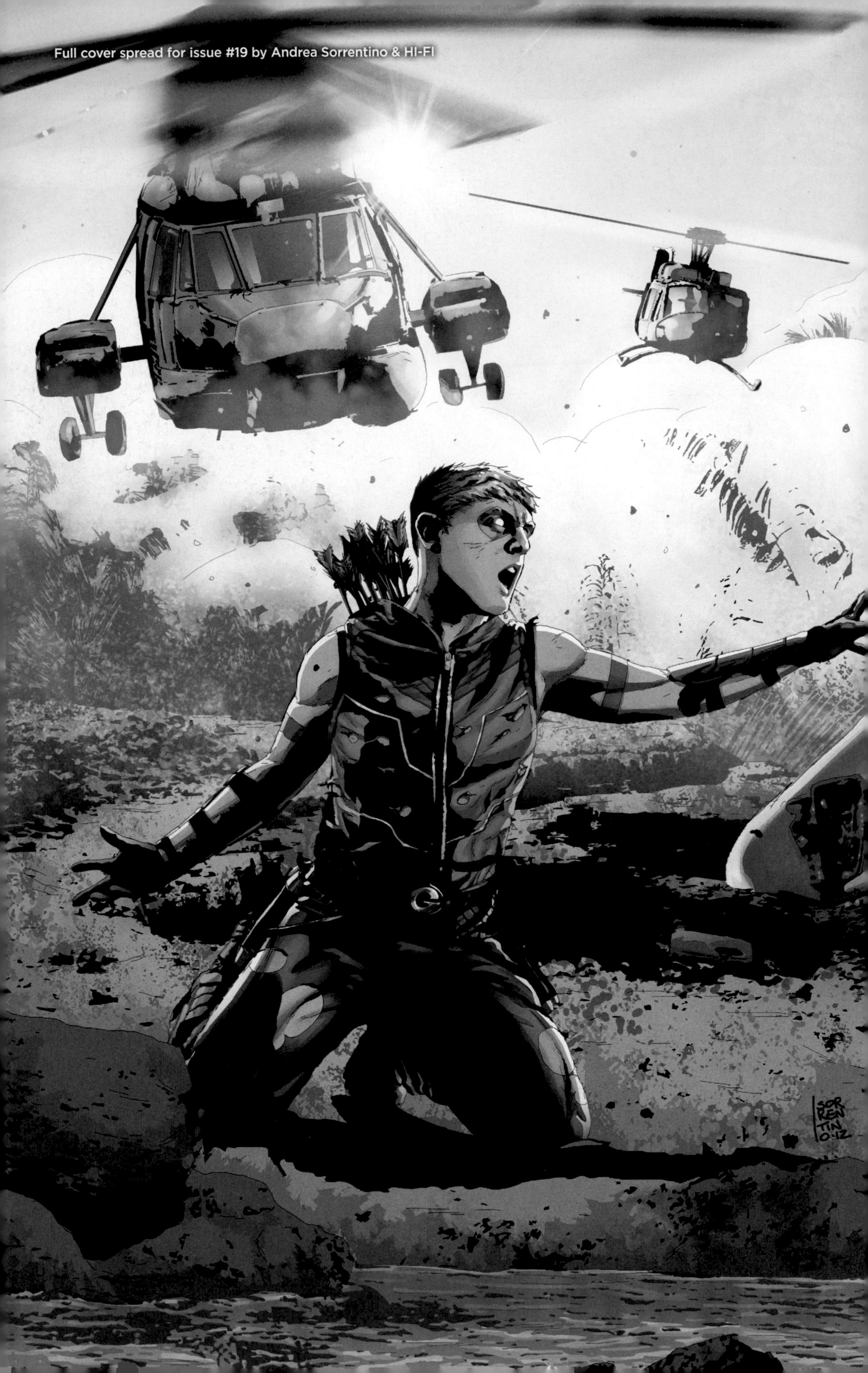
Full cover spread for issue #19 by Andrea Sorrentino & HI-FI

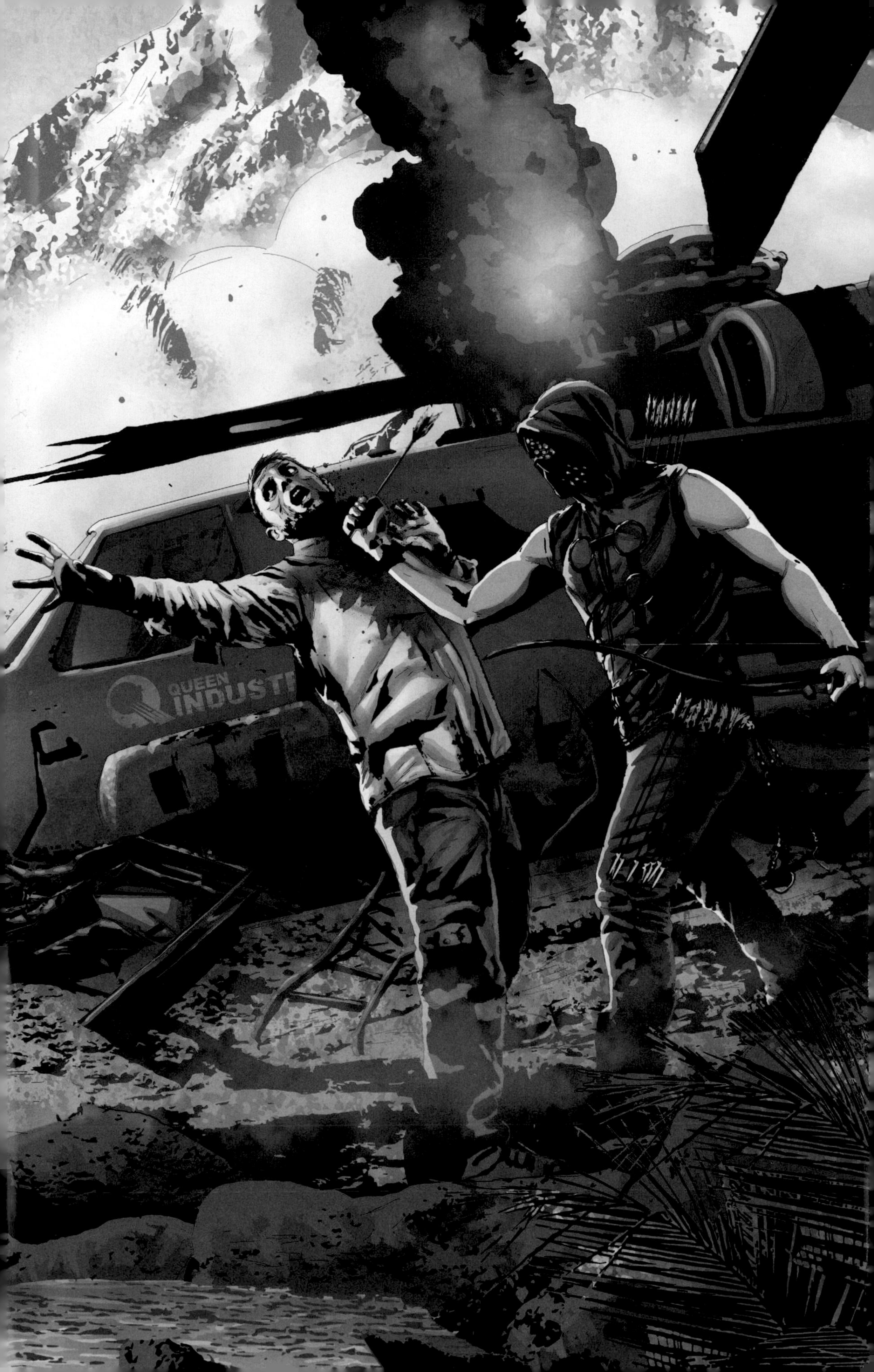
QUEEN
INDUSTR

GREEN ARROW

GREEN ARROW CHARACTER DESIGN BY ANDREA SORRENTINO

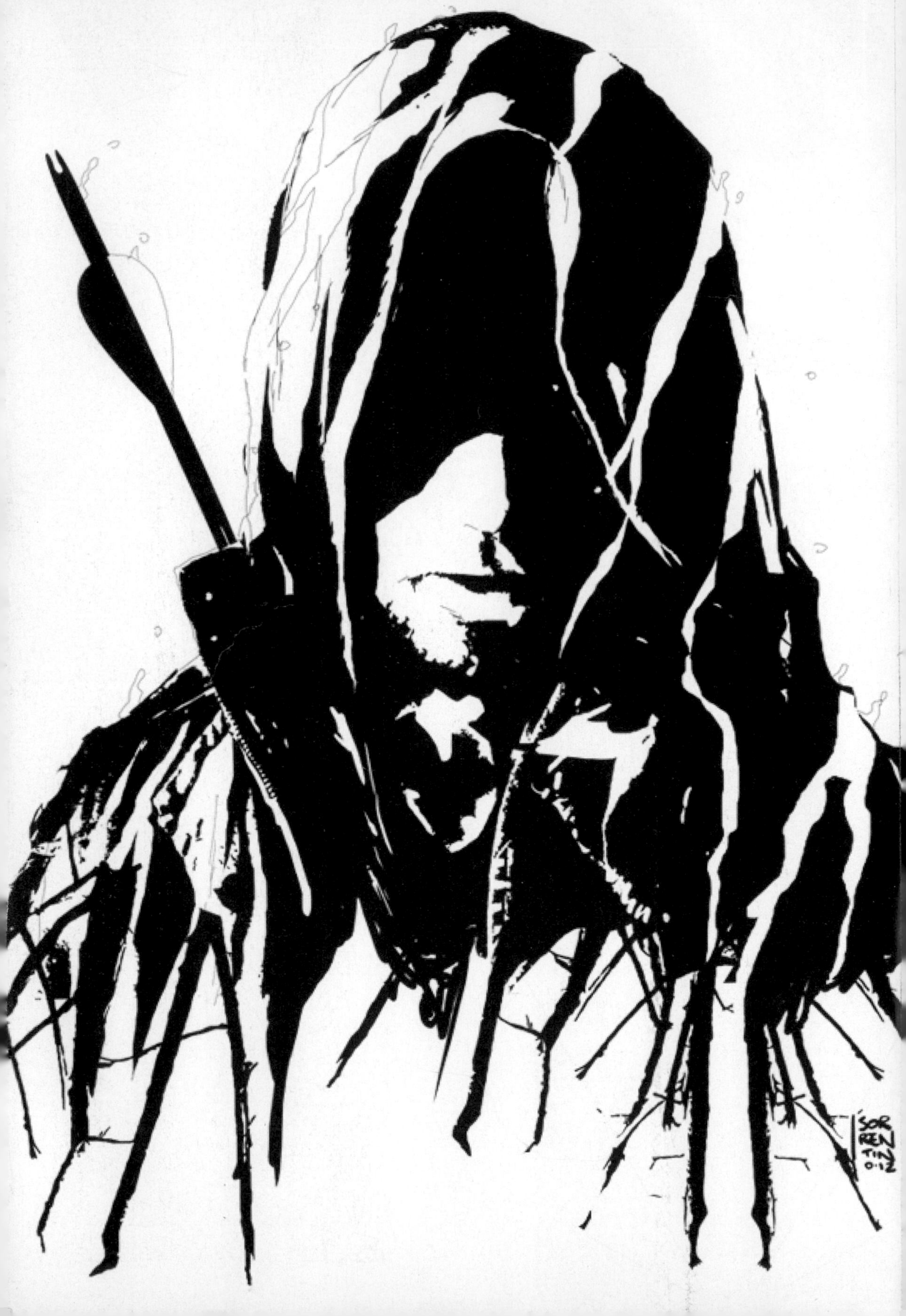